Fixing Windows Vista®

Jean Andrews, Ph.D.

COURSE TECHNOLOGY
CENGAGE Learning™

Australia • Brazil • Japan • Korea • Mexico • Singapore • Spain • United Kingdom • United States

COURSE TECHNOLOGY
CENGAGE Learning™

Fixing Windows Vista®
Jean Andrews, Ph.D.

Vice President, Career and Professional Editorial: Dave Garza

Director of Learning Solutions: Matthew Kane

Executive Editor: Stephen Helba

Managing Editor: Marah Bellegarde

Acquisitions Editor: Nick Lombardi

Senior Product Manager: Michelle Ruelos Cannistraci

Developmental Editor: Jill Batistick

Editorial Assistant: Sarah Pickering

Vice President, Career and Professional Marketing: Jennifer McAvey

Marketing Director: Deborah S. Yarnell

Marketing Manager: Erin Coffin

Marketing Coordinator: Shanna Gibbs

Production Director: Carolyn Miller

Production Manager: Andrew Crouth

Content Project Manager: Jessica McNavich

Art Director: Kun-Tee Chang

Cover designer: Robert Pehlke

Cover photo or illustration: Photodisc Photography/Veer

Production Technology Analyst: Jamison MacLachlan

Manufacturing Coordinator: Denise Powers

Copyeditor: Andrew Therriault

Proofreader: Harold Johnson

Compositor: Integra, Inc.

For product information and technology assistance, contact us at
Cengage Learning Customer & Sales Support, 1-800-354-9706

For permission to use material from this text or product,
submit all requests online at **cengage.com/permissions**
Further permissions questions can be emailed to
permissionrequest@cengage.com

Microsoft® and Windows® are registered trademarks of the Microsoft Corporation.
ExamView is a registered trademark of eInstruction Corp.

Library of Congress Control Number: 2008936787
ISBN-13: 978-1-428-32043-7
ISBN-10: 1-428-32043-1

Course Technology
25 Thomson Place
Boston, MA 02210
USA

Cengage Learning is a leading provider of customized learning solutions with office locations around the globe, including Singapore, the United Kingdom, Australia, Mexico, Brazil, and Japan. Locate your local office at: **international.cengage.com/region**

Cengage Learning products are represented in Canada by Nelson Education, Ltd.

For your lifelong learning solutions, visit **course.cengage.com**
Visit our corporate website at **cengage.com.**

Some of the product names and company names used in this book have been used for identification purposes only and may be trademarks or registered trademarks of their respective manufacturers and sellers.

Microsoft and the Office logo are either registered trademarks or trademarks of Microsoft Corporation in the United States and/or other countries. Course Technology, a part of Cengage Learning, is an independent entity from the Microsoft Corporation, and not affiliated with Microsoft in any manner.

Any fictional data related to persons or companies or URLs used throughout this book is intended for instructional purposes only. At the time this book was printed, any such data was fictional and not belonging to any real persons or companies.

Course Technology, the Course Technology logo, and the Shelly Cashman Series® are registered trademarks used under license.

Adobe, the Adobe logos, Authorware, ColdFusion, Director, Dreamweaver, Fireworks, FreeHand, JRun, Flash, and Shockwave are either registered trademarks or trademarks of Adobe Systems Incorporated in the United States and/or other countries. All other names used herein are for identification purposes only and are trademarks of their respective owners.

Course Technology, a part of Cengage Learning, reserves the right to revise this publication and make changes from time to time in its content without notice.

The programs in this book are for instructional purposes only. They have been tested with care, but are not guaranteed for any particular intent beyond educational purposes. The author and the publisher do not offer any warranties or representations, nor do they accept any liabilities with respect to the programs.

Printed in the United States of America
1 2 3 4 5 6 7 12 11 10 09 08

Brief Contents

Table of Contents

Introduction

Fixing Windows Vista® was written to help make your life with computers easier and more fun! Like it or not, in our present society we're all, to one degree or another, dependent on computers. And life has enough frustrations without a broken computer being one of them. After having studied this book, think how wonderful life can be the next time you're faced with a broken computer and you can confidently say, "Hey, I know what caused that problem, and I know how to fix it!" Well, that's the goal of this book—to put that power in your hands. I've written this book for those computer users who want to take charge of their own computer problems. Consider this book your ultimate take-charge tool!

When I first came up with the idea for this book, I made several trips to the shelves of computer bookstores to compare the idea to what was already written. Browsing through the offerings, I found books at two extremes. There were books written on how to use Windows and books written for Windows support technicians and developers. However, I didn't find a single book that hit in between these two extremes of expertise and lack thereof. This book targets the reader in the middle: You're beyond the how-to-use-the-OS level, and yet not really interested in the extremely technical intricacies of the OS. You just want to know how to fix the darn thing when it breaks! Well, you found your book! This book expects you to know how to use Windows Vista, but doesn't assume any technical expertise beyond that. And, yes, using this book, you *will* learn how to fix the darn thing when it breaks.

FEATURES

To make the book function well for the individual reader as well as in the classroom, you'll find these features:

▲ **Learning Objectives and Focus Problems:** Every chapter opens with a list of learning objectives and a Focus Problem that set the stage for the goals and content of the chapter.

▲ **Step-by-Step Instructions:** Detailed information on installation, maintenance, optimizing system performance, and troubleshooting are included throughout the book.

▲ **Art Program:** A wide array of photos, drawings, and screen shots support the text, displaying in detail the exact hardware and software features you will need to understand, fix, and maintain Windows Vista.

 ▲ **Notes:** Note icons highlight additional helpful information related to the subject being discussed.

 ▲ **Caution Icons:** These icons highlight critical safety information. Follow these instructions carefully to protect the PC and its data and also for your own safety.

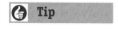 ▲ **Tip Icons:** These icons highlight additional insights and tips to remember.

◢ **End-of-Chapter Material:** Each chapter closes with the following features, which reinforce the material covered in the chapter and provide real-world, hands-on testing of the chapter's skill set.

- **Chapter Summary:** This bulleted list of concise statements summarizes all the major points of the chapter.

- **Key Terms:** The new, important terms introduced in the chapter are defined at the end of the chapter. The definitions of all terms are also included at the end of the book in a full-length glossary.

- **Reviewing the Basics:** A comprehensive set of review questions at the end of each chapter check your understanding of fundamental concepts.

- **Thinking Critically:** These sections present you with scenarios that require you to use both real-world common sense and the concepts you've learned in the chapter to solve problems or answer questions.

- **Hands-On Projects:** Several in-depth, hands-on projects are included at the end of each chapter, designed to ensure that you not only understand the material, but can apply what you've learned.

- **Real Problems, Real Solutions:** These projects give you valuable practice in applying the knowledge you've gained in the chapter to real-world situations, often using your own computer or one belonging to someone you know.

INSTRUCTOR RESOURCES

The following supplemental materials are available when this book is used in a classroom setting. All of the supplements available with this book are provided to the instructor on a single CD-ROM.

Electronic Instructor's Manual: The Instructor's Manual that accompanies this textbook includes additional instructional material to assist in class preparation, including suggestions for classroom activities, discussion topics, and additional projects.

Solutions: Answers to all end-of-chapter material, including the Review Questions, and where applicable, Hands-On Projects, are provided

ExamView®: This textbook is accompanied by ExamView, a powerful testing software package that allows instructors to create and administer printed, computer (LAN-based), and Internet exams. ExamView includes hundreds of questions that correspond to the topics covered in this text, enabling students to generate detailed study guides that include page references for further review. The computer-based and Internet testing components allow students to take exams at their computers, and also save the instructor time by grading each exam automatically.

PowerPoint® presentations: This book comes with Microsoft PowerPoint slides for each chapter. These are included as a teaching aid for classroom presentation, to make available to students on the network, for chapter review, or to be printed for classroom distribution. Instructors, please feel at liberty to add your own slides for additional topics you introduce to the class.

Figure files: All of the figures in the book are reproduced on the Instructor Resources CD, in bit-mapped format. Similar to the PowerPoint presentations, these are included as a teaching aid for classroom presentation, to make available to students for review, or to be printed for classroom distribution.

ORGANIZATION

This book is organized to address the most common problems with Windows Vista home and business editions. I call them Focus Problems, and you'll see them mentioned at the beginning of each chapter that tackles each problem. Here are the Focus Problems and the chapters that show you exactly what to do to solve each problem.

> **Focus Problem**
>
> "My Windows Vista system is really slow and I need a quick fix!"

- Chapter 1: "My Windows Vista system is really slow and I need a quick fix!"
- Chapter 2: "My Windows Vista startup is sluggish and gives me strange error messages."
- Chapter 3: "I'm under attack! Nasty software has attacked my system. How do I clean up the mess?"
- Chapter 4: "I need better security for my Windows Vista computer or small network."
- Chapter 5: "I need to connect to a wireless or wired network. I want to set up my own network."
- Chapter 6: "My applications or devices give errors, won't work, won't install, or won't uninstall."
- Chapter 7: "Windows won't start up! I have data in there somewhere!"

In the chapters, I've tried to stick to the bottom-line information of how to fix the problem at hand. But if you'd really like to know a bit more of what happens under the hood, check out Appendix D, "How Windows Vista Works." Also, in a classroom setting, you might be called on to install Vista at the beginning of the course. Appendix E, "Installing Windows Vista," shows you how to do that.

ACKNOWLEDGMENTS

When the idea for this book was being kicked around at Cengage Learning, Steve Helba, the Executive Editor, said this to me that made my heart jump with joy: "I want this book to be Jean Andrews unleashed! Write like you want to write, use as many pages as you want to use, and have fun with it!" Well, Steve, I did just that! Thank you! And, yes, it *was* fun.

Many thanks to Nick Lombardi, Michelle Ruelos Cannistraci, Jessica McNavich, and Steve Helba at Cengage Learning. Thank you, Jill Batistick, the Developmental Editor, for your careful attention to every detail of the book and for thoughtfully questioning its every move. Thank you, Tintu Clare Thomas and your team at Integra Software Services for your hard work in the production process. And thank you, John Bosco and your team at Green Pen Quality Assurance for checking and rechecking each technical detail of the book as well as your contributions to its organization and approach. The following reviewers all provided invaluable insights and showed a genuine interest in the book's success: Thank you to Brian Bridson (Baker College of Flint), Paul Carlson, Bruce Case (Thomas Jefferson High School), Sandra Daniels (New River Community College), Dr. Zareen Farooqi (University of Akron), Dean Farwood (Heald College), Ron Handlon (Remington College, Tampa, FL), John Krytus (Penta Career Center), and Hermine Turner (The Answer People).

And especially thank you to Sandra Daniels for contributing the graphical diagrams used in Chapter 7 to describe Vista startup. I'm very grateful for everyone's contributions.

This book is dedicated to the covenant of God with man on earth.

- Jean Andrews, Ph.D.

WANT TO WRITE THE AUTHOR?

If you'd like to give any feedback about the book or suggest what might be included in future books, please feel free to email Jean Andrews at jean.andrews@buystory.com.

PHOTO CREDITS

Unless otherwise stated in the photo credits table, all photographs were made by my daughter, Joy Dark.

Figure	Caption	Credit Request
Figure 5–59	This wireless access point by D-Link supports 802.11b/g	Photo Courtesy of D-Link Systems, Inc.

Windows Vista Quick Fixes

Personal computers using a Windows operating system have become just about the most valuable tools on our desktops today, making our work easier and more efficient, giving us a way to stay in touch with friends and family around the world, providing fun and games, and creating easy access to global information. They're great! But when things go wrong, many times the results are frustration, frantic attempts at fixing the problem, and just plain helplessness. If you've ever experienced this frustration, then this book is for you.

In the book, I'm assuming that you're a knowledgeable Windows Vista user, able to install and use applications, and that you're comfortable with common Windows tools such as Windows Explorer. I'm also assuming that you're new to Windows troubleshooting. And finally, I'm assuming you might be planning to use these skills not only to fix your own Windows Vista problems, but also to help users other than yourself. Based on this last assumption, where it's appropriate, I've given some suggestions on how to relate to users and especially how to protect their data as you work.

And I've made one more assumption: I've assumed that you are more focused on how to fix a Windows problem than you are on understanding how Windows works. For this reason, you're not going to find a lot of explanation of concepts in this book. But just in case you're interested in understanding concepts, you'll find Appendix D, "How Windows Vista Works," to be a great resource.

One of the most common Windows Vista problems creeps up on us over time as we install and uninstall software and use our computers for all sorts of things—Windows just gets tired and slow. Most often, this problem is caused by poor maintenance. You'll learn how to make Windows young again using some simple and easy-to-use Windows Vista tools. Next, you'll learn how to *keep* it young, using some necessary routine maintenance tasks. I consider the fixes in this chapter to be Vista quick fixes. If the problem is complex, we can "quick fix" it by applying a patch so that we can move on. For example, if a device or program is giving problems, we can disable it and then worry about the fix later. In later chapters, we'll deal with how to fix underlying problems. Lastly in this chapter, you'll learn how to approach a Windows problem, how to set your priorities, and how to plan your fix. In remaining chapters, we'll dig deeper into more complicated problems with more complicated solutions. By the end of this book, you can be a technically savvy Vista fixer-upper, confident and capable of dealing with the nastiest Vista problems.

> **⊠ Focus Problem**
>
> "My Windows Vista system is really slow and I need a quick fix!"

HOW TO MAKE WINDOWS YOUNG AGAIN

When you first purchased that new computer, Vista loaded quickly, software installed with no errors, and the system worked like a breeze. But now, after a few months or even a few years, you've noticed startup is slow and gives funny error messages, or boxes pop up out of nowhere. Then, when you're using your system, it just doesn't seem as fast as it once was, and strange things often happen that you can't explain. As with most users, you probably have not taken the time to do the routine and necessary maintenance tasks on your system that would keep it in top-notch condition. And when helping other users with their PC problems, one of the most common Vista complaints you'll hear is, "My Windows Vista system is just slow and sluggish. I'd love to see it working as fast as the day I bought it."

Unfortunately, the problem of a slow and sluggish Vista system is pretty open-ended and probably has more than one cause. Most likely, to solve the problem, you'll find yourself doing a lot of different things that, together, clean up the system. In other words, there's no magic bullet, but rather many little things for you to do. A Windows system can be slow and sluggish because of these reasons:

◢ *Reason 1*: Too many applications are running in the foreground or background. A program running independently in the background is called a service. Windows comes with many services, and services can also be added when you install an application, a device driver, or utility software. (Viruses also can install themselves as services.) A device driver is software that tells the OS exactly how to communicate with a hardware device.

◢ *Reason 2*: Device drivers might be corrupted or outdated, or the hardware device might have gone bad. Both problems can slow down performance.

◢ *Reason 3*: Viruses, adware, worms, and other malicious software might be pulling the system down.

◢ *Reason 4*: The hard drive does not have enough free space to work. Windows needs a certain amount of free hard drive space to use for temporary files. How much free space depends on how you use Vista, but keep at least 15 percent of the Vista drive free for normal operations and for maintenance. For large drives, that can be a lot of free space!

◢ *Reason 5*: The hard drive might be fragmented, which can slow down Windows performance.

> **✎ Note**
>
> Appendix D, "How Windows Vista Works" is for the reader who really wants to understand this stuff. But the appendix is relegated to the end of the book to keep it politely out of the way of those readers who don't have the time or patience for more in-depth study; these readers just want the bottom-line fix and want it now. This appendix has a very interesting discussion on how Windows uses a service or device driver, both of which are key terms mentioned in this section.

▲ *Reason 6*: You might not have enough available RAM, or your memory settings might not be correct. A heavily used Windows Vista computer probably needs as much as 2 GB of RAM and can benefit from more.

▲ *Reason 7*: In general, the system might not be robust enough to handle Windows Vista. Microsoft recommends you have a processor rated at least 1 GHz and at least 1 GB of RAM. But experience says you need more power than this for Vista not to bog down.

Here's what to do and the order in which I would do these things for a system that needs a general cleanup and doesn't have a major problem that stands out above the rest:

1. To begin solving the problem of a slow and sluggish system, you need to take a quick look at how the system is configured and how it performs just to get a lay of the land and decide what to do first.

2. Reduce the startup process to bare bones by running the System Configuration Utility (**MSconfig.exe**).

3. Clean up the hard drive, deleting unwanted files, defragmenting the hard drive, and scanning it for errors.

4. Use the Programs and Features window in Control Panel to uninstall any applications or utilities that are no longer needed.

5. Run antivirus software to scan the system for viruses, and run anti-adware and/or anti-spyware software.

6. Download and install Windows Vista updates, patches, and service packs.

7. Make one last check to verify the system is moving at a fast enough pace and is error free.

Now let's look at how to do all this in detail. If you run into errors as you work, know that the next chapters cover how to handle drastic Windows Vista problems and errors other than a slow and sluggish system.

STEP 1: SPY OUT THE LAND

No general worth his salt would send his army into battle without first spying out the land. He would not only know the enemy before him, but also would make it his business to find out about other less-obvious contributing factors that might affect the battle.

This advance preparation is the same with PC problems. You don't jump in with your fix until you have given that PC a quick once over. The idea is that you need to know about the PC's general condition so that you can be ready for any potential gotchas just around the corner as you work. Based on your quick examination of the system, you might decide to change the order in which you would do something so that you can address the most pressing problems first. You also need to know about any serious underlying problems that might mean additional, more intensive solutions are necessary.

Here are the things to do to examine the system so that you can get a general idea of what's going on:

1. *Get a pad and pen.* You'll need them to take notes as you go. Documenting what is happening and what you're doing is one mark of a truly professional technician. Besides that, documenting helps keep the work organized and efficient.

2. *Find out the administrator password.* Fixing most Windows problems requires administrator privileges, so plan to log on to the system using an administrator account. If

you're working on someone else's system, ask the user for the administrator password. Let the user know that as soon as you finish fixing the system, she can and should change the password.

3. ***Begin with a hard boot***. Several users who didn't log off and left applications open might be the cause of a sluggish system. A reboot cleans up the mess. Write down the time the hard boot takes from the time you press the power-on button until the Windows desktop is fully loaded and the spinning wait circle on the mouse pointer stops. If you want to get serious about this, use a stopwatch and document the seconds required for startup. Also write down any error messages you see and anything else that looks abnormal.

4. ***Did you receive hardware errors during the boot***? If you did receive an error message and the device is essential, you might have to solve the hardware problem before you can deal with the Vista problem. However, if the device is nonessential, go into Device Manager and disable it for now. Get Windows in good shape, and then you can return to Device Manager to deal with the hardware problem. To disable a device using Device Manager, click **Start**, type **devmgmt.msc** in the Start Search box, respond to the UAC box, and press **Enter**. (Yes, I know there are other ways to get to Device Manager, but typing the command is faster if you memorize it.) Right-click the device and click **Disable** from the shortcut menu (see Figure 1-1).

5. ***What processor and RAM are installed***? You can quickly get this information from the System window or System Information window. For the System window,

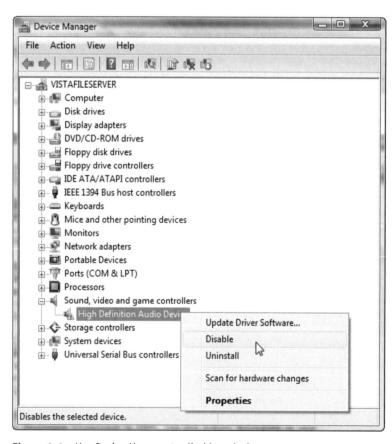

Figure 1-1 Use Device Manager to disable a device

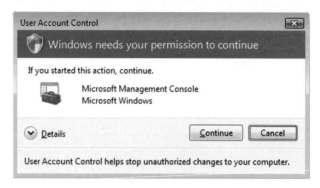

One important method Vista uses to protect itself from malware installing without the user's knowledge or from careless users making unauthorized changes is the User Account Control (UAC) box (see Figure 1-2). This box appears whenever software or hardware is about to be installed or the user opens an administrative tool such as Device Manager that can make changes to the Windows configuration. When the box appears, if you are logged on to the system as an administrator, click **Continue.** If you are not logged on to as an administrator, enter an administrator password and then click **Continue.**

User Account Control

🛡 Windows needs your permission to continue

If you started this action, continue.

Microsoft Management Console
Microsoft Windows

⌄ Details   Continue   Cancel

User Account Control helps stop unauthorized changes to your computer.

Figure 1-2   The User Account Control box appears whenever administrator permission is required

click **Start,** right-click **Computer** and select **Properties** from the shortcut menu. For example, for the system in Figure 1-3, a 2.4 GHz Pentium 4 processor is installed with 511 MB of RAM. Not exactly a screaming system, but for normal Vista use, it should do—except, with so little memory, the user won't see the nice Aero interface. If

Figure 1-3   The System window gives information about the hardware and currently installed OS

you'd like more detailed information, including the drive and directory where Vista is installed, use the System Information window. Click **Start**, enter **msinfo32.exe** in the Start Search box, and press **Enter** (see Figure 1-4).

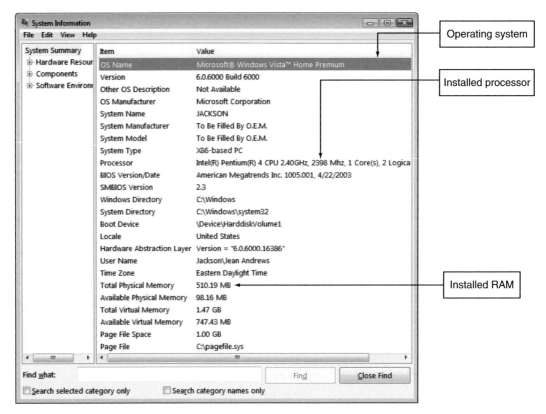

Figure 1-4 Use the System Information window for detailed information about the hardware and Vista

6. *What Windows Vista service packs and updates are installed*? On the screen shown in Figure 1-3, under Windows edition, note that no service packs are listed as installed. As of the writing of this book, Microsoft has released one service pack for Windows Vista. Write in your notes that you need to download and install Service Pack 1 before you're done with this system. To see how many updates are waiting to be installed, in the System window, click the **Windows Update** link in the left pane. In Figure 1-5, notice that this system has important updates not yet installed. These updates most likely will need installing before you can install Service Pack 1.

7. *How is Windows Update configured*? While you have the Windows Update window up, click the **Change settings** link in the left pane to see how Windows installs updates. Note in Figure 1-6 that this system is set so that updates are not automatically installed. For sure, you'll need to manually download and install all updates on this computer, and then ask the user for permission to set updating to install automatically. Make that note in your documentation. (One reason some users would not set updating to automatic is if the user has a slow Internet connection that is only connected when he is working on the PC, and he doesn't want to be bothered with downloading updates as he works. Also, some more experienced users don't trust all Vista updates and want to read up on them before they are installed, or they know that a particular update does not apply to their system.)

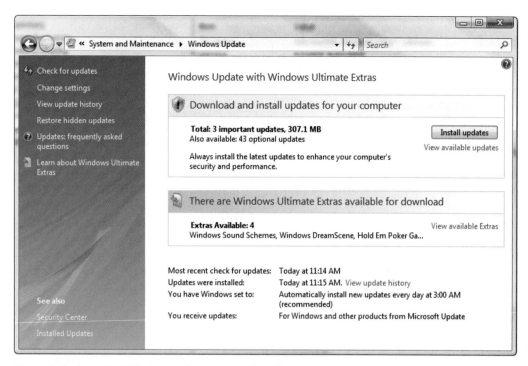

Figure 1-5   Important Windows updates are not installed

Figure 1-6   Use the Change settings link in the Windows Update window to note how Windows updates are set to be installed

8. *How much free hard drive space do you have?* Open Windows Explorer and look at the volume on which Windows is installed, most likely drive C. Right-click the drive and select **Properties** from the shortcut menu. Look at the amount of free space on the drive. For example, free space on drive C in Figure 1-7 is only 1.59 GB. Yikes! No wonder the user is complaining of a slow system. Even for a small drive, you need at least 3 GB of free space, and you're likely to need much more. As you can

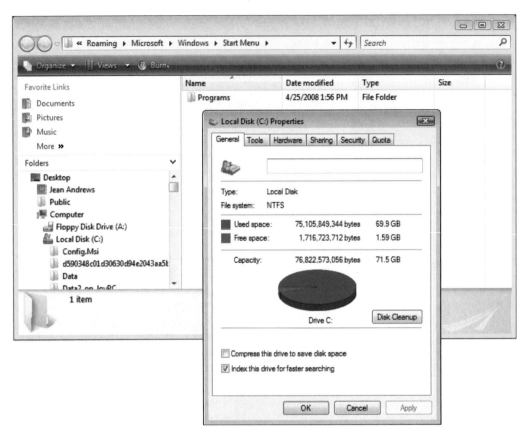

Figure 1-7 Use Windows Explorer to find out how much free space is on drive C

see in the figure, the size of the volume is 71.5 GB, which is a pretty large drive to be so full. Are there other partitions on the drive or other hard drives installed that can hold some of this data? To know for sure, turn to Disk Management.

9. *What size is the hard drive?* To view the size of a hard drive, how it is partitioned, and how much space is free, use Windows Disk Management. Click **Start**, right-click **Computer**, select **Manage** from the shortcut menu, and respond to the UAC box. In the Computer Management window, click **Disk Management**. (Or you can type **diskmgmt.msc** in the Start Search box and press **Enter**.) Figure 1-8 shows that the only hard drive installed has two partitions and the second partition is only about 3 GB. Even if you delete drive F and expand drive C to include this 3 GB, there still won't be enough free space on drive C. Make a note to discuss with the user the need to move some data on drive C to another media so that Windows has some room to breathe. You might also ask the user why drive F exists, since it appears mostly empty. If the user is not aware of a use for drive F and agrees to the change, you can use Disk Management to delete drive F and extend drive C so that the entire hard drive is included in drive C.

10. *What's showing in the notification area?* Icons in the notification area represent some, but not all, of the background processes that are currently running. To take a look at these icons, first you need to expand the notification area, because Vista won't normally show you everything hiding there. To do that, click the **left-pointing arrow** to the left of the notification area (see Figure 1-9). If you're not familiar with an icon you see in the notification area, use your mouse to hover over it to help identify it. You can also try right-clicking the icon to get a shortcut menu, which might tell you about the service the icon represents.

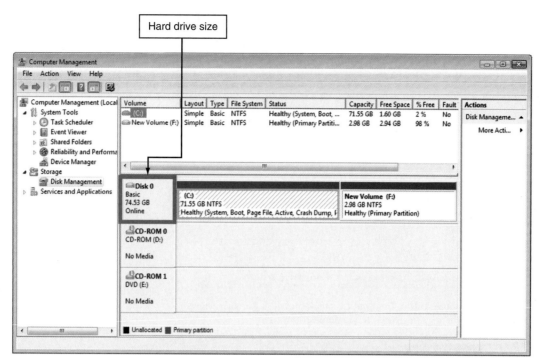

Figure 1-8   Use Disk Management to find out the size of the installed hard drive and how it is partitioned

Figure 1-9   Expand the notification area to see all the icons

Another alternative is to double-click the icon to open a window. Take note of any icons that represent processes you might not need and record that in your documentation. For example, you might find two icons for chat software such as an AOL Instant Messenger icon and one for MSN Messenger. It's possible that the user doesn't use both or is not even aware that both are taking up resources. Make a note to find out whether the user uses AOL Instant Messenger, MSN Messenger, or both. If necessary, you can remove the unused one later.

11. *What applications are currently running?* Use Task Manager (Taskmangr.exe) to see what applications are running. To open Task Manager, right-click a blank area of the taskbar and select **Task Manager** from the shortcut menu. When the Task Manager window opens, click the **Applications** tab, if necessary. Note and document any applications that are open. Because you haven't opened any yourself, you know that they had to be opened during startup. Make note of them so you can find out if the user really wants the system set this way. Opening applications at startup might mean they stay open even when the user doesn't really need or want them. In an ideal world, at this point there should be no running applications, as shown in Figure 1-10. In Chapter 2, you'll learn how to use the Processes tab of Task Manager to search deeper for unwanted processes. Note that a process is a program that runs with the resources needed by the running program.

Figure 1-10 The Applications tab of Task Manager shows no running applications

> **Note**
>
> Three ways to open Task Manager are: (1) right-click a blank area on the taskbar, and then select **Task Manager** on the shortcut menu, (2) press **Ctrl+Shift+Esc**, and (3) press **Ctrl+Alt+Delete**. Using the last option, depending on how Windows logon is configured, Task Manager opens or the Windows Security window opens. If the Windows Security window opens, click **Start Task Manager**. One good use of Task Manager is to deal with the situation of an application not responding, such as the one shown in Figure 1-11. To close an application that is locked up, in the Task Manager window on the Applications tab, select the application and click **End Task**.

Figure 1-11 Use Task Manager to stop a program that is not responding

12. *What services or other programs are currently running?* Use Windows Defender to find out what programs, including services or applications, are currently running. In Control Panel under Programs, click **Change startup programs**. Windows Defender

opens with Software Explorer listing the category, Startup Programs. In the drop-down list for Category, select **Currently Running Programs** as shown in Figure 1-12. When you select a program listed on the left, information about that program appears on the right, including the filename of the program. For example, notice in Figure 1-12 that acrotray.exe is the program filename for AcroTray, a helper application for Adobe Acrobat.

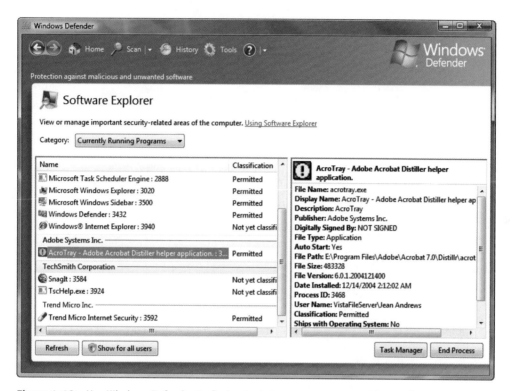

Figure 1-12   Use Windows Defender to find out what programs are currently running

As you smoke out unnecessary or unwanted programs that are slowing down a system, it helps to know which ones you definitely want to keep. Table 1-1 lists the minimum number of programs that you would find running in a barebones Windows Vista system immediately after startup. Any other programs you find listed in Software Explorer should be considered guilty of unnecessarily using resources until you've checked them out and found them to be needed or wanted.

13. *What programs are launched at startup?* In the Windows Defender Software Explorer window, under the Category drop-down menu, select **Startup Programs** to find out what applications or services are launched at startup. When you select a program on the left, notice on the right side you can see how the program is launched at startup. For example, in Figure 1-14, the selected program is launched by way of a registry entry. Some programs can be temporarily disabled using this window. You'll learn more about that in later chapters.

For a well-used Vista system, it's likely you'll see many nonessential programs launched at startup. To really clean up the system, you'll need to get to the bottom of these programs—what are they, why were they installed, and are they needed? And if they're not needed, how do you remove them? By the time you have this system running in top-notch shape, this window should show only a few programs. However, in this chapter, we're going to take a shortcut and simply disable all programs that are

> **Note**
>
> In this book, I'm assuming that Control Panel is using the Vista default view (see Figure 1-13). However, if you are using the Classic View for Control Panel, you will need to alter the steps in Control Panel to find a window. To change Control Panel from Classic View to its default setting, in the left pane of the Control Panel window, click **Control Panel Home**.

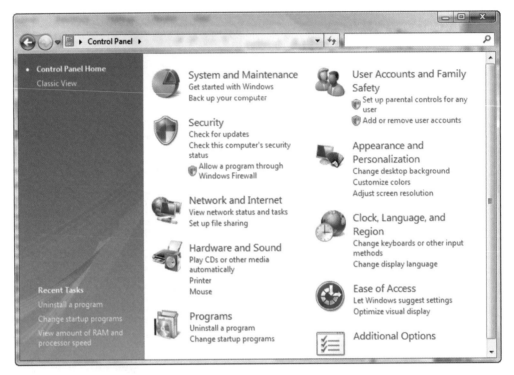

Figure 1-13   Window Vista Control Panel

Program	Description	Startup Programs	Currently Running Programs
Userinit.exe	Userinit Logon Application	X	
Explorer.exe	Windows Explorer	X	X
MSASCui.exe	Windows Defender	X	X
Dwm.exe	Desktop Window Manager		X
Taskeng.exe	Task Scheduler		X

Table 1-1   Programs launched at startup on a barebones Vista system

started when Windows is loaded and that are not part of the required Windows components. Then, in the next chapter, you'll learn to pick from the running programs the ones to keep and the ones to throw out.

As you worked through the tasks of examining the system using the System window, Information System window, Windows Explorer, Windows Defender, and Task Manager, you had a chance to see just how slow the system is. You also have seen which problems appear to be worse than others. As you read in the next section how to clean up Windows, you might want to change the order of what you do so that you address the worst problems first.

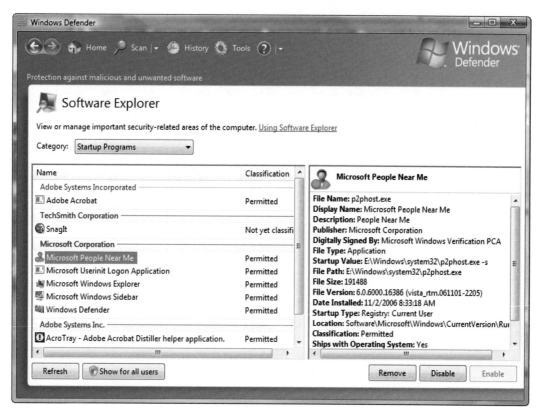

Figure 1-14 Use Windows Defender to find out what programs are launched at startup

STEP 2: REDUCE STARTUP TO ESSENTIALS

Now that you have a general idea about what you're up against, you're ready to clean things up. As you work, keep in mind that in the next chapter you'll learn about the many different ways applications and services can get launched at startup. You'll also learn how to figure out how these processes got set up to launch in the first place and how to remove the ones you don't want at this root level. But for now, we're going to take a quick-and-dirty approach to cleaning up the mess and just stop them all!

The tool we'll use is the System Configuration Utility, more commonly called MSconfig (pronounced "m-s-config") after the program name, MSconfig.exe. MSconfig works in a similar way to Windows Safe Mode; it reduces the startup process to essentials, but it's not intended to be a permanent solution to a problem. The idea is to use it to stop all nonessential processes and services from launching at startup. If the problem goes away, then you can add them back one at a time until the problem reappears. It's a great Windows troubleshooting tool, but should not be considered a permanent solution to a problem.

Here's how to use MSconfig:

1. To launch MSconfig, click **Start**, type **msconfig.exe** in the Start Search dialog box and press **Enter**. Respond to the User Account Control box. The System Configuration Utility window opens. Click the **Startup** tab, as shown in Figure 1-15.

2. To disable all nonessential startup tasks, click **Disable All**.

3. Now click the **Services** tab (see Figure 1-16). Notice that this tab also has a Disable All button. If you use that button, you'll disable all nonessential Windows services

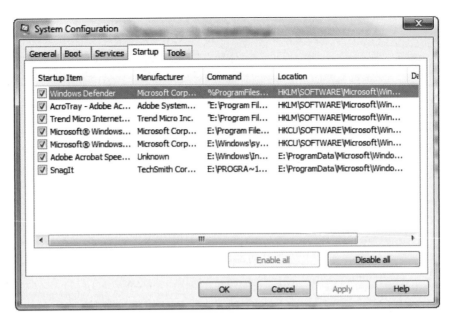

Figure 1-15 Use the System Configuration Utility (MSconfig) to temporarily disable a startup

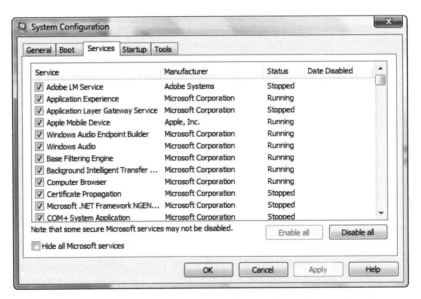

Figure 1-16 Use the System Configuration Utility to view and control services launched at startup

as well as third-party services such as virus scan programs. Use it only for the most difficult Windows problems, because you'll disable some services that you might really want, such as Windows Task Scheduler, Print Spooler, Automatic Updates, and the System Restore Service.

4. To view only those services put there by third-party software, check **Hide All Microsoft Services**. If you have antivirus software running in the background (and you should), you'll see that listed as well as any service launched at startup and put there by installed software. Uncheck all services that you don't recognize or know you don't want. You might not recognize something that you later realize you need, but for now, it's safe to disable it. Later, you'll need to investigate each service you don't recognize to decide if you really need it or not.

5. Click **Apply** to apply your changes. Now click the **General** tab and you should see Selective startup selected, as shown in Figure 1-17. MSconfig is now set to control the startup process. Click **OK** to close the MSconfig window.

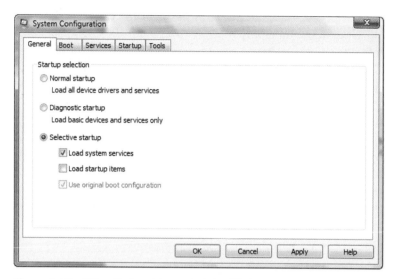

Figure 1-17 MSconfig is set to control the Windows startup process

6. After you apply a fix, reboot before you complicate matters with fixes on top of fixes so that you can see what happens.

7. When Windows starts up, you'll see the bubble window in Figure 1-18 that says Windows has blocked some startup programs. Remember, using MSconfig is recommended only as a temporary fix, and this bubble reminds us of that.

Figure 1-18 The System Configuration Utility has blocked some startup programs

Watch for error messages during the boot that indicate you've created a problem with our fix! For instance, after the boot, if you can no longer use that nifty little utility that came with your digital camera, you need to find out which service or program you stopped that you need for that utility. Go back to the MSconfig tool and enable that one service and reboot. In the next chapter, you'll learn how to permanently remove the ones you don't want. At that point, you will no longer need MSconfig and can return it to normal startup mode.

STEP 3: CLEAN UP THE HARD DRIVE

The next step in cleaning up a slow and sluggish system is to clean up the hard drive. To do that, we'll use three Windows Vista maintenance tools for hard drives to delete temporary files, defrag the drive, and scan it for errors. These tools are discussed next.

DISK CLEANUP

Temporary or unneeded files accumulate on a hard drive for a variety of reasons. For instance, an installation program might not clean up after itself after it finishes installing an application. And cached Web pages can take up a lot of disk space if you don't have the Internet settings correct. In addition, don't forget about the Recycle Bin; deleted files sit there taking up space until you empty it.

Vista needs free space on the hard drive for normal operation, for defragging the drive, for burning CDs and DVDs, and for a variety of other tasks, so it's important to delete unneeded files occasionally. Disk Cleanup is a convenient way to delete temporary files on a hard drive. To access Disk Cleanup, right-click the drive in Windows Explorer, and select **Properties** from the shortcut menu. The Disk Properties window appears, as shown in Figure 1-19. On the General tab, click **Disk Cleanup**. A dialog box opens asking if you want to clean up only your files or files from all users on this computer. Click on your choice. If you have selected to clean up the files of all users, you'll need to respond to the UAC box. Next, Disk Cleanup calculates how much space can be freed and then displays the Disk Cleanup window, also shown in Figure 1-19. From this window, you can select nonessential files to delete in order to save drive space.

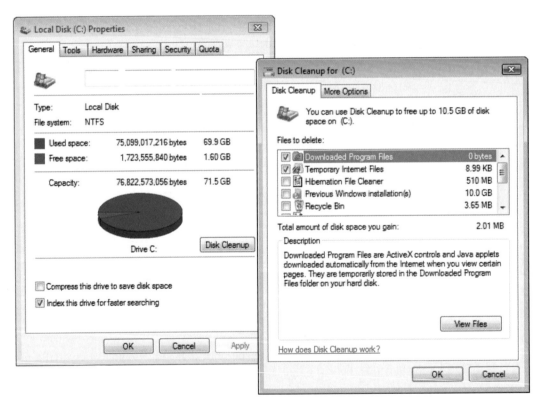

Figure 1-19 The Properties window for a drive provides Disk Cleanup, a quick and easy way to delete temporary files on a hard drive

Notice in Figure 1-19 the option to delete files from a Previous Windows installation(s), which can free up 10.0 GB of hard drive space. This 10 GB is used by the Windows.old folder. When Vista is installed on a system to replace or upgrade a previous Windows installation, it stores the old Windows, Program Files, and Documents and Settings folders in the Windows.old folder. If the user assures you that no information, data, or settings are needed from the old Windows installation, it's safe to delete these files to free up the 10 GB.

WINDOWS DISK DEFRAGMENTER AND DEFRAG

Another problem that might slow down your hard drive is fragmentation. Fragmentation happens over time as Windows writes files, deletes files, and writes new files to your drive. Files end up in fragmented segments all over the drive. Then, when Windows reads a fragmented file, the drive must work hard to move its read-write head all over the drive to retrieve the file. Also, if a file becomes corrupted, data recovery utilities are less likely to be able to find all the pieces to the file if the file is fragmented rather than written on the drive in one location. For these reasons, you should defragment your hard drive every week as part of a good maintenance plan. Defragging rearranges files on the drive into as few segments as possible.

Depending on how fragmented the drive and how large the drive, defragging it can take less than an hour or as long as all night. Therefore, it's best to start the defrag utility when you aren't going to be using your PC for a while. Vista is set to automatically defrag a drive every Wednesday at 1:00AM. To find out if this setting has been changed or to manually defrag the drive, close all open applications and then, using Windows Explorer, open the Properties box for the drive and click the **Tools** tab. Click **Defragment Now**. In the Disk Defragmenter window (see Figure 1-20), verify that Vista is set to defrag every Wednesday night. You can also click **Defragment now** to defrag the drive immediately.

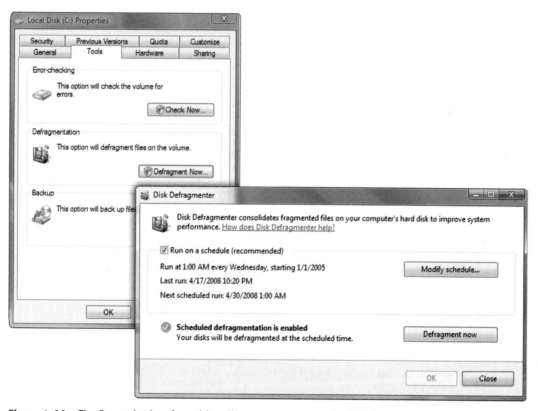

Figure 1-20   The Properties box for a drive allows you to manage the Disk Defragmenter

Generally, defragmenting a hard drive should be done when the hard drive is healthy; that is, it should be done as part of routine maintenance. To fully defrag the drive, 15% of the drive must be free. If there is less free space than 15%, Vista will partially defrag the drive. If you get an error message when attempting to defrag, try the utilities discussed next to repair the hard drive and then try to defrag again.

WINDOWS VISTA ERROR CHECKING AND CHKDSK

Next, to make sure the drive is healthy, you need to search for and repair file system errors, using the Windows Chkdsk utility. (In Windows Explorer, the Chkdsk utility is called Error Checking.) As with defragging, error checking and repair can take a long time depending on the size of the drive and how many files are present.

To launch the Chkdsk utility, use one of two methods:

◢ Using Windows Explorer, right-click the drive, and select **Properties** from the shortcut menu. Click the **Tools** tab, as shown in Figure 1-21, and then click **Check Now**. Respond to the UAC box. The Check Disk dialog box appears, also shown in Figure 1-21. Check the **Automatically fix file system errors** and **Scan for and attempt recovery of bad sectors** check boxes, and then click **Start**. For the utility to correct errors on the drive, it needs exclusive use of all files on the drive, which Windows calls a locked drive. If files are open, a dialog box appears telling you about the problem and asking your permission to scan the drive the next time Windows starts. Reboot the system and let her rip.

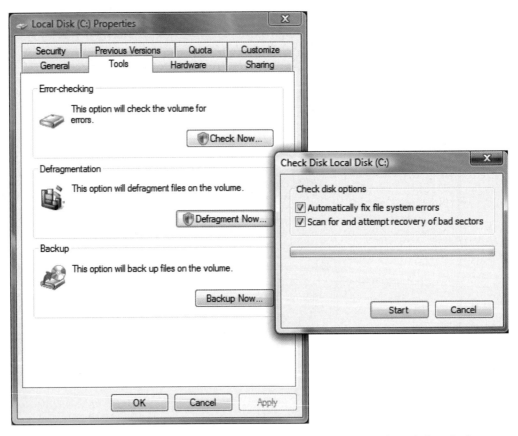

Figure 1-21 Vista repairs hard drive errors under the drive's Properties box using Windows Explorer

◢ Using an **elevated command prompt**, which has more privileges than a normal command prompt window, enter the Chkdsk command to check for and fix file system errors and to search out bad sectors and recover the data from them if possible. To access the elevated command prompt window, click **Start**, click **All Programs**, and click **Accessories**. Right-click **Command Prompt**, select **Run as administrator** from the shortcut menu, and respond to the UAC box. Then enter this Chkdsk command:

```
chkdsk c:/r
```

Before you move on to the next step in cleaning up an old and tired Windows Vista installation, reboot the system and verify all is well. If the drive was heavily fragmented with errors and unneeded files, you should now see a marked improvement in performance.

> **Tip**
>
> The Chkdsk command is also available from the Windows Vista Recovery Environment.

> **Note**
>
> The Chkdsk command searches for sectors that have already been marked as bad and attempts to recover data from them. It does not mark any new sectors as bad, and it cannot actually repair a bad sector.

FREE UP ADDITIONAL HARD DRIVE SPACE

Use Windows Explorer to find out how much free space is on the drive. There is no set minimum free space for Vista because the amount depends on how Vista and its applications are used. A good rule of thumb is to shoot for at least 15% of the drive to be free. If you still don't have that much, you can consider the following to get some additional space:

Move some data to other drives or devices

Most of us enjoy our digital cameras and we tend to keep a lot of photos on a hard drive. To free up that space, gather them all up and burn them to a few CDs or DVDs. Home videos or movies installed on a hard drive can take up tons of space. Consider an external hard drive to hold them all, or burn them to DVDs.

Consider drive or folder compression

If a volume is formatted using the NTFS file system, you can compress folders on the drive to save space, including the drive that Vista is installed on. However, know that drive compression will slow down a system because every file that is opened must be decompressed before it can be used. To avoid this problem, it's better to upgrade to a large hard drive or move some data to another media. If you do decide to compress a folder, right-click the folder and select **Properties**. On the General tab, click **Advanced**. In the Advanced Attributes box, click **Compress contents to save disk space** and click **OK** and then click **Apply** (see Figure 1-22). If you decide to compress the entire drive, right-click the drive and click **Properties** from the shortcut menu. On the General tab, click **Compress contents to save disk space** and click **Apply**.

Add a second hard drive

Consider installing a second hard drive to be used for the data and possibly for backups. How to install an external second hard drive is covered in Chapter 4.

Repartition the drive

Does the drive have more than one partition? If so, you can move some data or applications to another partition. To move applications from one partition or hard drive to another, you'll first have to uninstall the application. Most applications install their program files in the C:\Program Files folder, but during installation, they suggest this location and give you

> **Note**
>
> Vista installs on an NTFS volume, but if a second volume on the drive is formatted using the FAT32 file system, you can convert the volume to NTFS. For large drives, NTFS is more efficient and converting might improve performance. NTFS also offers better security and file and folder compression. For two Microsoft Knowledge Base articles about converting from FAT to NTFS, go to support.microsoft.com and search on articles 314097 and 156560.

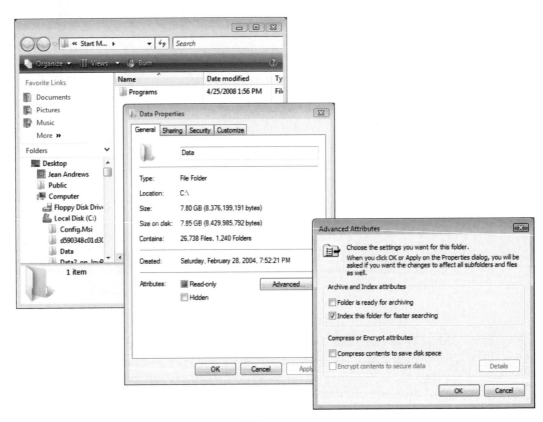

Figure 1-22 Compress folders or files to save disk space

the opportunity to change it. You can then point to a different drive or partition in the system to hold the application.

If the Windows partition is too small and the hard drive has unused space, you can enlarge the Windows partition using the Disk Management tool (see Figure 1-23). In the Disk Management window, right-click the **volume**, select **Extend Volume** from the shortcut menu, and follow directions on screen to select how much unused space to use.

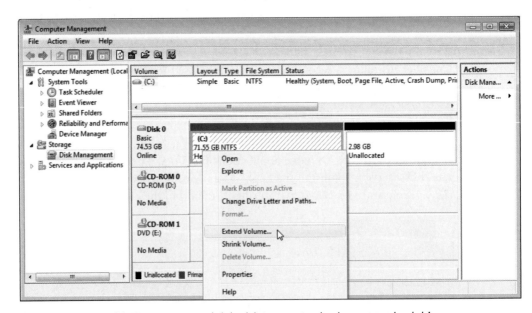

Figure 1-23 Use Disk Management to shrink, delete, or extend volumes on a hard drive

Move Pagefile.sys

Windows uses a file, Pagefile.sys, in the same way it uses memory. This file is called virtual memory and is used to enhance the amount of RAM in a system. Normally, the file is a hidden file stored in the root directory of drive C. To save space on drive C, you can move Pagefile.sys to another partition on the same hard drive or to a different hard drive, but don't move it to a different hard drive unless you know the other hard drive is at least as fast as this drive. Also, make sure the new volume has plenty of free space to hold the file—at least three times the amount of installed RAM.

To change the location of Pagefile.sys, follow these steps:

1. Click **Start,** right-click **Computer,** and click **Properties.** The System window appears.

2. Click **Advanced system settings** and respond to the UAC box. The System Properties box appears (see Figure 1-24).

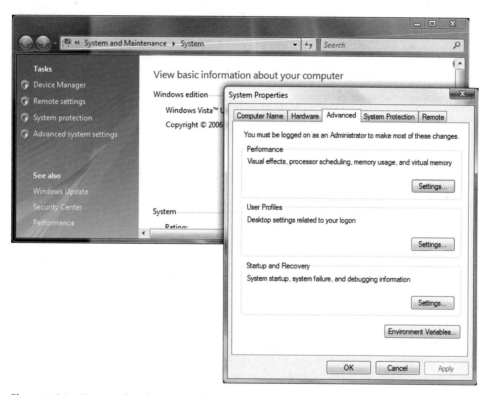

Figure 1-24 Manage virtual memory using the System Properties box

3. On the Advanced tab in the Performance section, click **Settings.** In the Performance Options box on the Advanced tab, click **Change.** The Virtual Memory dialog box appears.

4. Uncheck **Automatically manage paging file size on all drives** (see Figure 1-25). Select the drive and click **Set.** Don't dictate the size of the paging file; let Vista manage the size.

5. Click **OK.** Vista informs you that you must restart the system for the change to take effect.

6. Click **Apply** and **OK** to close the Performance Options box. Click **OK** to close the System Properties box and then restart the system.

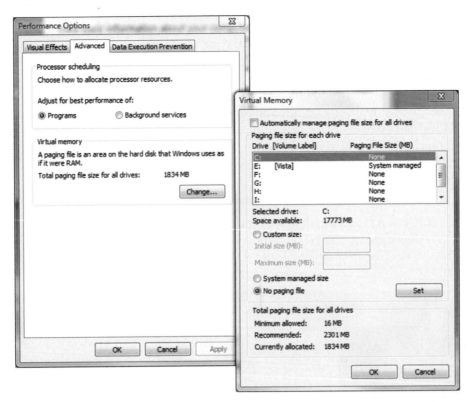

Figure 1-25   Move Pagefile.sys to a different drive

Limit space used by Internet Explorer

Here are some things you can do to save space on your primary Windows partition that is normally used by Internet Explorer:

▲ *Suggestion 1*: Reduce the amount of space Internet Explorer is allowed to use to cache files. In Internet Explorer, click **Tools**, then **Internet Options**. The Internet Options window opens. On the General tab under Browsing history, click **Settings**. In the Settings dialog box, change the amount of disk space to use (see Figure 1-26). Microsoft recommends that you not reduce the size below 50 MB.

▲ *Suggestion 2*: If you have some room on a second partition, you can move the Internet Explorer cache folder to that partition. Normally, this folder is C:\Users*username*\AppData\Local\Microsoft\Windows\Temporary Internet Files. To move it somewhere else, on the General tab of the Internet Options window under Browsing history, click **Settings**. In the Settings dialog box, click **Move folder**. In the Browse for Folder box, select the destination folder and click **OK** three times to close all boxes.

▲ *Suggestion 3*: You can also set IE to empty the cache folder each time you close the browser. To do that, on the Internet Options window, click the **Advanced** tab. Scroll down to the Security section, check **Empty Temporary Internet Files folder when browser is closed** and click **Apply** (see Figure 1-27). This setting is also good to use when you're using a public computer and want to make sure you don't leave tracks about your private surfing habits.

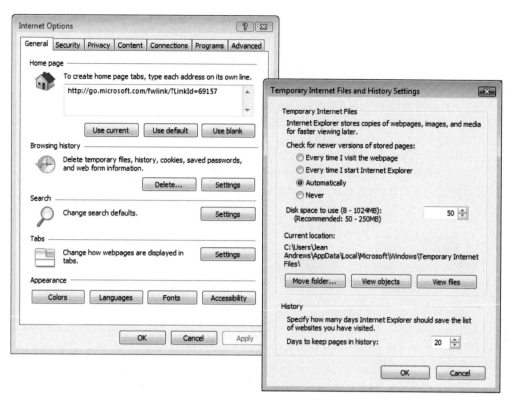

Figure 1-26 Allocate hard drive space to be used for temporary Internet files

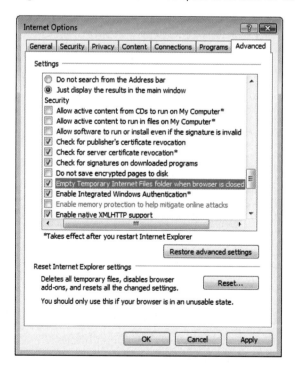

Figure 1-27 Set Internet Explorer not to keep a cache after the browser is closed

Remove unneeded or unwanted applications installed on drive C

Even though an application can be installed in any folder on the hard drive, by default, all applications are installed in the C:\Program Files folder. Using Windows Explorer, right-click the **Program Files** folder and select the **Properties** box, which lists the size of the folder. This size gives you a general idea of how much of the hard drive is being used by applications. How to remove unwanted software is covered in the next section.

STEP 4: REMOVE UNWANTED SOFTWARE

The next step in our quick-fix list of making Windows young again is to uninstall any unwanted software. To do that, open Control Panel, and click **Uninstall a program** under the Programs group. The Programs and Features window opens (see Figure 1-28). Notice the far-right column where you can see how much hard drive space the application is taking up. Besides taking up hard drive space, also consider that an application might start a program at startup that is taking up system resources.

> **Note**
>
> When a table column is missing in a Vista window, right-click the column headings area to see the shortcut menu that lists all columns available for this table. Check the missing column to make it appear in the table. For example, if the Publisher column is missing in the Programs and Features window, right-click in the column heading area and select Publisher from the shortcut menu. The Publisher column the appears.

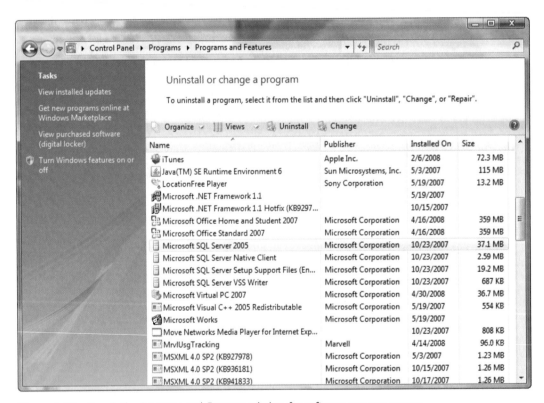

Figure 1-28 Search the Programs and Features window for software you can remove

As an example of a program that is launched at startup but serves no good purpose, look at the Microsoft SQL Server 2005 software in Figure 1-28. The user installed this software for a project that is finished. It's no longer needed and taking up space. We need to uninstall it. You'll find similar situations on most PCs that have been used for a while.

If you see software listed that you don't recognize, enter the title in a Google search (*www.google.com*). Don't remove software unless you know you won't need it later. This is especially true for laptop computers because the manufacturer often installs all kinds of software specific to the system. For example, check out all the Sony and Vaio software installed on the laptop in Figure 1-29. You would want to search on each product to find out why it's there before you remove it.

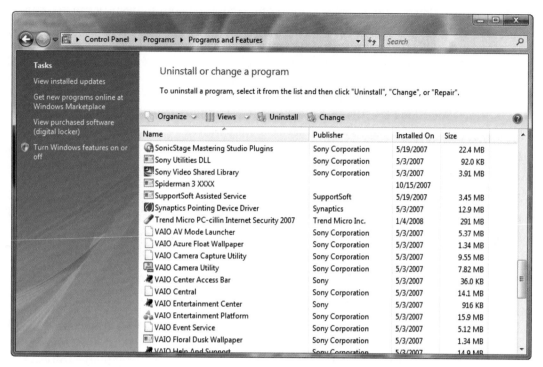

Figure 1-29 Manufacturers often preload many programs on their laptops

To remove a program, select it, and, at the top of the list, click **Uninstall** or **Uninstall/Change** (some programs combine the two functions into a single button). Then respond to the UAC box and follow the directions onscreen. During the uninstall process, a message might appear in the Remove Shared Component dialog box asking permission to delete a shared file as shown in Figure 1-30 for the program Belarc Advisor. If you have no other programs installed in the \Program Files\Belarc folder, it is safe enough to delete this file. To delete the file, click **Yes**.

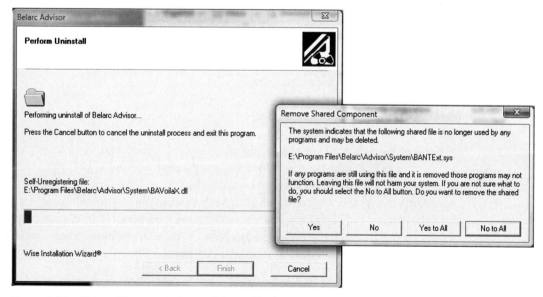

Figure 1-30 Vista asking permission to delete a file that might be needed by other programs

Well-behaved software like Belarc Advisor will uninstall with no problems, but this is not always the case with many shareware (download and try before you buy) and freeware (download for free or with a donation) applications and utilities. In fact, it's my opinion that many software producers purposely make their uninstall routines buggy so you have to keep the darn things. Also, when you attempt to remove stubborn software, it can do strange things to your system, such as pulling down your Windows Firewall. If an application or utility refuses to uninstall or gives errors when uninstalling, you might have to manually delete the program files and edit the registry to remove entries pertaining to the program. (I know you're probably tired of hearing me say something will be covered in later chapters, but we can't do *everything* in Chapter 1.) Removing buggy software is covered in Chapter 2.

Something else you can do to speed up Windows is to uninstall device drivers you no longer use and update older device drivers with newer versions. To uninstall a device you no longer need, open **Device Manager**, right-click the device, and select **Uninstall** from the shortcut menu. How to update device drivers is covered in Chapter 6.

STEP 5: SCAN THE SYSTEM FOR VIRUSES, ADWARE, AND SPYWARE

The next step in cleaning up a system is to scan it for viruses, adware, and spyware. You first scan for viruses because they can do a system the most harm, and then scan for adware and spyware.

SCAN THE SYSTEM FOR VIRUSES

Every computer connected to a network or the Internet needs to run antivirus (AV) software. When selecting a product, consider the effectiveness, hard drive space it requires, ease of use, customer support, and the cost. Table 1-2 lists a few antivirus software products designed for desktop or laptop computers.

Antivirus Software	Web Site
BitDefender Antivirus	*www.bitdefender.com*
Kaspersky Antivirus	*www.kaspersky.com*
McAfee VirusScan by McAfee Associates, Inc.	*www.mcafee.com*
Norton AntiVirus by Symantec, Inc.	*www.symantec.com*
AntiVirus plus AntiSpyware by Trend Micro	*www.trendmicro.com*
Windows Live OneCare	*onecare.live.com*

Table 1-2   Antivirus software and Web sites

Here's how to use antivirus software:

1. If you already have antivirus software installed, connect to the Internet, open the antivirus software main window, and execute the command to download any needed updates and virus definitions. For example, Figure 1-31 shows the main window for AntiVirus by Trend Micro, which is set to automatically download updates and scan the system. However, you can manually download updates by clicking **Update Now** or scan the system by clicking **Scan Now**. Viruses are released every day and your antivirus software is only as current as its latest update.

2. If you don't have antivirus software installed, you need it! Buy the software online or on CD and install it. When you're installing it, most likely the software will also scan for viruses as part of the installation process.

3. Run the antivirus software on the entire hard drive. Be sure to set it to check all folders and all types of files. If it finds a virus, run it again to make sure nothing new crops up.

4. Now set the antivirus software to run in the background of your system to keep it virus free. If it has the option, set it to scan e-mail before the e-mail or attachments are opened.

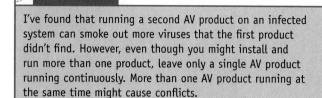

> **Note**
>
> I've found that running a second AV product on an infected system can smoke out more viruses that the first product didn't find. However, even though you might install and run more than one product, leave only a single AV product running continuously. More than one AV product running at the same time might cause conflicts.

5. If it offers the option, set the software to automatically keep updates current. For example, when you click the **Other Settings** link in Figure 1-31, you can change the way the software automatically downloads updates.

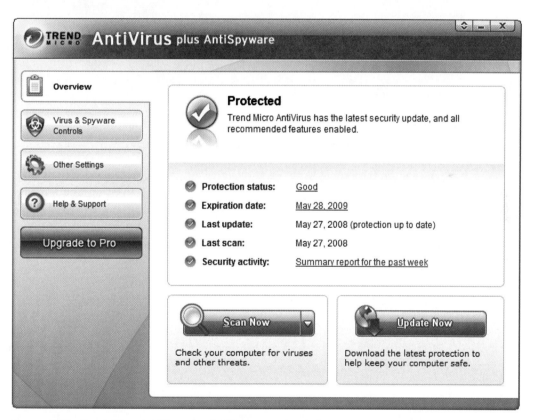

Figure 1-31   Trend Micro AntiVirus plus AntiSpyware main window

> **Note**
>
> If you have problems updating or running the antivirus software, try booting into Safe Mode and running the software from there. Safe Mode loads Windows with a rather plain, vanilla-flavored configuration, which might eliminate a problem that keeps the software from running. In fact, many AV software manufacturers recommend that if you suspect a system is infected, run the AV software in Safe Mode. To get to Safe Mode, reboot and press the **F8** key repeatedly while Windows is loading. The Advanced Boot Options menu appears, as shown in Figure 1-32. Select **Safe Mode with Networking** and press **Enter**.

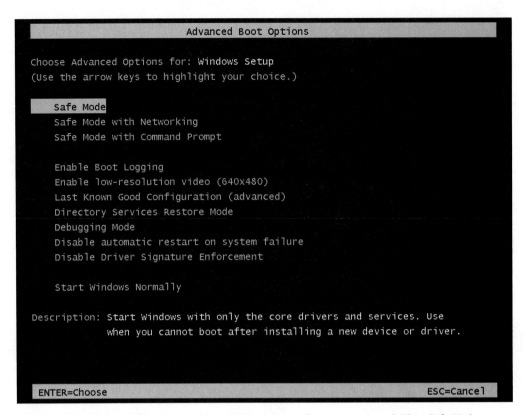

Figure 1-32 Windows Vista Advanced Boot Options menu allows you to launch Vista Safe Mode

SCAN FOR ADWARE AND SPYWARE

The distinction between adware and spyware is slight. Sometimes a malicious software program is displaying pop-up ads and also spying on you. Even though most popular AV software can find and remove adware and spyware, I've learned that what one product doesn't find another product might, so it pays to use more than one product.

There are tons of adware- and spyware-removal products available on the Web, but I recommend the two listed below. They both can catch adware, spyware, cookies, browser hijackers, dialers, keyloggers, and Trojans. All these types of nasty software are explained in Chapter 3, but for now, all you need to know is that you don't want them. To get rid of them, download and install one of these products:

> **Caution**
>
> One common problem that allows viruses and adware inside a computer is that users assume that, just because they have installed AV software on their computers, the AV software is doing its job. However, if the software is not kept updated, it gets pretty useless pretty fast. Also, users might assume the software is running in the background when it is not. Open the AV software main menu and verify that the AV software is turned on, and set it to automatically download and install updates.

▲ Ad-Aware by Lavasoft (*www.lavasoft.com*) is one of the most popular and successful adware- and spyware-removal products. It can be downloaded without support for free.

▲ Spybot Search & Destroy by PepiMK Software (*www.safer-networking.org*) does an excellent job of removing malicious software and it's free.

If you have scanned your system with AV software and then scanned using one of these products, but you still have a problem, download and run another product.

In Figure 1-33, you can see the results of when Spybot Search & Destroy scanned a system; it found a tracking cookie put there by *data.coremetrics.com*. A tracking cookie is used by the Web site that placed it on your PC without your knowledge to spy on your surfing habits in order to generate marketing statistics. To delete this cookie, check it and click **Fix selected problems**. You'll learn more about how to search for and remove cookies in Chapter 3.

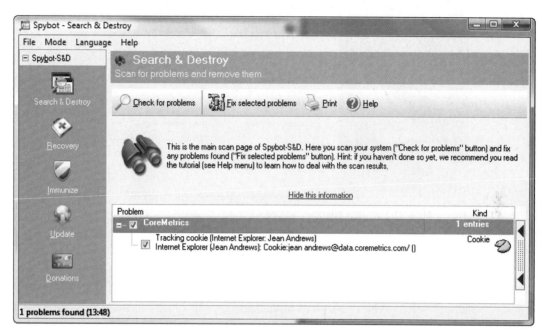

Figure 1-33 Spybot Search & Destroy scans for ads, keyloggers, dialers, browser hijackers, tracking cookies, and other malware

STEP 6: UPDATE WINDOWS

The Microsoft Web site offers patches, fixes, and updates for known problems and has an extensive knowledge base documenting problems and their solutions. It's important to keep these updates current on your system to fix known problems and plug up security holes to keep viruses and worms out.

HOW TO INSTALL UPDATES

To launch Windows Update, connect to the Internet and then click **Start**, point to **All Programs**, and click **Windows Update**. Depending on how automatic updating has been set, the updates might or might not be listed. If updates are not listed, click **Check for updates** in the left pane. If updates are listed, click **Install updates**. Follow directions on screen to download and install updates. During the process, if you see a window similar to that in Figure 1-34, click **Install now** to download and install the software needed to install updates.

If the PC hasn't been updated in a while, Windows selects the updates in the order you can receive them and will not necessarily list all the updates you need on the first pass. After you have installed the updates listed, go back and start again until Windows Update tells you there is nothing left to update. It might take two or more passes to get the PC entirely up to date.

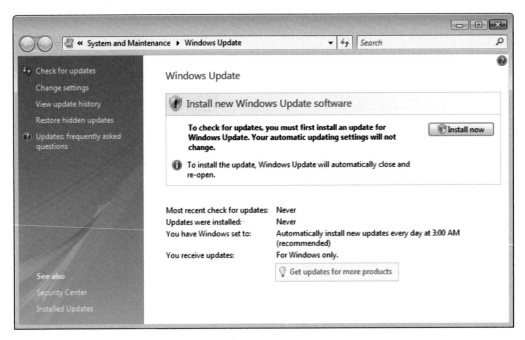

Figure 1-34 Install new Windows update software

If you later have a problem with Windows or another Microsoft product and think it might be caused by an installed update, you can uninstall the update. To do that, in the Windows Update window, click **View update history** and then click **Installed Updates**. In the Installed Updates window, select the update and click **Uninstall** (see Figure 1-35).

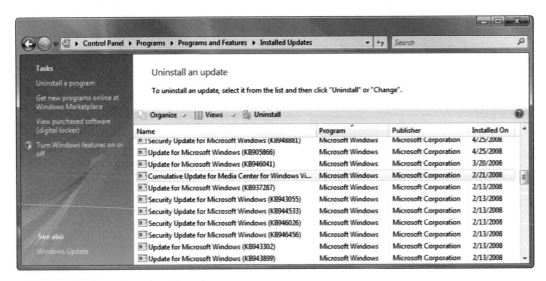

Figure 1-35 Uninstall a Microsoft update

WINDOWS VISTA SERVICE PACK 1 (SP1)

So far, Microsoft has released one service pack for Windows Vista. Service Pack 1 makes some improvements in Vista performance, plugs up some security holes, and solves some problems with hardware. As you work your way through the Windows Update process, when the system is ready to receive Service Pack 1, you'll see it listed as the only available update (see Figure 1-36). It will take some time and one or more reboots to complete the process of installing Service Pack 1. You'll need at least 4.5 GB of free space on the drive for the installation. After the service pack is installed, the System window shows it installed (see Figure 1-37).

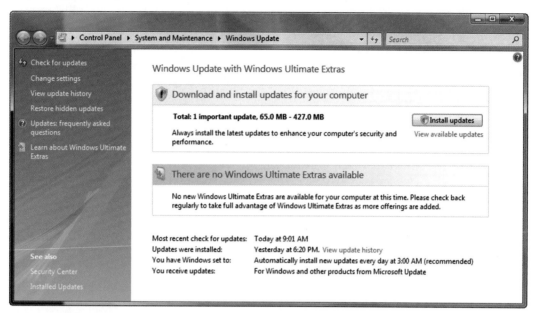

Figure 1-36 Service Pack 1 is available as an important update

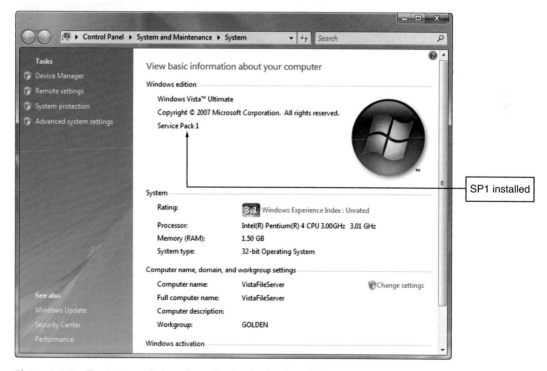

Figure 1-37 The System window shows Service Pack 1 installed

AUTOMATIC UPDATES

After you've gotten Windows Vista current with all its updates, set the system so that it will stay current. To do that, click **Start,** point to **All Programs,** and click **Windows Update.** In the Windows Update window shown in Figure 1-36, click **Change settings.** Using the Change settings window shown in Figure 1-38, configure these automatic update settings

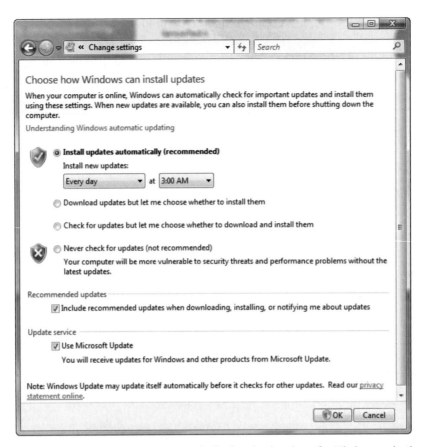

Figure 1-38 Set Windows to automatically download updates for Windows and other Microsoft products

according to how the PC connects to the Internet and user habits. For an always-up broadband connection (such as cable modem or DSL), select **Install updates automatically (recommended)** and choose to automatically download and install updates every day. If the PC's Internet connection is not always up (such as with a dial-up connection), you might want to select **Check for updates but let me choose whether to download and install them**. This option works better if a user doesn't want to be bothered with a long and involved download when the PC first connects to the ISP using a slow dial-up connection, or if you want more control over which updates are installed. Discuss the options with the user. Make sure the user understands that if the update process is not fully automated, he or she needs to take the time to do the updates at least once a week. And explain to the user that important security updates need to be installed daily.

> **Note**
>
> When updating Vista on a laptop computer, be aware that Windows service packs for laptops are often customized by the laptop manufacturer and made available on the manufacturer's web site. To get the download, look for a link on the All Programs menu. For example, for one Sony VAIO laptop, click **Start**, point to **All Programs**, and click **Go to VAIO Web Support**. The browser opens to a page on the *sony.com* site where you can download Vista Service Pack 1.

Notice in Figure 1-38 that you can choose to receive updates for other Microsoft products such as Microsoft Office. Ask the user for permission to receive these updates as well.

STEP 7: MAKE ONE LAST CHECK

By now, the system should be clean and purring. To make sure all is well, reboot and check for errors. Take another look at Task Manager and verify that it looks clean. Remember, you used MSconfig to control the startup process, and this is just a temporary fix until you can get to the root of all those processes bogging down startup. If you still see problems or performance hasn't improved, here are some more things you can do or try, and, in Chapter 2, you'll find other in-depth solutions.

USE SYSTEM FILE CHECK (sfc.exe)

Windows might have corrupted system files, which calls for a more drastic measure. Try using System File Check (sfc.exe) to scan the installation for corrupted or missing system files. The command-line utility must be launched from an elevated command prompt. To access this window, click **Start**, click **All Programs**, and click **Accessories**. Right click **Command Prompt**, select **Run as administrator** from the shortcut menu, and respond to the UAC box. An Administrator Command Prompt window opens. Then enter the command **sfc /scannow** to immediately scan all system files to make sure they're not corrupted. Or you can use sfc /scanonce to scan the system at the next reboot. You might be required to provide the Windows Vista setup DVD. How to repair a corrupted Windows installation is covered in Chapter 7.

> **Note**
>
> If you're responsible for several PCs in a small office or home office, you might find it difficult to keep track of which setup CD belongs to which system. I keep a brown manila envelope for each PC in my office. In the envelope are all the setup CDs for hardware and the OS on that one system and also any user manuals. It also contains a list of any changes I've made to the system, such as changes to CMOS setup. Also, if you purchased a system with Vista already installed and it did not come with a Vista DVD, you might consider purchasing the setup DVD from the computer manufacturer just in case problems later arise. The price should be only a few dollars.

CONSIDER A HARDWARE UPGRADE

You might need to upgrade memory or the processor, or you might consider a second hard drive. Vista needs much more memory than previous operating systems.

Windows should now be running faster and smoother. And now you're ready to set Windows so it is better protected to stay fit and clean.

KEEPING WINDOWS FIT

Now that Windows is all cleaned up, you'll want to keep it that way. And, if you're helping someone else clean up his or her computer, be sure to teach this user what to do to keep Windows fit and how to make good backups of important data. The best troubleshooting practice is to prevent problems from happening to begin with. Here are a few tips to practice and to teach other users:

◢ *Tip 1*: Keep good backups of data and protect the computer from mischief. How to schedule automated backups is covered in Chapter 4. Most Windows problems are caused by user error or malicious attacks that could have been prevented if proper protective measures had been taken. How to secure a desktop or notebook computer is covered in Chapter 4.

▲ *Tip 2*: Keep Windows updates current. Set Windows Update to Automatic so that you don't have to remember to perform the updates.

▲ *Tip 3*: Know and practice defensive measures when using the Internet. Make sure each network has a hardware firewall to the Internet connection and that each PC has Windows Firewall enabled. Configure AV software to continually run in the background and automatically download and install updates.

▲ *Tip 4*: Clean up your hard drive on a regular basis.

▲ *Tip 5*: Be a responsible Web surfer and e-mail and chat room user. Don't expose the system by downloading and installing freeware from untrustworthy sites. Don't open an e-mail attachment unless you trust the sender and have scanned it for viruses. Don't enter personal information into an e-mail message or on a Web site that you don't trust. Other ways to protect your privacy, your computer, and your identity are covered in Chapters 4 and 5.

▲ *Tip 6*: To protect your hardware, don't smoke around your computer; don't jar or move the computer case while the hard drive is active; protect your CDs and DVDs, and use a surge protector and adequate grounding.

▲ *Tip 7*: Even though Windows Defender monitors some suspicious activities, consider installing a second startup and registry monitor such as WinPatrol by BillP Studios (*www.winpatrol.com*). A little black Scotty dog woofs when the registry is about to be invaded or startup services added. Then an alert window appears and you can approve or stop the change (see Figure 1-39). Some AV or antispyware software, such as Trend Micro AntiVirus or Spybot Search & Destroy, will do the same thing.

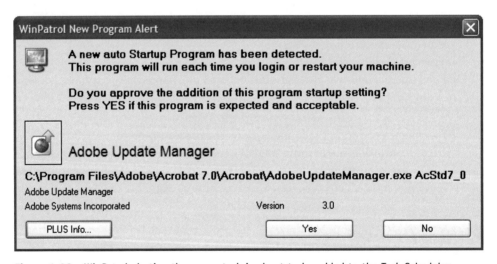

Figure 1-39   WinPatrol alerting the user a task is about to be added to the Task Scheduler

▲ *Tip 8*: When working with other users, ask permission to configure Windows and AV software so that the firewall is up and updates are kept current. Teach users how to back up data, how to clean up the hard drive, how to protect hardware, and how to use the Internet responsibly. Encourage users not to "tinker" with Windows unless they know what they're doing. For users who tend to use the Internet without restraint, ask permission to install a startup and registry monitor, such as WinPatrol.

1

WHAT TO EXPECT FROM THE REST OF THIS BOOK

In this chapter, you've seen how to solve a common Windows Vista problem, most likely caused by poor maintenance, and how to keep the problem from reoccurring. Let's now take a look at how to approach a Windows problem in general. We will use this approach throughout the rest of the book.

HOW TO APPROACH A WINDOWS PROBLEM

Generally, when trying to fix a Windows problem (or any problem, for that matter), the process begins by asking questions and finding answers. Based on the answers, take appropriate action and then evaluate the result. And, if you really want to be an expert troubleshooter, become a fanatic at documentation. Take good notes about what you are doing and learning so you can better remember it when dealing with future computer problems. See Figure 1-40.

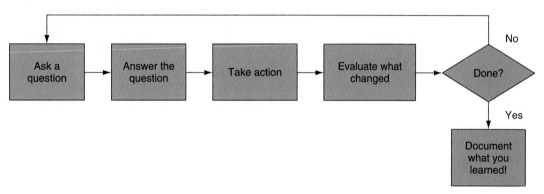

Figure 1-40 Learn to be an effective problem solver

ASK YOURSELF OR THE USER SOME QUESTIONS

If the PC you're fixing is your own, you might be tempted to skip this step, but don't. Step back and ask yourself the same questions you would ask other users if they came to you with their PC problem.

Don't begin actual problem solving until you know if there is valuable data on the PC that's not backed up. If there are no backups, absolutely, positively do all you can to back up that data before you do anything else. Sometimes the most valuable thing on a PC is the data. Then begin troubleshooting by isolating the problem into one of two categories: pre-boot problems that prevent the PC from booting and post-boot problems that occur after a successful boot.

As you talk with the user, please be careful not to accuse him or her of causing the problem. You want to build a team with the user. For example, rather than asking, "Did you move the computer recently?" a less accusing question is, "Has the computer been moved recently?" Here are some good questions to help you learn as much as you can:

▲ *Question 1*: Please describe the problem. What error messages, unusual displays, or failures did you see? (Possible answer: I see this blue screen with a funny looking message on it that makes no sense to me.)

▲ *Question 2*: When did the problem start? (Possible answer: When I first booted after loading this neat little screen saver I downloaded from the Web.)

◢ *Question 3*: What was the situation when the problem occurred? (Possible answers: I was trying to start up my PC. I was opening a document in MS Word. I was researching a project on the Internet.)

◢ *Question 4*: What programs or software were you using? (Possible answer: I was using Internet Explorer.)

◢ *Question 5*: Has the computer been moved recently? (Possible answer: Well, yes. Yesterday I moved the computer case from one side of my desk to the other.) By the way, if someone told me that, my next question would be: Was the system powered down before it was moved? If they answered no, I'd begin by suspecting a crashed hard drive.

◢ *Question 6*: Has there been a recent thunderstorm or electrical problem? (Possible answer: Yes, last night. Then when I tried to turn on my PC this morning, nothing happened.)

◢ *Question 7*: Do you think any hardware, software, or configuration changes have been made? (Possible answer: Could be. I think my sister might have.)

◢ *Question 8*: Has someone else used your computer recently? (Possible answer: Sure, my son uses it all the time.)

◢ *Question 9*: Is there some valuable data on your system that is not backed up that I should know about before I start working on the problem? (Possible answer: Yes! Yes! My term paper! It's not backed up! You gotta get me that!)

◢ *Question 10*: Can you show me exactly how to reproduce the problem? (Possible answer: Yes, let me show you what to do.) Remember that many problems stem from user error. As the user shows you how to reproduce the problem, watch what the user is doing and ask questions.

Based on the answers to your questions, you're ready to set your priorities and address the problem. As you work on the problem, at the top of your priority list should be to protect any important data that is not backed up.

PROTECT THE DATA

If valuable data is at stake, don't do anything to jeopardize it. Back it up as soon as possible. If you must take a risk with the data, let it be the user's decision to do so, not yours. Here are some examples of the urgency of protecting the data and what you might do to protect it:

◢ Mary's only copy of her term paper is on the hard drive, and Windows is giving strange errors when she opens Internet Explorer. Before you do anything to solve the IE problem, copy her term paper to a flash drive or burn it to a CD and hand it to her for safekeeping. She can now relax while you work.

◢ Zack is responsible for a huge database that is not currently backed up, and Windows is giving an error and refusing to boot. You believe the only way to solve the Windows problem is to reinstall the OS. Before you do that, remove the hard drive from the system, install it as a second hard drive in another PC, and copy the database to the primary hard drive in the working system. Then move the hard drive back to the original PC and begin working on the Windows boot problem.

◢ Isaac tells you the only important data on his desktop computer's hard drive is his e-mail, the e-mail attachments, and his e-mail address book. He uses Eudora as his e-mail software, which is configured to store all that information in the C:\Email folder. Before you begin upgrading his OS from Windows XP to Windows Vista, copy the contents of the C:\Email folder to Isaac's notebook computer. Install Eudora on the notebook and have Isaac verify that he can

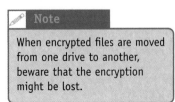

Note

When encrypted files are moved from one drive to another, beware that the encryption might be lost.

access all the e-mail there. Now you're free to upgrade his desktop OS. You'll learn more about backing up and recovering e-mail data in Chapter 4. In Chapter 5, you'll learn how to connect two computers to copy data from one to the other using a super-simple network.

After the data is safe, you can begin troubleshooting the problem. At this point, you might not want the user watching, especially if you're new at this and someone watching might make you nervous. You can say to the user something like "Okay, now I just need to work on the problem. I'll let you know if I need something or have more questions."

TIPS WHEN PROBLEM SOLVING

Following the steps the user showed you earlier, reproduce the problem as you carefully observe what happens. Here are some useful tips:

- *Tip 1*: Keep a pad and pencil handy as you work. Take notes as you work so that you can backtrack if need be, and so that you can keep track of what you've already tried or not tried. Once you fix the problem, you'll also have a valuable document to take into the next troubleshooting situation.
- *Tip 2*: Remember that copying data not backed up to another media is top priority. If you suspect the hard drive is failing, don't do anything else, including rebooting the system, until the data is safely copied.
- *Tip 3*: Start troubleshooting with a reboot. Many problems go away with a reboot. However, if the problem still exists, you know your starting point. The exception to this rule is when a user points out a problem currently displayed onscreen that he or she doesn't know how to reproduce. In addition, when a problem comes and goes at odd times (called an intermittent problem) and you finally see it displayed, take the time to investigate as much as you can about the current situation before you reboot.
- *Tip 4*: As you attempt to solve the problem, first reproduce the problem and learn what you can as you go. Start at the beginning. Watch everything carefully—error messages, lights, and so forth. Take good notes. Be a careful observer.
- *Tip 5*: Does the problem occur during the boot? If the problem occurs during the boot, is it hardware or software related? Does the problem occur with hardware before the OS load begins? Is the problem related to loading the OS?
- *Tip 6*: If the problem occurs after the boot, is it related to hardware or software? Has the hardware or application ever worked?
- *Tip 7*: Simplify and isolate the problem. For example, if you have a problem with an application, close all other applications.
- *Tip 8*: As you try one thing after another, reboot between fixes. You might have solved the problem with your fix, or you might have created a new problem. At the least, each reboot gives you a fresh perspective on what's going on. Also, for external devices such as printers or routers, turn them off and then back on to begin fresh.
- *Tip 9*: Use the Internet for research. You'll see many examples in this book of how the Internet can be useful when problem solving. Search the Web site of the device or software manufacturer, open a chat session with the site's technical support staff, or use a search engine such as Google to research an error message or symptom. For just about any PC problem, someone somewhere has had the same problem. It can be particularly useful to use a search engine such as Google to search for specific text from error messages, which often goes directly to the problem. For example, if an error message appears and includes a reference to the program "badpc.exe," simply searching for "badpc.exe" on Google may bring up numerous pages that identify this file as a known malicious program. Also, newsgroups can be very helpful in researching problems.

◢ *Tip 10*: Don't stop until you know you're done. If you think the problem is fixed, test the fix and the system. Make sure all is working before you stop. Then have the user verify the problem is solved.

TOOLS OF THE TRADE

In this book, we're going to use all kinds of resources. You'll learn to use some Windows utilities and some third-party utilities, and you'll also learn how to research a problem using the Internet and other sources. Here's a summary of these tools and resources:

◢ Perhaps the most powerful and useful tool for solving problems with Windows is the Internet. Appendix A lists Web sites that contain helpful information when solving computer problems. The most important is the Microsoft support site (*support.microsoft.com*). This site is extremely useful in finding information on software and hardware problems and solutions. Windows updates are also available from the site.

◢ Windows Vista comes with many utility tools. In this chapter, you already learned about Task Manager, System Configuration (MSconfig), Device Manager, Disk Management, Safe Mode, Windows Defender, and System File Checker. In later chapters, you'll learn to use many other Windows utility tools such as the Recovery Environment and the Registry Editor.

◢ A third-party utility is software not written by Microsoft (although Microsoft has purchased much of it recently). You can download it from the Web and install it on your system to help get behind the scenes in Windows and to solve problems. Many third-party utilities are shareware (download and try before you buy) or freeware (download for free or with a donation). You'll learn to use several third-party utilities in this book; most of them can be downloaded for free. This software is generally divided into two categories:

◢ Software that runs in the background to defend and protect. Examples are Norton Antivirus by Symantec (*www.symantec.com*) and Ad-Aware by Lavasoft (*www.lavasoft.com*); both are discussed in this chapter.

◢ Software used by a technician to examine a system and manually fix a problem. For example, Process Explorer by Mark Russinovich (*technet.microsoft.com* and formally owned by Sysinternals) can be used to track processes running on your PC and gives more information than does Task Manager.

◢ Use this book as your most valuable Windows troubleshooting tool. In the book, you'll learn step-by-step strategies to solve the most difficult and most common Windows problems. As you follow these steps, you're going to learn an awful lot about how Windows works and how to get inside its guts to fix it. With this knowledge comes power. You can take what you've learned and apply it to other Windows problems and build on it to learn even more about how Windows works and how to fix it.

TOP SEVEN WINDOWS PROBLEMS

In this and the remaining chapters, we'll take each problem one at a time, give you the insights and understanding you need about the problem, and step you through the process of fixing the problem. It's going to be fun! So here are the top seven complaints you'll hear when supporting Windows:

1. My Windows system is sluggish and slow.

2. When I start up Windows, it's slow and clunky, and I see strange messages.

3. I'm under attack! Nasty software has attacked my system!

4. I need better security for my computer or small network, but I don't know how to get it.

5. I can't connect using wireless or wired networks.

6. My applications or devices give errors, won't work, won't install, or won't uninstall.

7. Windows won't start up at all. And I have data in there somewhere!

Let the fun begin!

>> CHAPTER SUMMARY

▲ A sluggish Windows system is most likely caused by poor maintenance resulting in too many applications and services loading at startup, too little free hard drive space, a fragmented hard drive, or not enough memory or powerful enough processor.

▲ Before you start trying to fix a Windows problem, take a few minutes to examine the system so you know what essential hardware is present, how much free space on the hard drive is available, and what programs and processes are running.

▲ Clean up a sluggish Windows system by first using the System Configuration Utility (MSconfig) to stop all nonessential and non-Windows processes from loading at startup. Later you'll need to allow those to start that you really want.

▲ Clean up the hard drive by deleting unwanted files, defragging the drive, and scanning it for errors.

▲ To clean up the system, remove any unwanted software, scan for viruses and other malicious software, and download and install Windows updates, patches, and fixes.

▲ Routine maintenance of a system includes keeping Windows current with updates and patches, using a firewall and antivirus software, and using good judgment when using the Internet or tinkering with Windows settings.

▲ When solving a Windows problem, interview the user and protect any important data not backed up.

▲ Classify a computer problem as a pre-boot problem (occurs during the boot) or post-boot problem (occurs after the Windows desktop is loaded).

▲ Key troubleshooting tools include the Internet for research, Windows tools, third-party tools, and this book.

>> KEY TERMS

device driver   A program stored on the hard drive that tells the computer how to communicate with a hardware device such as a printer or modem.

device manager   A Windows tool to view and manage installed hardware devices and drivers and the resources they use.

devmgmt.msc   The Microsoft Management Console program that launches Device Manager.

diskmgmt.msc   The Microsoft Management Console program that launches Disk Management

elevated command prompt   A command prompt window that allows commands to run at the privileged administrative level.

freeware   Software you can download for free.

MSconfig.exe   A Windows troubleshooting utility that launches the System Configuration Utility used to reduce startup to essentials.

msinfo32.exe   The Windows utility program that launches the System Information window.

process   A Program that is running together with the resources needed by the running program.

service   A program running in the background that provides support to Windows, an application, or a device (for more explanation, see Appendix D).

shareware   Software you can download and try before you buy.

Taskmgr.exe   The Windows utility program that launches Task Manager.

third-party utility   Software not written by Microsoft that you can install on your system to help solve a Windows problem.

tracking cookie   A cookie placed on your PC without your knowledge by a Web site to spy on your surfing habits in order to generate marketing statistics.

>> REVIEWING THE BASICS

1. A PC problem can be divided into what two main categories?

2. What Windows utility do you use to find out how a hard drive is partitioned?

3. What Windows utility can easily let you see how much free space is available on drive C?

4. When someone asks you for help solving a Windows problem, what is the first thing you should do?

5. Why is it important to keep notes as you solve a Windows problem?

6. What Vista utility can be used to see a list of all programs launched at startup and how the program is launched?

7. What Windows tool can you use to see which processor is installed and how much RAM is installed?

8. What Vista tool lets you quickly see if a service pack has been applied to Windows?

9. What are two reasons why a user might not want to turn on Automatic Updates for Windows?

10. How much memory does Microsoft say Windows Vista must have for normal operation?

11. What are three things you can do to clean up a hard drive?

12. What Windows utility can give a list of open applications?

13. Using Task Manager, which tab gives a list of running applications?

14. In Software Explorer, how can you see the name of the program file that was used to launch a running program?

15. When trying to run antivirus software, if you get errors, what can you do to solve the problem(s)?

>> THINKING CRITICALLY

1. You are helping a user who is suddenly having trouble printing. Select the steps you should take in attempting to solve this problem, and list them in the appropriate order:

   a. Reboot the system.
   b. Have the user demonstrate how he or she is trying to print.
   c. Interview the user about how the problem started.
   d. Close unnecessary applications.

2. Jason notices that drive C is very full and has many applications installed. A second partition on the same drive, named drive F, has plenty of space. Answer these questions:

   a. Can Jason move the Program Files folder to drive F? Why or why not?
   b. Can Jason move the Pagefile.sys file to drive F? Why or why not?
   c. What tool can Jason use to reduce the size of drive F and increase the size of drive C?

3. You have a system with a 2 GHz Pentium 4 processor, 512 MB of RAM, and a 20GB hard drive. Which upgrade (processor, RAM, or hard drive) would most benefit your system and what, if anything, does this depend on?

>> HANDS-ON PROJECTS

PROJECT 1-1: Investigating Running Processes

Open Task Manager and click the **Processes** tab to view the processes running under your current user's account and write down each of them. Next, use the Internet to research each of these processes and determine what they do and what (if any) applications they are associated with. Identify which processes belong to Windows Vista.

PROJECT 1-2: Checking for Spyware

Go to *www.lavasoft.com* and download the latest version of Ad-Aware. Once it is installed, use it to remove any spyware that has infected your PC. Then run Spybot Search & Destroy (*www.safer-networking.org*). Did Search & Destroy find anything that Ad-Aware left behind?

PROJECT 1-3: Cleaning Up Your Hard Drive

Log onto Vista using an account with Administrator rights. Open **Windows Explorer** and right-click drive C. On the shortcut menu, click **Properties** and then click **Disk Cleanup** in the properties window. Clean up files for all users. In the Disk Cleanup window, select **Downloaded Program Files, Temporary Internet Files, Recycle Bin**, and **Temporary files** and click **OK**.

   Next, log onto the system using an account that does not have Administrator rights. How are you limited in the way you can perform a Disk Cleanup? Why do you think this limitation exists?

PROJECT 1-4: Running System File Checker

Open an elevated command prompt window and type **sfc/scannow** to scan your system for corrupted or missing system files. Document any error messages that appear. Next, try to use the command from a regular command prompt window. What error message do you receive?

>> REAL PROBLEMS, REAL SOLUTIONS

REAL PROBLEM 1-1:   Examining a Windows Vista Computer

Begin this project by rebooting your system. Then, following directions given in the chapter, answer the following questions. The answers to these questions are intended to give you a quick survey of the condition of a Windows Vista computer and to determine its maintenance needs:

1. What processor is installed?

2. How much RAM is installed?

3. What Windows Vista service packs are installed?

4. What is the size of the hard drive? How much free space is on the primary drive partition (drive C)? Are there other volumes on this same hard drive?

5. Are there any installed devices that don't appear to be running or that have a problem?

6. What applications or processes are currently running that appear as though they might not be necessary or might be malicious?

7. List some quick fixes presented in this chapter that might improve performance. List them in the order that you would do them.

REAL PROBLEM 1-2:   Cleaning Up a Sluggish Windows Vista System

Using all the tools and techniques presented in this chapter, clean up a sluggish Windows Vista system. Take detailed notes as you go, showing what you checked before you started to solve the problems, what you did to solve the problems, and what the results were of your efforts. What questions did you have along the way? Bring these questions to class for discussion.

Making Windows Vista Boot Like New

In Chapter 1, you saw how to clean up a slow and sluggish Windows Vista system. For the most part, we fixed the problems using routine maintenance tools such as Defrag and Chkdsk. If a problem wasn't easy to solve, we simply applied a quick patch and moved on. For example, if a program were launched at startup and we didn't think we really needed it, we just temporarily disabled it from the startup process—we didn't take the time to get at the underlying problem of how or why the program got there to begin with and remove it at its root. In this chapter, we go for the roots. That is, in this chapter you'll learn how a program gets into the lineup of startup processes, how to determine if you really want it there, and how to permanently reduce startup to the essentials.

This chapter is organized as a how-to chapter to make your work as easy as possible. First, you'll learn about some quick-and-dirty solutions to startup problems that might clean things up easily for you. Then you'll learn about the most common ways to clean up the startup process. These methods are presented to you in the order you should use them. Next, we'll dig a little deeper into some more complex solutions that you'll need to use only in the most difficult of situations. Last, after the problem is solved, you'll learn how to keep the problem from coming back—that is, you'll learn about some things you can do to keep the startup process clean as a whistle.

Focus Problem

"My Windows Vista startup is sluggish and gives me strange error messages."

QUICK FIXES FOR DRASTIC STARTUP PROBLEMS

Sometimes you have to put out a fire or two before you can begin solving an underlying problem. This section is about some things you can do if you have an immediate Vista startup problem that you need to deal with before you work on the underlying problem. If your Vista startup is generally just slow and is not giving errors, you can skip this section and move on to the next, "Clean Up Startup." However, if you've got an error message staring you in the face, try the quick-and-dirty solutions presented in this part of the chapter. If your problem is still not solved, then you need to move on to Chapter 7, "Resurrecting the Dead." That chapter pulls out the big guns to solve the really nasty startup problems that prevent a system from booting.

The tools covered in the following subsections are the Last Known Good Configuration, Safe Mode for running antivirus software, System Restore, and the System Configuration Utility. Let's get started with the first one, which you can try if Windows Vista won't boot to the Windows desktop.

LAST KNOWN GOOD CONFIGURATION

If Vista won't boot to the Windows desktop, you can try to use the Last Known Good Configuration on the Advanced Boot Options menu. Windows considers the startup to be a good startup just after a user successfully logs onto the system. At that time, it saves the configuration it used for that startup in a place in the registry and calls this information the **Last Known Good Configuration**, which most technicians simply call the Last Known Good. If you are having a problem starting up Windows, you can have Windows revert to the Last Known Good. Here's what to do:

1. While Windows is loading, repeatedly press the **F8** key. The Windows Advanced Boot Options Menu shown in Figure 2-1 appears.

2. On the menu, highlight **Last Known Good Configuration** (**advanced**) and press **Enter**.

The system reboots and the Last Known Good is applied. This step sequence will solve your startup problem if these things are true:

▲ *The problem is caused by the Vista startup configuration.* The Last Known Good is good only for solving a problem caused by an error in the Windows Vista configuration, such as when you just installed a bad device driver or other program that has corrupted the registry.

▲ *The Last Known Good snapshot of the startup configuration was taken before the problem occurred.* Recall that the Last Known Good is taken immediately after a user logs on. If you've logged on several times after the problem started, you've probably overwritten the Last Known Good that was good. Therefore, it's important to try the Last Known Good early, after the problem has first started.

If applying the Last Known Good doesn't solve your problem, then try Safe Mode.

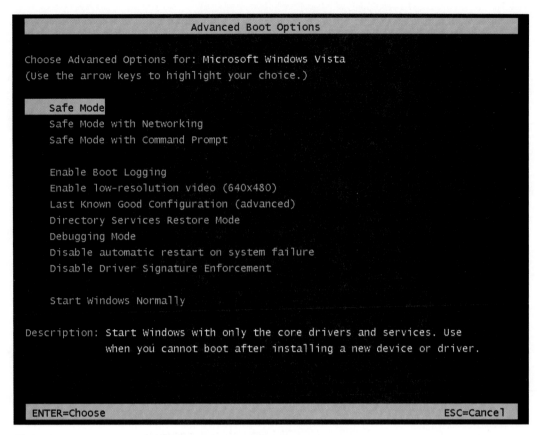

```
                        Advanced Boot Options

Choose Advanced Options for: Microsoft Windows Vista
(Use the arrow keys to highlight your choice.)

    Safe Mode
    Safe Mode with Networking
    Safe Mode with Command Prompt

    Enable Boot Logging
    Enable low-resolution video (640x480)
    Last Known Good Configuration (advanced)
    Directory Services Restore Mode
    Debugging Mode
    Disable automatic restart on system failure
    Disable Driver Signature Enforcement


    Start Windows Normally

Description: Start Windows with only the core drivers and services. Use
            when you cannot boot after installing a new device or driver.




ENTER=Choose                                            ESC=Cancel
```

Figure 2-1   Press F8 to see the Advanced Boot Options Menu

SAFE MODE ON THE ADVANCED BOOT OPTIONS MENU

If you think you know the cause of the problem preventing Windows from starting normally, you can try to start Windows in Safe Mode and fix the problem there. When you start Windows Vista in **Safe Mode**, it uses only the core device drivers needed to operate essential hardware devices and does not load installed applications or third-party services. In other words, Windows loads using a bare-bones configuration. If the Windows desktop will not load normally, but does load in Safe Mode, you can conclude that the problem is caused by non-essential hardware devices, startup applications, malware, or non-essential Windows components or features.

To start Windows in Safe Mode, press **F8** while Windows is loading to display the Windows **Advanced Boot Options Menu**, which allows you to select options when starting Windows Vista. Select **Safe Mode with Networking**. When you see a logon screen, log on using an administrator account. Figure 2-2 shows what the Windows desktop looks like in Safe Mode. Notice the black background with Safe Mode written in all four corners of the screen.

Here are some problems and what you can do to fix them while Vista is loaded in Safe Mode:

   ◢ *Problem 1: A hardware device is preventing the system from booting normally.* If you have just installed a new hardware device, use Device Manager to disable the device. If the problem doesn't go away, then uninstall the device. If this solves the problem, then try to find updated device drivers for the device. Search the Microsoft Web site for known problems with the device or search the device manufacturer Web site.

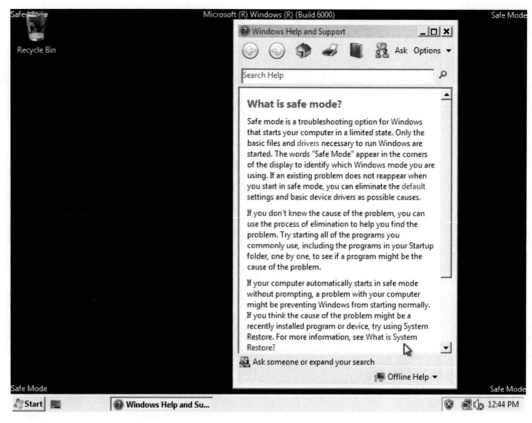

Figure 2-2 Safe Mode loads a minimum Vista configuration

Try updating the device drivers. If you have just updated a device driver, the update might be causing the problem. Open Device Manager and use Driver Rollback to restore the old drivers.

▲ *Problem 2: A startup application is causing errors.* If you have just installed a new application or utility program, you can use Software Explorer to disable the startup program, or in Control Panel, you can use the Programs and Features page to uninstall the program. If the problem goes away, try reinstalling the software. If the problem comes back, go to the software manufacturer's Web site and download and install any updates or fixes.

▲ *Problem 3: The hard drive does not have enough free space for a normal startup.* When the hard drive is full or has errors, a normal startup that launches several applications or services can give errors. In Safe Mode, you can clean up the hard drive and check the drive for errors. To do that, using Windows Explorer, open the Properties box for drive C and perform a Disk Cleanup. Then, on the Tools tab of the Properties box, check for errors using the Check Now button.

▲ *Problem 4: Malware is preventing a normal boot.* Some really nasty viruses can prevent Vista from starting normally. In Safe Mode, the malware might not load, making it possible for you to run antivirus software to remove it. Also, if you don't have antivirus software installed on your system, installing it in Safe Mode might mean you have a better chance of success.

▲ *Problem 5: Windows is corrupted.* In Safe Mode, you can change Windows settings, change startup options, or use System Restore to restore the system to a previous state. How to use System Restore is covered in the next section of this chapter.

▲ *Problem 6: The source of a startup problem is unknown.* If you don't know the source of a problem that prevents a normal startup, but you can launch Safe Mode, you can investigate the problem while in Safe Mode. Use Event Viewer and other detective tools to find information saved during previously failed startups that can help you identify the source of a problem. How to use Event Viewer and other Windows investigating tools is covered in Chapter 7.

Here are some tips about loading Safe Mode that you need to be aware of:

▲ From the Advanced Boot Options menu, first try Safe Mode with Networking. If that doesn't work, try Safe Mode. And if that doesn't work, try Safe Mode with Command Prompt. What to do when you've loaded Safe Mode with Command Prompt is covered in Chapter 7.

▲ Know that Safe Mode won't load if core Windows components are corrupted. In this situation, you need to proceed to Chapter 7.

SYSTEM RESTORE

Ever wish you could backtrack to a previous point in time when things were nice? That's what System Restore can do for you—well, sometimes anyway System Restore restores the system to its condition at the time a snapshot was taken of the system settings and configuration. These snapshots are called restore points. If System Restore is turned on, Windows automatically creates a restore point before you install new software or hardware or make other changes to the system. You can also manually create a restore point at any time.

If you restore the system to a previous restore point, user data on the hard drive will not be altered, but you can affect installed software and hardware, user settings, and OS configuration settings. When you use System Restore to roll back the system to a restore point, any changes made to these settings after the restore point was created are lost; therefore, always use the most recent restore point that can fix the problem so that you make the least intrusive changes to the system.

USING A PREVIOUS RESTORE POINT

To restore the system configuration to an earlier time, depending on the severity of the problem, you can start System Restore using one of these methods:

▲ *Using the normal Windows desktop.* From the Windows desktop, click **Start**, point to **All Programs**, click **Accessories**, click **System Tools**, click **System Restore**, and then respond to the UAC box. The System Restore window opens, as shown in Figure 2-3. Notice that System Restore is recommending that I use the latest restore point, which is normally the correct choice.

▲ *Using Safe Mode.* If you cannot start Vista normally, try starting in Safe Mode, which loads a minimum system configuration. When you get to the Safe Mode desktop, use System Restore there. How to start Vista in Safe Mode was covered earlier in the chapter.

▲ *Using Windows RE.* The Windows Recovery Environment (Windows RE) is an operating system that is loaded from the Vista setup DVD when Windows cannot be started from the hard drive. After Windows RE is loaded, you can use System Restore and several other troubleshooting tools to fix the problem and/or recover data. How to load and use Windows RE is covered in Chapter 7.

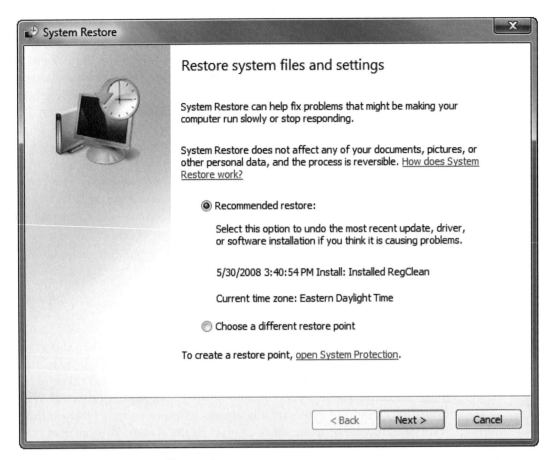

Figure 2-3 System Restore utility opening screen

Regardless of how you launched System Restore, to return the system to a previous restore point, in the System Restore window, click **Next** to use the recommended restore point. If you don't want to use the recommended restore point, select **Choose a different restore point**, click **Next**, and select a restore point from a list (see Figure 2-4). Click **Finish** to apply the restore point.

When selecting a restore point, choose a point as close to the present as you can so that as few changes to the system as possible are lost. The system will require a reboot for the changes to take effect. Data files are not affected, but any installation or configuration changes made after the restore point are lost. If the changes don't work, you can use System Restore to try a new restore point or to undo your changes.

POINTS TO REMEMBER ABOUT SYSTEM RESTORE

System Restore is a great tool to try to fix a device that is not working, restore Windows settings that are giving problems, or solve problems with applications. Although it's a great tool in some situations, it does have its limitations. Keep these points in mind:

- *Point 1*: System Restore works to recover from errors only if the registry is somewhat intact, because restore points replace certain keys in the registry but cannot completely rebuild a totally corrupted registry.
- *Point 2*: The restore process cannot help you recover from a virus or worm infection unless the infection is launched at startup, and even then it probably won't totally remove the infection.

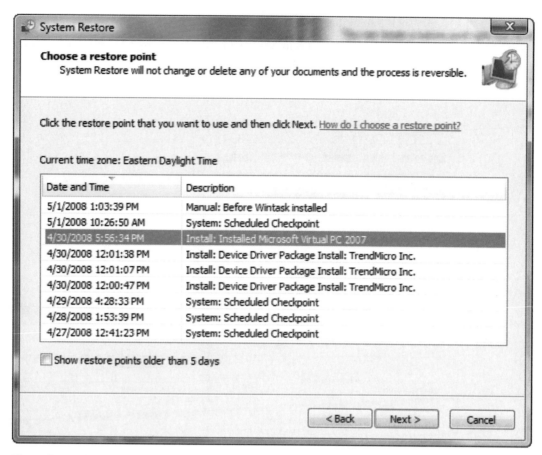

Figure 2-4 Select a restore point

▲ *Point 3*: System Restore might create a new problem. I've discovered that whenever I use a restore point, my antivirus software gets all out of whack and sometimes even needs reinstalling. Thus, use restore points sparingly.

▲ *Point 4*: Before using System Restore to undo a change, if the change was made to a hardware device, first try Driver Rollback so that as few changes as possible to the system are lost. Driver Rollback is covered in Chapter 6.

▲ *Point 5*: System Restore won't help you if you don't have restore points to use. Normally, a Windows component called System Protection creates restore points without your knowledge. How to make sure System Protection is turned on is covered later in the chapter.

▲ *Point 6*: Restore points are kept in a hidden folder on the hard drive. If that area of the drive is corrupted, the restore points are lost. Also, if a user turns System Protection off, all restore points are lost.

▲ *Point 7*: Viruses and other malware sometimes hide in restore points. To completely clean an infected system, you need to delete all restore points by turning System Protection off and back on.

To manually create a restore point, follow these steps:

1. Click **Start**, right-click **Computer**, and select **Properties** from the shortcut menu. The System window opens.

2. Click **Advanced system settings** and respond to the UAC box. The System Properties box opens.

3. Click the **System Protection** tab (see the left side of Figure 2-5). Click **Create**.

4. In the System Protection box (right side of Figure 2-5), enter a description of the restore point and click **Create**.

5. Click **OK** twice to close both boxes. Close the System window.

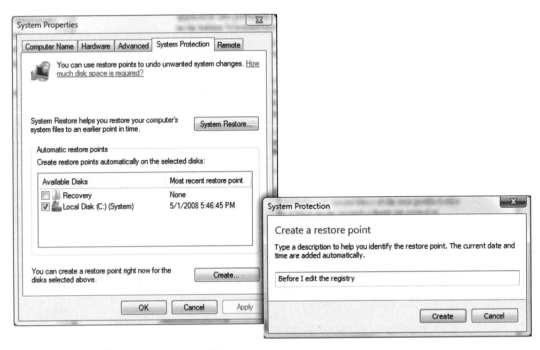

Figure 2-5   Manually create a restore point

SYSTEM CONFIGURATION UTILITY (MSCONFIG)

Recall from Chapter 1 that we used the System Configuration Utility (MSconfig.exe) to disable many processes that normally would load at startup. Although we used it there to temporarily control an out-of-control startup, it should not be considered a permanent fix. Once you've identified the process that is causing the problem, use other tools to permanently remove it from the startup process.

As you learned in Chapter 1, to use MSconfig, click **Start** and enter **msconfig.exe** in the Start Search box, press **Enter,** and respond to the UAC box. The Msconfig window opens. The two more important tabs used to temporarily control startup are the Services tab and the Startup tab. The Services tab contains a list of services automatically launched at startup, and the Startup tab contains a list of programs started by entries in the registry or in startup folders. The Startup tab is shown in Figure 2-6. You learned to use these two tabs in the last chapter.

To troubleshoot a startup problem, check the items you want to start and uncheck the ones you want to temporarily disable; apply your changes; close the utility; and reboot your system. If this solves your problem, go back to Msconfig and enable one service at a time until the problem reappears. You've then discovered the service that is your problem. You'll need to investigate this service. If you don't recognize it, try entering its name in an Internet

> **Note**
>
> If you suspect a Windows system service is causing the problem, you can use Msconfig to disable the service. If this works, then replace the service file with a fresh copy from the Windows setup CD.

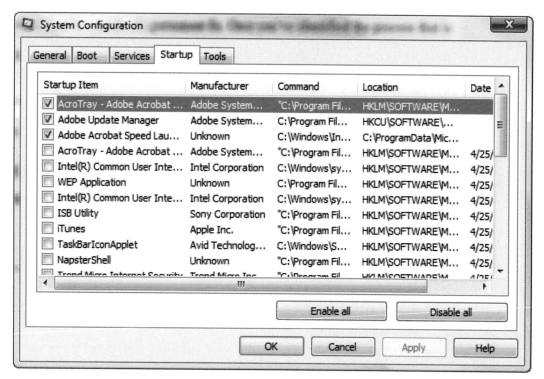

Figure 2-6 Use the Msconfig utility to temporarily disable programs and services from loading at startup

search engine such as Google (*www.google.com*) to learn about the service. To stop a service permanently, you can use the Services console, which you'll learn to use later in the chapter.

CLEAN UP STARTUP

In the previous section, you learned how to deal with pressing problems that need a quick fix. In this section, you'll learn step-by-step procedures to clean up the Windows startup process. The idea is to start at the highest and easiest level of tools and methods to use to affect the startup process. If that doesn't do the job, we must dig deeper using more technical tools and work behind the scenes to manage startup. Another goal is to strike at the root of the tree rather than its branches. In other words, we want not just to kill a process or block it from loading at startup; we want to remove altogether the unwanted application or driver, or at least change its startup parameters.

If you're following along at your computer while you're reading this chapter, before continuing in this section, open the Msconfig window of your computer and verify that Normal Startup is selected on the General tab. In this section, we want to use Task Manager to examine the startup processes when all processes have been turned loose on the system.

In this part of the chapter, I'm assuming you can start Windows with no errors. If you are having trouble loading Windows, it's best to address the error first rather than to use the tools described here to do a general cleanup.

KNOW YOUR STARTING POINT

To know your starting point, perform a cold boot to start Windows Vista. If you have a stopwatch handy or a watch with a second hand, time the seconds required to get to the

Windows desktop when all the spinning wait circle icons have disappeared and Windows is ready to use. Write that time down in your documentation of your work. Also write in your notes 1) the windows on the desktop and 2) the items in the notification area that appear when you start up. All these things will be our measuring stick to show the progress we're making as we work.

PERFORM ROUTINE MAINTENANCE

It might seem pretty mundane, but the first things you need to do to begin the actual cleaning of Windows startup are the obvious routine maintenance tasks. Begin by doing these things:

- ◢ As always, if valuable data is not backed up, back it up before you do anything else. Don't risk the data without the user's permission.
- ◢ If you suspect a virus is present that might be affecting the startup, boot into Safe Mode and run antivirus software.
- ◢ If you see an error message, respond to it. If you've made a change to the system, such as installing software or hardware, assume the installation is the guilty party until it's proven innocent.
- ◢ Clean up the hard drive, deleting unwanted files and using Defrag and Chkdsk, as you learned to do in Chapter 1. If the system is slow while trying to do this, boot into Safe Mode and do these maintenance tasks from there.

UNINSTALL OR DISABLE UNWANTED PROGRAMS

Now let's uninstall any unwanted software. If you don't want to uninstall the software, you might want to disable it as a startup program. We'll begin by using Software Explorer to find out the programs set to run at startup. Then we'll use Control Panel's Programs and Features window to uninstall unwanted software.

To open Software Explorer, from the Control Panel, under the Programs group, click **Change startup programs**. The Windows Defender window opens, showing Software Explorer. If necessary, select **Startup Programs** from the Category list. The list of startup programs is on the left. Click on an item to see its description on the right (see Figure 2-7).

Look at each program in the list and decide if you want to leave it alone, uninstall it or disable it from running at startup. You might need to investigate a program. For example, in Figure 2-7, entice.exe is listed but not much information is given about it. However, on the right, you can see that it is stored in the \Intuit\SimpleStartEntice folder. A quick search on the Internet shows that this program is related to the QuickBooks software. We also notice one more program, qbupdate.exe, that belongs to Intuit QuickBooks. The user tells us that he does not use or want QuickBooks and did not know that it was installed on his PC. We're on the trail of software unnecessarily bogging down his system!

In Control Panel, click **Uninstall a program**. The Programs and Features window opens. Here we find QuickBooks Simple Start Free Starter Edition listed (see Figure 2-8). This PC came with this free software preloaded, which is the practice for many desktop and laptop manufacturers.

The user does not want the software, so we can uninstall it by selecting it and then clicking **Uninstall/Change** in the menu bar of the Programs and Features window. We could have simply disabled the two startup programs in the Software Explorer window, but that would have still left the underlying software installed. Better to dig out the root and uninstall it.

Figure 2-7 Use Software Explorer to list programs that launch at startup

It's handy to keep the two windows, Software Explorer and Programs and Features, open side by side. Look for programs in startup in the Software Explorer window that you don't want. Then find each one in the Programs and Features window to uninstall it.

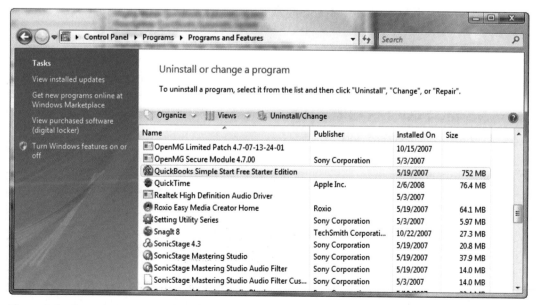

Figure 2-8 Several programs came preloaded on this PC

You might decide to leave software installed, but disable it from startup. To do that, select the software in the Software Explorer window and click **Disable**. Some programs don't allow you to do this. If Disable is grayed, you can still disable it using the Msconfig utility. After making a change to the system, reboot the system before moving on to the next fix.

All these steps are pretty simple things to do to generally clean up the startup process. But some programs are not so easily disabled or removed, so now let's turn our attention to looking for startup tasks in other, more remote locations.

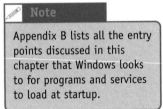

Note

Appendix B lists all the entry points discussed in this chapter that Windows looks to for programs and services to load at startup.

STARTUP FOLDERS

Certain folders are designated as startup folders for all user accounts or a particular user account. Scripts, programs, or shortcuts to programs can be placed in these startup folders by the user, by an administrator, or by a program without the user's knowledge. For example, Figure 2-9 shows a startup folder with all kinds of services placed there by Windows and other software.

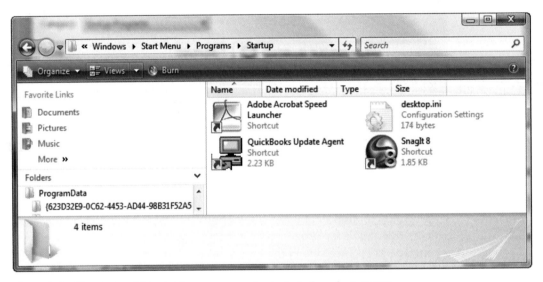

Figure 2-9   The startup folder holds programs or shortcuts to launch at startup

As you clean up startup, look in each startup folder mentioned in this section. If you find a program or shortcut there that you don't think you want, unless you know it's malicious, move it to a different folder rather than deleting it. Later, if you like, you can return it to the startup folder, or you can start the program manually from the new folder.

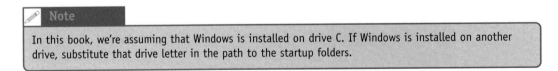

Note

In this book, we're assuming that Windows is installed on drive C. If Windows is installed on another drive, substitute that drive letter in the path to the startup folders.

CURRENT USER STARTUP FOLDER

A program file or a shortcut to it can be placed in this folder:

C:\Users*username*\AppData\Roaming\Microsoft\Windows\Start Menu\Programs\Startup

Each time this particular user logs on, the program is launched. The user who owns the folder and users with administrator privileges can place programs or shortcuts in this folder.

ALL USERS STARTUP FOLDER

Someone with administrator privileges can place a program file or shortcut in this folder so that the startup event applies to all users:

C:\ProgramData\Microsoft\Windows\Start Menu\Program\Startup

The program starts up when any user logs on.

After you check these two folders for startup processes you don't want, you then can move on to the next thing to check, the scheduled task folder.

SCHEDULED TASK FOLDER

Windows offers a Task Scheduler that can be set to launch a task or program at a future time, including at startup. Tasks are scheduled using the Task Scheduler console (Taskschd.msc), which stores them in a file stored in the C:\Windows\System32\Tasks folder. For example, in Figure 2-10, there are four scheduled tasks showing and other tasks are stored in three folders.

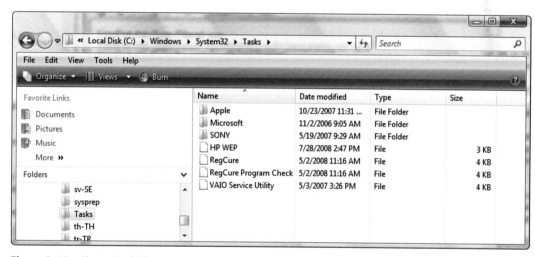

Figure 2-10   The Tasks folder can contain tasks that launch at startup

To view a list of scheduled tasks, click **Start** and enter **Taskschd.msc** in the Start Search box, press **Enter**, and respond to the UAC box. The Task Scheduler window opens as shown in Figure 2-11. For a bare-bones Vista system, the Microsoft folder will be the only item listed in the Task Scheduler Library on the left. But for this system, other folders and tasks are present. To see details about a task, including what triggers it, what actions it performs, the conditions and settings related to the task, and the history of past actions, select the task and then click the tabs in the lower-middle pane. For example, in Figure 2-11 you can see that the HP WEP task is scheduled to run at 5:48 PM daily.

Tasks can be scheduled to run when users log on, when Windows launches, or at a particular time of day, week, or month. Tasks can be scheduled to run one time or many times. Tasks can be applications, services, or other background processes, and tasks can be scheduled to download e-mail or open Internet Explorer and download a Web page.

> **Note**
>
> Tasks can be hidden in the Task Scheduler window. To be certain you're viewing all scheduled tasks, unhide them. In the menu bar, click **View**, then **Show Hidden Tasks**.

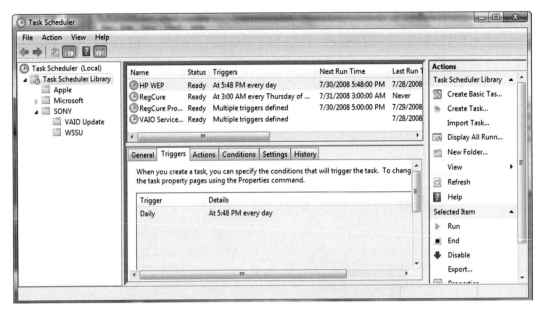

Figure 2-11 View and manage tasks from the Task Scheduler window

Tasks can also consist of batch programs or Windows scripting. Using the Task Scheduler window, you can add, delete, or change a task, and these actions can also be performed at a command prompt.

All this information is helpful when researching scheduled tasks to unravel the mystery of processes or activities that fail or bog down a system. In cleaning up startup, be sure to check the Task Scheduler window *after* you have run antivirus software and disabled or uninstalled all startup programs you don't want. If you still find scheduled tasks present in the Task Scheduler window, research each task by searching for information about it on the Internet. (Be sure you use reliable Web sites to get your information.) If you decide you don't want a task, rather than deleting it, select the task and click **Disable** in the Actions pane so that you can undo your change if necessary. The exception to this rule is if you know the task is malware; in this case, definitely delete it!

> **Note**
>
> When searching the Internet for information about a process, be sure to use reliable web sites to get your information. Some sites will tell you a good process is a bad one just so you'll purchase their software to scan the system for errors.

You're now ready to move on to the next step to clean up startup, which is to look for services launched at startup that you don't need.

SERVICES

Recall that a service is a program that runs in the background to support other programs. Services are managed by the Services console (Services.msc). Use the Services console to see what services have been set to automatically start when Windows loads. To launch the Services console, type **Services.msc** in the Start Search box, press **Enter**, and respond to the UAC box to open the Services window, as shown on the left side of Figure 2-12.

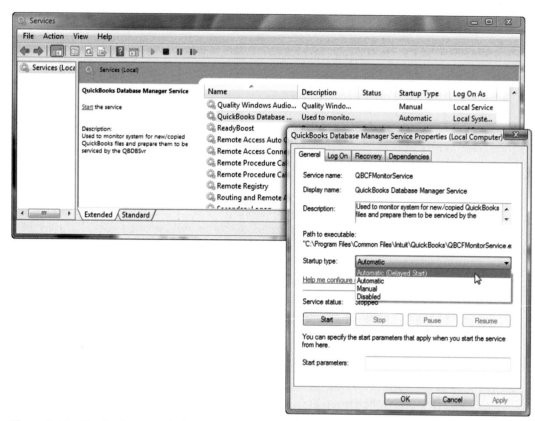

Figure 2-12 The Services console is used to start, stop, and schedule services

To learn more about a service, right-click it and select **Properties** from the shortcut menu. In the resulting Properties window, also shown in Figure 2-12 for one selected service, you can see the name of the program file and its path. From this window, you can start and stop the service and change the startup type. Choices for the startup type are shown in the drop-down list in the figure and are Automatic Delayed Start (launched late in startup so as not to slow down the user logon), Automatic (automatically launched at startup), Manual (can be started after Windows is launched by a user or by another program), or Disabled (cannot be started). You can also start and stop a service by right-clicking the service in the Services console window and selecting the appropriate action on the shortcut menu.

If you are having trouble with a service, you can sometimes solve the problem by pausing or stopping the service and then resuming or starting it. For example, suppose a print job is stuck in the print spooling window. Pausing and resuming, or stopping and starting the Print Spooler might solve the problem. Beware, however, that when you stop a service, other services that this

> **Note**
>
> Recall that you can stop a service using the Task Manager, and you can use Msconfig to stop it from starting at startup. However, all these solutions should be considered temporary fixes. To permanently deal with a service, use the Services console or the Windows component responsible for the service, such as an applet in Control Panel.
> For third-party services, such as software to update an application or software to download digital photos, the application is likely to have a management utility to control the service.

service needs to work are also stopped. This can result in some service being stopped that another service is also dependent on. To see a list of services that a service depends on, click the **Dependencies** tab in the service's Properties window.

When investigating a service, try using a good search engine on the Web to search for the name of the service or the name of the program file that launches the service. Either can give you information you need to snoop out unwanted services. If you're not sure you want to keep a certain service, use Msconfig to temporarily disable it at the next boot so that you can see what happens.

When you permanently disable a service using the Services console or some other tool, don't forget to reboot to make sure everything works before moving on to the next tool to use in cleaning up startup: Group Policy.

GROUP POLICY

When using certain versions of Windows Vista, an administrator can use the Group Policy console (Gpedit.msc) to manage many computers on a network, limiting the way users can use Windows and applications and control Windows settings and features. Group Policy is available on Vista Small Business, Professional, Enterprise and Ultimate editions. It is not available on Vista Home Premium or Home Basic because these versions are normally not used on a corporate network.

Besides working on a corporate network, Group Policy can also be used to manage a single standalone computer and can be used to launch programs at startup. Group Policy works by making entries in the registry, applying scripts to the Windows startup, shutdown, and logon processes, and affecting security settings. To access the Group Policy console, enter **gpedit.msc** in the Start Search box, press **Enter**, and respond to the UAC box. Notice in the left pane of the Group Policy window (see Figure 2-13) that there are two main groups of policies: Computer Configuration and User Configuration. There is some overlap in policies

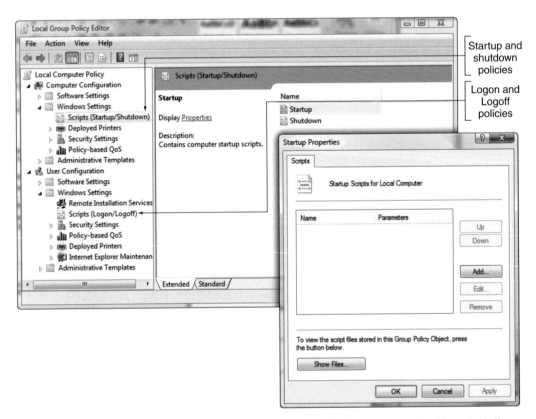

Figure 2-13 Using Group Policy console, you can control many Windows events and settings, including the startup process

between these two groups. When this happens, Computer Configuration takes precedence. Group Policy also takes precedence over any settings you make using Windows menus.

Also in Figure 2-13, you can see four ways a script can be launched using Group Policy: at startup, at shutdown, when a user logs on, or when a user logs off. Because a script can launch a program, Group Policy can be used to launch a program. These scripts are stored in one of these four folders:

▲ C:\WINDOWS\System32\GroupPolicy\Machine\Scripts\Startup
▲ C:\WINDOWS\System32\GroupPolicy\Machine\Scripts\Shutdown
▲ C:\WINDOWS\System32\GroupPolicy\User\Scripts\Logon
▲ C:\WINDOWS\System32\GroupPolicy\User\Scripts\Logoff

To add or remove a Group Policy that is executed at logon or at startup, open the Group Policy console (Gpedit.msc) and do the following:

1. In the Group Policy window, under either Computer Configuration or User Configuration, open the policy you want to change. For example, to change the Administrative Templates policy for Logon, under **Administrative Templates,** open **System,** and then open **Logon** (see the left side of Figure 2-14).

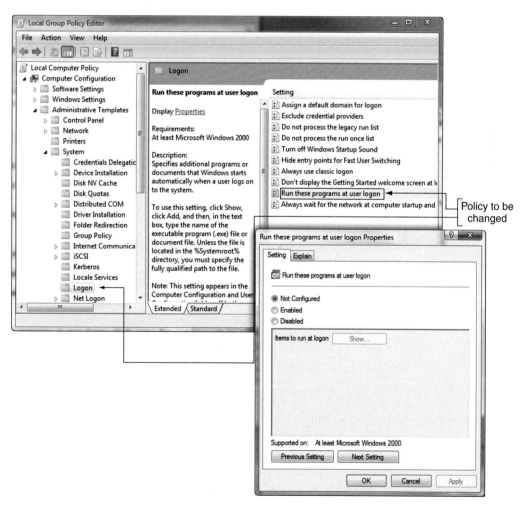

Figure 2-14 Use Group Policy to launch a program or script at logon

2. In the right pane, double-click **Run these programs at user logon**, which opens the properties window shown on the right side of Figure 2-14. Select **Enabled** and then click **Show**. The Show Contents dialog box opens, as shown in Figure 2-15.

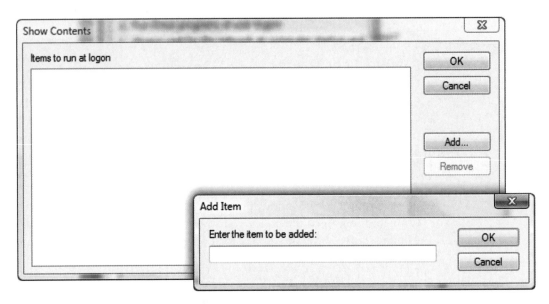

Figure 2-15 Add or remove a logon policy

3. To add a script or executable program to the list of items to run at logon, click **Add** and enter the item. To remove an item from the list, select it and click **Remove**. Click **OK** to close the dialog box and **Apply** to apply the changes. Click **OK** to close the Properties window.

When someone makes one of the above changes using Group Policy, an entry is made in the registry. When you want to reverse a Group Policy setting, it is best to not do it by editing the registry, for a couple of reasons. First, editing the registry is dangerous, because it is so easy to make mistakes and any change is immediately applied. Second, Group Policy might undo your changes because Group Policy stores its settings in alternate locations in the registry and routinely refreshes settings to other keys that apply the policies.

After making a change to Group Policies, be sure to reboot and check for errors before moving on to the next step in cleaning up the startup process: uninstalling unused fonts.

UNINSTALL UNUSED FONTS

Another thing you can do to clean up the startup process is uninstall fonts that you don't use. When Windows Vista is installed, it comes with a group of fonts that can be used for the Windows desktop and in a variety of other places. Some applications install additional fonts, and you can purchase and manually install other fonts. All installed fonts are loaded at startup, so if a system has had many new fonts installed, these can slow down startup.

Windows Vista keeps installed fonts in files in the C:\Windows\Fonts folder. You can access this folder using Windows Explorer, or, in the Control Panel, by clicking **Appearance and Personalization** and then clicking **Fonts**. In the Fonts folder, to see a font, double-click the fonts file as shown in Figure 2-16. To install or uninstall a font, you simply move the fonts file in or out of this folder. When Windows starts up for the first time after the Fonts folder has been changed, it rebuilds the fonts table, which means the first reboot after a font change is slowed down.

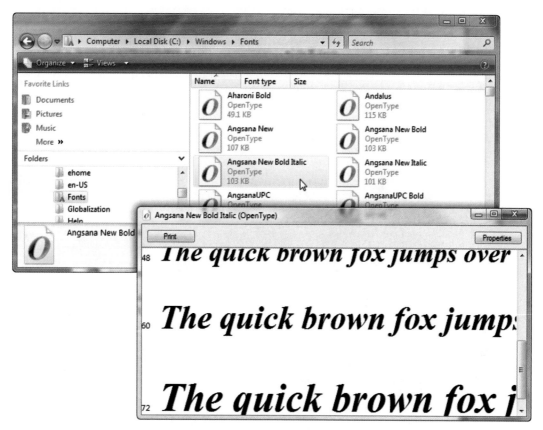

Figure 2-16 Fonts are kept in the C:\Windows\Fonts folder

Check the C:\Windows\Fonts folder. If you see more than 1,000 files in this folder, loading all these fonts is most likely slowing down Vista. You can try moving some files to a different folder to reduce the number of fonts loading at startup. Actually, you can move all the files out of this folder and Windows will still work because it doesn't keep the one system font here. But then, your documents will look pretty plain. If you change the Fonts folder, don't forget it will take the second reboot before you notice any improvement in startup.

CLEAN THE REGISTRY

When software is installed, used, reconfigured, and uninstalled, not all of the registry entries made by the software are cleaned up. Over time the registry can become cluttered with invalid entries, which can lead to a slow startup and slow system performance. If the Vista startup is slow, you might want to consider purchasing and using a registry cleaner. Many registry cleaners are available on the Internet, some free and some not. Some of these "cleaners" are actually adware, spyware, or viruses; therefore, you must be careful which you download and use. Before using a registry cleaner, be sure to search the Internet for warnings about the product, and especially search antivirus sites for information. However, using a good and safe registry cleaner might improve the overall speed of your system.

Three registry cleaners that are safe and good are RegClean (*www.regclean.com*), RegCure (*www.regcure.com*), and RegSweep (*www.regsweep.com*). Before you use a registry cleaner, be sure to back up the registry first so that you can backtrack if cleaning the registry creates errors. How to back up the registry is covered in the next section. After the registry is backed up, to use a registry cleaner, download the cleaner, install it, and run it.

Figure 2-17 shows that RegCure has found 1,077 errors in a registry. Notice the highlighted error that shows a reference to napster.exe. The Napster software was previously uninstalled and left behind an orphaned entry in the registry. This type of error is typical of errors that can slow down startup as Windows attempts to find the missing napster.exe file. If you decide to allow the cleaner to clean the registry, click Fix Errors. If you have not already purchased the product, you are taken to the RegCure web site to purchase it.

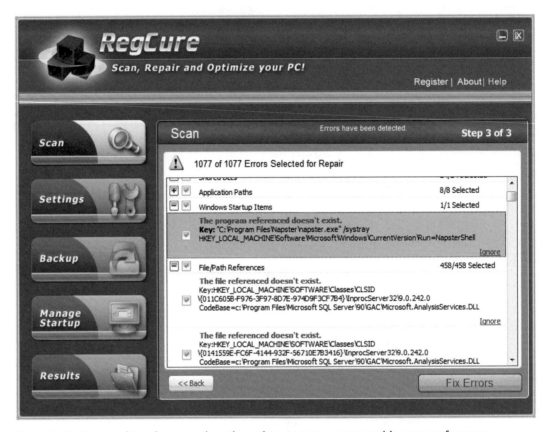

Figure 2-17 Use a registry cleaner to clean the registry to remove errors and improve performance

After you have cleaned the registry, reboot the system and check for any error messages at startup. If you see any, you can restore the registry from backup. One more point about using a registry cleaner: if the cleaner reports hundreds of errors, don't be alarmed. Many of these errors are harmless; in fact, if you run a registry cleaner immediately after a Vista installation, the cleaner will most likely still report "errors."

Unless you have some unusually difficult problems to solve, your Windows Vista startup should now be smooth and fast. However, you might have to dig deeper into some more complex issues. That's the subject of the next section.

DIG DEEPER INTO STARTUP PROCESSES

In this section, you'll learn to search the registry and remove startup tasks left there by software that has been uninstalled incorrectly or by malicious software. You'll also learn how to remove software that won't politely uninstall when you use the Programs and Features window in Control Panel.

EDITING THE REGISTRY

As you have seen, many actions, such as Group Policy changes or installing application software, can result in changes to the registry. These changes can create new keys, add new values to existing keys, and change existing values. For really difficult problems, you might need to edit or remove a registry key. This section looks at how the registry is organized, which keys might hold entries causing problems, and how to back up and edit the registry.

HOW THE REGISTRY IS ORGANIZED

The most important Windows component that holds information for Windows is the registry. The **registry** is a database designed with a tree-like structure (called a hierarchical database) that contains configuration information for Windows, users, software applications, and installed hardware devices. During startup, Windows builds the registry in memory and keeps it there until Windows shuts down. During startup, after the registry is built, Windows reads from it to obtain information to complete the startup process. After Windows is loaded, it continually reads from many of the subkeys in the registry.

Windows builds the registry from the current hardware configuration and from information it takes from these files:

▲ Five files stored in the C:\Windows\System32\config folder; these files are called hives, and they are named the Sam, Security, Software, System, and Default hives
▲ The file C:\Users*username*\Ntuser.dat, which contains the current user's preferences

After the registry is built in memory, it is organized into five tree-like structures. Each of the five segments is called a key. Each key can have subkeys, and subkeys can have more subkeys and can be assigned one or more values.

Here are the five keys and their purposes:

▲ *HKEY_LOCAL_MACHINE (HKLM)* is the most important key and contains hardware, software, and security data. The data is taken from four hives: the SAM hive, the Security hive, the Software hive, and the System hive. In addition, the HARDWARE subkey of HKLM is built when the registry is first loaded based on data collected about the current hardware configuration.

Note

Device Manager reads data from the HKLM\HARDWARE key to build the information it displays about hardware configurations. You can consider Device Manager to be an easy-to-view presentation of this HARDWARE key data.

▲ *HKEY_CURRENT_CONFIG (HKCC)* contains Plug and Play information about the hardware configuration that is used by the computer at startup. Information that identifies each hardware device installed on a PC is kept in this area. Some of the data is gathered from the current hardware configuration when the registry is first loaded into memory. Other data is taken from the HKLM key, which got its data from the System hive.
▲ *HKEY_CLASSES_ROOT (HKCR)* stores information that determines which application is opened when the user double-clicks a file. This process relies on the file's extension to determine which program to load. For example, this registry key might hold the information to cause Microsoft Word to open when a user double-clicks a file with a .doc file extension. Data for this key is gathered from HKLM key and the HKCU key.
▲ *HKEY_USERS (HKU)* contains data about all users and is taken from the Default hive.

Tip

For a better explanation of how the registry is organized, how it is built, and how Windows uses it, see Appendix D, "How Windows Vista Works."

▲ *HKEY_CURRENT_USER (HKCU)* contains data about the current user. The key is built when a user logs on using data kept in the HKEY_USERS key and data kept in the Ntuser.dat file of the current user. The Ntuser.dat file is stored in the C:\Users*username* folder.

BEFORE YOU EDIT THE REGISTRY, BACK IT UP!

As you investigate startup problems and see a registry entry that needs changing, remember that it is important to use caution when editing the registry. If possible, make the change from the Windows tool that is responsible for the key—for example, by using Group Policy or the Programs and Features window in Control Panel. If that doesn't work and you must edit the registry, always back up the registry before attempting to edit it. Changes made to the registry are implemented immediately. *There is no undo feature in the registry editor, and no opportunity to change your mind once the edit is made.*

There are basically three ways to back up the registry:

▲ *Use System Protection to create a restore point.* A restore point keeps information about the registry, and you can restore the system to a restore point to undo registry changes as long as the registry is basically intact and not too corrupted.

▲ *Back up a single registry key just before you edit the key.* This method, called exporting a key, should always be used before you edit the registry. How to export a key is coming up in this chapter.

▲ *Make an extra copy of the C:\Windows\System32\config folder.* This is what I call the old-fashioned shotgun approach to backing up the registry. This backup will help if the registry gets totally trashed. You can boot from the Vista DVD and use Windows RE to restore the folder from your extra copy. This method is drastic and not recommended except in severe cases. But, still, just to be on the safe side, I make an extra copy of this folder just before I start any serious digging into the registry.

In some situations, such as when you're going to make some drastic changes to the registry, you'll want to play it safe and use all three backup methods. Extra registry backups are always a good thing! Now let's look at how to perform the first two backup methods.

Create a restore point

Recall that restore points are automatically made before software or hardware is installed, but you can manually create a restore point at any time. Follow these steps:

1. Click **Start**, right-click **Computer**, and select **Properties** from the shortcut menu. The System window opens.

2. In the left pane, click **System protection** and respond to the UAC box. The System Properties box opens. Click **Create**.

3. Enter a description of the restore point and click **Create**. The restore point is created.

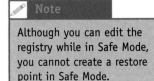

Note

Although you can edit the registry while in Safe Mode, you cannot create a restore point in Safe Mode.

4. Click **OK** twice to close both boxes.

Recall that if you need to restore the system to a restore point, use System Restore, which you learned to use earlier in the chapter.

2

Backing up and restoring individual keys in the registry

A less time-consuming method of backing up the registry is to back up a particular key that you plan to edit. However, know that if the registry gets corrupted, having a backup of only a particular key most likely will not help you much when trying a recovery. Also, although you could use this technique to back up the entire registry or an entire tree within the registry, it is not recommended.

To back up a key along with its subkeys in the registry, follow these steps:

1. Open the registry editor. To do that, click **Start** and type **regedit** in the Start Search dialog box, press **Enter**, and respond to the UAC box. Figure 2-18 shows the registry editor with the five main keys and several subkeys listed. Click the triangles on the left to see subkeys. When you select a subkey, such as KeyboardClass in the figure, the names of the values in that subkey are displayed in the right pane along with the data assigned to each value.

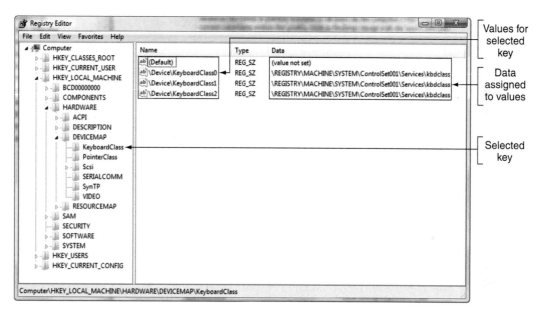

Figure 2-18 The registry editor showing the five main keys, subkeys, values, and data

2. Suppose we want to back up the registry key that contains a list of installed software, which is HKLM\Software\Microsoft\Windows\CurrentVersion\Uninstall. (HKLM stands for HKEY_LOCAL_MACHINE.) First click the appropriate triangles to navigate to the key. Next, right-click the key and select **Export** on the shortcut menu, as shown in Figure 2-19. The Export Registry File dialog box appears.

3. Select the location to save the export file and name the file. A convenient place to store an export file while you edit the registry is the desktop. Click **Save** when done. The file saved will have a .reg file extension.

4. You can now edit the key. Later, if you need to undo your changes, exit the registry editor and double-click the saved export file. The key and its subkeys saved in the export file will be restored. After you're done with an export file, delete it.

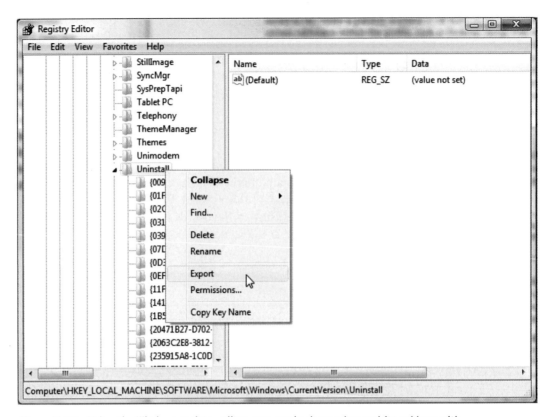

Figure 2-19 Using the Windows registry editor, you can back up a key and its subkeys with the Export command

EDITING THE REGISTRY

When you make a change in Control Panel, Device Manager, or many other places in Windows Vista, the registry is modified automatically. This is the only way most users will ever change the registry. However, on rare occasions, you might need to edit the registry manually.

Before you edit the registry, you should use one or more of the three backup methods just discussed so that you can restore it if something goes wrong. To edit the registry, open the registry editor and locate and select the key in the left pane of the registry editor, which will display the values stored in this key in the right pane. To edit, rename, or delete a value, right-click it and select the appropriate option from the shortcut menu. For example, in Figure 2-20,

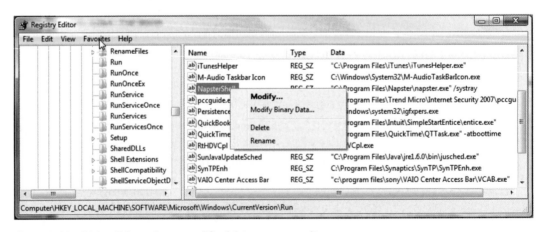

Figure 2-20 Right-click a value to modify, delete, or rename it

2

I'm ready to delete the value NapsterShell and its data. Changes are immediately applied to the registry and there is no undo feature. Notice in Figure 2-20 that the selected key is displayed in the status bar at the bottom of the editor window. If the status bar is missing, click **View** on the menu bar and make sure **Status Bar** is checked. To search the registry for keys, values, and data, click **Edit** on the menu bar and then click **Find**.

Now let's look at a situation where it is appropriate to edit the registry to remove unwanted software entries.

MANUALLY REMOVING SOFTWARE

Just about every uninstall routine I've ever known, includ- ing some I've written myself, leaves behind some files or registry entries here and there in a Windows system. Even Microsoft, in Knowledge Base Article 254250, lists more than 100 files, folders, and registry keys left behind when Microsoft Office 97 uninstalls itself! The article shows you how to manually delete each one! This is good because when you install and uninstall software, most likely the end result is going to be more files and folders and a larger registry than you had before you installed the software.

> **Note**
>
> Before uninstalling software, make sure it's not running in the background. Antivirus software can't be uninstalled if it's still running. You can use Task Manager to end all processes related to the software, and you can use the Services console to stop services related to the software. Then remove the software.

In this section, we focus on getting rid of programs that refuse to uninstall or give errors when uninstalling. In these cases, you can manually uninstall a program. Doing so often causes problems later, so use the methods discussed in this section only as a last resort after the Programs and Features window has failed.

FIRST TRY THE UNINSTALL ROUTINE

Most programs written for Vista have an uninstall routine which can be accessed from the Programs and Features window or in the All Programs menu. For example, in Figure 2-21 you can see in the All Programs menu that Uninstall is an option for the

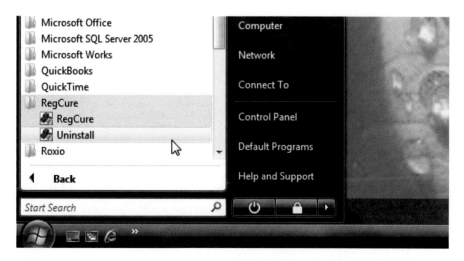

Figure 2-21 Most applications have an uninstall utility included with the software

RegCure software installation. Click this option and follow the directions onscreen to uninstall the software. Alternately, using the Programs and Features window, you can select the software and click **Uninstall** or **Uninstall/Change** in the menu bar to remove the software.

MANUALLY DELETE THE PROGRAM FILES

If the uninstall routine does not work or is missing, as a last resort, you can manually delete the program files and registry entries used by the software you want to uninstall. In our example, we'll use the RegCure software by ParetoLogic, Inc. Follow these steps:

1. Most likely, the program files are stored in the C:\Program Files folder on the hard drive (see Figure 2-22). Using Windows Explorer, look for a folder in the Program Files folder that contains the software. In Figure 2-22, you can see the RegCure folder under the Program Files folder. Keep in mind, however, that you might not find the program files you're looking for in the C:\Program Files folder because when you install software, the software installation program normally asks you where to install the software. Therefore, the program files might be anywhere, and you might need to search a bit to find them.

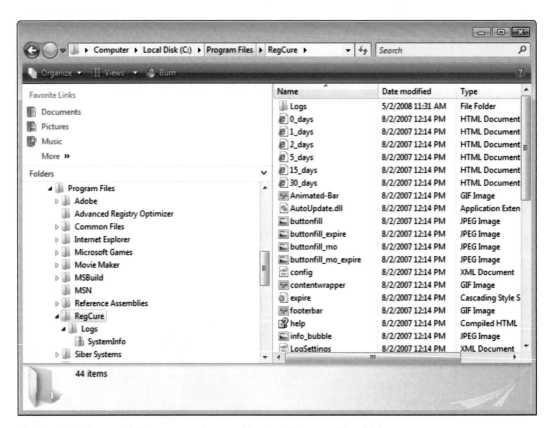

Figure 2-22   Program folders are usually stored in the C:\Program Files folder

2. Delete the RegCure folder and all its contents. You'll need to confirm the deletion several times as Windows really doesn't like your doing such things.

DELETE REGISTRY ENTRIES

Editing the registry can be dangerous, so do this with caution! Do the following to delete registry entries for a program that cause it to be listed as installed software in the Programs and Features window of Control Panel:

1. Click **Start,** type **regedit** in the Start Search box, press **Enter,** and respond to the UAC box.

2. Locate this key, which contains the entries that comprise the list of installed software in the Programs and Features window: HKEY_LOCAL_MACHINE\Software\ Microsoft\Windows\CurrentVersion\Uninstall.

3. Back up the Uninstall key to the Windows desktop so that you can backtrack if necessary. To do that, right-click the Uninstall key and select **Export** from the shortcut menu (refer back to Figure 2-19).

4. In the Export Registry File dialog box, select the **Desktop.** Enter the filename as **Save Uninstall Key,** and click **Save.** You should see a new icon on your desktop named Save Uninstall Key.reg.

5. The Uninstall key can be a daunting list of all the programs installed on your PC. When you expand the key, you might see a long list of subkeys in the left pane, which have meaningless names that won't help you find the program you're looking for. Select the first subkey in the Uninstall key and watch its values and data display in the right pane (see Figure 2-23). Step down through each key, watching for a meaningful name of the subkey in the left pane or meaningful details in the right pane until you find the program you want to delete.

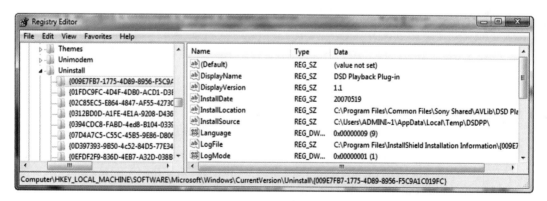

Figure 2-23 Select a subkey under the Uninstall key to display its values and data in the right pane

6. To delete the key, right-click the key and select **Delete** from the shortcut menu (see Figure 2-24). When the Confirm Key Delete dialog box appears asking you to confirm the deletion, click **Yes.** Be sure to search through all the keys in this list because the software might have more than one key. Delete them all and exit the registry editor.

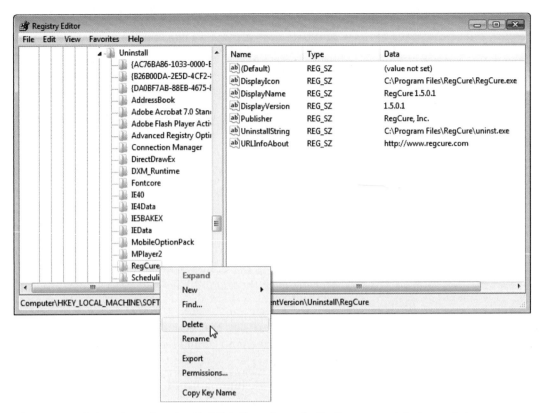

Figure 2-24 Delete the registry key that lists the software in the Programs and Features window

7. Open the Programs and Features window and verify that the list of installed software is correct and the software you are uninstalling is no longer listed.

8. If the list of installed software is not correct, to undo your change to the registry, double-click the **Save Uninstall Key.reg** icon on your desktop to restore the Uninstall key.

9. As a last step when editing the registry, clean up after yourself by deleting the Save Uninstall Key.reg icon and file on your desktop. Right-click the icon and select **Delete** from the shortcut menu.

REMOVE THE PROGRAM FROM THE ALL PROGRAMS MENU

To remove the program from the All Programs menu, right-click it and select **Delete** from the shortcut menu (see Figure 2-25). Click **Yes** and then **Continue** to confirm the deletion and respond to the UAC box.

REGISTRY KEYS THAT AFFECT STARTUP AND LOGON EVENTS

You have just seen how you can manually edit the registry to remove the entries that identify software as installed software. Listed in this section are some registry keys where startup processes can be located. As one step in cleaning up startup, you can search through

Figure 2-25 Delete the program from the All Programs menu

these registry keys for processes left there by uninstalled or corrupted software that might be giving startup problems.

As you read through this list of registry keys to search, know that the list is not exhaustive. With experience, you'll learn that the registry is an ever-changing landscape of keys and values.

Registry keys that affect the startup and logon events are listed in the bulleted list below. Your registry might or might not have all these keys. As you search the registry for entries in these keys, don't forget to first back up the registry. Because you'll be searching all over the registry and not just in one particular place, it's a good idea to create a restore point as well as back up the C:\Windows\System32\config folder so that the entire registry will be backed up.

These keys cause an entry to run once and only once at startup:

- HKLM\Software\Microsoft\Windows\CurrentVersion\RunOnce
- HKLM\Software\Microsoft\Windows\CurrentVersion\RunServiceOnce
- HKLM\Software\Microsoft\Windows\CurrentVersion\RunServicesOnce
- HKCU\Software\Microsoft\Windows\CurrentVersion\RunOnce

Check each key in the list above and move on to the next list.

Group Policy places entries in the following keys to affect startup:

◢ HKCU\Software\Microsoft\Windows\CurrentVersion\Policies\Explorer\Run
◢ HKLM\Software\Microsoft\Windows\CurrentVersion\Policies\Explorer\Run

Windows loads many DLL programs from the following key, which is sometimes used by malicious software. Entries in this key are normal, so don't delete one unless you know it's causing a problem:

◢ HKLM\Software\Microsoft\Windows\CurrentVersion\ShellServiceObjectDelayLoad

Entries in the keys listed next apply to all users and hold legitimate startup entries. Don't delete an entry unless you suspect it to be bad:

◢ HKLM\Software\Microsoft\Windows\CurrentVersion\Run
◢ HKCU\Software\Microsoft\Windows NT\CurrentVersion\Windows
◢ HKCU\Software\Microsoft\Windows NT\CurrentVersion\Windows\Run
◢ HKCU\Software\Microsoft\Windows\CurrentVersion\Run

This key and its subkeys contain entries that pertain to background services that are sometimes launched at startup:

◢ HKLM\Software\Microsoft\Windows\CurrentVersion\RunServices

The following key contains a value named BootExecute, which is normally set to autochk. It causes the system to run a type of Chkdsk program to check for hard drive integrity when it was previously shut down improperly. Sometimes another program adds itself to this value, causing a problem. For more information about this situation, see the Microsoft Knowledge Base article 151376, "How to Disable Autochk If It Stops Responding During Reboot" at *support.microsoft.com*.

◢ HKLM\System\CurrentControlSet\Control\Session Manager

Here is an assorted list of registry keys that have all been known to cause various problems at startup. Remember, before you delete a program entry from one of these keys, research the program filename so that you won't accidentally delete something you want to keep:

◢ HKCU\Software\Microsoft\Command
◢ HKCU\Software\Microsoft\Command Processor\AutoRun
◢ HKCU\Software\Microsoft\Windows\CurrentVersion\RunOnce\Setup
◢ HKCU\Software\Microsoft\Windows NT\CurrentVersion\Windows\load
◢ HKLM\Software\Microsoft\Windows NT\CurrentVersion\Windows\AppInit_DLLs
◢ HKLM\Software\Microsoft\Windows NT\CurrentVersion\Winlogon\System
◢ HKLM\Software\Microsoft\Windows NT\CurrentVersion\Winlogon\Us
◢ HKCR\batfile\shell\open\command
◢ HKCR\comfile\shell\open\command
◢ HKCR\exefile\shell\open\command
◢ HKCR\htafile\shell\open\command
◢ HKCR\piffile\shell\open\command
◢ HKCR\scrfile\shell\open\command

DIGGING EVEN DEEPER FOR STARTUP PROCESSES

Unless you have some really tricky malware or corrupted software, your Vista startup process should be clean, fast, and error free. However, in this section we leave no stone unturned to give you every possible tool to find even the most elusive startup process. Well, actually there are a few more tools available to root out stubborn malware, but they're covered in the next chapter. For now, let's look at Task Manager, Msconfig, and two third-party utilities designed to help you smoke out startup processes you don't want or need.

EXAMINE STARTUP PROCESSES USING TASK MANAGER AND MSCONFIG

In Chapter 1, you learned how to use Task Manager to see what's running after the system starts and to use Msconfig (the System Configuration utility) to control startup processes, so we won't cover that again here. But it's worth mentioning here that if you still are bothered by a slow startup or by startup errors, you can use Task Manager immediately after the Windows desktop loads to view the currently running processes. And you can use Msconfig to give you a list of startup programs and services. Msconfig also gives you information about how the program or service was started, and you then can use this information to root out the source of the problem.

So far in this book, we've used only Windows tools to examine a system and fix it. But there are some great third-party tools that show you more about processes, services, and the guts of Windows than Windows allows you to see. In this part of the chapter, we take a look at two tools: Autoruns by Mark Russinovich and Bryce Cogswell and Startup Control Panel by Mike Lin. Both can help with startup problems better than Msconfig. In the next chapter, you'll learn about some third-party tools that improve on Task Manager.

AUTORUNS SEARCHES OUT STARTUP PROGRAMS

Autoruns by Mark Russinovich and Bryce Cogswell, formerly of Sysinternals but now part of Microsoft TechNet (*technet.microsoft.com*), can find startup and logon programs that Msconfig doesn't find. Also, Autoruns gives more information about a program than does Msconfig.

To download and use Autoruns, go to the TechNet Web site (*technet.microsoft.com*) and then search for and download the Autoruns zip file. When you run the program, the Autoruns window appears, as shown in Figure 2-26.

Looking at the Autoruns window, the first thing you notice is the number of entry points Autoruns tracks compared to Msconfig. This version of Autoruns is tracking more than 40 registry keys that can launch processes at startup, compared to the four registry keys tracked by Msconfig. (New versions of Autoruns are released as more entry points are discovered.) Also notice in Figure 2-26 that Autoruns gives more information about a running process than does Msconfig, and, by using the several tabs on this window, you can view information about programs launched while using Windows. This makes it a useful tool when tracking activities while using your browser or other applications.

Autoruns is also useful when searching for the way a listed item was started. Double-click an item and one of two things will happen: Regedit will launch and search for the registry key that was responsible for launching the item or Explorer will launch and locate the program file responsible for launching the item. Either way, you are conveniently taken to the root of a possible problem.

When you click **Options** on the menu bar, check **Hide Microsoft Entries,** and then click the **Refresh** icon near the top of the window, Autoruns refreshes the list to show those items installed on your system by third-party software, making it easier for you to locate a potential problem (see Figure 2-27).

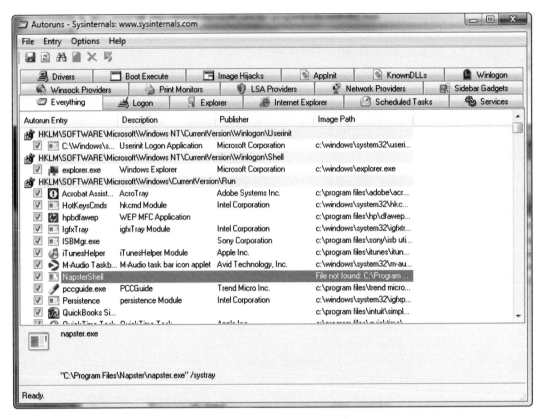

Figure 2-26   Use Autoruns to display and manage startup and logon items

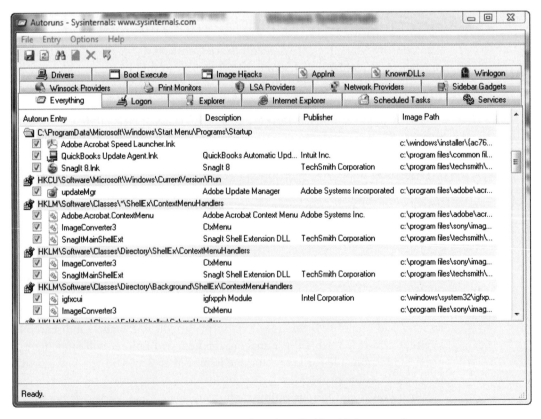

Figure 2-27   Autoruns can hide all items except those installed by third-party software

To cause an item not to launch at startup or logon, uncheck it on the left side of the screen. You can also save Autoruns information to a text file so that you can keep a record of a current state. To do that, click **File**, click **Save As**, and enter a path and filename to save the text data. All in all, Autoruns gives better and more complete information than does Msconfig and takes up very little hard drive space or system resources to run.

STARTUP CONTROL PANEL BY MIKE LIN

Another third-party product is Startup Control Panel by Mike Lin, which gives a very user-friendly presentation. Follow these directions to download and use the software:

1. Go to Mike Lin's Web site and download the Standalone EXE Version of Startup Control Panel at *www.mlin.net/StartupCPL.shtml.*

2. Extract the zip file and run the **Startup.exe** file. The Startup Control Panel window appears. Figure 2-28 shows the Startup Control Panel window with the HKLM / Run tab selected.

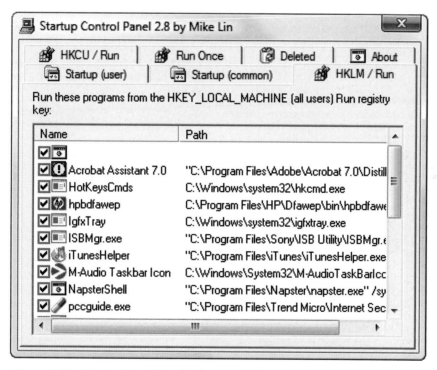

Figure 2-28   Startup Control Panel helps control the startup process

3. Tabs on the Startup Control Panel window are organized so that you can determine the source of a program more easily than you could with Msconfig. To disable a program from launching at startup, uncheck it.

KEEP VISTA STARTUP CLEAN AND PREPARE FOR DISASTER

After you have Windows startup squeaky clean, I know you want to keep it that way. In this section, you'll learn about things you can do to protect startup and to prepare in advance for problems.

MAKE SURE SYSTEM PROTECTION IS TURNED ON AND USE IT

Recall that System Restore can restore the system to a previously saved restore point. These restore points are normally automatically created by System Protection, and you can manually create a restore point at any time. You learned how to create restore points earlier in the chapter. System Protection creates restore points at regular intervals and just before you install software or hardware. However, to make sure System Protection has not been turned off, click **Start**, right-click **Computer**, and select **Properties** from the shortcut menu. In the System window, click **System protection** and respond to the UAC box (see Figure 2-29). Make sure the drive on which Windows is installed is checked, indicating that restore points are created automatically. If you make a change to this window, click **Apply** and then click **OK**.

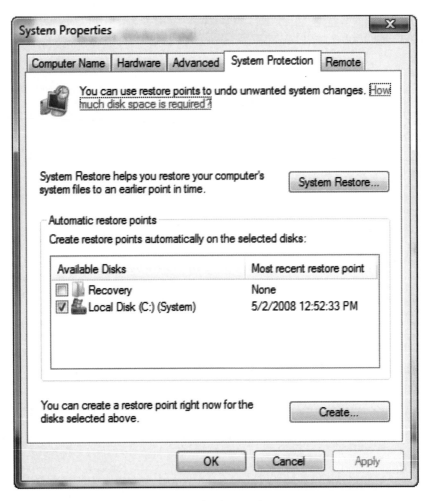

Figure 2-29 Make sure System Protection is turned on

Here is some useful information about how and when restore points are made: Restore points are normally kept in the folder C:\System Volume Information, which is not accessible to the user. Restore points are taken at least every 24 hours, and they can use up to 15 percent of disk space. If disk space gets very low, restore points are no longer made, which is one more good reason to keep about 15% or more of the hard drive free.

MONITOR THE STARTUP PROCESS

Once you've got the startup process the way you want it, you can use several third-party tools to monitor any changes to it. A good one is WinPatrol by BillP Studios (*www.winpatrol.com*), which you first learned about in Chapter 1. Download and install the free program to run in the background to monitor all sorts of things, including changes to the registry, startup processes, Internet Explorer settings, and system files. In Figure 2-30, you can see how WinPatrol alerted me when it detected that Adobe Update Manager was placing an entry in the registry to launch at startup to update the Adobe software. WinPatrol displays a little black Scotty dog in the notification area to indicate it's running in the background and guarding your system. Also, many antivirus programs monitor the startup process and inform you when changes are made.

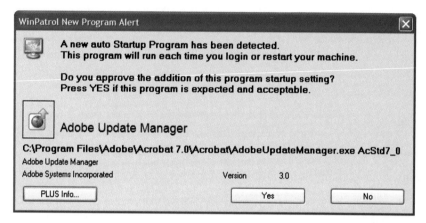

Figure 2-30 WinPatrol by BillP Studios alerts you when the startup process has been altered

>> CHAPTER SUMMARY

◢ When you're having trouble starting Windows Vista, use the Last Known Good Configuration on the Windows Advanced Boot Options menu to return the configuration to its settings at the last successful boot.

◢ Windows Vista Safe Mode boots the system using only the core device drivers and does not load installed applications or third-party services, so a failed boot can be troubleshooted or antivirus software can be run to detect viruses launched at startup.

◢ Using System Restore, you can return the system settings to a point in time when a snapshot of the system was taken.

◢ The System Configuration Utility (Msconfig) can be used to limit startup processes and services so that you can troubleshoot a problem with Windows startup.

◢ Before cleaning startup, measure the amount of time it takes Windows to start from a cold boot.

◢ Perform routine maintenance before the actual cleaning of Windows startup.

- Software Explorer, part of Windows Defender, can be used to view detailed information about and disable startup programs.

- The Internet is a powerful tool to use when identifying unknown processes or programs running on your system.

- When cleaning up a slow or error-prone startup, address any error messages before you begin a general cleanup.

- Services, scripts, and other programs can be launched when Windows starts up or a user logs on.

- Windows looks for items to launch in startup folders, entries in system files, and registry entries.

- Three folders used to contain startup programs and shortcuts are the all users startup folder, the current user startup folder, and the scheduled task folder.

- A service can be launched at startup by making an entry using the Services console, which causes an entry to be put into the registry. The Services console is the tool to use to manage Windows and some third-party services. Other third-party applications provide utilities to manage their services.

- Group Policy can affect startup or logon, launching scripts that can contain programs to run. Group Policy is managed using the Group Policy console, gpedit.msc. Scripts are stored in the GroupPolicy folder under \Windows\System32.

- Too many loaded fonts can slow down startup. Fonts are installed in the C:\Windows\Fonts folder.

- Most software does not clean up all the registry entries the software made as it is installed, used, reconfigured, and uninstalled. Using a good and safe registry cleaner can remove errors and improve performance.

- For really difficult problems, you might need to edit or remove a registry key.

- The most important Windows component that holds information for Windows is the registry. Windows builds the registry from the current hardware configuration and from information it takes from the C:\Windows\System32\config folder and the file C:\Users*username*\Ntuser.dat.

- The five files stored in the C:\Windows\System32\config folder are called hives, and they are named the Sam, Security, Software, System, and Default hives.

- Always back up the registry before making changes to it, because there is no undo feature in the registry editor.

- Some programs have an uninstall routine that can be executed to uninstall the software rather than using the Programs and Features applet.

- As a last resort, an application can be manually deleted by deleting the folder in which it is installed (this folder is most likely in the C:\Program Files folder), deleting its entries in the registry that identify it as installed software, and deleting its entry in the All Programs menu.

- Many registry keys exist that can affect the startup process. When searching out obscure locations for startup entries, all these keys need to be searched.

- Autoruns can find startup and logon programs that Msconfig doesn't find, and also gives more information about the programs.

◢ Startup Control Panel is a third-party product, which gives a very user-friendly presentation to help control the startup process.

◢ System Protection can automatically create a restore point at regular intervals and just before you install software or hardware.

◢ To monitor the startup process so items are not added without your knowledge, WinPatrol or some other third-party tool can be used.

>> KEY TERMS

Advanced Boot Options Menu A startup menu that lists advanced troubleshooting options used to diagnose Windows startup problems.

Last Known Good Configuration Configuration information about the Windows startup process saved in the registry immediately after the user logs on. The information can be used to reconfigure startup when the user chooses this option on the Advanced Boot Options menu.

registry A database designed with a tree-like structure (called a hierarchical database) that contains configuration information for Windows, users, software applications, and installed hardware devices.

restore point A snapshot of the Windows system settings and configuration, usually made before installation of new hardware or applications. *See also* System Restore.

Safe Mode An Advanced Boot Menu option that loads only the core device drivers needed to operate essential hardware at startup and does not load installed applications or third-party services.

System Restore A Windows utility used to create restore points and to restore the system from a restore point.

>> REVIEWING THE BASICS

1. When does Windows Vista save the Last Known Good Configuration settings?

2. What will be displayed if F8 is pressed while Windows is loading?

3. What is the complete path to the folder that contains startup items that are launched when a specific user logs on?

4. What is the complete path to the folder that contains startup items that are launched when any user logs on?

5. Tasks scheduled by the Scheduled Tasks applet are placed in what folder?

6. The ____ can be used to see what services have been set to automatically start when Windows loads.

7. What are the two main groups of policies managed by the Group Policy console?

8. What is the name of the executable program file used to manage group policies?

9. If the user has made a change to a Windows setting and Group Policy has made a different change, which value will be applied—the one made by the user, or the one made by Group Policy?

10. At what four events can Group Policy launch a script?

11. What Windows tool can be used to quickly see what group policies are currently applied?

12. Give an example of a registry key that causes a task to run only once at startup.

13. What has to be turned on for Windows to automatically create a restore point before you install new software or hardware or make other changes to the system?

14. List the five files stored in the C:\Windows\System32\config folder.

15. What command in the Windows registry editor can be used to back up a key?

16. A file holding the backup copy of a registry key has what file extension?

17. What is the name of the executable program file used to launch the System Configuration Utility?

18. List one of the tools that can be used to disable a startup program without uninstalling it.

19. When are all restore points erased?

20. What is an example of a third-party utility that gives better information than Msconfig about the startup process?

21. Which window in Control Panel is used to uninstall an application?

22. Which folder is most likely used to hold the program files for applications installed under Windows?

23. Which Windows tool should you use to temporarily disable a program from launching at startup?

24. Name a registry key into which Group Policy places entries to affect startup.

25. Which registry key contains entries listed in the Programs or Features window?

26. Which Windows registry subtree contains information about the currently logged-on user?

27. In Windows NT/2000/XP/Vista, a file that contains part of the Windows registry is called a(n) _____.

28. To which registry key does the HKEY_CURRENT_USER key point for information?

29. What is a restore point, and what is it used for?

30. What Windows Vista tool can be used to quickly see all of the currently running processes?

>> THINKING CRITICALLY

1. When cleaning up the startup process, which of these should you do first?

   a. Run Msconfig to see what processes are started.
   b. Investigate an error message that is displayed when you start Windows.
   c. After you have launched several applications, use Task Manager to view a list of running tasks.
   d. Run the Defrag utility to optimize the hard drive.

2. Using the Internet, investigate each of the following startup processes. Identify the process and write a one-sentence description.

   a. Acrotray.exe
   b. Ieuser.exe

3. Using Autoruns, you discover an unwanted program that is launched at startup. Of the items listed below, which ones might lead you to the solution to the problem? Which ones would not be an appropriate solution to the problem? Explain why they are not appropriate.

   a. Look at the registry key that launched the program to help determine where in Windows the program was initiated.
   b. Use Autoruns to disable the program.
   c. Search Task Scheduler for the source of the program being launched.
   d. Use Msconfig to disable the program.
   e. Search Group Policy for the source of the program.

>> HANDS-ON PROJECTS

PROJECT 2-1:   Researching Running Processes

Boot to the Windows desktop and then use Task Manager to get a list of all the running processes on your machine. Use the Vista Snipping Tool to save and print the Task Manager screens showing the list of processes. Next, boot the system into Safe Mode and use Task Manager to list running processes. Which processes that were loaded normally are not loaded when the system is running in Safe Mode?

PROJECT 2-2:   Editing and Restoring the Registry

Practice editing and restoring the registry by doing the following:

1. Export the registry key HKEY_CURRENT_USER\Software\Microsoft\Windows\ CurrentVersion\Explorer to an export file stored on the desktop.

2. To change the name of the Recycle Bin on the Windows Vista desktop for the currently logged-on user, click the following subkey, which holds the name of the Recycle Bin:

   HKEY_CURRENT_USER\Software\Microsoft\Windows\CurrentVersion\Explorer\ CLSID\645FF040-5081-101B-9F08-00AA002F954E

3. Double-click (**Default**) in the Name column in the right pane. The Edit String dialog box opens. The Value data text box in the dialog box should be empty. If a value is present, you selected the wrong value. Check your work and try again.

4. Enter a new name for the Recycle Bin. Click **OK**.

5. To see your change, right-click the desktop and select **Refresh** on the shortcut menu. The name of the Recycle Bin changes.

6. To restore the name to the default value, in the Registry Editor window, again double-click (**Default**) in the right pane. The Edit String dialog box opens. Delete your entry and click **OK**.

7. To verify the change is made, right-click the desktop and select **Refresh** on the shortcut menu. The Recycle Bin name should return to its default value.

8. Exit the registry editor and delete the exported key you saved to your desktop.

   From these directions, you can see that changes made to the registry take effect immediately. Therefore, take extra care when editing the registry. If you make a mistake and don't know how to correct a problem you create, then you can undo your changes by exiting the registry editor and double-clicking the exported key.

PROJECT 2-3: Monitoring Startup Items with WinPatrol

1. Using the System Configuration Utility (Msconfig), disable all the non-Windows startup items. Restart your computer.

2. Download and install Winpatrol from *www.winpatrol.com*.

3. Using the System Configuration Utility (Msconfig), enable all of the disabled startup items and restart the computer.

4. Are the startup programs able to start? What messages are displayed on the screen?

PROJECT 2-4: Using System Restore

Manually create a restore point. Make a change to the display settings. Restore the system using System Restore. Are the changes still in effect? Why or why not? Now undo the restore that you just performed. Were the changes made to the display settings restored? Why or why not?

PROJECT 2-5: Practicing Launching Programs at Startup

Do the following to practice launching programs at startup, listing the steps you took for each activity:

1. Configure Scheduled Tasks to launch NotePad each time the computer starts and any user logs on. List the steps you took.

2. Configure Group Policy to launch Paint each time the computer starts and any user logs on. List the steps you took.

3. Put a shortcut in a startup folder so that any user launches a command prompt window at startup.

4. Restart the system and verify that all three programs are launched. Did you receive any errors?

5. Remove the three programs from the startup process.

PROJECT 2-6: Using Boot Logs and System Information to Research Startup

Boot logs can be used to generate a list of drivers that were loaded during a normal startup and during the Safe Mode startup. By comparing the two lists, you can determine which drivers are not essential to startup. Also, the System Information utility (msinfo32.exe) can help you find out information about a driver or service. Do the following to research startup:

1. To turn on boot logging, boot to the Advanced Boot Options menu and choose Enable Boot Logging. Then boot to the normal Windows desktop. Print the file C:\Windows\ntbtlog.txt and save the file to a different location on the hard drive.

2. Reboot the system in Safe Mode. Print the file C:\Windows\ntbtlog.txt and save the file to a different location on the hard drive. By comparing the two lists, identify the drivers that were loaded normally but not loaded during Safe Mode.

2

3. Using the System Information utility (msinfo32.exe), identify the hardware components that use the drivers you discovered were not loaded during Safe Mode but are loaded during a normal startup. (To find a driver, you can drill down to each hardware component and/or you can use the search feature at the bottom of the System Information window.)

As you identify the drivers not loaded during Safe Mode, it might be helpful to know that these registry keys list the drivers and services that are loaded during Safe Mode:

◢ Lists drivers and services loaded during Safe Mode:
HKLM\System\CurrentControlSet\Control\SafeBoot\Minimal

◢ Lists drivers and services loaded during Safe Mode with Networking:
HKLM\System\CurrentControlSet\Control\SafeBoot\Network

PROJECT 2-7:   Researching Software to Compare Text Files

Comparing boot log files manually can be tedious work, and a utility that compares text files looking for differences can be a great help. Finding the best utility can, however, be a challenge. Vista offers the Comp command, and Windows XP support tools include Windiff.exe. Alternately, you can find and download another file comparison program from the Internet. Do the following to research file comparison programs:

1. In a command prompt window, use the Vista Comp command to compare the two log files you saved in Project 2-6.

2. Locate a file comparison program on the Internet, copy it to your Vista computer, and install it. Be sure to verify that the site you are using is reliable before you download a file from it—you don't want to download malware to your PC. Use the program to compare the two log files.

3. If you have access to a Windows XP computer that has the system tools installed, copy the Windiff.exe program to your Vista computer and use it to compare the two log files.

4. Which file comparison program do you like best? Why?

PROJECT 2-8:   Practicing Manually Removing Software

To practice your skills of manually removing software, install Startup Control Panel by Mike Lin (*www.mlin.net/StartupCPL.shtml*). Then following directions in the chapter, manually remove the software, listing the steps you used. After you have manually removed the software, reboot the system. Did you get any error messages?

>> REAL PROBLEMS, REAL SOLUTIONS

REAL PROBLEM 2-1:   Cleaning Up Startup

Using a computer that has a problem with a sluggish startup, apply the tools and procedures you learned in this chapter to clean up the startup process. Take detailed notes of each step you take and the results. (If you are having a problem finding a computer with a sluggish startup, consider offering your help to a friend, a family member, or a non-profit organization.)

CHAPTER 3

Removing Malicious Software

Malicious software, also called **malware** or a computer **infestation**, is any unwanted program that means you harm and is transmitted to your computer without your knowledge. The best-known malicious software is a **virus**, which is malicious software that can replicate itself by attaching itself to other programs. However, many types of malicious software have evolved over the past few years, such as adware, spyware, and worms, and there is considerable overlap in what they do, how they spread, and how to get rid of them. In this chapter, you'll learn enough about how malware works to help you deal with it at a technical level. For the average user, the solution to cleaning up an infected system is to run antivirus software, and that is the first and most important step to solving the problem. However, in some situations, you'll need to dig much deeper to root out some of the more difficult and stubborn malware problems. How to do all this is covered in this chapter.

After your system is clean, the next thing you want to do is to learn how to protect it from future problems. In the next chapter, we talk about all the many ways you can protect your home or small office computers and protect your laptop when traveling. Putting into place some solid security and knowing how to use that security are the ultimate solutions to protecting yourself. For now, however, let's concentrate on cleaning up an infected system.

⚒ Focus Problem

"I'm under attack! Nasty software has attacked my system. How do I clean up the mess?"

WHAT ARE WE UP AGAINST?

In this section, we'll look at Windows Vista symptoms that indicate you've got an infected system. Next, you'll learn about the different kinds of malware and how they work.

YOU'VE GOT MALWARE

Here are some warnings that suggest malicious software is at work:

- *Warning 1*: Pop-up ads plague you when surfing the Web.
- *Warning 2*: Generally, the system works much slower than it used to. Programs take longer than normal to load.
- *Warning 3*: The number and length of disk accesses seem excessive for simple tasks. The number of bad sectors on the hard drive continues to increase.
- *Warning 4*: The access lights on the hard drive turn on when there should be no activity on the devices. (However, sometimes Vista performs routine maintenance on the drive when the system has been inactive for a while.)
- *Warning 5*: Strange or bizarre error messages appear. Programs that once worked now give errors.
- *Warning 6*: Less memory than usual is available, or there is a noticeable reduction in disk space.
- *Warning 7*: Strange graphics appear on your computer monitor, or the computer makes strange noises.
- *Warning 8*: The system cannot recognize the DVD or CD drive, although it worked earlier.
- *Warning 9*: In Windows Explorer, filenames now have weird characters or their file sizes seem excessively large. Executable files have changed size or file extensions change without reason. Files mysteriously disappear or appear.
- *Warning 10*: Files constantly become corrupted.
- *Warning 11*: The OS begins to boot, but hangs before getting to the Windows desktop.
- *Warning 12*: Your antivirus software displays one or more messages.
- *Warning 13*: You receive e-mail messages telling you that you have sent someone an infected message.
- *Warning 14*: Task Manager shows unfamiliar processes running.
- *Warning 15*: When you try to use your browser to access the Internet, strange things happen and you can't surf the Web. Your IE home page has changed and you see new toolbars you didn't ask for.

✎ Note

Malicious software is designed to do varying degrees of damage to data and software, although it does not damage PC hardware. However, when boot sector information is destroyed on a hard drive, the hard drive can appear to be physically damaged.

HERE'S THE NASTY LIST

You need to know your enemy! Different categories of malicious software are listed next and are described in a bit more detail later in this section:

▲ *Category 1*: A virus is a program that replicates by attaching itself to other programs. The infected program must be executed for a virus to run. The program might be an application, a macro in a document, a Windows system file, or one of the small programs at the beginning of the hard drive needed to boot the OS. (These programs are called the boot sector program and the master boot program.) The damage a virus does ranges from minor, such as displaying bugs crawling around on a screen, to major, such as erasing everything written on a hard drive or stealing your credit card information. The best way to protect against viruses is to always run antivirus (AV) software in the background.

▲ *Category 2*: Adware produces all those unwanted pop-up ads. Adware is secretly installed on your computer when you download and install shareware or freeware, including screen savers, desktop wallpaper, music, cartoons, news, and weather alerts. Then it displays pop-up ads which might be based on your browsing habits (see Figure 3-1). Sometimes when you try to uninstall adware, it deletes whatever it was you downloaded that you really wanted to keep. And sometimes adware is also spying on you and collecting private information.

Figure 3-1   This popup window is luring the user to take the bait

▲ *Category 3*: Spam is junk e-mail that you don't want, didn't ask for, and which gets in your way.

▲ *Category 4*: Spyware is software that installs itself on your computer to spy on you and that collects personal information about you that it transmits over the Internet to Web-hosting sites. These sites might use your personal data in harmless or harmful ways such as tailoring marketing information to suit your shopping habits, tracking marketing trends, or stealing your identity for harm. Spyware comes to you by way of e-mail attachments, downloaded freeware or shareware, instant messaging programs, or when you click a link on a malicious Web site.

▲ *Category 5*: A **worm** is a program that copies itself throughout a network or the Internet without a host program. A worm creates problems by overloading the network as it replicates. Worms cause damage by their presence rather than by performing a specific damaging act, as a virus does. A worm overloads memory or hard drive space by replicating repeatedly. When a worm (for example, Sasser or W32.Sobig.F@mm) is loose on the Internet, it can cause damage such as sending mass e-mailings. The best way to protect against worms is to use a firewall. Antivirus software also offers protection.

▲ *Category 6*: A **browser hijacker**, also called a home page hijacker, does mischief by changing your home page and other browser settings. Figure 3-2 shows Internet Explorer after a user tried to install a free game downloaded from the Internet. The program installed two new toolbars in his browser and changed his home page. Browser hijackers can set unwanted bookmarks, redirect your browser to a shopping site when you type in a wrong URL, produce pop-up ads, and direct your browser to Web sites that offer pay-per-view pornography.

Figure 3-2   Internet Explorer with toolbars installed and home page changed

▲ *Category 7*: A **virus hoax** or e-mail hoax is e-mail that does damage by tempting you to forward it to everyone in your e-mail address book with the intent of clogging up e-mail systems or tempting you to delete a critical Windows system file by convincing you the file is malicious. Also, some e-mail scam artists promise to send you money if you'll circulate their e-mail messages to thousands of people. I recently received one that was supposedly promising money from Microsoft for "testing" the strength of the Internet e-mail system. Beware! Always check Web sites that track virus hoaxes before pressing that Send button! Your AV software Web site most likely keeps a database of virus hoaxes. Here are some other good sites to help you debunk a virus hoax:

▲ *www.hoaxkill.com* by Oxcart Software
▲ *www.snopes.com* by Barbara and David Mikkelson
▲ *www.viruslist.com* by Kaspersky Lab
▲ *www.vmyths.com* by Rhode Island Soft Systems, Inc.

▲ *Category 8*: **Phishing** (pronounced "fishing") is a type of identity theft where the sender of an e-mail message scams you into responding with personal data about yourself. The scam artist baits you by asking you to verify personal data on your bank account, ISP account, credit card account, or something of that nature. Often you are tricked into clicking a link in the e-mail message, which takes you to an official-looking site complete with corporate or bank logos where you are asked to enter your user ID and password to enter the site.

▲ *Category 9*: Scam artists use **scam e-mail** to lure you into their scheme. One scam e-mail I recently received was supposedly from the secretary of a Russian oil tycoon who was being held in jail with his millions of dollars of assets frozen. If I would respond to the e-mail and get involved, I was promised a 12% commission to help recover the funds.

▲ *Category 10*: A **dialer** is software installed on your PC that disconnects your phone line from your ISP and dials up an expensive pay-per-minute phone number without your knowledge. The damage a dialer does is an expensive phone bill.

▲ *Category 11*: A **keylogger** tracks all your keystrokes, including passwords, chat room sessions, e-mail messages, documents, online purchases, and anything else you type on your PC. All this text is logged to a text file and transmitted over the Internet without your knowledge. A keylogger is a type of spyware that can be used to steal a person's identity, credit card numbers, Social Security number, bank information, passwords, e-mail addresses, and so forth.

▲ *Category 12*: A **logic bomb** is dormant code added to software and triggered at a predetermined time or by a predetermined event. For instance, an employee might put code in a program to destroy important files if his or her name is ever removed from the payroll file.

▲ *Category 13*: A **Trojan horse** does not need a host program to work; rather, it substitutes itself for a legitimate program. In most cases, a user launches it thinking she is launching a legitimate program. Figure 3-3 shows a pop-up that appears when you're surfing the Web. Click OK and you might introduce a Trojan into your system. A Trojan is likely to introduce one or more viruses into the system. These Trojans are called downloaders.

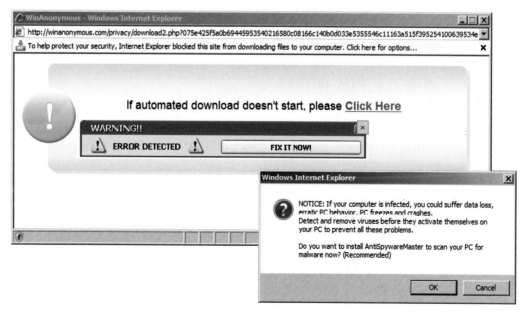

Figure 3-3 Clicking an action button on a pop-up window might invite a Trojan into your system

Last year, I got fooled with a Trojan when I got an e-mail message near the actual date of my birthday from someone named Emily, whom I thought I knew. Without thinking, I clicked the link in the e-mail message to "View my birthday card to you." Figure 3-4 shows what happened when I clicked.

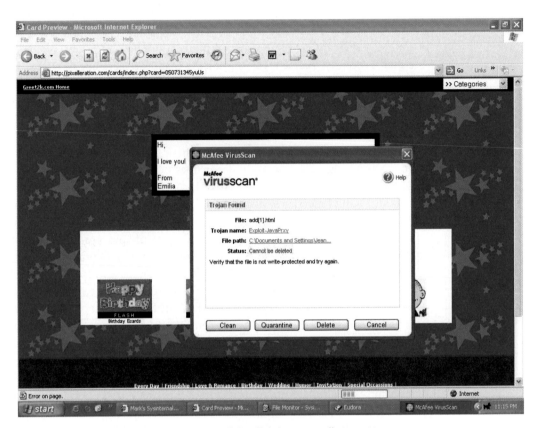

Figure 3-4 A Trojan can get in when you click a link in an e-mail message

In this next part of the chapter, let's look at the different types of malicious software and how they work; then we'll look at best practices to avoid them. Lastly, we'll look at how to get rid of them once we're under attack.

HOW A VIRUS WORKS

A virus attacks your computer system and hides in several different ways. A **boot sector virus** hides in the boot sector program of a hard drive or floppy disk, or in the master boot program in the very first sector of a hard drive called the master boot record (MBR). A **file virus** hides in an executable program having a .exe, .com, .sys, .vbs, or other executable file extension, or in a word-processing document that contains a macro. A **multipartite virus** is a combination of a boot sector virus and a file virus and can hide in either. A **macro** is a small program contained in a document that can be automatically executed either when the document is first loaded or later by pressing a key combination. For example, a word-processing macro might automatically read the system date and copy it into a document when you open the document. Viruses that hide in macros of document files are called macro viruses. **Macro viruses** are the most common viruses spread by e-mail, hiding in macros of attached document files. A **script virus** is a virus that hides in a script, which might execute when you click a link on a Web page or in an HTML e-mail message or when you attempt to open an e-mail attachment.

HOW MALWARE REPLICATES AND HIDES

A virus or other malware can use various techniques to load itself in memory and replicate itself. Also, malware attempts to hide from antivirus (AV) software by changing its distinguishing characteristics (its signature) and by attempting to mask its presence. Here are some techniques used by malware to start itself and prevent detection:

▲ *Technique 1*: A virus can search a hard drive for a file with an .exe extension and then create another file with the same filename but with a .com file extension. The virus then stores itself there. When the user launches the program, the OS first looks for the program name with the .com file extension. It then finds and executes the virus. The virus is loaded into memory and loads the program with the .exe extension. The user appears to have launched the desired program. The virus is then free to do damage or spread itself to other programs.

▲ *Technique 2*: Because AV software can detect a virus by noting the difference between a program's file size before the virus infects it and after the virus is present, the virus alters OS information to mask the size of the file in which it hides.

▲ *Technique 3*: The virus monitors when files are opened or closed. When it sees that the file in which it is hiding is about to be opened, it temporarily removes itself or substitutes a copy of the file that does not include the virus. The virus keeps a copy of this uninfected file on the hard drive just for this purpose. A virus that does this or changes the attributes of its host program is called a **stealth virus**.

▲ *Technique 4*: As a virus replicates, it changes its characteristics. This type of virus is called a **polymorphic virus**.

▲ *Technique 5*: Some viruses can continually transform themselves so they will not be detected by AV software that is looking for a particular characteristic. A virus that uses this technique is called an **encrypting virus**.

▲ *Technique 6*: The virus creates more than one process; each process is watching the others. If one process gets closed, it will be started up again by one of the other processes. (This method of preventing detection is also used by other forms of malware.)

▲ *Technique 7*: Entries are often made in obscure places in the registry that allow the software to start when you start up Windows or launch Internet Explorer. (This method is used by several types of malware.)

▲ *Technique 8*: One type of malware, called a **rootkit**, loads itself before the OS boot is complete. Because it is already loaded when the AV software loads, it is sometimes overlooked by AV software. In addition, a rootkit hijacks internal Windows components so that it masks information Windows provides to user mode utilities such as Task Manager, Windows Explorer, the registry editor, and AV software. This helps it remain undetected.

STEP-BY-STEP ATTACK PLAN

This section is a step-by-step attack plan to clean up an infected system. We'll first use AV software and anti-adware software to do a general cleanup. Then we'll use some Windows tools to check out the system to make sure all remnants of malware have been removed and the system is in tip-top order.

STEP 1: RUN AV SOFTWARE

A virus is often programmed to attempt to hide from antivirus (AV) software. It's also sometimes programmed to block downloading and installing the AV software if the software is not already installed. AV software can only detect viruses identical or similar to those it has been programmed to search for and recognize. Most AV software scans

Figure 3-5 Verify that your account has Administrator privileges

> ✎ **Note**
>
> Most of the tasks to rid a system of malware described in this chapter require that you be logged onto the Vista system using an account with administrator privileges. If you are not sure what type of account you are using, in Control Panel, click **User Accounts and Family Safety** and then click **User Accounts**. Look for "Administrator" under your account name (see Figure 3-5).

for unknown viruses by looking for suspicious activity typical of what viruses generally do. (This type of hit-or-miss, inaccurate scanning is called heuristic scanning.) AV software detects a known virus by looking for distinguishing characteristics called **virus signatures**, which is why AV software cannot always detect a virus it does not know to look for. For all these reasons, it's important to have AV software installed, have it running in the background, and regularly download updates to it.

Table 3-1 lists popular antivirus software and Web sites that also provide information about viruses.

Antivirus Software	Web Site
AVG Anti-Virus by Grisoft	*www.grisoft.com*
BitDefender Antivirus	*www.bitdefender.com*
F-Secure Antivirus by F-Secure Corp.	*www.f-secure.com*
Kaspersky Antivirus	*www.kaspersky.com*
McAfee VirusScan by McAfee Associates, Inc.	*www.mcafee.com*
NeatSuite by Trend Micro (for networks)	*www.trendmicro.com*
Norton AntiVirus by Symantec, Inc.	*www.symantec.com*
Panda Antivirus	*www.pandasoftware.com*
AntiVirus plus AntiSpyware by Trend Micro (for home use)	*www.trendmicro.com*
Windows Live OneCare by Microsoft	*onecare.live.com*

Table 3-1 Antivirus software and Web sites

When selecting AV software, find out if it can:

◢ Automatically download new software upgrades and virus definitions from the Internet so that your software is continually aware of new viruses

◢ Automatically execute at startup before the system connects to a network

◢ Detect macros in a word-processing document as it is loaded by the word processor

◢ Automatically monitor files being downloaded from the Internet, including e-mail attachments and attachments sent during a chat session, such as when using AOL Instant Messenger

◢ Scan both automatically and manually for viruses

◢ Scan for other types of malware, including adware, spyware, and rootkits

 Note

It's handy to have AV software on CD so that you don't need Internet access to download the software, but recognize that this AV software won't have the latest updates. You'll need these updates downloaded from the Internet before it will catch newer viruses.

Here are steps to use AV software on an infected system that does not already have AV software installed:

1. Purchase the AV software on CD (see Figure 3-6), or use another computer to download the AV software from its Web site and then burn the downloaded files to a CD. Don't make the mistake of using the infected PC to purchase and download AV software because keyloggers might be spying and collecting credit card information.

Figure 3-6 Having AV software on CD means you don't need Internet access to install the software

2. Insert the AV software CD. Most likely the AV main menu will be displayed automatically. If it does not, use Windows Explorer to locate and execute the setup program on the CD (see Figure 3-7).

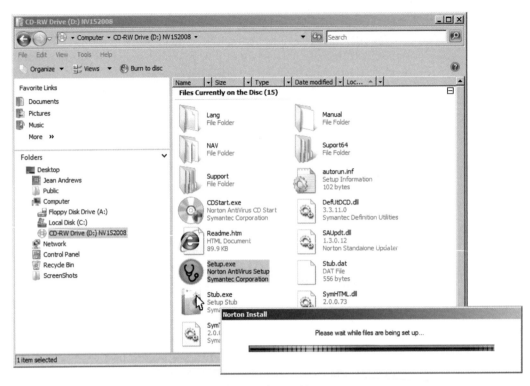

Figure 3-7   Execute the setup program on the AV software CD

3. When given the opportunity, choose to scan for infections before installing the software (see Figure 3-8). The software will ask for Internet access to download the latest updates.

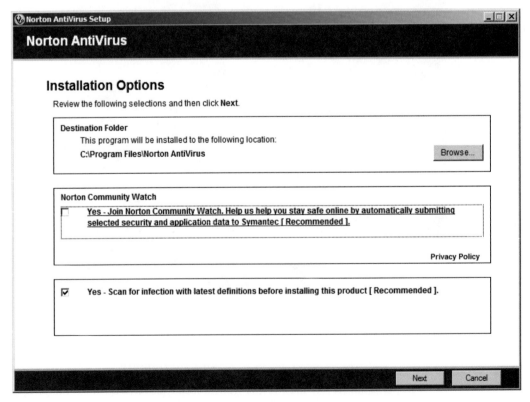

Figure 3-8   Choose to scan for infections before installing the AV software

4. The AV software gives you the chance to decide what to do with any problems it finds. Sometimes AV software detects a program that you know you have downloaded and want to keep, but the AV software recognizes it as potentially harmful. This type of software is sometimes called grayware or a PUP (potentially unwanted program). When the AV software displays the list of detected files, unless you recognize something you want to keep, I suggest you tell the AV software to delete them all.

5. The software might require a restart after the scan and before the installation completes.

6. After the reboot, allow the software to update itself again and then scan the system again. Most likely, some new malware will be discovered. For example, after AV software declared it had removed all malware it had found, on the next restart the window in Figure 3-9 appeared after Internet Explorer was launched. It's a bait window put there by malware proving the system is far from clean. Keep repeating the scan until you get a clean scan. Reboot between scans and take notes of any program files the software is not able to delete.

Figure 3-9 Evidence that malware is still infecting the system

7. After the AV software performs a scan and finds no problems, it's time to see where you stand. Reboot the system and look for any error messages or problems. If you still believe the system might be infected, reboot the PC in Safe Mode and scan again. (Recall that to boot into Safe Mode, press F8 while Windows starts and then choose Safe Mode with Networking from the Advanced Boot Options menu.)

It might be more fun to begin manually removing each program yourself, but it's probably quicker and more thorough to use anti-adware software next. I suggest you resist the temptation to poke around looking for the malware and move on to the next step.

> **Note**
>
> If viruses are launched even after you boot in Safe Mode and you cannot get the AV software to work, try searching for suspicious entries in the subkeys under HKLM\System\CurrentControlSet\Control\SafeBoot. Subkeys under this key control what is launched when you boot into Safe Mode. How to edit the registry is covered in Chapter 2.

STEP 2: RUN ADWARE OR SPYWARE REMOVAL SOFTWARE

Almost all AV software products today also search for adware and spyware. However, software specifically dedicated to removing this type of malware generally does a better job of it than does AV software. The next step in the removal process is to use anti-adware or anti-spyware software.

The distinction between adware and spyware is slight, and sometimes a malicious software program is displaying pop-up ads and also spying on you. There are tons of removal software products available on the Web, but I recommend those in the following list. They all can catch adware, spyware, cookies, browser hijackers, dialers, keyloggers, and Trojans.

- ◢ Ad-Aware by Lavasoft (*www.lavasoft.com*) is one of the most popular and successful adware and spyware removal products. It can be downloaded without support for free.
- ◢ Spybot Search and Destroy by PepiMK Software (*www.safer-networking.org*) does an excellent job of removing malicious software and it's free.
- ◢ Spy Sweeper by Webroot Software, Inc (*www.webroot.com*) is a very good product but does require you pay a yearly subscription.
- ◢ Windows Vista includes Windows Defender, which is antispyware software embedded in the OS.

Figure 3-10 shows what Search & Destroy discovered on one computer after AV software declared the system clean. Notice in the window that the software lists the exact registry keys that are infected.

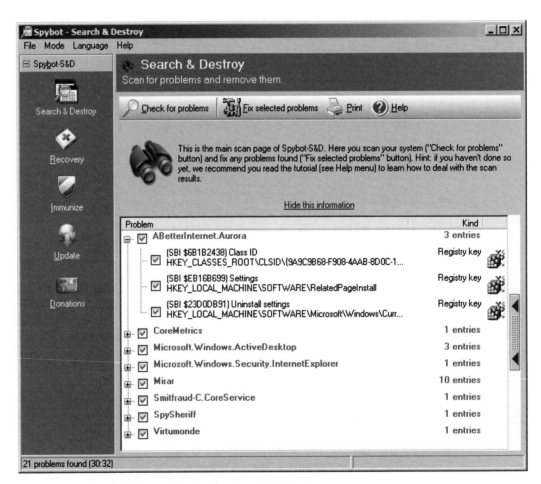

Figure 3-10 Search & Destroy showing details as it finds adware

To completely clean your system, you might have to run a removal product more than once or use more than one product. For example, what Ad-Aware doesn't find, Search & Destroy might, but what Search & Destroy doesn't find, Ad-Aware might find. To be sure, run two products.

STEP 3: CLEAN UP WHAT'S LEFT OVER

Next, you'll need to clean up anything the AV or anti-adware software left behind. Sometimes AV software tells you it is not able to delete a file or it deletes an infected file, but leaves behind an orphaned entry in the registry or startup folders. If the AV software tells you it was not able to delete or clean a file, first check the AV software Web site for any instructions you might find to manually clean things up. In this section, you'll learn about general things you can do to clean up what might be left behind.

RESPOND TO ANY STARTUP ERRORS

On the first boot after AV software and anti-adware software have declared a system is malware free, you might still find some startup errors caused by incomplete removal of the malware. One example of such an error is shown in Figure 3-11. Somewhere in the system, the command to launch OsisOijw.dll is still working even though this DLL has been deleted.

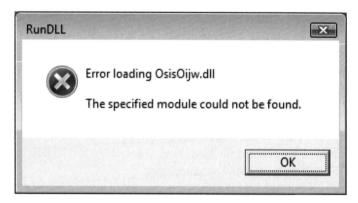

Figure 3-11 Startup error indicates an entry to launch malware has not been removed

One way to find this orphaned entry point is to use Msconfig. Figure 3-12 shows the Msconfig window showing us that the DLL is launched from a registry key.

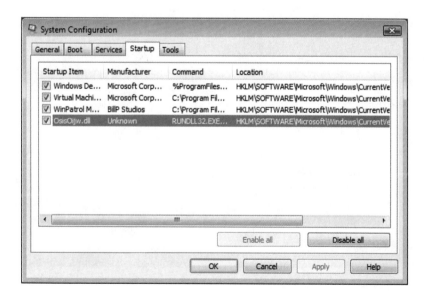

Figure 3-12 Msconfig shows how the DLL is launched during startup

The next step is to back up the registry and then use Regedit to find and delete the key (see Figure 3-13).

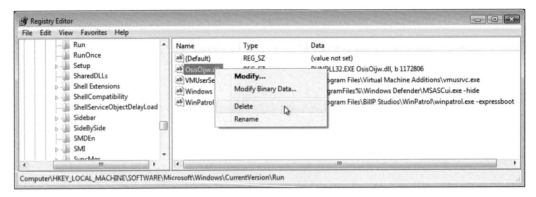

Figure 3-13   Delete the orphan registry entry left there by malware

DELETE FILES

For each program file the AV software told you it could not delete, try to delete the program file yourself using Windows Explorer. For peace of mind, don't forget to empty the Recycle Bin when you're done. You might need to open an elevated command prompt window and remove the hidden or system attributes on a file so that you can delete it. Recall that to open an elevated command prompt window, click **Start**, click **All Programs**, click **Accessories**, and right-click **Command Prompt**. Then select **Run as administrator** from the shortcut menu and respond to the UAC box. Figure 3-14 shows how to delete the file C:\INT0094.exe. Table 3-2 explains each command used.

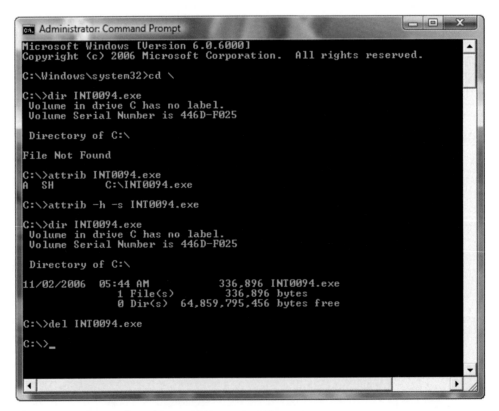

Figure 3-14   Commands to delete a hidden system file

Command	Explanation
cd \	Make the root directory of drive C the current directory
dir INT0094.exe	The file does not appear to be in the directory
attrib INT0094.exe	The file is actually present but hidden
attrib –h –s INT0094.exe	Remove the hidden and system attributes of the file
dir INT0094.exe	The dir command now displays the file
del INT0094.exe	Delete the file

Table 3-2 Commands to delete a hidden system file

If you are still not able to delete a file, open Task Manager and make sure the process is not running. A program file cannot be deleted if it is currently running. If you cannot end the process using Task Manager, know that later in the chapter you'll learn more about ending processes that refuse to be stopped by Task Manager.

To get rid of other malware files, you might need to delete all Internet Explorer temporary Internet files. Use one of these two methods:

▲ *Method 1*: Using Windows Explorer, open the Drive C: properties window and on the General tab window, click **Disk Cleanup**. Then choose to delete files for all users and respond to the UAC box. Next, from the Disk Cleanup window shown in Figure 3-15, make sure **Temporary Internet Files** is checked and click **OK**.

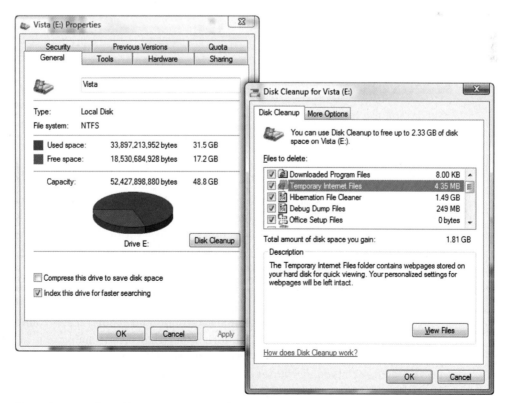

Figure 3-15 Delete all temporary Internet files

▲ *Method 2*: Click **Start**, right-click **Internet Explorer,** and select **Internet Properties** from the shortcut menu. The Internet Properties dialog box opens as shown on the left side of Figure 3-16. (You can also access this box from within Internet Explorer by clicking **Tools** and **Internet Options**.) On the Internet Properties box under Browsing History, click **Delete**. From the Delete Browsing History box shown on the right side of Figure 3-16, not only can you delete Temporary Internet Files, but also you can delete Cookies, History, Form data, and Passwords. Make your selections and follow directions on screen to complete the deletions. However, be aware that if you delete Cookies and Passwords, you will lose personal information saved by reputable sites such as your banking site.

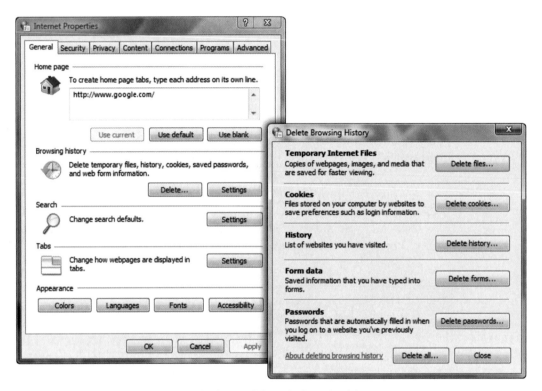

Figure 3-16   Use the Internet Properties box to delete the browsing history

PURGE RESTORE POINTS

Some malware hides its program files in the data storage area of the Windows Vista System Restore utility. Windows does not always allow AV software to look in this storage area when it is scanning for malware. To get rid of that malware, you must turn off System Protection, reboot your system, and turn System Protection back on. How to do that was covered in Chapter 2. Turning off System Protection causes the data storage area to be purged. You'll get rid of any malware there, but you'll also lose all your restore points.

If your AV software is running in the background and reports it has found a virus in the C:\System Volume Information_restore folder, that means malware is in a System Restore point (see Figure 3-17). Unless you desperately need to keep a restore point you've previously made, if you see a message similar to the one in Figure 3-17 or your AV software scan feature found lots of malware in other places on the drive, the best idea is to purge all restore points.

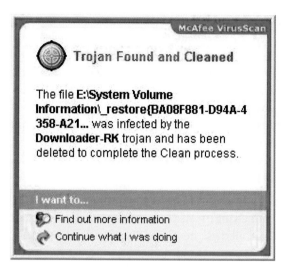

Figure 3-17 Malware found in a restore point

CLEAN THE REGISTRY

Earlier in the chapter, when we were responding to any startup errors found after the AV software had finished cleaning the system, we dealt with the startup error by manually deleting a registry key left there by malware. An easier way to deal with the problem as well as clean up the registry in general is to purchase and use a registry cleaner. You learned about three registry cleaners in Chapter 2: RegClean (*www.regclean.com*), RegCure (*www.regcure.com*), and RegSweep (*www.regsweep.com*). To remove orphaned entries in the registry left there by AV software, you can download and run one of these products. Don't forget to back up the registry before you run the product so that you can backtrack if necessary.

If you prefer to have more control over how the registry is changed, you can use Autoruns at Microsoft TechNet (*technet.microsoft.com*) to help you search for these orphaned registry entries. Figure 3-18 shows a screen shot where Autoruns is displaying an orphaned entry in

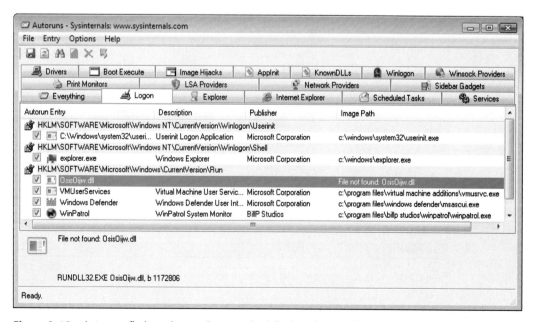

Figure 3-18 Autoruns finds orphan registry entries left there by AV software

the HKLM\Software\Microsoft\Windows\CurrentVersion\Run registry key used to launch the OsisOijw.dll malware program. AV software had already found and deleted this DLL file, but it left the registry key untouched.

Scan through the Autoruns window looking for suspicious entries. Research any entries that you think might be used by malware. To get rid of these entries, back up the registry and then use Regedit to delete unwanted keys or values.

After you have finished cleaning the registry, don't forget to restart the system to make sure all is well before you move on.

CLEAN UP INTERNET EXPLORER

Adware and spyware might install add-ons to Internet Explorer (including toolbars you didn't ask for), install cookie trackers, and change your IE security settings. Anti-adware and antivirus software might have found all these items, but as a good defense, take a few minutes to find out for yourself. Follow these directions to make sure Internet Explorer is error free:

1. Open Internet Explorer and look for unwanted toolbars and home pages. For example, looking back at Figure 3-2 shown earlier in the chapter, the browser has two toolbars the user doesn't want: one by Mirar and one by Google.

2. To remove these toolbars, open Control Panel and in the **Programs** group, click **Uninstall a program**. Select the toolbar program (see Figure 3-19) and click **Uninstall/Change**. Respond to the UAC box.

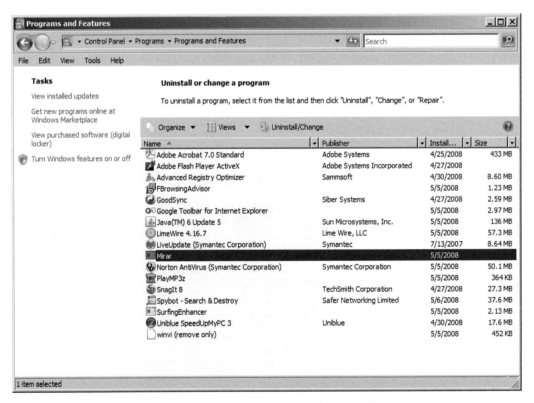

Figure 3-19 Use the Programs and Features window to uninstall an IE toolbar

3. You might be in for a few surprises. When I tried to uninstall the Mirar toolbar showing in Figure 3-19, I got the window showing in Figure 3-20. I decided to go ahead and take the risk of downloading and running the uninstaller program, which did uninstall the toolbar.

Figure 3-20   This software used a suspicious method to uninstall itself

4. Continue to uninstall any other software related to the browser that is listed in the Programs and Features window.

5. Restart Vista and open Internet Explorer. On the IE menu bar, click **Tools, Manage Add-ons,** and **Enable or Disable Add-ons.** The Manage Add-ons box appears (see Figure 3-21).

6. Suspect any item that lists a Publisher you don't trust or lists no publisher at all. To disable the add-on, select it and click **Disable.** ActiveX add-ons can be deleted from this window, but other add-ons can only be disabled. If you find a suspicious add-on, such as the one in Figure 3-21 named opnNEtSl.dll that does not declare its publisher, run the anti-adware product again.

7. Close Internet Explorer and reopen it. Verify that all is working as it should.

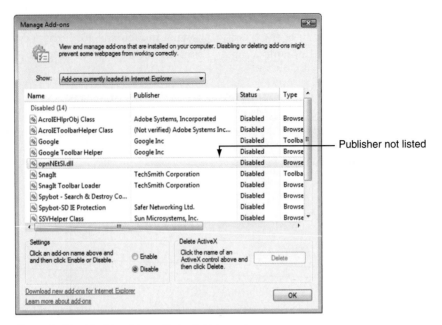

Publisher not listed

Figure 3-21   Disable add-ons that might be malware

8. To change your home page, in Internet Explorer, click **Tools** and click **Internet Options**. On the General tab under Home page, enter the new home page URL, beginning with http://. If you want IE to open two tabs with two different sites, use a second line for the second URL, as shown in Figure 3-22.

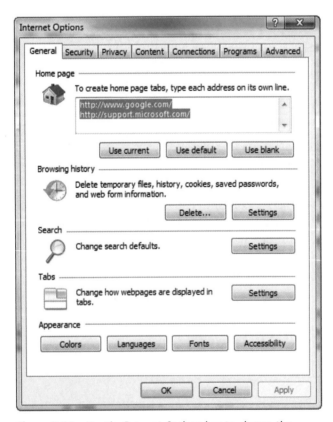

Figure 3-22   Use the Internet Options box to change the home page

DIGGING DEEPER TO FIND MALWARE PROCESSES

It is my hope you won't need this section! Hopefully, by now your system is malware free. However, occasionally you'll need to deal with a really nasty infection that won't be found or deleted by conventional means. In this section, you'll learn to look under the hood of Windows Vista to find processes that have eluded detection by other means. And, as you work through this section, you'll going to learn much about how Windows Vista works. You'll first see how Task Manager can be used to examine processes. Then we'll look at a third-party tool, Process Explorer by Sysinternals and Microsoft TechNet, that can be used to smoke out any lurking processes that elude normal methods of de-infesting a system.

LOOKING UNDER THE HOOD WITH TASK MANAGER

Recall from Chapter 1 that Task Manager can be used to examine running applications and processes and to end a process that is not responding. The easiest way to open Task Manager is to right-click the taskbar and select **Task Manager** from the shortcut menu. The Task Manager window opens. The Applications tab shows the list of currently opened applications. Sometimes the Applications tab shows only the name of the application, but not the program filename associated with it. To get that information, right-click the application in the Applications tab and select **Go To Process** from the shortcut menu (see Figure 3-23). This takes you to the correct process on the Processes tab of Task Manager.

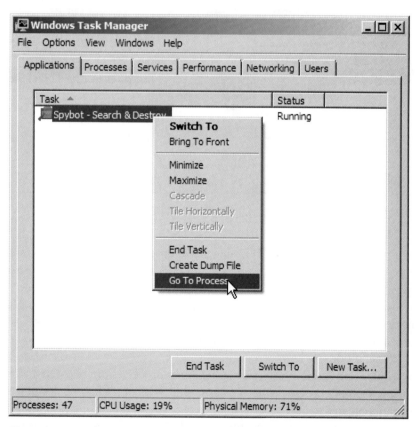

Figure 3-23   Task Manager shows all running applications

To see a list of processes currently running, click the **Processes** tab (see Figure 3-24). The Processes tab normally lists all processes running in user mode in Windows Vista.

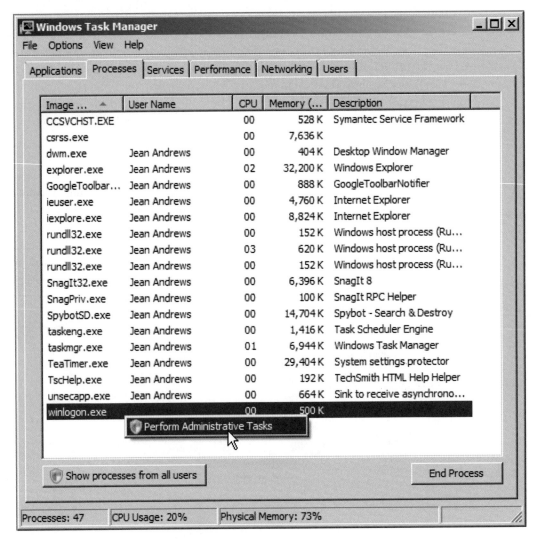

Figure 3-24   Processes currently running under Windows Vista

User mode is one of two modes in which OS programs and other programs can run. User mode has less access to hardware than the other mode, kernel mode. Applications normally run in user mode and device drivers normally run in kernel mode. Windows Vista programs can run in either mode depending on how the program is used by the OS. A virus or worm can run in either mode. Sometimes a malicious process shows up in Task Manager and sometimes it does not. One reason it does not show up is because it's running in kernel mode.

Looking back at Figure 3-24, you can see most processes are registered as running under a user name or user account. Core Windows processes don't list the account under which they are running and not all processes are listed. To get the full picture, right-click on an item that does not list a user name and select **Perform Administrative Tasks**, as shown in the figure, and respond to the UAC box.

The Task Manager window changes to show the accounts all processes are using as well as all processes currently running, include kernel mode processes (see Figure 3-25).

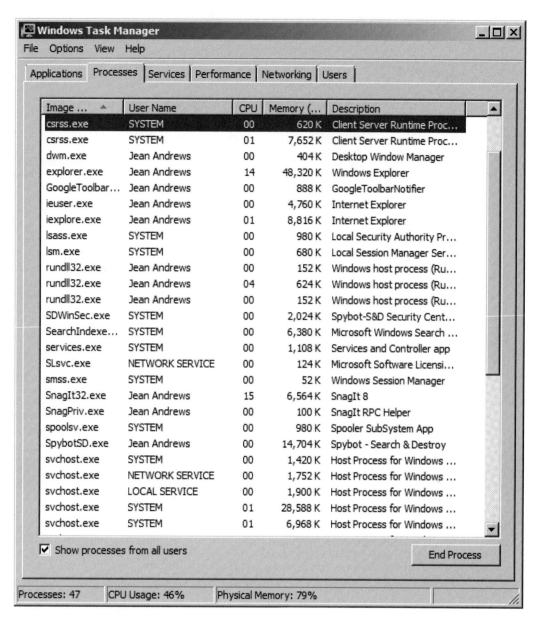

Figure 3-25 Task Manager set to show more information about processes

Accounts that a process can run under include the current user (Jean Andrews), System, Local Service, or Network Service account. Both the Local Service and Network Service accounts have lower privileges than the System account. Services that run under the System, Local Service, or Network Service accounts can't display a dialog box onscreen or interact with the user. To do that, the service must be running under a user account.

CORE WINDOWS PROCESSES

Figure 3-26 shows the Processes tab of Task Manager for a new installation of Windows Vista, before any changes are made or applications are installed.

As a good Windows troubleshooter, you should be familiar with all the processes showing in Figure 3-26, the path to each program file, which in most cases is C:\Windows\system32, and the account under which the process normally runs. Consider this list your starting point

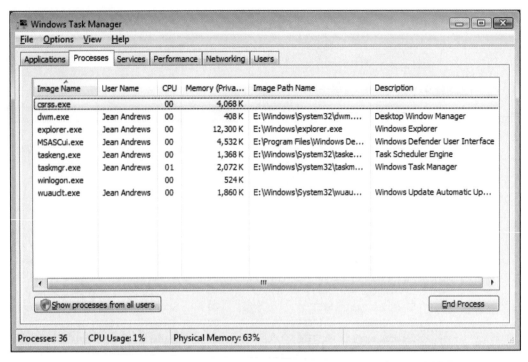

Figure 3-26 Processes showing under Task Manager for a fresh installation of Windows Vista

for learning to recognize legitimate Windows processes. Here is the list of processes, their purposes, and paths, including some processes not shown in Figure 3-26 that can be automatically launched depending on Windows settings:

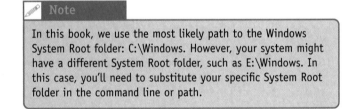

Note

In this book, we use the most likely path to the Windows System Root folder: C:\Windows. However, your system might have a different System Root folder, such as E:\Windows. In this case, you'll need to substitute your specific System Root folder in the command line or path.

▲ *Process 1: Taskmgr.exe.* This is the Task Manager utility itself. The program file is stored in C:\Windows\system32.

▲ *Process 2: Msmsgs.exe.* MSN Messenger, a chat application located in C:\Program Files\MSN Messenger. This process is not a core Windows process and can be easily removed if you don't use MSN Messenger.

▲ *Process 3: Svchost.exe.* This process manages each process that is executed by a DLL. One instance of Svchost runs for each process it manages. The program file is stored in C:\Windows\system32. To see a list of services managed by Svchost, enter this command in a command-prompt window: **tasklist /SVC**.

▲ *Process 4: Explorer.exe.* The Windows graphical shell that manages the desktop, Start menu, taskbar, and file system. The program file is stored in C:\Windows.

▲ *Process 5: Spoolsv.exe.* Handles Windows print spooling and is stored in C:\Windows\system32. Stopping and starting this process can sometimes solve a print spooling problem.

▲ *Process 6: Lsass.exe.* Manages local security and logon policies. The program file is stored in C:\Windows\system32.

▲ *Process 7: Services.exe.* Starts and stops services. This program file is stored in C:\Windows\system32.

▲ *Process 8: Winlogon.exe.* Manages logon and logof events. The program file is stored in C:\Windows\system32.

▲ *Process 9: Csrss.exe.* Client/server runtime server subsystem; manages many commands in Windows that use graphics. The program file is stored in C:\Windows\system32.

▲ *Process 10: Smss.exe.* Windows sessions manager; essential Windows process and is stored in C:\Windows\system32.

▲ *Process 11: Internat.exe.* Displays an icon in the notification area of the taskbar that can be used to switch from English to another language when supplemental language support is enabled using the Regional and Language Options applet in Control Panel.

▲ *Process 12: Mstask.exe.* The task scheduler that runs tasks at scheduled times.

▲ *Process 13: Winmgmt.exe.* A core Windows component that starts the first time a client process requests to connect to the system.

▲ *Process 14: System.* Windows system counter that shows up as a process, but has no program file associated with it.

▲ *Process 15: System Idle Process.* Appears in the Task Manager to show how CPU usage is allotted. It is not associated with a program file.

> **Note**
>
> A **DLL (dynamic link library)** is a program file that contains a collection of subroutines used by other programs. See Appendix D, "How Windows Vista Works," for more information.

> **Note**
>
> When your Windows desktop is locked up, you can sometimes solve the problem by using Task Manager to stop and start Explorer.exe. For more information about how the desktop works, see Appendix D, "How Windows Vista Works."

THE REAL THING AND THE COUNTERFEIT

Do you know how bank tellers recognize counterfeit money? By the time they've spent hours and hours handling the real thing, when a counterfeit bill passes through their hands, they quickly spot it. Becoming familiar with the real thing makes it much easier to recognize a counterfeit. In this book, you're going to see a lot of screen shots of Task Manager processes. After some practice, you'll be able to spot a true Windows process and a counterfeit one. You'll also learn how to investigate processes you don't recognize.

For example, sometimes a virus will disguise itself as Svchost.exe. You can recognize it as a counterfeit process if it's not running under System, Local Service, or Network Service. If you spot an Svchost.exe process running under a user name, suspect a rat. Also, if you notice the Svchost.exe program file is located somewhere other than C:\Windows\system32, this most likely means it's a counterfeit version put there to make trouble. And how do you know the path to a program file? Click **View** on the Task Manager menu and select **Select Columns**. In the Select Process Page Columns dialog box, check **Image Path Name** and click **OK** (see Figure 3-27).

INVESTIGATING AN UNKNOWN PROCESS

When trying to identify a process that shows in Task Manager, your very best tool to investigate the process is the Internet. There are several good online databases of processes, and many times a Google search turns up excellent information. Beware, however! Much information on the Web is written by people who are just guessing about what they are saying, and some of the information is put there to purposefully deceive. Check things out carefully, and learn which sites you can rely on. This section looks at some of these trustworthy sites and how to use them.

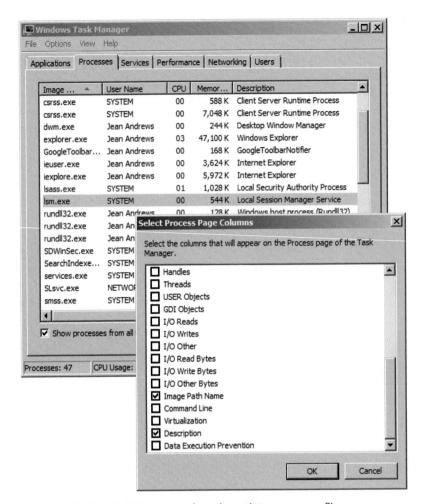

Figure 3-27   Set Task Manager to show the path to a program file

The most reliable site to use when researching processes is the Microsoft support site (*support.microsoft.com*). A search on a process name, an error message, a description of a process or problem with a process, or other related information can turn up a Knowledge Base article with the information you need.

However, Microsoft doesn't normally maintain information about processes other than its own, so for that you must go somewhere else. Suppose for example, when you look at the Processes tab under Task Manager, you see the list shown in Figure 3-28. You see a process you don't recognize, rwwnw64d.exe. You right-click the process and select **Properties** from the shortcut menu. The Properties box shows you little helpful information. But your search on the Web tells you the program is related to adware. Knowing this fact helps you set your priorities when cleaning up the system—begin by ending the process and running anti-adware software.

Some other useful sites that can be trusted to give you information about unknown processes are:

▲ Jim Foley, The Elder Geek at *www.theeldergeekvista.com*
▲ Process Library by Uniblue Systems Limited at *www.processlibrary.com*
▲ DLL Library by Uniblue Systems Limited at *www.liutilities.com*
▲ All the antivirus software sites listed earlier in the chapter in Table 3-1

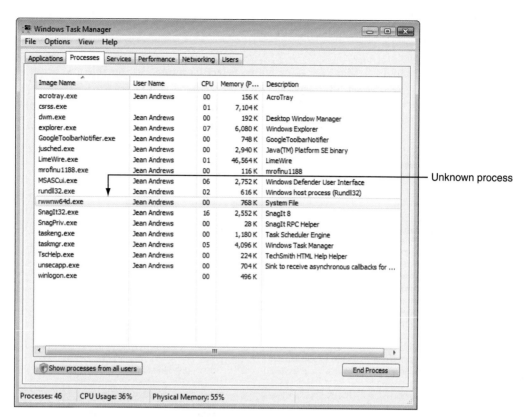

Unknown process

Figure 3-28 Processes you don't recognize can be researched on the Internet

HOW TO END A PROCESS

As you clean up startup, you might need to close an application or service. To close an application, normally you would use the menus within the application or click the Close button in the upper-right corner of the window in which the application is running. To close a service, under normal conditions, you would use the Services console, which is discussed in Chapter 2. However, if a process (application or service) is not responding or is giving errors, these normal methods might not work. To end a process that is not responding, first try to use Task Manager.

Here is what you can do to end a process that is giving you trouble:

▲ *Method 1*: Using Task Manager, to end a program that is not responding to the system, click the **Applications** tab, select the program (called a task in the window), and click **End Task**. This action is the same as if you had used a menu option on the application's window to close the application. If the problem with the application is not too drastic, you might have the opportunity to close data files that are open.

▲ *Method 2*: Sometimes the application is so locked up, clicking End Task will not close the application. In this case, click the **Processes** tab, select the application, and click **End Process**. This action is more drastic than End Task, because it closes the process immediately without giving you the opportunity to close open data files.

▲ *Method 3*: If clicking End Process does not work, the application might be locked up as it waits for your response to a dialog box displayed onscreen. Close the dialog box and then click **End Process**.

▲ *Method 4*: Sometimes when you try to end a service, you get an error message that access is denied and the process does not end. In this case, you might not have the right permissions. Try closing a service when you are logged in as an administrator.

◢ *Method 5:* If Task Manager cannot end a process, try using the Taskkill command. Follow these steps:

1. In Task Manager, click **View, Select Columns**. In the Select Process Page Columns box, check **PID (Process Identifier)** and click **OK**.
2. Note the PID of the process you want to kill. For example, in Figure 3-29, to kill the process TeaTimer.exe, use the PID 2212.

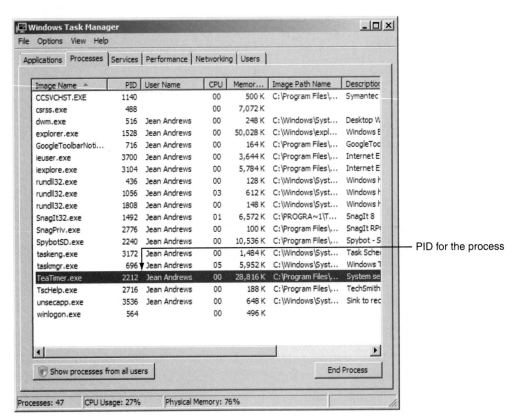

Figure 3-29   The PID identifies a process

3. To open a command prompt window, click **Start**, enter **cmd** in the Start Search box, and press **Enter**.
4. At the command prompt, enter the command **taskkill /f /pid:2212**, using the PID as seen in the Task Manager window. The /f parameter forcefully kills the process. Be careful using this command; it is so powerful that you can end critical system processes that will cause the system to shut down.

PROCESS EXPLORER AT MICROSOFT TECHNET

Process Explorer works like Task Manager, but takes us to another level of information. When you look at all the processes and services running in Task Manager, it's difficult if not impossible to know how these processes are related to each other. Knowing this can help you identify a process that is launching other processes, which is called a process tree. By identifying the original process, the one handling other processes, you can lay the ax to the root of the tree rather than swinging at branches. When one process calls another process into action, the process called into action is called a handle. An open handle is a relationship that has not yet completed. Process Explorer can help you find these open handles and identify the original process.

If you go to the Web site *technet.microsoft.com*, search for and download Process Explorer, and run it, the window in Figure 3-30 appears.

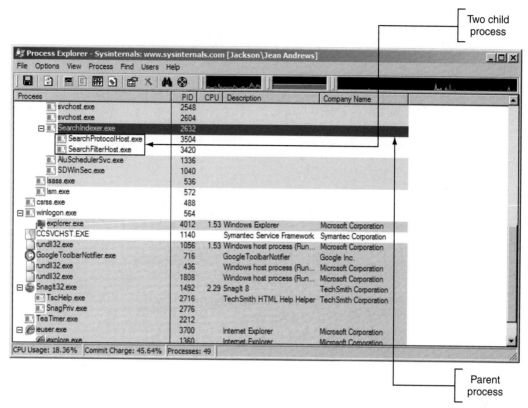

Figure 3-30 Process Explorer color codes child-parent relationships among processes and gives information about processes

On this system monitored by Process Explorer, a browser hijacker is at work changing Web pages and producing pop-ups. As I watched the browser jump from one Web page to another without my involvement, Processor Explorer showed me what was happening with the related processes. From the information we see in Figure 3-30, we see that the process, SearchIndexer.exe, has called two other processes shown in the figure. As the browser jumped from one Web page to another, these two processes completed and started up again. I was watching malware in action!

As you can see, Process Explorer gives much information about a process and is a useful tool for software developers when writing and troubleshooting problems with their software, installation routines, and software conflicts. You can use the tool to smoke out processes, DLLs, and registry keys that elude Task Manager.

DEALING WITH ROOTKITS

A rootkit is a program that uses unusually complex methods to hide itself on a system, and many spyware and adware programs are also rootkits. The term rootkit applies to a kit or set of tools used originally on Unix computers. In Unix, the lowest and most powerful level of Unix accounts is called the root account; therefore, this kit of tools was intended to keep a program working at this root level without detection.

Rootkits can prevent Task Manager from displaying the running rootkit process, or may cause Task Manager to display a different name for this process. The program filename might not be displayed in Windows Explorer, the rootkit's registry keys might be hidden from the registry editor, or the registry editor might display wrong information. All this hiding is accomplished in one of two ways, depending on whether the rootkit is running in user mode or kernel mode (see Figure 3-31). A rootkit running in user mode intercepts the API calls between the time when the API retrieves the data and when it is displayed in a window. A rootkit running in kernel mode actually interferes with the Windows kernel and substitutes its own information in place of the raw data read by the Windows kernel.

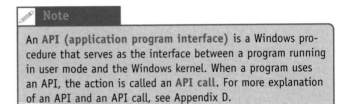

Note

An **API (application program interface)** is a Windows procedure that serves as the interface between a program running in user mode and the Windows kernel. When a program uses an API, the action is called an **API call**. For more explanation of an API and an API call, see Appendix D.

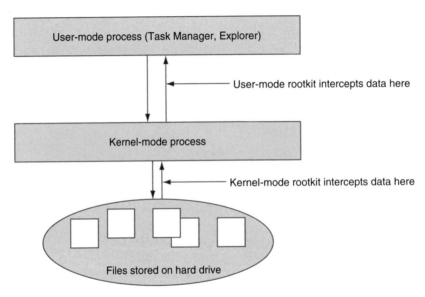

Figure 3-31 A rootkit can run in user mode or kernel mode

Because most AV software to one degree or another relies on Windows tools and components to work, the rootkit is not detected if the Windows tools themselves are infected. Rootkits are also programmed to hide from specific programs designed to find and remove them.

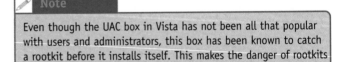

Note

Even though the UAC box in Vista has not been all that popular with users and administrators, this box has been known to catch a rootkit before it installs itself. This makes the danger of rootkits less when using Windows Vista.

Generally, anti-rootkit software works to remove rootkits after they are installed by using these two methods:

▲ The software looks for running processes that don't match up with the underlying program filename.

▲ The software compares files, registry entries, and processes provided by the OS to the lists it generates from the raw data. If the two lists differ, a rootkit is suspected.

Two good anti-rootkit programs are:

◢ Rootkit Revealer by Sysinternals available at TechNet (*technet.microsoft.com*)
◢ BackLight by F-Secure (*www.f-secure.com*)

After you have used other available methods to remove malware and you still believe you're not clean, you might want to download and run one of these products. Close all open applications, including your AV software, and launch the product. Figure 3-32 shows the Vista desktop while Rootkit Revealer scans for rootkits. While it works, it takes complete control of the system so that you cannot use your computer while it is running.

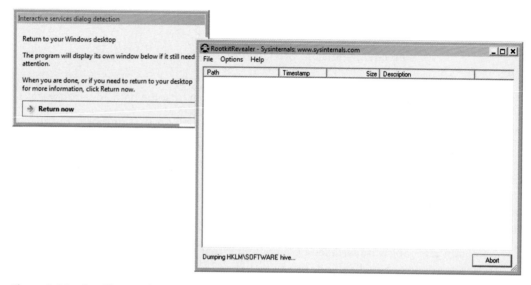

Figure 3-32 Rootkit Revealer scanning for rootkits

For best results when scanning for rootkits, run the anti-rootkit software from another networked computer so that the software is not dependent on the OS that might be infected. For example, you can share drive C on the network and then, from another computer on the network, run the anti-rootkit software and instruct it to scan drive C on the remote computer.

If the software detects a discrepancy that might indicate a rootkit is installed, you'll need to go to the TechNet or F-Secure Web site or do a general Web search to find information about the potential rootkit and instructions for removing it. Follow the instructions to manually remove the program and all its remnants. Sometimes the removal is so complicated, you might decide it makes more sense to just start over and reinstall Windows.

If you have tried all the techniques and products in this chapter and still have malware, I'm sorry to say the next suggestion I have to offer is to back up your data, completely erase your hard drive, reinstall Windows and all your applications, and then restore your data.

Once your system is clean, you'll certainly want to keep it that way. There's so much to say about protecting a computer from malware, I've devoted the entire next chapter to the subject.

>> CHAPTER SUMMARY

◢ Types of malicious software include viruses, Trojan horses, worms, adware, spyware, keyloggers, browser hijackers, dialers, and downloaders.

◢ The first defense against malicious software is antivirus software. If you cannot access the Internet, install the AV software from CD.

◢ If AV software will not run on a PC because the PC is so badly infected, try running the software while in Safe Mode.

◢ Adware and spyware removal software sometimes finds malware that AV software does not find.

◢ AV software sometimes cannot delete a malware program and you must manually delete it.

◢ AV software might leave orphaned registry entries behind that you can manually delete using the registry editor.

◢ Purging all restore points can rid the system of some malicious software.

◢ Rootkits can be detected by software designed for that purpose, and then the rootkits can be manually removed.

◢ Some systems become so highly infected, the only solution is reinstall Windows.

>> KEY TERMS

adware   Software installed on a computer that produces pop-up ads using your browser; the ads are often based on your browsing habits.

API (application program interface)   A predefined Windows procedure that allows a program to access hardware or other software.

API call   A request made by software to the OS to use an API procedure to access hardware or other software.

boot sector virus   A virus that hides in one or both of the small programs at the beginning of the hard drive used to initiate the boot of the operating system.

browser hijacker   A malicious program that infects your Web browser and can change your home page or browser settings. It can also redirect your browser to unwanted sites, produce pop-up ads, and set unwanted bookmarks.

dialer   Malicious software that can disconnect your phone line from your ISP and dial an expensive pay-per-minute phone number without your knowledge.

DLL (dynamic link library)   A group or library of programs packaged into a single program file that can be called on by a Windows application. A DLL file can have a .dll, .fon, .ocx, .drv, .nls, .evt, or .exe file extension.

encrypting virus   A type of virus that can continually transform itself so that it is not detected by AV software.

file virus   A virus that hides in an executable program (for example, .exe, .com, or .sys) or in a word-processing document that contains a macro.

handle   A relationship between a process and a resource it has called into action.

infestation   *See* malicious software.

kernel mode   The Windows privileged processing mode that has access to hardware components.

keylogger   A type of spyware that tracks your keystrokes, including passwords, chat room sessions, e-mail messages, documents, online purchases, and anything else you type on your PC. Text is logged to a text file and transmitted over the Internet without your knowledge.

logic bomb   A type of malicious software that is dormant code added to software and triggered at a predetermined time or by a predetermined event.

macro   A small sequence of commands, contained within a document, that can be automatically executed when the document is loaded, or executed later by using a predetermined keystroke.

macro virus   A virus that can hide in the small programs embedded in a document file. These small programs are called macros.

malicious software   Any unwanted program that is transmitted to a computer without the user's knowledge and that is designed to do varying degrees of damage to data and software. Types of infestations include viruses, Trojan horses, worms, adware, spyware, keyloggers, browser hijackers, dialers, and downloaders.

malware   *See* malicious software.

multipartite virus   A combination of a boot sector virus and a file virus. It can hide in either type of program.

open handle   A handle that is still in progress. (A handle is the relationship between a process and a resource it has called into action.)

phishing   Sending an e-mail message with the intent of getting the user to reveal private information that can be used for identify theft.

polymorphic virus   A type of virus that changes its distinguishing characteristics as it replicates itself. Mutating in this way makes it more difficult for AV software to recognize the presence of the virus.

process tree   A process and all the processes it has launched or other processes beneath it have launched.

rootkit   A type of malicious software that loads itself before the OS boot is complete and can hijack internal Windows components so that it masks information Windows provides to user-mode utilities such as Windows Explorer or Task Manager.

scam e-mail   E-mail sent by a scam artist intended to lure you into a scheme.

script virus   A type of virus that hides in a script which might execute when you click a link on a Web page or in an HTML e-mail message, or when you attempt to open an e-mail attachment.

spam   Junk e-mail you don't ask for, don't want, and which gets in your way.

spyware   Malicious software that installs itself on your computer to spy on you. It collects personal information about you that it transmits over the Internet to Web-hosting sites that intend to use your personal data for harm.

stealth virus   A virus that actively conceals itself by temporarily removing itself from an infected file that is about to be examined, and then hiding a copy of itself elsewhere on the drive.

Trojan horse   A type of malicious software that hides or disguises itself as a useful program, yet is designed to cause damage at a later time.

user mode   In Windows, a processing mode that provides an interface between an application and the OS and that has access to hardware resources only through programs running in kernel mode.

virus   A malicious program that often has an incubation period, is infectious, and is intended to cause damage. A virus program might destroy data and programs or damage a hard drive's boot sector.

virus hoax   E-mail that does damage by tempting you to forward it to everyone in your e-mail address book with the intent of clogging up e-mail systems or by persuading you to delete a critical Windows system file by convincing you the file is malicious.

virus signature   The distinguishing characteristics of malicious software that are used by AV software to identify a program as malicious.

worm   Malicious software designed to copy itself repeatedly to memory, on drive space, or on a network, until little memory or disk space remains. The attack can result in the system not being able to function.

>> REVIEWING THE BASICS

1. Define and explain the differences between viruses, worms, logic bombs, and Trojans.

2. Where can viruses hide?

3. What is the best way to protect a computer or network against worms?

4. What is the best way to determine if an e-mail message warning about a virus is a hoax?

5. Name three ways that a virus can hide from antivirus software.

6. What is the most likely way that a virus will get access to your computer?

7. List two products to remove malicious software that can deal with adware and spyware.

8. Why might it be useful to run AV software in Safe Mode?

9. What registry key keeps information about services that run when a computer is booted into Safe Mode?

10. What does AV software look for to determine that a program or a process is a virus?

11. What Windows tool can you use to solve a problem of an error message displayed at startup just after your AV software has removed malware?

12. What folder is used by Windows to hold System Restore restore points?

13. How can you delete all restore points and clean up the restore points data storage area?

14. Name two anti-rootkit products.

15. What is the major disadvantage of using an AV software installation CD to install the AV software to rid a system of viruses?

16. How does a rootkit running in user mode normally hide?

17. What is the difference between spyware and adware?

18. When one process calls another process, this relationship is called a(n) _____.

19. If a process cannot be ended using Task Manager, what command can you use to end the process?

20. What utility program can be used to find out dependencies among processes to help you discover a process that is starting other processes?

>> THINKING CRITICALLY

1. A virus has attacked your hard drive and now when you start up Windows, instead of seeing a Windows desktop, the system freezes and you see a "blue screen of death" (an error message on a blue background). You have extremely important document files on the drive that you cannot afford to lose. What do you do first?

   a. Try a data recovery service even though it is very expensive.
   b. Remove the hard drive from the computer case and install it in another computer.
   c. Try GetDataBack by Runtime Software (*www.runtime.org*) to recover the data.
   d. Use Windows utilities to attempt to fix the Windows boot problem.
   e. Run antivirus software to remove the virus.

2. Just after you reboot after running AV software that found much malware, an error message is displayed that contains a reference to a strange DLL file that is missing. Which two options should you use to begin troubleshooting?

   a. Run the AV software again.
   b. Run Msconfig and look for startup entries that are launching the DLL.
   c. Run Regedit and look for keys that refer to the DLL.
   d. Search the Internet for information about the DLL.

>> HANDS-ON PROJECTS

PROJECT 3-1: Researching Running Processes

Boot to the Windows desktop and then use Task Manager to get a list of all the running processes on your machine. Get a print screen of this list. Make a written list of each process running and write a one-sentence explanation of the process. Note that you most likely will need to use the Internet to research some of these processes.

Next, boot the system into Safe Mode and use Task Manager to list running processes. Which processes that were loaded normally are not loaded when the system is running in Safe Mode?

PROJECT 3-2: Learning to Use Autoruns

Download Autoruns by TechNet and Sysinternals (*technet.microsoft.com*) and run it on your PC. How many registry keys does Autoruns list that contain startup items on your PC? Use Msconfig to get a similar list. Compare the list of startup items to that generated by Msconfig. Describe any differences between the two lists.

PROJECT 3-3: History of Rootkits

Rootkits became widely known when Sony included a rootkit with some of its audio CDs. The rootkit was intended to detect and prevent ripping or illegally copying of the CDs. The rootkit was also written so that it could not be detected or uninstalled by normal means. Use the Internet to research and answer these questions:

1. What are some of the audio CDs by Sony that contained the rootkit?

2. What are two software products that might be hidden on a Sony CD that contained the rootkit?

3. Describe Sony's response when consumers angrily protested the rootkit installation without their knowledge.

4. If you have used your computer to play a Sony audio CD that contained the rootkit, how can you best rid your computer of the rootkit?

PROJECT 3-4:   Using the Internet to Learn About Viruses

One source of information about viruses on the Web is F-Secure Corporation. Go to the Web site *www.f-secure.com/v-descs/*, shown in Figure 3-33, for information about viruses; the viruses are listed alphabetically with complete descriptions, including any known sources of the viruses. Print a description of three viruses from this Web site, with these characteristics:

- ▲ One virus that destroys data on a hard drive
- ▲ One harmless virus that only displays garbage on the screen
- ▲ One virus that hides in a boot sector

Figure 3-33   For comprehensive virus information, see the F-Secure Web site

The site also lists information about the most recent viruses. Search the Web site at *www.f-secure.com*, list five recent viruses, and describe their payloads.

<u>**PROJECT 3-5:** Configuring Your AV Software</u>

If you own antivirus software, do the following to learn about and set its configuration:

1. Download the latest antivirus (AV) definition list from the Internet. For example, for Trend Micro AntiVirus plus AntiSpyware, open the main window and click Update Now (see Figure 3-34).

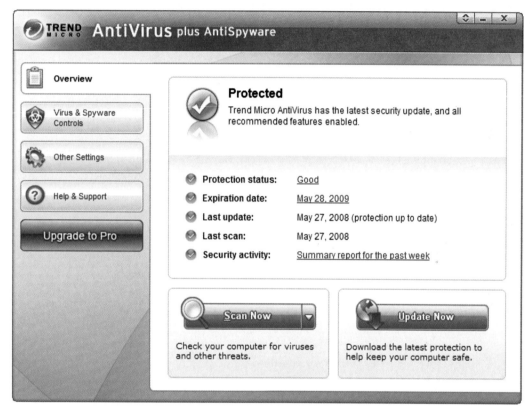

Figure 3-34 Trend Micro AntiVirus software offers a button to update the virus definitions

2. Verify that the software is set to automatically download updates. List the steps you took.

3. Verify that the software is automatically checking incoming and outgoing e-mail. List the steps you took.

4. Does the software offer the option to schedule a full scan of the system? If so, schedule a full scan weekly at 1:00AM on Friday. List the steps you took.

5. Does the software offer the option to filter spam? If so, turn the option on. Describe how the spam filter works. What spam filtering options does it provide? Which options do you think are appropriate for your needs?

6. Does the software offer the option to set a password so that others cannot change settings? If so, list the steps to set the password.

7. Does the software keep logs of its activity? If so, list these logs. For how long are the logs kept?

8. Can you use the software to scan another computer on the network for malware? If so, list the steps to do that.

>> REAL PROBLEMS, REAL SOLUTIONS

REAL PROBLEM 3-1:   Cleaning Your System of Malware

Using the tools and techniques presented in this chapter, thoroughly clean your system of any malware. Take notes as you work and list any malware detected.

CHAPTER 4

Vista Pest Control

In the last chapter, you learned how to get rid of malware that has infected a system. In this chapter, you learn how to keep the stuff from getting inside in the first place. As hackers and identity thieves get more and more sophisticated and dangerous, securing your notebook or desktop computer is absolutely essential in today's world. The most common parasites come in by way of the Internet, so our focus is on protecting yourself from malware getting to you from that avenue. However, you also need to be able to secure a system from natural causes (such as your system being struck by lightning) and ill-intended hacking, stealing, deception, and harassment, so these problems also will be discussed.

The very best defense against all these predators is to be prepared in the event you lose important data and user preferences. Therefore, the last part of the chapter is devoted to keeping good backups of what is likely to be your most valuable computer asset: your data.

SEVENTEEN WAYS TO SECURE YOUR DESKTOP OR LAPTOP COMPUTER

In today's computing environment, we all need to know how to keep our shields up. This chapter focuses on the tools and methods you need to know to protect yourself. However, knowledge won't help much unless you use it. Be sure to apply what you're about to learn. Here are my 17 methods of securing a computer:

- ◢ *Method 1*: Always use a personal firewall.
- ◢ *Method 2*: Set AV software to run in the background and keep it current.
- ◢ *Method 3*: Keep Windows updates current.
- ◢ *Method 4*: Keep Windows Defender turned on.
- ◢ *Method 5*: Keep that pesky UAC box turned on.
- ◢ *Method 6*: Use alternate third-party client software and monitoring tools.
- ◢ *Method 7*: Practice sensible Internet habits.
- ◢ *Method 8*: Take advantage of Internet Explorer security settings.
- ◢ *Method 9*: Protect against Trojan programs by not hiding file extensions.
- ◢ *Method 10*: Use folder and file encryption.
- ◢ *Method 11*: Consider BitLocker Encryption for drastic security measures.
- ◢ *Method 12*: Hide a shared folder.
- ◢ *Method 13*: Limit use of the administrator accounts.
- ◢ *Method 14*: Make a password reset disk.
- ◢ *Method 15*: Physically protect your equipment.
- ◢ *Method 16*: Secure your wired or wireless network.
- ◢ *Method 17*: Keep good backups.

USE A PERSONAL FIREWALL

Never, ever connect your computer to an unprotected network without using a firewall. A firewall is software or hardware that prevents worms or hackers from getting into your system. A network is normally secured by a hardware firewall (a device that stands between the network and another network, including the Internet), and a single computer is normally secured by a software firewall (software installed on your computer that protects it from outsiders). A software firewall is a personal firewall, such as McAfee Personal Firewall or Windows Firewall.

Let's first look at how worms work and how a firewall stands up against them. Then, we'll look at some firewalls and how to use them.

HOW A WORM GETS INTO YOUR COMPUTER

Most worms come to your computer or network through the Internet. A computer communicates with other computers on the Internet by using 1) IP addresses that identify each computer and 2) port numbers that identify each program that is using the network and that is running on each computer. For example, your laptop computer might have one IP address assigned to it and be using one port for your Web browser and another port for your e-mail software. These ports provide a way for programs, such as a Web server or e-mail server on another computer, to communicate with the counterpart program on your laptop. You can think of a port as similar to a post office box number that serves as an address for a program to receive mail (see Figure 4-1).

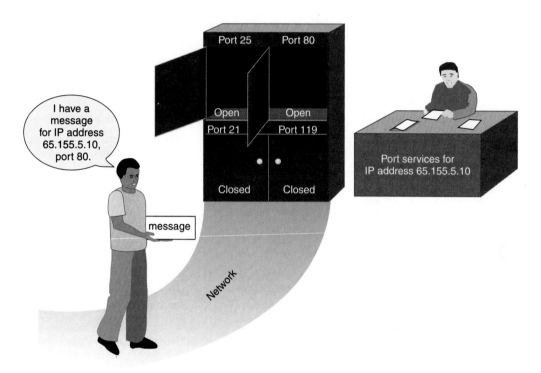

Figure 4-1 A computer receives communication over a network by way of an IP address that identifies the computer and ports that identify a communication service running on the computer

When a computer is configured for network or Internet communication, it opens a series of port numbers to send and receive messages. One computer will say to the other, "I have a message for your port 25." If the receiving computer is not protected against worms, it will receive any message from any computer to any port it has opened for service. Worms on the Internet routinely perform "port scanning," meaning that they are constantly looking for open, unprotected ports through which they can invade a system. Once they are in the computer, they are free to download other software, move to other computers on the internal network, or produce mass e-mailings to bog down the network or Internet.

Table 4-1 lists some port numbers for several common services used on the Internet. For a complete listing of well-known and registered port number assignments, see the Internet Assigned Numbers Authority (IANA) Web site at *www.iana.org/assignments/port-numbers*.

HOW A FIREWALL WORKS

Recall that a firewall can be either a software firewall or a hardware firewall. A hardware firewall is a device that stands between a network and another network such as the Internet, or it can stand between a single computer and a network. The firewall filters or stops all port service requests that have not been initiated by computers inside the protected area.

Port	Protocol	Service	Description
20	FTP	FTP	File transfer data
21	FTP	FTP	File transfer control information
22	SSH	Secure Shell	Remote control to a networked computer
23	Telnet	Telnet	Telnet, a mostly outdated application first used by Unix computers to control a computer remotely
25	SMTP	E-mail	Simple Mail Transfer Protocol; used by client to send e-mail
80	HTTP	Web browser	World Wide Web protocol
109	POP2	E-mail	Post Office Protocol, version 2; used by client to receive e-mail
110	POP3	E-mail	Post Office Protocol, version 3; used by client to receive e-mail
119	NNTP	News server	News servers
143	IMAP	E-mail	Internet Message Access Protocol, a newer protocol used by clients to receive e-mail
194	IRC	Chat	Internet Relay Chat Protocol
443	HTTPS	Secured Web browser	Secured HTTP uses TLS (Transport Layer Security) or SSL (Secure Sockets Layer) encryption
3389	WBT	MS WBT server	Listening port for Vista Remote Desktop and Remote Assistance

Table 4-1   Common TCP/IP port assignments for well-known services

The device used most often for this purpose is a combo device like the one in Figure 4-2, and it does a lot more than just serve as a firewall. Using a device like this one is the best

Figure 4-2   This combo device by Linksys is a firewall to protect a network, a router that allows computers on the network to share a broadband Internet connection, and a wireless access point for computers with wireless adapters

way to protect a small network, and in the next chapter you'll learn how to set one up and use it.

A software firewall is an application or OS utility installed on a single computer that protects that computer. A software firewall will not allow communication from another computer unless one of two things is true: (a) The computer being protected initiated the communication and another computer is simply responding to the request or (b) the firewall has been set to open a certain port (called port filtering). For example, if you want to allow chat sessions to be initiated by others, you would tell your firewall software to open port 194. Figure 4-3 illustrates a software firewall.

Figure 4-3   A software firewall protecting a computer

Software firewalls don't usually protect a computer as well as hardware firewalls, but you need to use a software firewall for a number of reasons: to protect your computer from worms that might be inside a network protected by a hardware firewall, to protect your computer against malicious programs running on it and doing further damage, and to protect your computer when a hardware firewall is not present. Software firewalls are particularly useful when you're traveling with a laptop or when you connect your computer at home directly to a cable modem or DSL modem or use a dial-up connection.

THIRD-PARTY SOFTWARE FIREWALL

Windows Vista offers good firewall protection, but for added protection features, you might want to use third-party firewall software. Some examples of firewall software for personal computers are ZoneAlarm (see Figure 4-4) by Zone Labs (*www.zonelabs.com*), Norton Personal Firewall by Symantec (*www.symantec.com*), McAfee Personal Firewall by McAfee (*www.mcafee.com*), Personal Firewall Pro by Sygate (*www.sygate.com*), and Windows Live OneCare (*onecare.live.com*). When evaluating firewall software, look for its ability to control traffic coming from both outside and inside the network. Sometimes you want to allow communication initiated by others, such as to play an online multiplayer game. In such cases, look for the software's ability to open a certain port that a game might use.

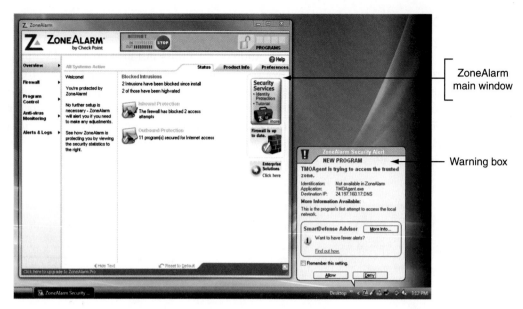

Figure 4-4   ZoneAlarm allows you to determine the amount of security the firewall provides

There's a problem with some software firewalls. They might do too good of a job protecting your computer and block communication that you really want to allow—such as when you've got shared folders on your computer and want to allow others on a local network to access these folders. For example, ZoneAlarm might block two computers on your network from file sharing until you add the remote PC to the ZoneAlarm trusted zone list. Also, by default ZoneAlarm displays messages like the one in the lower-right corner of Figure 4-4 each time Windows or other software attempts Internet access. It's interesting and sometimes even critical to your computer's security to see what software is requesting access, but these messages can really get in your way after a while. To be more selective about the types of alerts given, click **Firewall** in the left pane.

HOW TO MANAGE WINDOWS FIREWALL

Vista comes with a built-in software firewall: Windows Firewall. Vista automatically configures Windows Firewall based on the type of network it believes you are connected to; it can assign you a public profile, a private profile, or a domain profile. A **public profile** offers the highest level of protection when you are connected to a public network. A **private profile** offers moderate protection when you are connected to a private network, and the least protection is used for a **domain profile** when your PC is on a domain and security is managed by the domain's operating system, such as Windows Server 2008. In this section, I'm assuming your computer is not connected to a domain. For this situation, when the PC first connects to a new network, Vista asks you if the network is a public or private network (see Figure 4-5). It saves this response and applies it each time you reconnect to this network.

To see how firewall protection is set for a public or private network, look at the Network and Sharing Center window and the Windows Firewall window by following these steps:

1. Click **Start,** right-click **Network,** and select **Properties** from the shortcut menu. The Network and Sharing Center window opens.

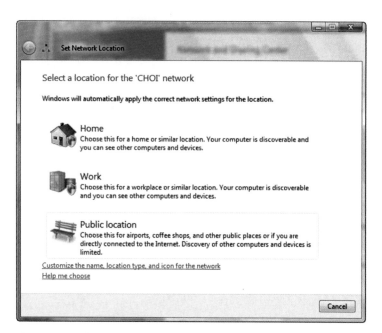

Figure 4-5 Vista is asking how to set firewall protection on this new network

2. For the window showing in Figure 4-6, the PC is connected to a wired and wireless network. The wired network is set to Private and the wireless network is set to Public. Because the PC is connected to a public network, the Sharing and Discovery settings at the bottom of the window are turned off. To change the security setting for the Public network, click **Customize**.

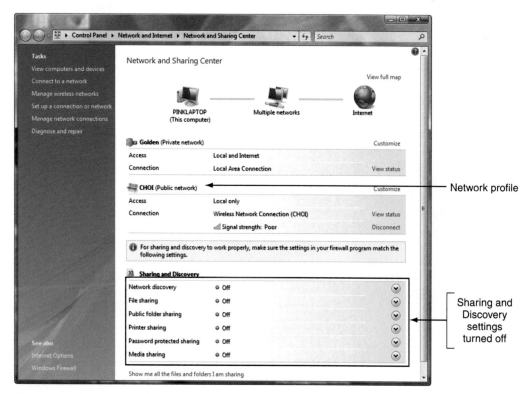

Figure 4-6 Security is high when connected to a public network

3. The Set Network Location box appears (see Figure 4-7). To allow for less security and more communication on the network, click **Private** and then click **Next**.

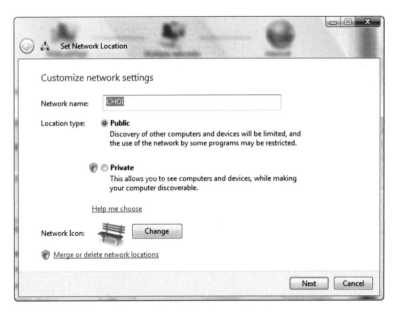

Figure 4-7 Change the security setting for a network

4. Sharing and Discovery settings are now less secure, allowing the PC to be seen on the network (Network discovery), files on the PC to be shared with others on the network (File sharing), and printers installed on this PC to be shared (Printer sharing). These are the standard settings for a private network. To change a setting under the Sharing and Discovery group, click the down arrow to the right of the item and turn the item on or off (see Figure 4-8).

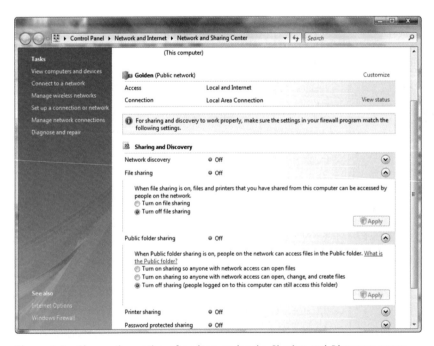

Figure 4-8 Change the setting of an item under the Sharing and Discovery group

5. To see how Windows Firewall is configured, in the left pane, click **Windows Firewall**. The Windows Firewall window opens (see Figure 4-9). No matter how secure the network, Windows Firewall should always be turned on unless you are using a third-party software firewall instead of Windows Firewall.

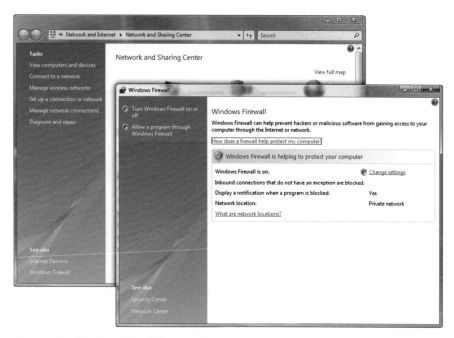

Figure 4-9 Windows Firewall is turned on

6. To see the details of how Windows Firewall is working, click **Change settings** and respond to the UAC box. The Windows Firewall Settings box opens (see Figure 4-10).

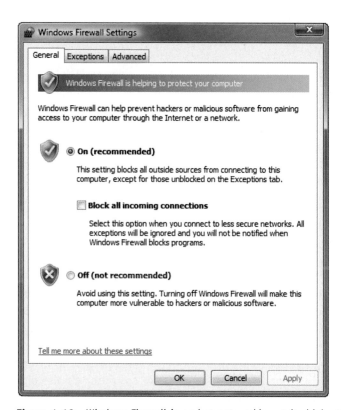

Figure 4-10 Windows Firewall is on but not working at its highest security level

7. Notice the check box for *Block all incoming connections*, which controls communication initiated from another computer. For a private network, Vista does not check this box. When connected to a public network, the box is checked. To see what incoming connections are allowed, click the **Exceptions** tab (see Figure 4-11).

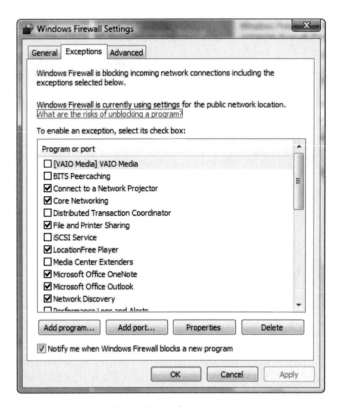

Figure 4-11   Exceptions allowed for incoming connections

8. Notice in Figure 4-11 that File and Printer Sharing is checked. This means that another computer can initiate communication with this computer to access a shared file or printer. You can change individual settings on this Exceptions tab by checking or unchecking items. Recall earlier in the chapter that a computer uses a port number to control incoming activity on the network. This Exceptions box controls these ports. Each item in the list is associated with one or more ports, which are opened or closed based on the settings on this tab.

9. After you have Windows Firewall configured the way you want it, click **Apply** and click **OK** to close the Windows Firewall Settings window.

USE AV SOFTWARE

I know you're probably tired of reading this, but I'll say it just one more time: install and run antivirus (AV) software and keep it current. Configure the AV software so that it automatically downloads updates to the software and runs in the background. To be effective, AV software must be kept current and must be turned on. Set the AV software to automatically scan e-mail attachments. You can find a list of AV software in the previous chapter, so I won't repeat it here.

Because AV software does not always stop adware or spyware, it's also a good idea to run anti-adware software in the background.

KEEP WINDOWS UPDATES CURRENT

Although Unix, Linux, and the Apple Mac OS sometimes get viruses, Windows is plagued the most, by far, for two reasons. First, Windows is the most popular OS for desktop and notebook computers. Being the most popular also makes it the most targeted by authors of malware. Second, Windows is designed with highly integrated components and many user-level entry points into those components. Once a program has penetrated a Windows user-mode process, it is possible to infect more than one component. Security holes are being found all the time, and Microsoft is constantly releasing patches to keep up, but you have to download and install those patches before they'll help you.

Keep Windows updates current by using the Web site *windowsupdate.microsoft.com*. The easiest way to start the process is to click **Start**, point to **All Programs**, and click **Windows Update**. You can also set Windows Vista to download and install most updates in the background automatically without your involvement. To install updates and configure automatic updating, follow these steps:

1. Click **Start**, right-click **Computer**, select **Properties** on the shortcut menu, and then click the **Windows Update** in the left pane. Notice that in Figure 4-12, even though this PC is set for automatic updating, some updates are waiting to be installed until the user gives permission. To install these updates, click **Install updates**.

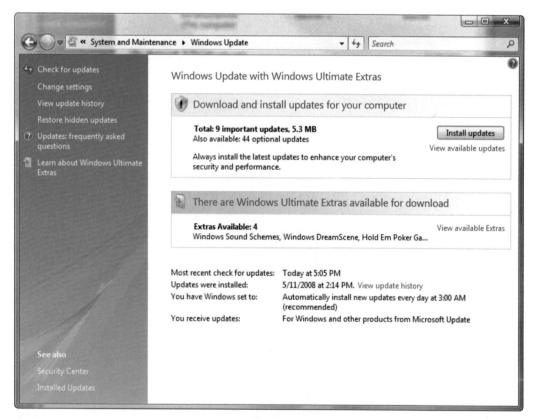

Figure 4-12 Windows Update shows updates ready to be installed

2. To see how Vista updating is configured, in the left pane, click **Change settings**. The window in Figure 4-13 appears. Unless you have a good reason to do otherwise (such as a slow Internet connection that is not always up or you want total control over updating), the best choice is to **Install updates automatically**.

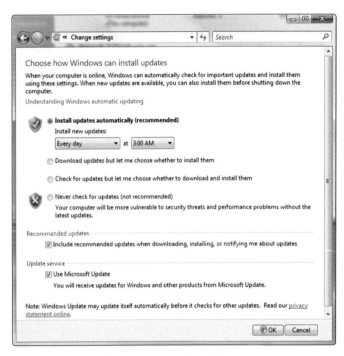

Figure 4-13 Set Vista for automatic updating

 Note

When updating Vista on a laptop computer, be aware that service packs for laptops are often customized by the laptop manufacturer and made available on the manufacturer's Web site. For example, click **Start** and **Go to VAIO Web Support** to download Vista Service Pack 1 to a Sony laptop computer (see Figure 4-14).

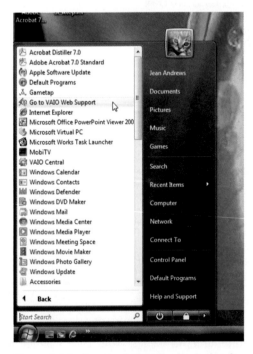

Figure 4-14 Download Vista Service Pack 1 from the laptop manufacturer

3. If other Microsoft products are installed, such as Microsoft Office, also check **Use Microsoft Update** to get updates for these products as well.

4. Click **OK** to close the window.

KEEP WINDOWS DEFENDER TURNED ON

Windows Defender is anti-adware and anti-spyware software integrated into Windows Vista. Its chief job is to act as a police officer who constantly watches for malicious software trying to install itself on your PC without your knowledge. By default, it is configured to work in two ways:

▲ Defender automatically downloads updates and then scans your system every day at 2:00AM by default. It does a quick scan, checking the registry and memory. However, you can manually perform a full scan, which checks all files on the computer, at any time.

▲ Defender continually monitors a computer and notifies the user when a process is attempting to make changes to the system or install itself. Defender reports suspicious activity using a bubble that appears in the lower-right corner of your screen (see Figure 4-15).

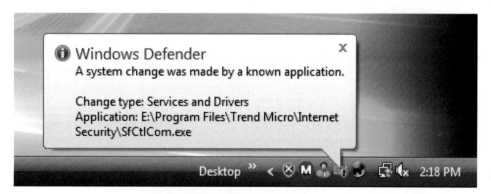

Figure 4-15 Windows Defender alerts the user to a system change

Defender monitors these activities:

▲ Any changes to startup processes
▲ Any changes to security settings that are designed to protect a system against malware
▲ Suspicious activity by services and drivers
▲ Suspicious activity when an application is launched
▲ When an application registers itself to automatically start at any time
▲ When attempts are made to install Windows add-ons or background utilities
▲ Attempts to install an add-on to Internet Explorer; sometimes when you click on a link on a Web site, the site attempts to install an add-on without your knowledge
▲ Changes to Internet Explorer security settings; malware sometimes attempts to change these settings without your knowledge
▲ When Internet Explorer attempts to download files

To use Windows Defender to manually perform a quick or full scan of your system and explore other tools provided by Defender, do the following:

1. In Control Panel, click **Security**. The Security window shown in Figure 4-16 appears.

Figure 4-16   Use the Security window to manage many security features of Vista

2. Click **Windows Defender**. If Defender is turned on, the Windows Defender window appears as shown in Figure 4-17. If Defender is turned off, the dialog box in Figure 4-18 appears. When this dialog box appears, click **Turn on and open Windows Defender** to turn on Defender.

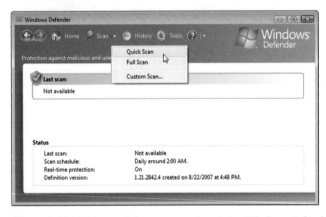

Figure 4-17   Three ways to scan a system using Windows Defender

Figure 4-18   Defender is asking to be turned on

3. To see scanning options, click the down arrow beside **Scan** to see the drop-down menu shown in the figure. When you select **Custom Scan**, you can choose which drives or folders to scan. Alternately, to perform a quick scan of the system, simply click **Scan** in Figure 4-17.

4. Click **Tools**, and the Tools and Settings window in Figure 4-19 appears. Using this window, you can change Defender settings, view quarantined and allowed items, access online information and options regarding Defender, and use Software Explorer. You learned to use Software Explorer in Chapter 2.

Figure 4-19 Windows Defender Tools and Settings window

5. To change Defender settings, click **Options**, and the window in Figure 4-20 opens. Using this window, you can set how often, when, and how Defender will scan the system and decide if all users, or only those with administrative rights, can perform manual scans. You can also turn Defender on and off using this window. For added security, keep Defender turned on.

KEEP THE UAC BOX TURNED ON

Even though you can disable that pesky UAC box, don't do it. Not only does it make you think before you make some drastic change to your system, but also it might prevent malware from installing. For example, if you're logged on as an administrator with the UAC box turned off and you click a malicious link on a Web site, the hacker can install malware without your knowledge and might get admin privileges on your computer. If you're logged on as a standard user with the UAC box turned off, the malware might still install but with lesser privileges. However, the best practice is to have the UAC box enabled so that an administrator or a standard user is warned and given the chance to bail out before malware installs.

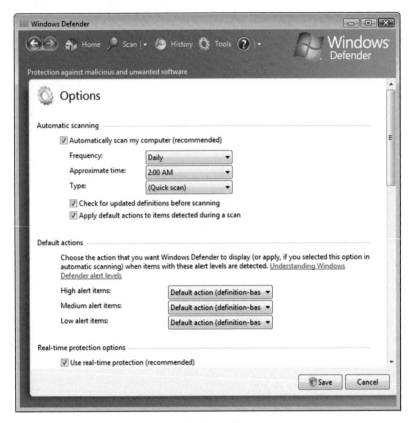

Figure 4-20   Configure Windows Defender options

Also, keeping the UAC box turned on has proven to be an excellent defense for preventing rootkits from installing themselves without user knowledge. The UAC box stands as a gatekeeper to malware installing behind your back because someone has to click the UAC box before the installation can proceed.

It's also interesting to know the color codes that the UAC box uses to help you decide if software being installed is safe:

- ◢ If the top of the UAC box is red, Vista does not trust this program one bit and is not happy with your installing it. In fact, it refuses to allow the installation to continue.
- ◢ If the top of the UAC box is yellow (see Figure 4-21), Vista doesn't know or trust the publisher. It will allow you to continue, but with a serious warning.
- ◢ If the top of the UAC box is green, Vista is happy to accept one of its own Windows components to be installed.
- ◢ If the top of the UAC box is gray, the program has signed in with Microsoft and Vista is happy to install it.

USE ALTERNATE CLIENT SOFTWARE AND MONITORING TOOLS

Using alternate client software, including browsers and e-mail clients, can give you an added layer of protection from malicious software that targets Microsoft's products. You can add even another layer of protection by installing third-party software to monitor any additions to your startup process. Both these security measures are discussed in this section.

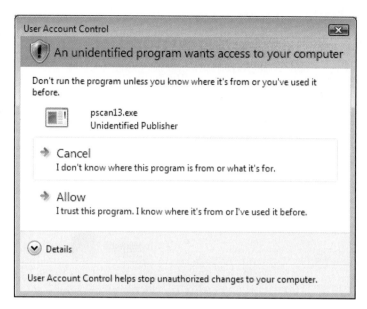

Figure 4-21 This UAC box using a yellow bar indicates the program has not been approved by Microsoft

BROWSER SOFTWARE

Internet Explorer (IE) gets attacked by malware more than any other browser product for these reasons:

◢ Internet Explorer is by far the most popular browser, and, therefore, writers of malware know they are more likely to get more hits than when they write malware for less popular browsers.

◢ Internet Explorer is written to integrate more closely with Windows components than other browsers. When malware penetrates IE, it can then get to other Windows components that are inherently tied to IE.

◢ Internet Explorer is written to use ActiveX controls. An ActiveX control is a small program that can be downloaded by a Web site to your computer (sometimes without your knowledge). Microsoft invented ActiveX controls so that Web sites could use some nifty multimedia features. However, ActiveX controls allow Web pages to execute program code on your machine—and there's no way for you to know ahead of time whether that code is harmless or a malicious attack on your computer.

For these reasons, you might consider using a different browser than Internet Explorer. One excellent browser is Firefox by Mozilla (*www.mozilla.com*). It's free and easy to use. See Figure 4-22.

If you do decide to stay with Internet Explorer, be sure to take advantage of its security features, which are described later in the chapter.

E-MAIL CLIENTS

Outlook and Outlook Express by Microsoft are probably the most popular e-mail clients. That means they're also the most often attacked. They also support ActiveX controls and

Figure 4-22 Firefox by Mozilla is not as vulnerable to malware as is Internet Explorer

are closely integrated with Windows components, making your system more vulnerable to malware. To help stay out of the line of fire, you can use alternate e-mail clients. Personally, I use Eudora by Qualcomm (*www.eudora.com*). Mozilla offers Thunderbird, which is also a great product.

MONITORING TOOLS

Remember from Chapter 2 that you can install some third-party monitoring tools to monitor the startup processes and let you know when installation software attempts to add something to your startup routines. Two good products are WinPatrol by BillP Studios (*www.winpatrol.com*) and StartupMonitor by Mike Lin (*www.mlin.net*). You saw a screen shot of WinPatrol in Chapter 2. I've used this utility successfully for years.

> **Note**
>
> When you have to give an e-mail address to companies that you suspect might sell your address to spammers, use a second e-mail address that you don't use for normal e-mailing. That way, your primary e-mail address is protected from spam and stays private.

PRACTICE RESPONSIBLE INTERNET HABITS

For several years it appeared that hackers and malware authors were more interested in bragging rights from having successfully caused damage than in the fruits of their labor. But times are changing and now it appears these criminals are seriously trying to steal your identity, your banking information, your credit card information, and whatever else they can use to make money as thieves. There appears to be less satisfaction with writing malware that merely displays bugs crawling across the screen or bogs down e-mail servers. For these reasons, you need to be especially careful with what information you give on the Internet and how you protect data on your PC from attack. In this section, we'll look at some best practices that, for the most part, simply equate to using good judgment when using the Internet to keep you out of harm's way.

Here is a list of what I'll call the Ten Commandments for using the Internet:

1. *You shall not open e-mail attachments without scanning them for viruses first.* In fact, if you don't know the person who sent you the attachment, save yourself a lot of trouble and just delete it without opening it.

2. *You shall not click links inside e-mail messages.* Copy and paste the link to your browser address bar instead.

3. *You shall not forward an e-mail message warning without first checking to see if that warning is a hoax.* Save us all the time of having to delete the thing from our inbox.

4. *You shall always check out a Web site before you download anything from it.* Freeware isn't so free if you end up with an infected computer. Download only from trusted sites.

5. *You shall never give your private information to just any ol' Web site.* Use a search engine and search for information about a site before you trust it with your identity.

6. *You shall never trust an e-mail message asking you to verify your private data on a Web site with which you do business.* If you receive an e-mail that looks like it came from your bank, your PayPal account, or your utility company, don't click those links in that message. If you think it might be legitimate, open your browser, type in the link to the business's Web site, and check out the request.

7. *You shall always reboot a computer in a public place before you use it (that includes computers in school labs).* You never know who just used the thing and what he or she might have left there. Unless you are prohibited from doing so, use a hard boot, not just a soft boot, to erase all memory-resident programs (including a memory-resident virus) from memory. Don't trust public computers with your private information.

8. *You shall never use the Internet without having your firewall turned on and your AV software working in the background.* For good measure, run anti-adware software, too.

9. *You shall never trust your valuable data to just one storage media.* Sooner or later, it will let you down. Always keep backups. How to make backups is covered later in the chapter.

10. *You shall never blindly trust your recovery routine.* It does no good to have backups, only to find out after a disaster that the backups don't work. Before disaster strikes, test your backups to make sure they're good and you know how to use them.

HOW TO DEBUNK AN E-MAIL HOAX

An e-mail hoax is itself a pest because it overloads network traffic when naïve users pass it on. Figure 4-23 shows an example of a virus hoax e-mail message I received.

Viruses grow more powerful every day, but this message is just absurd. It is unlikely that a virus can render computer components useless. No virus has been known to do actual physical damage to hardware, although viruses can make a PC useless by destroying programs or data, and a few viruses have been able to attack system BIOS code on the motherboard.

What's most important is not to be gullible and take the bait by forwarding the message to someone else. The potential damage a hoax like this can do is to overload an e-mail system with useless traffic, which is the real intent of the hoax. When I received this e-mail, over a hundred names were on the distribution list, sent by a friend who was innocently trying to help us all out.

Refer to Chapter 3 for a list of Web sites that specialize in debunking virus hoaxes.

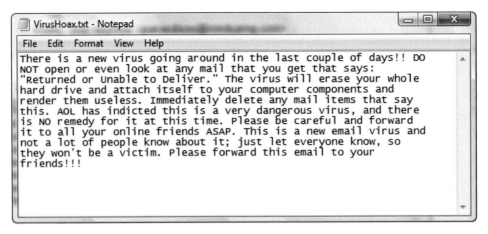

Figure 4-23   An example of hoax e-mail text

TAKE ADVANTAGE OF INTERNET EXPLORER SECURITY SETTINGS

Be sure to take advantage of Internet Explorer's security features. The features described in the following come with Internet Explorer version 7, which is included with Windows Vista.

TURN ON POP-UP BLOCKER

Adware and malware bait sometimes get in your face in a pop-up window while you're surfing the Web. IE Pop-up Blocker gives you control over these windows. To verify that Pop-up Blocker is turned on, open Internet Explorer, click **Tools**, and point to **Pop-up Blocker**, as shown in Figure 4-24. The first item in the menu toggles between turning Pop-up Blocker on and off. To change settings, click **Pop-up Blocker Settings**. From the Pop-up Blocker Settings window that appears, you can create a list of Web sites that are allowed to present pop-ups and control how Pop-up Blocker informs you when it blocks a pop-up.

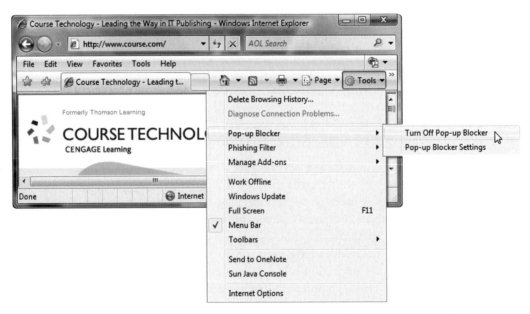

Figure 4-24   Internet Explorer Pop-up Blocker can be turned on or off and you can adjust its settings

If Pop-up Blocker is turned on, you might have a problem when you try to download something from a Web site. Sometimes the download routine tries to open a Security Warning window to start the download, and your pop-up blocker suppresses this window and causes an error. To solve the problem, you can (a) hold down the **Ctrl key** while clicking on a link, which allows a pop-up window to appear, (b) temporarily turn off Pop-up Blocker before you begin the download, or (c) allow the Information Bar to appear. When the bar appears, click it and select **Download File** as shown in Figure 4-25.

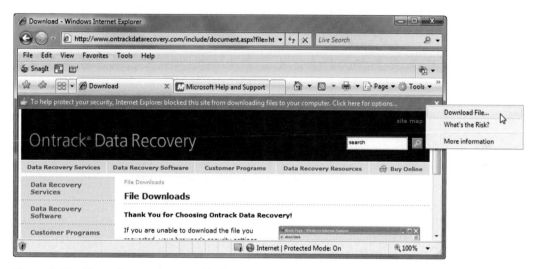

Figure 4-25   If your browser is set to block pop-ups, a message appears under the address bar of your browser

MANAGE IE SECURITY LEVELS

Internet Explorer offers several security options and levels. To set them, on the **Tools** menu, click **Internet Options**, and then click the **Security** tab (see Figure 4-26). Using the sliding bar on the left side of this window, you can choose the security level. The Medium-high level is about right for most computers. If you click the **Custom level** button, you can see exactly what option is being monitored and controlled by this security level and change what you want. These settings apply to ActiveX plug-ins, downloads, Java plug-ins, scripts, and other miscellaneous settings. Adware or spyware can make changes to these security settings without your knowledge. These settings are not password protected, so they will not help if you are trying to secure the browser from what other users of this computer can do. In Figure 4-26, also note the option to Enable Protected Mode, which is discussed next.

INTERNET EXPLORER PROTECTED MODE

By default, Internet Explorer runs in Protected Mode to help prevent malware from secretly installing itself in the system. When IE is in Protected Mode, it can write files to the Temporary Internet Files folder only and change only insignificant registry keys. But sometimes a user might want IE to install an add-on. To handle this situation, IE asks the user permission to move to a higher access level to perform the task. An information bar

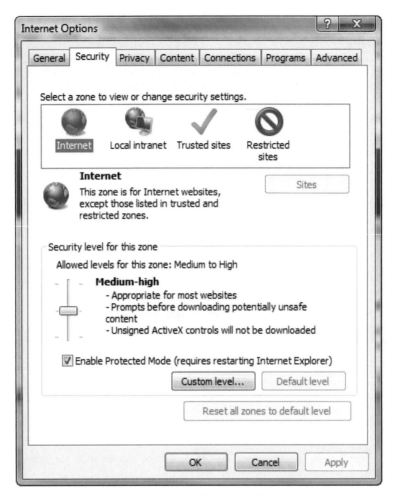

Figure 4-26 Set the security level of Internet Explorer using the Internet Options window

appears below the IE menu bar, as shown in Figure 4-27. When you click on the bar, the drop-down menu appears as shown in the figure. Click **Run ActiveX Control** to allow the add-on to be installed.

MANAGE ADD-ONS

Sometimes problems arise with corrupt or malicious add-ons. Using Internet Explorer 7, you can temporarily disable all add-ons so that they can be eliminated as the source of an Internet Explorer problem.

Do the following to manage Internet Explorer add-ons:

1. Click **Start, All Programs, Accessories, System Tools,** and **Internet Explorer (No Add-ons).** Internet Explorer opens showing the information bar message in Figure 4-28.

2. You can now find out if the problem with Internet Explorer has disappeared. If it has disappeared, then you can assume the source of the problem is an add-on. You can next try disabling one add-on after another until you discover the one giving the problem.

3. To return to running Internet Explorer with add-ons, close the window and then open Internet Explorer as usual.

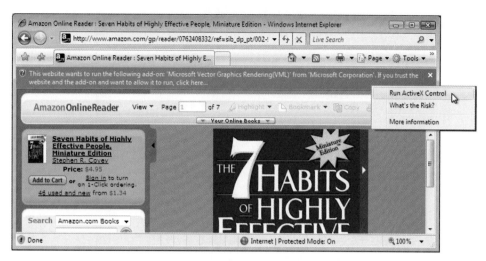

Figure 4-27 Internet Explorer is asking permission to install an add-on

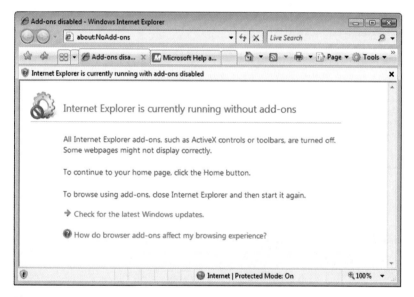

Figure 4-28 Internet Explorer is running without add-ons

To disable a specific add-on, do the following:

1. Open Internet Explorer. Click **Tools,** point to **Manage Add-ons,** and click **Enable or Disable Add-ons** (see Figure 4-29). The Manage Add-ons window opens as shown in Figure 4-30.

2. The window displays currently loaded add-ons, but you can also display add-ons that have been used by IE. To disable any add-on, select it and click **Disable.** You can also delete ActiveX controls by selecting them and clicking **Delete.**

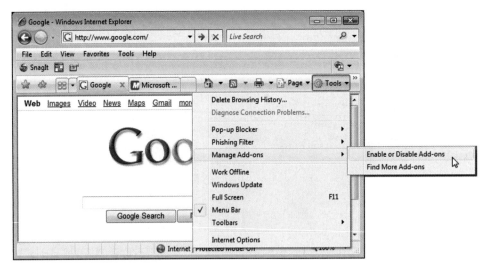

Figure 4-29 Manage add-ons using the Tools menu of Internet Explorer

Figure 4-30 Use the Manage Add-ons window to disable or delete add-ons

USE THE PHISHING FILTER

Swindlers and cons have gone electronic, and lots of phishing Web sites are trying to lure in naïve users. Internet Explorer 7 offers a phishing filter to help you decide whom you can trust. It works in three ways:

- ◢ It compares the current Web site to a list of trusted sites stored on this computer.
- ◢ It checks the current site for characteristics that indicate it is a phishing site.
- ◢ It compares the site against an online database kept by Microsoft of known phishing sites.

You can use and manage the phishing filter using the Tools menu. Click **Tools** and **Phishing Filter** and the menu in Figure 4-31 appears. Using this menu, you can check the current Web site, turn the filter off and on, report a site to be a phishing site, and manage filter settings.

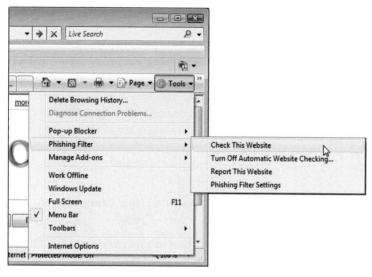

Figure 4-31   Use the Internet Explorer Phishing Filter to protect yourself against phishing

CLEAN THE BROWSER HISTORY

Next time you surf the Web on a computer and don't know or don't trust the next users, you might want to consider protecting your privacy by cleaning out your browser history. Follow these steps:

1. In Internet Explorer, click **Tools** and **Internet Options**. The Internet Options dialog box appears as shown on the left in Figure 4-32.

2. Under Browsing history, click **Delete**. The Delete Browsing History dialog box appears as shown on the right in Figure 4-32. You can select particular items to delete or click **Delete all** to clean out the entire browsing history.

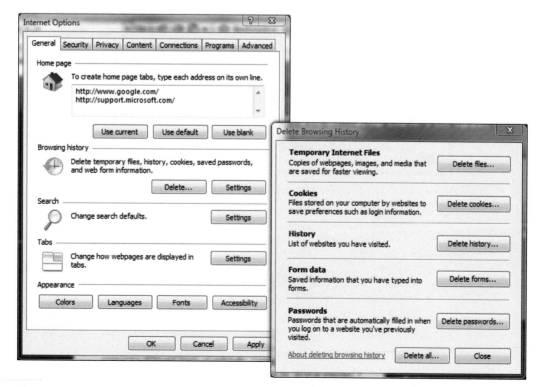

Figure 4-32   Internet Options dialog box

PROTECT AGAINST TROJAN PROGRAMS

One popular Trojan technique to spread a virus or worm is to mask a malicious program as a picture file, music file, or other type of multimedia file. The file comes to you as an attachment to an e-mail message, or you download it to your PC from a Web site. Then when you double-click it, thinking to view a picture or play music, you spread a virus or worm, or install adware onto your PC. The Trojan program is able to hide as a harmless multimedia file because the file extension is hidden. (Program files end with extensions such as .exe, .com, .sys, or .bat.) Thus, you might see the Trojan file as Coolpic.jpg, when the filename is in fact Coolpic.jpg.exe. You can set Vista to display the file extensions of all files by doing the following:

1. To open the Computer window, click **Start** and click **Computer**. (Alternately, you can click Computer in the Windows Explorer window.)

2. On the Computer window (see the left side of Figure 4-33), click **Organize** and click **Folder and Search Options**. The Folder Options box opens.

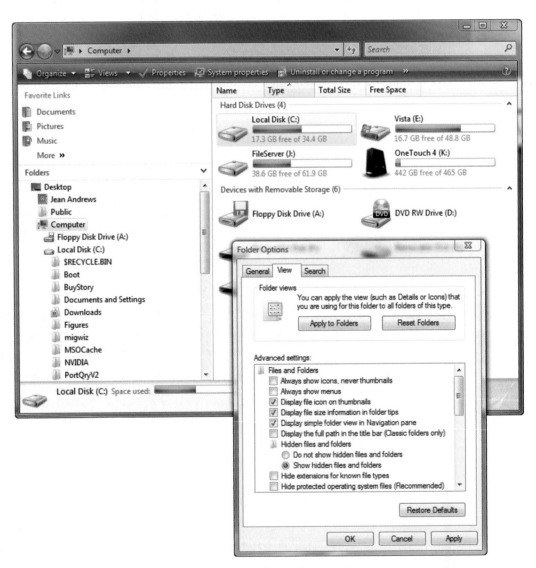

Figure 4-33 Use the Folder Options box to display known file extensions

3. Click the **View** tab (see the right side of Figure 4-33). Clear the check box **Hide extensions for known file types** and click **Apply**. Click **OK** to close the box.

USE FOLDER AND FILE ENCRYPTION

Encryption puts data into code that must be translated before it can be accessed. If you are using Windows Vista Business, Enterprise, or Ultimate editions with the NTFS file system on your hard drive partition, you can encrypt either folders or files. (Windows Vista Home Basic and Home Premium editions do not provide encryption.) If a folder is marked for encryption, every file created in the folder or copied to the folder will be encrypted. At the file level, each file must be encrypted individually. Encrypting at the folder level is considered a best practice because it provides greater security: any file placed in an encrypted folder is automatically encrypted so that you don't have to remember to encrypt it. An encrypted file remains encrypted if you move it from an encrypted folder to an unencrypted folder on the same or another NTFS volume.

To encrypt a file or folder on an NTFS drive, do the following:

1. Right-click the folder or file you want to encrypt and select **Properties** from the shortcut menu. The Properties window for that file or folder opens (see Figure 4-34).

2. Click the **Advanced** button. The Advanced Attributes dialog box appears, also shown in Figure 4-34.

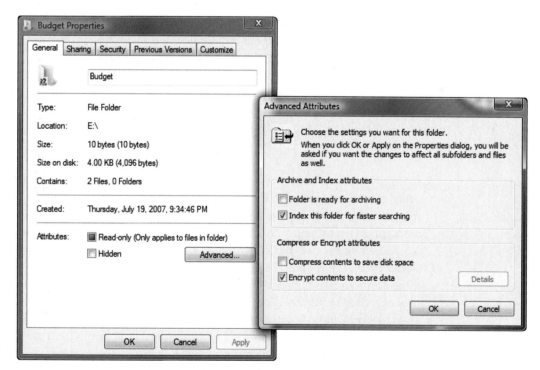

Figure 4-34   Encrypt a file or folder using the Properties window

3. To encrypt the folder or file, check **Encrypt contents to secure data** and click **OK**. On the Properties window, click **Apply**. If the folder contains subfolders, the dialog box shown in Figure 4-35 appears, asking you if you want the encryption to apply to the folder's subfolders. Make your choice and click **OK**.

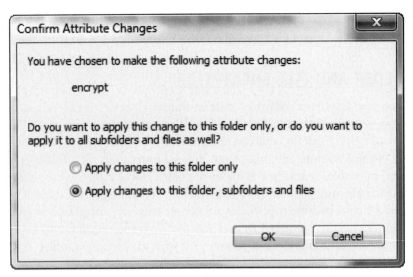

Figure 4-35 Encryption can apply to subfolders or just to one folder

If some other user who is not an administrator attempts to access the encrypted file or folder, an "Access Denied" message appears.

FOR HIGHEST SECURITY, CONSIDER BITLOCKER ENCRYPTION

BitLocker Encryption locks down a hard drive by encrypting the entire Vista volume and any other volume on the drive. It's a bit complicated to set up and beyond the scope of this book; however, if you have some really important and sensitive data to protect, know that BitLocker Encryption is available with Windows Vista Enterprise or Ultimate editions. It is intended to work in partnership with file and folder encryption to provide data security.

There are three ways to use BitLocker Encryption depending on the type of protection you need and the computer hardware available:

- *Computer authentication.* Many notebook computers have a chip on the motherboard called the TPM (Trusted Platform Module) chip. BitLocker is designed to work with this chip; the chip holds the BitLocker encryption key (also called the startup key). If the hard drive is stolen from the notebook and installed in another computer, the data would be safe because BitLocker would not allow access without the startup key stored on the TPM chip. Therefore, this method authenticates the computer. However, if the motherboard fails and is replaced, you'll need a backup copy of the startup key to access data on the hard drive.
- *User authentication.* For computers that don't have TPM, the startup key can be stored on a USB flash drive (or other storage device the computer reads before the OS is loaded), and the flash drive must be installed before the computer boots. This method authenticates the user. For this method to be the most secure, the user must never leave the flash drive stored with the computer. (Instead, the user might keep the USB startup key on his or her key ring.)
- *Computer and user authentication.* For *best* security, a PIN or password can be required at every startup in addition to TPM. Using this method, both the computer and the user are authenticated.

BitLocker Encryption provides great security, but security comes with a price. For instance, you risk the chance your TPM will fail or you will lose all copies of the startup key. In these events, recovering the data can be messy. Therefore, use BitLocker only if the risks of BitLocker giving problems outweigh the risks of stolen data. And, if you decide to use BitLocker, be sure to make extra copies of the startup key and/or password and keep them in a safe location.

For detailed instructions on how to set up BitLocker Encryption, see Microsoft Knowledge Base article 933246 at *support.microsoft.com*.

HIDE A SHARED FOLDER

If you share folders on your computer with others on your local network, there is a way to hide those shared folders on the network so that other users can't see them. Only users who know the path and name of hidden shared folders can find and use them.

To hide a shared folder, use a dollar sign at the end of the folder name like this: C:\Private$. When you share the folder, it will not show up in Windows Explorer or the Network window. A user on the network can access the folder by entering \\*computername*\ *foldername*$ in the Start Search box. For example, in Figure 4-36, the name of the computer is JOY and the folder name is Private$.

Figure 4-36 Accessing a hidden, shared folder on the network

LIMIT THE USE OF THE ADMINISTRATOR ACCOUNTS

Another thing you can do to secure your computer is to limit the use of the more powerful administrator accounts. A **user account** defines a user to Windows and records information about the user, including the username, password used to access the account, groups that the account belongs to, and rights to use certain Windows features, utilities, and commands. Also, permissions to access and use a resource such as a folder, file, or printer are granted to user accounts or groups of accounts. In short, permissions assigned to a user account control what the user can and cannot do in Windows.

In Windows Vista, there are three types of user accounts:

- An **administrator account** has complete access to the system and can make changes that affect the security of the system and other users.
- A **standard user** account can use software and hardware and make some system changes, but cannot make changes that affect the security of the system or other users.
- A **guest account** has few privileges and is normally disabled.

Just after you complete a Windows Vista installation or you buy a new computer with the OS already installed, Vista has automatically created three accounts: the Administrator account (the account name is Administrator and the account has administrator privileges), one more account that has administrator privileges (for computers purchased with Vista installed, the account name is NewOwner or something similar), and a Guest account.

By default, no standard account is created. Also by default, the Administrator account and the Guest account are disabled, and not normally used. Therefore, when you log onto your system, you see only the one account that has administrative privileges, which we call an administrator account. And, as you learned in Chapter 1, you must log onto the system using an administrator account before you can install hardware or software or change settings that affect all users.

When we're logged on as an administrator, a program can run with more authority and privileges than when we're logged on as a standard user. Therefore, if a malware program is at work while we're logged on as an administrator, it has the ability to do more damage than if we had been logged on under a less powerful standard account. For that reason, it's a good idea to create at least one account that has standard privileges to use for your everyday normal computer activities. Then use only an administrator account when you need to do maintenance or installation chores that require the power of the administrator account.

HOW TO CREATE A USER ACCOUNT

You must be logged on as an administrator to create a new user account. Follow these steps:

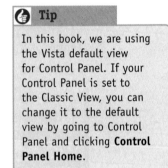

Tip

In this book, we are using the Vista default view for Control Panel. If your Control Panel is set to the Classic View, you can change it to the default view by going to Control Panel and clicking **Control Panel Home**.

1. Log on to the computer using an administrator account.

2. From Control Panel, under User Accounts and Family Safety, click **Add or remove user accounts** and respond to the UAC box. The Manage Accounts window appears, as shown in Figure 4-37.

Figure 4-37 Use the Manage Accounts window to create accounts and set parental controls

3. Click **Create a new account**. On the Create New Account window shown in Figure 4-38, enter the account name and select the type of account (Standard user or Administrator). Then click **Create Account**.

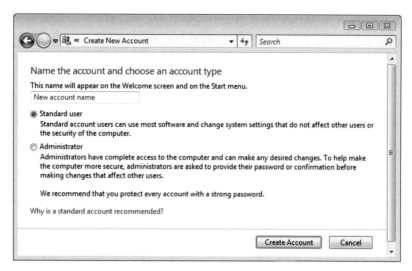

Figure 4-38 Name the account and select the account type

4. The account now displays in the Manage Accounts window. Click the account to see a list of changes you can make to the account. The Change an Account window appears, as shown in Figure 4-39. If you want to set a password for the new account, click **Create a password** and enter the password on the next screen.

Figure 4-39 Make changes to an account

MAKE A PASSWORD RESET DISK

If you or another user forgets his or her password to a standard or administrator account, you can log onto the system using another administrator account and use the Control Panel to reset the user's password. However, resetting a password under Windows Vista causes the OS to lock out the user from files or e-mail that have been encrypted or from Internet passwords stored on the computer. If you need to reset a password for a user who has encrypted data, first remove the encryption status on the folder or file before you reset the password. To reset the password, follow these steps:

1. In Control Panel, click **User Accounts and Family Safety** and then click **User Accounts**. In the User Accounts window, click **Manage another account** and respond to the UAC box.

2. Select the account and then click **Change the password**. The Change Password window appears (see Figure 4-40).

Figure 4-40 Reset the password for another user account

A user, including an administrator, can create a password reset disk, which he can use to reset his own password if it is forgotten. To create the disk, click **User Accounts and Family Safety** in Control Panel and then click **User Accounts**. In the User Accounts window (see Figure 4-41), click **Create a password reset disk**. The Forgotten Password Wizard launches. Follow the steps in the wizard to create the disk. You can use any removable media including CD, USB drive, or floppy disk for the disc, but insert the media before you launch the wizard. After the disk is created, store it in a safe, protected place.

> **Note**
>
> If you forget your password to the administrator account and don't have a password reset disk, as far as Windows is concerned, you're not going to get in the door and Microsoft suggests you reinstall Windows! However, recall from Chapter 1 that you can use one of several third-party utilities to log onto the system. How to do that is covered in Chapter 1.

> **Caution**
>
> The password reset disk can be used by anyone to get access to the computer, so be sure to keep it in a protected place.

If you enter a wrong password at logon, a message appears. When you click OK to the message, the logon screen includes a link to use the disk (see Figure 4-42). Insert the disk, click **Reset password**, and the Password Reset Wizard launches to use the disk and reset your password. Because Windows is protecting you from others using the password reset disk without your knowledge to gain access to your private data, when the password reset disk is used to log onto the system, encrypted files and encrypted e-mail are not accessible.

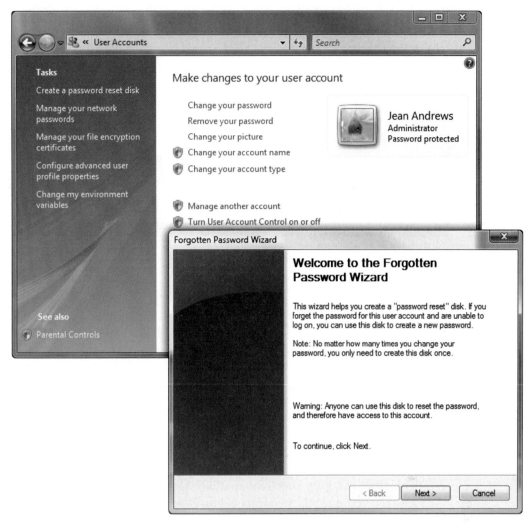

Figure 4-41   Create a password reset disk

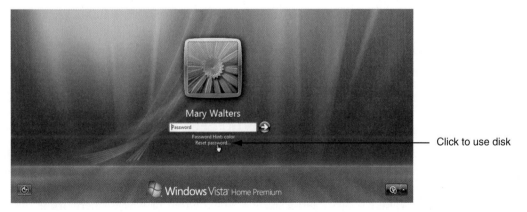

Figure 4-42   Use the password reset disk to reset your password

PHYSICALLY PROTECT YOUR EQUIPMENT

It's only common sense, but worth mentioning anyway: There are some things you can do to physically protect your computer equipment. Here is my list of dos and don'ts. You can probably add your own tips to the list:

◢ *Tip 1: Don't move or jar your computer when the hard drive is in use.* Before you move the computer case even a foot or so, make sure the hard drive is not in use. One way to make sure is to put the PC in Vista sleep mode. (Click **Start** and the sleep button, shown in Figure 4-43.) Don't put the computer case under your desk where it might get bumped or kicked. Although modern hard drives are sealed and much more resistant to vibration than earlier models, it's still possible to crash a drive by banging into it while it's reading or writing data.

Figure 4-43 Vista sleep mode stops all hard drive activity

◢ *Tip 2: Don't smoke around your computer.* Tar from cigarettes can accumulate on fans, causing them to jam and the system to overheat.

◢ *Tip 3: Don't leave the PC turned off for weeks or months at a time.* Once my daughter left her PC turned off for an entire summer. At the beginning of the new school term, the PC would not boot. We discovered that the boot record at the beginning of the hard drive had become corrupted. PCs, like old cars, can give problems after long spans of inactivity.

◢ *Tip 4: High humidity can be dangerous for hard drives.* I once worked in a basement with PCs, and hard drives failed much too often. After we installed dehumidifiers, the hard drives became more reliable.

◢ *Tip 5: In CMOS setup, disable the ability to write to the boot sector of the hard drive.* This alone can keep boot viruses at bay. However, before you upgrade your OS, such as when you upgrade Windows XP to Windows Vista, be sure to enable writing to the boot sector, which the OS setup will want to do.

◢ *Tip 6: If your data is really private, keep it under lock and key.* You can use all kinds of security methods to encrypt, password protect, and hide data, but if it really is that important, one obvious thing you can do is store the data on a removable storage device such as a flash drive and, when you're not using the data, put the flash drive in a fire-proof safe. And, of course, keep two copies. Sounds simple, but it works.

◢ *Tip 7: Keep magnets away from your computer.* Don't work inside the computer case with magnetized screwdrivers or set magnets on top of the computer case.

SECURE YOUR WIRED OR WIRELESS NETWORK

Unsecured networks are like leaving your front door open when you go to work in the morning or signing every check in your checkbook and then leaving it lying around in a coffee shop. Don't even think about it! If you're responsible for a home or small office network, take security seriously. Securing a wired or wireless network is covered in the next chapter. Read it with the intention of deciding on the best way to secure your network and then buy the equipment you need to do it. Most often, the device you'll want is a router that can be used to secure a wired network or provide a secured wireless network. Routers don't cost that much nowadays, and the investment is well worth it. However, after you buy it and set it up, be sure you implement what you'll learn in the next chapter to configure it for good security.

We have been discussing the top 17 methods to secure your desktop or laptop computer. The last method is to keep good backups. Because there is so much to say about keeping backups, I've devoted the entire next section to the subject.

KEEPING GOOD BACKUPS

When it comes to computers, we all need a Plan B. For peace of mind and to be prepared for the worst-case scenario, we all need to keep data backed up. If you can't get along without it, back it up! For example, suppose the hard drive on your computer stopped working. It's totally dead and everything on it is lost. How would that affect you? What would be lost and what would that cost you in time, stress, and money? The time to prepare for disaster is before it happens. As a rule of thumb, if you can't get along without those data files, e-mail address lists, or e-mail attachments, back them up.

As a general rule of thumb, back up your data for every eight to ten hours of data entry. That might mean you back up once a day, once a week, or once a month. If you work for a large corporation, chances are the company has a data backup policy and backup media already in place. If that's the case, follow your IT department's instructions for keeping good backups. If you travel with a corporate notebook, you might need to get your notebook in sync with the corporate server on a regular basis, say daily. Syncing up your notebook is, in effect, backing up your data. Don't assume that your data is backed up, unless you've checked with your IT department for specific policies and procedures and you understand and use those procedures. In this section, I'm assuming you don't have these backup methods available and that you're responsible for your own backups.

In this part of the chapter, you'll learn how to back up data and how to use those backups when you need them, using the Vista backup utility and a third-party utility. And for really serious backer-uppers, you will learn how to back up the entire Vista volume on the hard drive. In addition, recall from earlier chapters that System Protection and System Restore can be used to back up and recover parts of the Vista system. Let's begin our discussion of backups by taking a look at the different backup media.

BACKUP MEDIA

The most popular media for backing up data on a personal computer are second hard drives; USB devices including flash memory; CDs; and DVDs, including the newer Blu-ray DVDs. For large volumes of data, tape drives can be used. Although they are more difficult to use than other methods, tapes are less expensive than other media if you have a ton of data to back up. Backing up to a second hard drive is the most convenient method, but for the best security, you need to keep the backed-up data off site, and that's not convenient when using a second hard drive. Flash memory is a great choice for small amounts of data. CDs and DVDs are good choices if you don't have too much data to back up. The newer Blu-ray DVDs are still expensive, but they do hold up to 25 GB on a single layer disk or 50 GB on a dual layer disk. Optical media are easy to use and easy to store in an off-site location. Flash memory is a great choice for small amounts of data.

If you don't have a CD or DVD burner on your computer, you might want to consider buying an external device that can use an available USB or Firewire port. Unfortunately, several DVD technologies exist, so be sure to match the blank DVDs to the DVD type that the burner can use.

To back up to a second hard drive, you can use an external hard drive that connects to your computer by way of a FireWire or USB port (see Figure 4-44), a hard drive in another computer on your network, or a second drive installed inside your computer. And for really large backup needs, you can buy a group of hard drives housed in a case that connects to your network.

Figure 4-44 This Maxtor external hard drive holds 500 GB and uses a high-speed USB 2.0 connection

Even though it's easy to do, don't make the mistake of backing up your data to another partition or folder on your same hard drive. When a hard drive crashes, most likely all partitions go down together and you will have lost your data and your backup. Back up to another medium and, for extra safety, store it at an off-site location.

If you travel a lot, keeping good backups of data on your notebook computer might be a problem. Several Internet companies have solved this backup-on-the-go problem by providing remote backup services over the Internet. In a hotel room or other remote location, connect to the Internet and back up your data to a Web site's file server. If data is lost, you can easily recover it by connecting to the Internet and logging onto your backup service Web site. If security is a concern, be sure you understand the security guarantees of the site.

> **Note**
>
> A hard drive is organized into one or more partitions. A **partition** can be a primary partition or an extended partition (see Figure 4-45). A primary partition can have only one logical drive (for example, drive C), and an extended partition can have one or more logical drives (for example, drives D and E). Each **logical drive** (also called a **volume**) is formatted with a file system (NTFS or FAT32), and each logical drive has its own root directory and subdirectories.

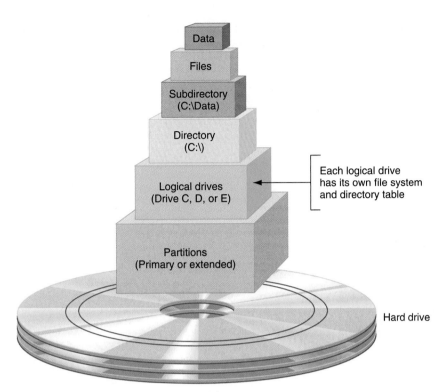

Figure 4-45 A hard drive is divided and organized at several levels

Two online backup services are @Backup (*www.backup.com*) and Remote Backup Systems (*www.remote-backup.com*).

 Note

> Two good sites to check out when purchasing any hardware device are CNET, at *reviews.cnet.com*, and Tom's Hardware, at *www.tomshardware.com*. Also, if you do a search on "Hardware reviews," you'll turn up a bunch of other review sites. Before you make your decision, be sure to check some retail sites to compare prices on the drive and the media (tapes or blank CDs or DVDs). My favorite retail site is TigerDirect, at *www.tigerdirect.com*.

BACK UP FILES AND FOLDERS USING WINDOWS VISTA BACKUP UTILITY

The Windows Vista backup utility limits your decisions about which files and folders on a Vista system you can back up. You are forced to back up data for all users. Follow these steps to back up files and folders:

1. Connect your backup device to your PC. If you are using an external hard drive, use Windows Explorer to verify you can access the drive.

2. From Control Panel, under System and Maintenance, click **Back up your computer**. The Backup and Restore Center window appears as shown in Figure 4-46.

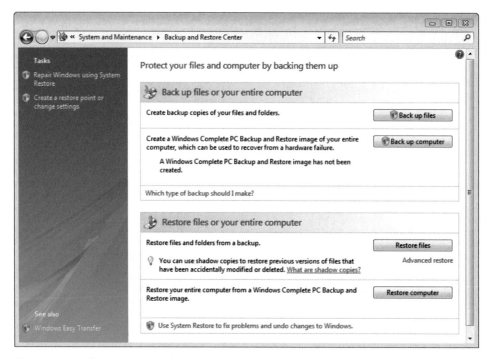

Figure 4-46   Windows Vista Backup and Restore Center

3. Click **Back up files** and respond to the UAC box. On the next window (see Figure 4-47) select where you want to save your backup and click **Next**.

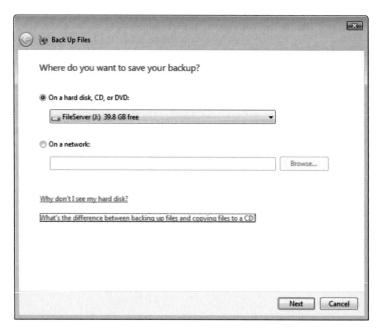

Figure 4-47   Select your backup location for files and folders

4. On the next window, select the volumes on your computer that contain folders or files you want to back up and click **Next**.

5. On the next window, shown in Figure 4-48, select the type of files you want to back up and click **Next**.

6. The next window lets you select how often (daily, weekly, or monthly), what day (day of week or day of month), and what time of day to schedule automatic incremental backups of today's full backup. Make your selections and click **Save settings and start backup.**

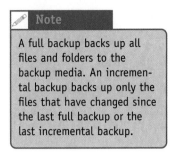

> **Note**
>
> A full backup backs up all files and folders to the backup media. An incremental backup backs up only the files that have changed since the last full backup or the last incremental backup.

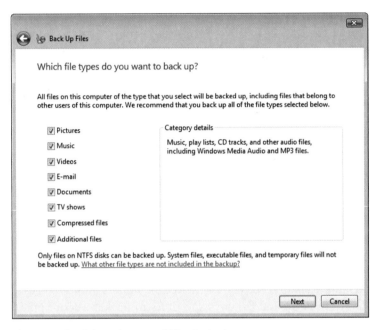

Figure 4-48   Select the type of files to back up

To see the status of the last backup, click **Start, All Programs, Accessories, System Tools, Backup Status and Configuration**. The Backup Status and Configuration window opens as shown in Figure 4-49. Using this window, you can change the backup settings. When you change the settings, a new, full backup is created.

To restore files from backup, on the Backup Status and Configuration window, click **Restore Files** and follow directions on screen to select a specific backup and specific folders or files to restore.

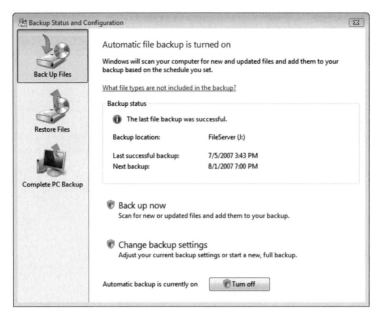

Figure 4-49   Backup Status and Configuration window

BACK UP FOLDERS USING A THIRD-PARTY BACKUP UTILITY

Because Windows Vista backup gives you so little control over the folders you choose to back up, many people turn to third-party backup utilities. Let's look at one example by Maxtor. The bundled backup utility that comes loaded on the Maxtor external hard drive shown back in Figure 4-44 installs when you first plug in the drive to a USB port. The software creates an icon in the notification area. When you click the icon, the main menu in Figure 4-50 appears.

When you click the Backup icon, you can select the folders and file types (identified by the file extension) to back up and the days and times to backup. Besides the folders that contain your documents, spreadsheets, databases, and other data files, you also might want to back up these folders:

▲ *Your e-mail messages and address book.* For Windows Mail, back up this folder: C:\Users*username*\AppData\Local\Microsoft\Windows Mail
▲ *Your Internet Explorer favorites list.* To back up your IE favorites list, back up this folder: C:\Users*username*\Favorites.

At scheduled times, the utility copies the files and folders to the external hard drive, keeping 10 levels of backups. At any time, if you push the button on the front of the drive, a backup is created on the spot. Later if you need to recover a file or folder, you can use the backup utility to help you find it on the drive or you can use Windows Explorer to find it yourself.

COMPLETE PC BACKUP USING THE VISTA BACKUP UTILITY

A Complete PC backup makes a backup of the entire volume on which Vista is installed and can also back up other volumes. The best practice to protect a Windows Vista system is

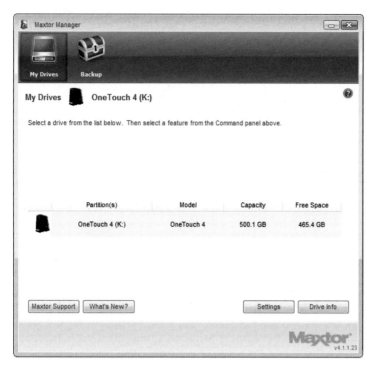

Figure 4-50 Maxtor Manager software manages backups to the drive

to make a Complete PC backup after you have installed Vista, all hardware devices, and all applications. This backup works similar to recovery DVDs that come with a brand name computer used to recover from a failed hard drive to return the system to its original state at the time of purchase.

The Complete PC backup must be saved to a local device such as an external hard drive or to DVDs. Don't back up the volume to another partition on the same hard drive. After the initial backup is made, Vista will automatically keep this backup current by making incremental backups. Vista does not keep multiple copies of backups made using the Complete PC backup method, as it does when backing up files and folders.

Follow these steps to create the initial Complete PC backup:

> 👍 **Tip**
>
> Complete PC backup is not available in Vista Starter or Vista Home versions.

1. Connect your backup device to your PC. If you're using an external hard drive, use Windows Explorer to verify you can access the drive.

2. From Control Panel, under System and Maintenance, click **Back up your computer**. The Backup and Restore Center window appears as shown earlier in Figure 4-46.

3. Click **Back up computer** and respond to the UAC dialog box. Vista searches for available backup devices and then displays the list. Select the backup media and click **Next**.

4. In the next window, Vista Backup shows you the Vista volume it will backup and gives you the opportunity to select other volumes it finds to include in the backup. Make your selections and click **Next**.

5. On the next window (see Figure 4-51), the backup tells you the maximum amount of space expected for the backup, assuming no compression and room for housekeeping data about the backup. If you are backing up to DVDs, the backup tells you about how many DVDs are required. Click **Start backup** to begin the backup.

Figure 4-51 Confirm your backup settings and begin the backup

In the event your hard drive fails or Vista is so corrupted you cannot recover it, you can restore the volume or volumes from your Complete PC backup. Because the entire Vista volume will be overwritten, you must perform the operation from the Vista setup DVD using the Windows Recovery Environment (Windows RE).

Follow these steps to recover the system from backup:

1. Because this process will erase everything on the Vista volume and any other volumes included in the Complete PC backup, make every attempt to save any important data on these volumes before you continue with these steps.

2. Connect the backup device to your computer.

3. Boot from the Vista DVD and select your language and keyboard layout preferences, as shown in Figure 4-52. Click **Next**.

Figure 4-52 Select language and keyboard preferences

4. The Install Windows screen appears. Click **Repair your computer** (see Figure 4-53).

Figure 4-53 Opening menu when you boot from the Vista DVD

5. System Recovery searches for an installed OS. If it finds one, select it and click **Next**. If it does not find an installed OS, just click **Next**.

6. If System Recovery presents a logon dialog box, log onto the system using an administrator account and password.

7. The System Recovery Options window shown in Figure 4-54 appears. Click **Windows Complete PC Restore,** and follow directions on screen to restore the system from backup.

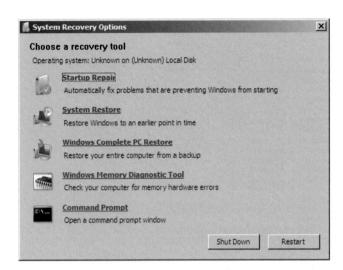

Figure 4-54   Restore the system to previous Complete PC backup

In Chapter 7, you'll learn more about the Windows Recovery Environment, including how to use all the options shown in Figure 4-54, and what you can do to recover a failed Vista system without having to revert to the last Complete PC backup.

>> CHAPTER SUMMARY

◢ A firewall is software or hardware that stands between your computer system and the Internet, protecting it against uninvited communication.

◢ A port is a number that is used to allow a program on another computer to communicate with your computer. A firewall closes all ports or only allows communication on selected ports.

◢ Hardware firewalls offer more protection than software firewalls, but software firewalls are useful when a hardware firewall is not present, such as when you are traveling with a notebook computer or you are on a local network and need protection from other computers on the network.

◢ Vista comes with a built-in firewall that is automatically configured based on the type of network it believes that you are connected to, assigning you a public, private, or domain profile.

◢ For AV software or anti-adware software to be effective, it must be kept current and must be turned on.

◢ Security holes are being found all the time in Windows Vista, but Microsoft is constantly releasing patches to fix the vulnerabilities. These patches have to be downloaded and installed for them to help. The best choice is to allow Vista to install updates automatically.

◢ Windows Defender is an anti-adware and anti-spyware software integrated into Vista, constantly watching for malicious software trying to install itself on your PC without your knowledge.

◢ It is not a good idea to disable the UAC box, because it makes you think before making drastic changes to the system and it stands as a gatekeeper, not allowing malware to install behind your back.

◢ Internet Explorer and Windows Mail, Outlook, or Outlook Express are most often targeted by malicious software. Using less popular clients such as Firefox by Mozilla (a browser) or Eudora by Qualcomm (an e-mail client) might mean you are less likely to be attacked.

◢ Practice and teach responsible Web surfing, such as never opening an e-mail attachment from unknown senders and never downloading from Web sites you have not carefully checked out.

◢ There are several security options offered in Internet Explorer that can be used to decrease the chance of a malware infection.

◢ To make it less likely you'll launch a malicious script on your computer, set Windows to display file extensions of scripts.

◢ File and folder encryption provides a high level of defense against data theft. Some versions of Vista come with BitLocker, a feature that locks a hard drive if stolen.

◢ Create and use a less powerful account than an administrator account for most activities so that you will not unknowingly allow malicious software to use a more powerful administrator account.

◢ Make a password reset disk so a forgotten password can easily be reset.

◢ The best practice to protect a Windows Vista system is to make a Complete PC backup after you have installed Vista, all hardware devices, and all applications.

>> KEY TERMS

administrator account A type of user account that has complete access to the system and can make changes that affect the security of the system and other users.

BitLocker Drive Encryption A Vista feature that locks down a hard drive if it is stolen. It encrypts the entire system volume and is designed to be used in conjunction with file and folder encryption for high security requirements.

domain profile The profile settings that Windows Firewall uses when the computer is logged onto a domain and security is managed by the domain controller.

encryption Used to protect sensitive data, the conversion of data into code that must be translated before it can be accessed.

firewall Software or a hardware device that protects a computer or network from unsolicited communication. A hardware firewall stands between two networks or a computer and a network. A software firewall is installed on a single computer to protect it, and is called a personal firewall.

guest account An account that has few privileges and that is normally disabled.

logical drive A portion or all of a hard drive partition that is treated by the operating system as though it were a physical drive. Each logical drive is assigned a drive letter, such as drive C, and contains a file system. Also called a *volume*.

partition A division of a hard drive that can be used to hold logical drives (for example, drive C).

password reset disk A Windows Vista disk created to be used to reset a password in the event the user forgets the user account password to the system.

port A number assigned to an application or other process on a computer so that the process can be found by TCP/IP. Also called a *port address* or *port number*.

private profile The profile settings that Windows Firewall uses when the computer is not logged onto a domain and all active networks (wired and wireless, including Bluetooth) are configured as private networks. The profile uses a medium level of protection. Also see *public profile*.

Protected Mode An operating mode used by Internet Explorer to protect the system from malware where files can only be written to the Temporary Internet Files folder and only insignificant registry keys can be changed.

public profile The profile settings that Windows Firewall uses when Vista recognizes the computer is connected to a public network. This profile offers the highest level of protection. Also see *private profile*.

standard user A type of user account that can use software and hardware and make some system changes, but cannot make changes that affect the security of the system or other users.

user account The information that defines a Windows Vista user, including username, password, memberships, and rights.

volume *See* logical drive.

>> *REVIEWING THE BASICS*

1. Which of the three Windows Firewall profiles offers the highest level of protection?
2. Why is using an ActiveX control considered a security risk?
3. Why is it a good idea to not leave the computer under your desk?
4. Name one browser other than Internet Explorer by Microsoft.
5. Name two e-mail clients other than Windows Mail, Outlook, or Outlook Express by Microsoft.
6. What is the best way to protect a computer or network against worms?
7. When connecting your laptop to an access point on a secured network, and you want to give others access to a shared folder, which profile setting should be used?
8. How many logical drives can a primary partition hold?
9. Why might someone see better security when using a browser other than Internet Explorer?
10. Name four types of media that can be used to hold backups of data.
11. Where does a Complete PC backup need to be saved?
12. What two accounts are created by the Windows Vista setup process, but are disabled by default?
13. What folder can you back up in order to back up e-mail messages and the address book used by Windows Mail?
14. To back up your IE favorites list, what folder do you back up?
15. What is the best way to determine if an e-mail message warning about a virus is a hoax?

>> *THINKING CRITICALLY*

1. If you have Windows Firewall set not to allow any exceptions and keep all ports closed, which of the following activities will be allowed, and which will not be allowed? Explain your answer.

   a. You receive e-mail.
   b. You receive an MSN Messenger notice that a friend wants to have a chat session with you.
   c. Your antivirus software informs you a new update has just been downloaded and installed.

2. You are about to install Windows Vista on a new 120 GB hard drive. You plan to use the system as a file server for a small business network and you estimate the capacity required for data stored on the file server will not exceed 60 GB. How many and what size partitions should the drive have? Explain your answer.

   a. One 120 GB partition
   b. One 20 GB partition and one 100 GB partition
   c. One 60 GB partition and one 60 GB partition
   d. One 20 GB partition, one 60 GB partition, and the remaining space not partitioned

>> *HANDS-ON PROJECTS*

PROJECT 4-1:   E-Mail Hoax

Search through your spam and junk mail for an e-mail you think might be a hoax. (Please don't click any links or open any attachments as you search.) Using the Web sites listed earlier in the chapter for debunking virus hoaxes, search for information about this potential hoax. You might need to enter the subject line in the e-mail message into a search box on the Web site.

PROJECT 4-2:   Using Firefox

Go to the Mozilla Web site (*www.mozilla.com*) and download and install Firefox. Use it to browse the Web. How does it compare to Internet Explorer? What do you like better about it? What do you not like as well? When might you recommend to someone that they use Firefox rather than Internet Explorer? Also, download the FoxFilter plug-in from www.mozilla.com and install it. What are the differences between FoxFilter and the IE content filter?

PROJECT 4-3:   Using a Port Scanner

This project will require the use of two computers on the same network to practice using port scanning software. Do the following:

1. Download and install Advanced Port Scanner by Famatech at *www.radmin.com* on Computer 1.

2. On Computer 2, make sure that Windows Firewall is turned on and that **Block all incoming connections** box is checked. Also, disable any third party personal firewalls.

3. On Computer 1, start Advanced Port Scanner and make sure that the range of IP addresses includes the IP address of Computer 2. Then click **Scan**.

4. Browse the list and find Computer 2. List the number and purpose of all open ports found on your Computer 2.

5. On Computer 2, turn Windows Firewall off.

6. On Computer 1, rescan and list the number and purpose of each port now open on Computer 2.

7. If Computer 2 has another personal firewall installed, turn on that firewall. On Computer 1, rescan and list the number and purpose of each port now open on Computer 2 when the personal firewall is running.

PROJECT 4-4: Scheduling Backups

For large volumes of data, tapes are the best choice for backups because they are inexpensive and can easily be stored off-site. Using Table 4-2 as your guide, set up Windows Vista backup schedules to create backups of user data for all users. Notice in the table that a full backup is called a parent backup and an incremental backup is called a child backup. Assume the data for all users is stored in the C:\Users folder. Print the details of each scheduled backup.

Name of Backup	How Often Performed	Storage Location	Description
Child backup	Daily	On-site	Keep four daily backup tapes of data that has changed that day, and rotate the tapes each week. Label the four tapes Monday, Tuesday, Wednesday, and Thursday. A Friday daily (child) backup is not made, because on Friday you make the parent backup.
Parent backup	Weekly	Off-site	Perform a full backup each week on Friday. Keep five weekly backup tapes, one for each Friday of the month, and rotate them each month. Label the tapes Friday 1, Friday 2, Friday 3, and Friday 4.
Grandparent backup	Monthly	Off-site, in a fireproof vault	Perform the monthly backup on the last Friday of the month. Make a full backup of data and the system state. Keep 12 tapes, one for each month. Rotate them each year. Label the tapes January, February, and so on.

Table 4-2 The Child, Parent, Grandparent Backup Method

PROJECT 4-5:   Managing User Accounts

Do the following to experiment with managing user accounts:

1. Create a Standard user account and log on using that account. Can you view the contents of the Documents folder for an account with Administrator privileges?

2. Using the Standard account, try to install a program. What message do you receive?

3. What happens if you try to create a new account while logged on under the Standard account?

PROJECT 4-6:   Recovering From a Forgotten Windows Password

Forgotten passwords can be a messy problem if you have not made a password reset disk. If you have forgotten the password for a Vista user account and you know the password for an administrator account, you can log on as an administrator and reset the forgotten password. If you don't know a password for any Vista account, here are some password recovery utilities that can help. Research each utility and describe its approach to helping with forgotten passwords and how much the utility costs. Which of the three utilities would you select for purchase and why?

▲ Ophcrack by phpBB Group at *ophcrack.sourceforge.net*
▲ Active Password Changer at *www.password-changer.com*
▲ Windows Password Reset at *ResetWindowsPassword.com*

>> REAL PROBLEMS, REAL SOLUTIONS

REAL PROBLEM 4-1:   Securing Your Computer

Using as many of the suggestions in the chapter as apply to your system, make your computer as secure as possible. Take notes as you work and record any problems you encounter. What other measures would you like to take to secure your computer that you don't know how to do or that cost too much?

Wired and Wireless Made Easy

This chapter is more of a how-to chapter than others in this book. Yes, I know this book is mostly focused on fixing what's broken, but understanding how to set up a network correctly is by far your strongest resource when troubleshooting network problems. Many beginners tend to use wizards to configure a network without really understanding what they are doing. When things go wrong and connections fail, this lack of understanding becomes a hindrance. In this chapter, you'll become armed with a solid understanding of how networks are configured and how to troubleshoot their problems.

We'll start by going through the step-by-step processes of connecting a single computer to the Internet and then networking two or more computers using a wired or wireless connection. At the end of the chapter, we'll talk about tools and techniques you can use when things that are set up correctly won't work. Security is always a major concern when networking, so we'll also cover how to secure both wired and wireless networks.

HOW TO CONNECT A COMPUTER TO THE INTERNET

For individual computers and for small networks at home or in a small office, the entry point to the Internet is an Internet Service Provider (ISP), as shown in Figure 5-1. That ISP can provide one or more ways to connect to the Internet. The four most popular methods are DSL, cable modem, satellite, and phone lines. Phone lines are the cheapest and slowest method. Satellite might work for you if you live in a remote location where DSL and cable modem are not available. The choice between DSL and cable modem depends on several factors, and sometimes it's a toss-up between the two.

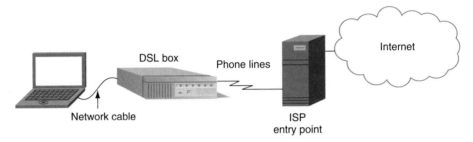

Figure 5-1 Use an ISP to connect to the Internet

The major differences and similarities between cable modem and DSL are:

- Cable modem (also called cable Internet) uses TV cable lines for transmission. You can subscribe to cable modem in a bundle with your TV cable subscription and possibly with VoIP (Voice over Internet Protocol, a type of Internet telephone service). On the other hand, DSL uses phone lines for transmission and is bundled with your local phone service.
- Cable modem and DSL both can be purchased on a sliding scale depending on the bandwidth you want to buy. Also, both subscriptions offer residential and more expensive business plans. Generally, with business plans, you get better service and more bandwidth.
- With cable modem, you share the TV cable infrastructure with your neighbors, so your service can become degraded if many people in your neighborhood are using cable modem at the same time. I once used cable modem in a neighborhood where I found I needed to stay away from Web surfing between 5–7pm when folks were just coming in from work and using the Internet. With DSL, you're using a dedicated phone line, so your neighbors' surfing habits don't interfere.
- With DSL, static over phone lines in your house can be a problem. The DSL company provides filters to install at each phone jack, but the problem still might not be fully solved. Also, some phone lines (called "dirty" lines) have so much static on them that DSL just won't work. Your phone company can test your line to see if it is clean enough to qualify for DSL.
- Setup of cable modem and DSL works about the same way using either a cable modem or a DSL modem for the interface between the broadband jack (TV jack or phone jack) and the PC.

◢ With either installation, the cable modem or DSL provider can send you the broadband modem and you can follow the instructions to install it, or you can have the provider do the entire installation for you at an additional cost. If you pay for this installation service, a service technician comes to your home, installs all equipment, including a network card if necessary, and configures your PC to use the service.

Personally, I subscribe to two ISPs. I use one ISP to provide dial-up connections when I travel to remote locations, and I use another ISP, my local cable company, to provide broadband high-speed Internet access to my home office. Because I absolutely must have Internet access when I'm working, I use my dial-up connection as a backup connection when cable is down. I used to use DSL for my broadband connection, but we had so much trouble with static and other interference on my phone lines, I switched to cable. However, I'm not criticizing DSL; I think the problem might have been with my home phone wiring job. I know others who switched from cable to DSL because cable gave them grief. What works best for you largely depends on the wiring in your house and your neighborhood and the services and infrastructure of your local providers. If you're trying to decide between going with DSL or cable modem for your high-speed Internet connection, ask several neighbors on your street which one they use and why.

Now let's turn our attention to how to connect to the Internet using cable modem, DSL, and dial-up. We begin by looking at how communication happens at three levels.

COMMUNICATION AT THREE LEVELS

Let's talk about the big picture for a moment. When your computer at home is connected to your ISP off somewhere in the distance, your computer and a computer on the Internet are communicating at three levels. The computers need a way to address each other at each level. These three levels and the addresses used at each level are diagrammed in Figure 5-2.

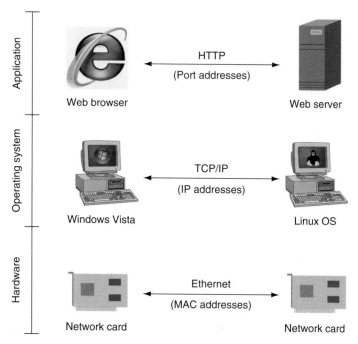

Figure 5-2 Internet communication happens at three levels

Listed next is a description of each level of communication:

◢ *Level 1: Hardware level.* At the root level of communication is hardware. The hardware or physical connection might be wireless or might use network cables, phone lines (for DSL or dial-up), or TV cable lines (for cable modem). For local wired or wireless networks, a network adapter (also called a network card, network interface card, or NIC) inside your computer is part of this physical network. The rules for communication are predetermined and these rules are called protocols. Currently, the most common networking standard for local networks at the hardware level is called Ethernet. So that network cards can identify each other on the network, each card contains a unique number—a 48-bit (or 6-byte) address called a MAC address. An example of a MAC address is 00–0C-6E-4E-AB-A5. Each of the six bytes is presented as a two-character hexadecimal (base 16) numeral. Part of the MAC address refers to the manufacturer, and the rest of the address is a serial number assigned by the manufacturer. Therefore, by design, no two adapters will have the same MAC address. Most likely the MAC address is written on the adapter, as shown in Figure 5-3. At the lowest level of communication, one NIC is searching on its network for another NIC with a specific MAC address.

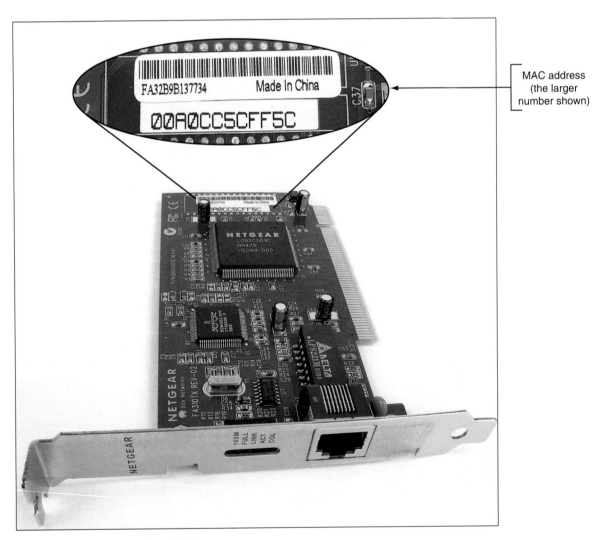

Figure 5-3 A network card's MAC address

▲ **Level 2: Operating system level.** An OS is responsible for managing communication between it and another computer, using rules for communication that both operating systems understand. This group, or suite, of communication protocols is collectively called TCP/IP. One OS addresses the other OS using addresses called IP addresses. An IP address is a 32-bit string used to identify a computer on a network. These 32 bits are organized into four groups of eight bits each, which are presented as four decimal numbers separated by periods, such as 72.56.105.12. A network can use static IP addressing, in which each computer is assigned an IP address that never changes, or dynamic IP addressing, in which each time the computer connects to the network, it gets a new IP address (called leasing the IP address).

▲ **Level 3: Application level.** When you use the Internet to surf the Web or download your e-mail, you are using an application on your computer called an Internet client. For Web surfing, that client, such as Internet Explorer or Firefox, is called a browser. The client communicates with another application somewhere on the Internet, called a server. Examples of server applications are your e-mail server at your ISP or a Web server anywhere on the Web. Recall from earlier chapters that each server is installed under the OS as a third-party service. Web browsers and servers use the HTTP protocol, and e-mail clients and servers can use POP, SMTP, and IMAP protocols. A client identifies

> **📝 Note**
>
> When you enter a domain name such as *www.microsoft.com* in a browser address box, that name is translated into an IP address followed by a port number. It's interesting to know that you can skip the translation step and enter the IP address and port number in the address box. See Figure 5-5.

a server by the IP address of the computer and a port number. Web servers are normally assigned port 80 and e-mail servers are assigned port 25. See Figure 5-4.

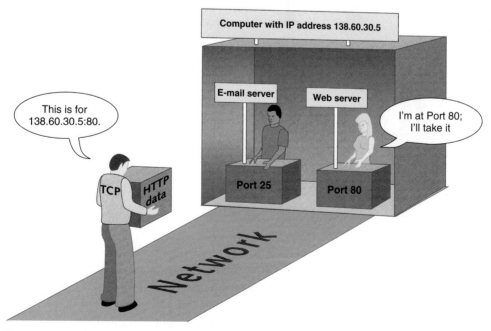

Figure 5-4 Each server running on a computer is addressed by a unique port number

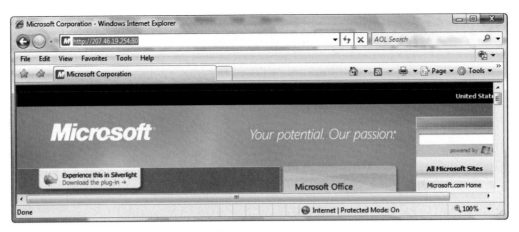

Figure 5-5 A Web site can be accessed by its IP address and port number

Figure 5-6 shows how communication moves from a browser to the OS to the hardware on one computer and on to the hardware, OS, and Web server on a remote computer. As you set up a small network that consists of your computer connected to the ISP, keep in mind that the network must be set up at all three levels. And when things don't work right, it helps to understand that you must solve the problem at one or more levels. In other words, the problem might be with the physical equipment, with the OS, or with the application.

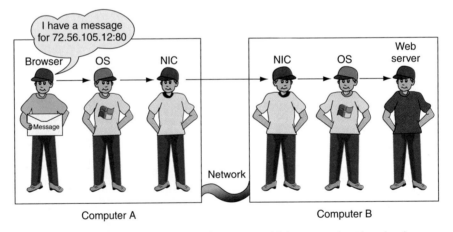

Figure 5-6 How a message gets from a browser to a Web server using three levels of communication

When you first purchase a subscription to your ISP, you might receive an installation CD from your ISP. If so, you'll want to follow the installation setup routine on this CD instead of the manual procedures outlined in this chapter. The order of doing things might differ from instructions here.

When first connecting to the Internet, the installation generally goes like this:

1. Physically connect your PC to the cable modem, DSL modem, or phone jack.
   (Sometimes the ISP will ask you to install software before you connect equipment.)

2. Using Windows, configure the TCP/IP settings for the connection to the ISP. To configure Windows correctly, you'll need to know these things:

   a. Your username and password for the ISP. (This username and password might be required to connect to the ISP, or it might just be used to manage your ISP account on the ISP Web site. Your ISP will let you know how to use it.)

   b. For dial-up connections, you'll need the phone number to the ISP that your modem will dial.

   c. An ISP might use static IP addressing or dynamic IP addressing. If it uses static IP addressing, you will be told the IP address to give Windows. If it uses dynamic IP addressing (which is more likely), you can set Windows to ask for an IP address each time it connects to the ISP.

   d. If your ISP has you set up for static IP addressing, the ISP will also tell you the subnet mask and the IP addresses of the default gateway and of the DNS servers.

3. Test the connection by using a browser to surf the Web.

Here is a quick explanation of the terms subnet mask, default gateway, and DNS server:

▲ A **subnet mask** is a group of four 8-bit numbers separated by periods that, when combined with an IP address, indicate what network a computer is on. An example of a subnet mask is 255.255.255.0.

▲ A **default gateway** is a computer on a network that acts as an access point, or gateway, to another network. Depending on the context, this can refer to the computer at the ISP that you go through to get to the Internet, or to the router on your own network that is connected to the cable modem or DSL modem.

▲ A **DNS (Domain Name System)** server matches up domain names with IP addresses. For example, when you enter *www.delmarlearning.com* in your browser address box, the DNS server will look up that domain name in one of its available tables and translate it into the IP address of the Delmar server that is named www.delmarlearning.com.

CONNECT TO THE INTERNET USING A CABLE MODEM

Note

When setting up a new network connection to the Internet, first log onto the system using an administrator account.

Most cable modem connections use dynamic IP addressing and are always up. Always-up connections don't require a user name or password to connect. You'll first learn how to make the connection using these most-likely assumptions. Then later in the chapter, after the "Connect to the Internet Using DSL" section, we'll look at how to configure static IP addressing and on-demand connections.

A cable modem broadband connection uses a network port or a USB port on the PC to connect to the cable modem. Figure 5-7 shows the setup for a cable modem connection using a network cable between the PC and the cable modem.

Follow these instructions to connect a computer to the Internet using a cable modem connection and an Ethernet cable to connect the PC to the modem:

1. Select the TV wall jack that will be used to connect your cable modem. You want to use the jack that connects directly to the point where the TV cable comes into your home, with no splitters between this jack and the entrance point. Otherwise, in-line

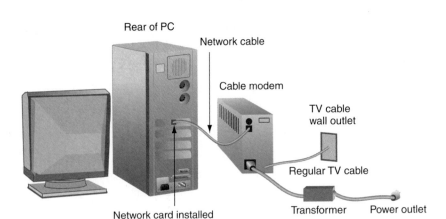

Figure 5-7 Cable modem connecting to a PC through a network card installed on the PC

splitters can degrade the signal quality and make your connection erratic. The cable company can test each jack and tell you which jack is best to use for the cable modem—one good reason to have a technician come and hook you up for the first time. Later, if your cable modem connection is constantly going down, you might consider that you've chosen the wrong jack for the connection.

> **Note**
>
> When setting up cable modem, you might want to connect your TV to the same jack that the cable modem is using. In this situation, connect a splitter to the jack and then connect the cable modem and TV cables to the splitter. If the connection gives problems, try removing the splitter.

2. Using coaxial cable, connect the cable modem to the TV wall jack. Plug in the power cord to the cable modem.

3. When using a network port on your PC, connect one end of the network cable to the network port on the PC, and the other end to the network port on the cable modem. Vista makes a valiant effort to automatically configure the network connection that it now senses is present. If your ISP uses dynamic IP addressing and you have an always up connection, most likely Vista is able to configure the connection without your help.

Follow these directions if you are using a USB cable to connect your cable modem to your computer:

1. When using a USB port on your PC, first read the directions that came with your cable modem to find out if you install the software before or after you connect the cable modem, and follow that order. For most installations, you begin with connecting the cable modem.

2. Connect the USB cable to your PC and to the cable modem. Plug in and turn on the cable modem and Windows Vista will automatically detect it as a new USB device. When the Found New Hardware Wizard launches (see Figure 5-8), click **Locate and install driver software**, respond to the UAC box, and insert the USB driver CD that came with your cable modem. The wizard searches for and installs these drivers.

Figure 5-8 When using a USB cable to connect to the cable modem, the Found New Hardware Wizard will install the cable modem drivers

3. Vista automatically creates a new network connection and displays the Set Network Location window shown in Figure 5-9. Select the location, most likely **Home**. Close the two windows left there by Set Network Location and Found New Hardware.

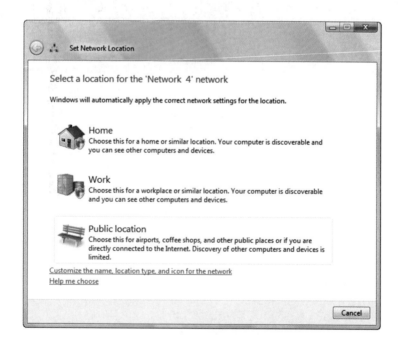

Figure 5-9 Vista asks for the location of the new connection so that it can configure the firewall

4. Connect the cable modem to the TV wall jack. Vista automatically configures the new connection for dynamic IP addressing and an always-up connection.

You are now ready to activate your service and test the connection. Do the following:

1. The cable company must know the MAC address of the cable modem you have installed. If you have received the cable modem from your cable company, the company already has the MAC address listed as belonging to you and you can skip this step. If you purchased the cable modem from another source, look for the MAC address somewhere on the back or bottom of the cable modem. See Figure 5-10. Contact the cable company and tell them the new MAC address.

Figure 5-10   Look for the MAC address of the cable modem printed on the modem

2. Test the Internet connection using your Web browser. If you are not connected, try the following:

   a. Open the Network and Sharing Center window, select **Diagnose and Repair** under Tasks. This will walk you through a few basic steps to try to resolve the issue.
   b. If this doesn't work, turn off the PC and the cable modem. Wait a full five minutes until all connections have timed out at the cable Internet company. Turn on the cable modem and wait for the lights on the front of the modem to settle in. Then turn on the PC. After the PC boots up, again check for connectivity.
   c. Try another cable TV jack in your home.

3. If this doesn't work, call the cable Internet help desk. The technician there can release and restore the connection at that end, which might restore service. If this doesn't work, there might be a problem with the cable company's equipment, which the company will need to repair.

CONNECT TO THE INTERNET USING DSL

DSL service and an older technology, ISDN, are provided by the local telephone company. (An up-and-coming, second-generation DSL, called DSL over Fiber in the Loop [DFITL], uses dedicated fiber optic cable to bring DSL to your neighborhood.) As with cable modem, a technician from the phone company can install DSL for you, or the company can send you a kit for you to install yourself. If you do the installation yourself, know that it works pretty much the same way as cable modem.

Here are the steps that are different:

1. Read the directions that came with the DSL modem and follow them. If your DSL modem came with a setup CD, you can run that setup to step you through the installation, including installing the drivers for a modem that uses a USB connection. You might be instructed to run a setup CD on your PC before you connect the modem, or you might need to install the modem first.

2. Install a telephone filter on every phone jack in your house that is being used by a telephone, fax machine, or dial-up modem. See Figure 5-11.

Figure 5-11   Filters are needed on every phone jack
when DSL is used in your house

3. Connect the DSL modem as shown in Figure 5-12. If necessary, you can use a Y-splitter on the wall jack (as shown on the left in Figure 5-11) so that a telephone can use the same jack. Plug the DSL modem into the DSL port on a filter or directly into a wall jack. (Don't connect the DSL modem to a telephone port on the filter; this setup would prevent DSL from working.) Plug in the power to the DSL modem. Connect a network cable or USB cable between the DSL modem and the PC.

To telephone

DSL modem

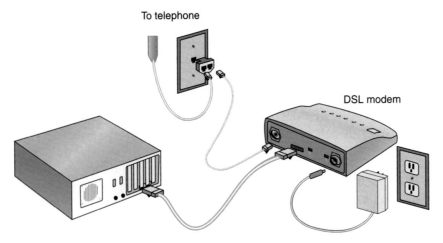

Figure 5-12 Sample setup for DSL

4. Vista automatically configures the new network connection for dynamic IP addressing and an always-up connection. If this is your situation and you received the DSL modem from the telephone company, most likely the connection is completed. Open your browser and surf the Web to test the connection.

5. If you did not receive the DSL modem from the telephone company, you might need to call the DSL help desk and give them the MAC address of the modem and have them reset the connection on their end.

If your DSL connection requires a user name and password or static IP addressing, see the next section on how to configure these connections.

CONNECT TO THE INTERNET USING AN ON-DEMAND BROADBAND CONNECTION OR STATIC IP ADDRESSING

Most broadband connections today are always up and use dynamic IP addressing, which are the assumptions that Vista makes when it automatically creates and configures a new network connection. But some business services for cable modem or DSL use static IP addressing, and a less expensive DSL service might use an on-demand connection.

When you connect a cable modem or a DSL modem to a PC and to the ISP, Vista automatically creates an always-up network connection. In the following steps, you will manually create a new connection using a user name and password.

Follow these steps to create an on-demand broadband connection to the Internet:

1. Follow directions given in this chapter to connect the cable modem or DSL modem to the PC and to connect the modem to the wall jack. Vista will automatically create a new connection configured with dynamic IP addressing and an always-up connection.

2. Click **Start**, right-click **Network**, and select **Properties** from the shortcut menu. The Network and Sharing Center window opens. See Figure 5-13.

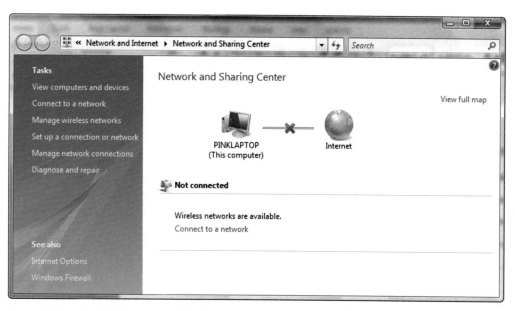

Figure 5-13 Use the Network and Sharing Center to create and manage network connections

3. Click **Set up a connection or network**. On the next screen (see Figure 5-14), select **Connect to the Internet** and click **Next**.

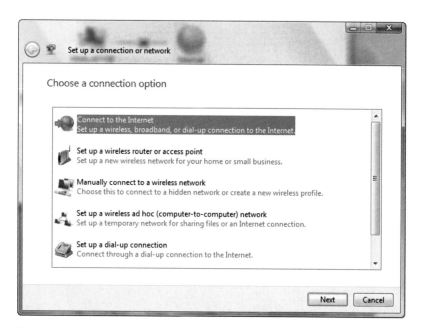

Figure 5-14 Select the type of network you want to set up

📝 **Note**

An on-demand broadband connection that is not always up requires that a user name and password be authenticated at the ISP each time you make the connection. The logon is managed by a protocol called PPPoE (Point-to-Point-Protocol over Ethernet), which is why the connection is sometimes called a PPPoE connection.

4. On the next screen (see Figure 5-15), select **No, create a new connection** and click **Next**.

5. On the next screen shown in Figure 5-16, click **Broadband (PPPoE)**.

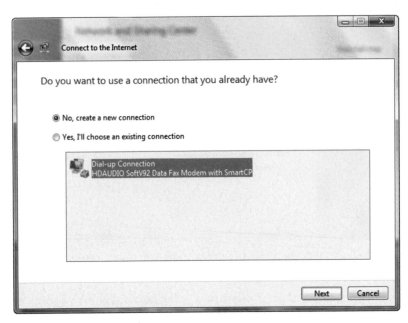

Figure 5-15 Choose the option to create a new network connection

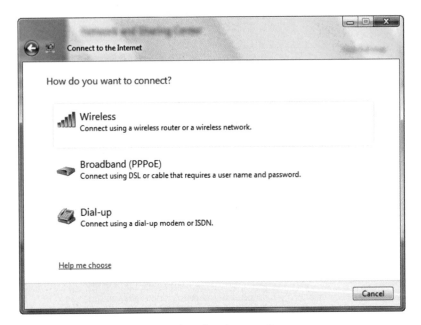

Figure 5-16 Choose to create a broadband connection

6. On the next screen (see Figure 5-17), fill in the information for the User name and Password given to you by your ISP. The Connection name can be any name you like. At the bottom of the screen there is also a check box that will allow other users on this computer to use the connection. Click **Connect**.

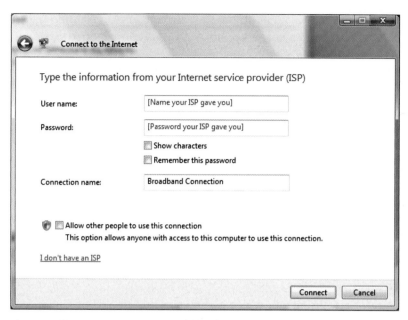

Figure 5-17   Enter the information given to you by your ISP

7. Vista assumes the connection will use dynamic IP addressing and attempts to make the connection. If you are using static IP addressing, the connection will fail and you will see the screen in Figure 5-18. For that situation, click **Set up the connection anyway**. On the next screen, click **Close**.

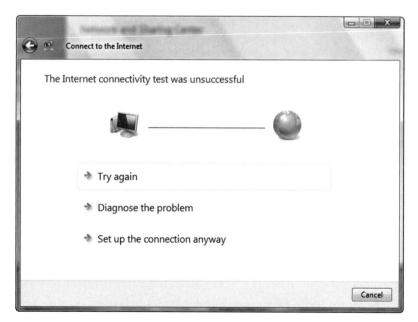

Figure 5-18   The connection failed

Follow these steps to configure any network connection for static IP addressing:

1. In the Network and Sharing Center window, click **Manage network connections**. The Network Connections window appears, showing each network the computer

has set up (see Figure 5-19). Right-click **Broadband Connection** and select **Properties** from the shortcut menu. The Broadband Connection Properties box appears.

Figure 5-19   Use the Network Connections window to manage these connections

2. Select the **Networking** tab, which is shown in the left side of Figure 5-20. On this tab, select **Internet Protocol Version 4 (TCP/IPv4)** and click **Properties**. The properties box appears, as shown on the right side of Figure 5-20.

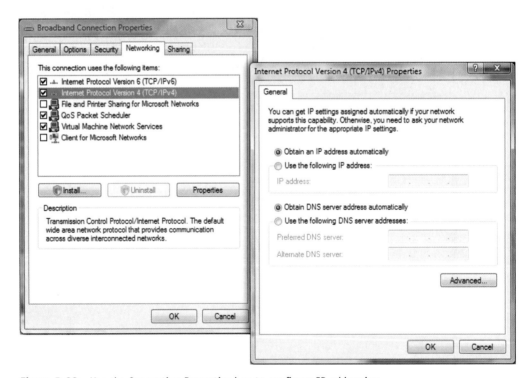

Figure 5-20   Use the Connection Properties box to configure IP addressing

3. For static IP addressing, select **Use the following IP address** and enter the IP address given to you by your ISP. Then enter the IP addresses given to you by your ISP for the first two DNS servers. If your ISP gave you IP addresses for a third or fourth DNS server, click **Advanced** and enter those IP addresses on the DNS tab in the Advanced TCP/IP Settings box.

4. Click **OK** three times to close all three dialog boxes. Then close the Network Connections window.

Because it's so important to make sure your firewall is set properly, before you close the Network and Sharing Center window, in its left pane, click **Windows Firewall** and verify that the firewall is up and configured correctly. Then close the Windows Firewall window and the Network and Sharing Center window.

CONNECT TO THE INTERNET USING A DIAL-UP CONNECTION

Dial-up connections are painfully slow, but many times we still need them when traveling to remote locations, and they're good at home when our broadband connection is down or we just plain want to save money. To connect a computer to the Internet using a dial-up modem, follow these directions:

1. Plug the phone line into the modem port on your computer and into the wall jack.

2. Open the Network and Sharing Center window and click **Set up a connection or network**.

3. On the next window, select **Set up a dial-up connection** and click **Next**.

4. On the next window (see Figure 5-21), enter the phone number to your ISP, your ISP username and password, and the name you decide to give the dial-up connection, such as the name and city of your ISP. If you want other users of this computer to be able to use the connection, check **Allow other people to use this connection**. Then click **Connect**.

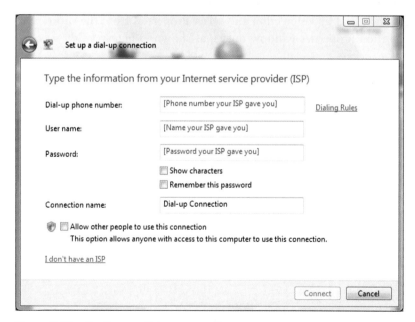

Figure 5-21   Configure a dial-up connection

To use the connection, go to the Network and Sharing Center and click **Connect to a network**. Select the dial-up connection, and click **Connect**. The Connect dialog box appears (see Figure 5-22). Click **Dial**. You will hear the modem dial up the ISP and make the connection.

Figure 5-22   Make a dial-up connection to your ISP

To view or change the configuration for the dial-up connection, do the following:

1. In the Network and Sharing Center, click **Manage network connections**, and then right-click **Dial-up connection** and select **Properties** from the shortcut menu. The connection Properties window opens, as shown in Figure 5-23.

Figure 5-23   Configure an Internet connection using the Properties window of the connection icon

2. Use the tabs on this window to change Internet connection sharing options (Sharing tab), configure TCP/IP (Networking tab), control the way Windows attempts to dial the ISP when the first try fails (Options tab), and change other dialing features.

If the dial-up connection won't work, here are some things you can try:

◢ Is the phone line working? Plug in a regular phone and check for a dial tone. Is the phone cord securely connected to the computer and the wall jack?

◢ Check the Dial-up Connection Properties box for errors. Is the phone number correct? Does the number need to include a 9 to get an outside line? Has a 1 been added in front of the number by mistake? If you need to add a 9, you can put a comma in the field like this "9,4045661200", which causes a slight pause after the 9 is dialed.

◢ Try dialing the number manually from a phone. Do you hear beeps on the other end?

◢ Try another phone number.

◢ When you try to connect, do you hear the number being dialed? If so, the problem is most likely with the phone number, the phone line, or the username and password.

◢ Does the modem work? Check Device Manager for reported errors about the modem. Does the modem work when making a call to another phone number (not your ISP)?

◢ Is TCP/IP configured correctly? Most likely you need to set it to obtain an IP address automatically.

◢ Reboot your PC and try again.

◢ Try removing and reinstalling the dial-up connection. If that doesn't work, try using Device Manager to uninstall the modem and install it again. (Don't do this unless you have the modem drivers on CD or on the hard drive.)

> **Note**
>
> If you want to disable call waiting while you're connected to the Internet, enter *70 in front of the phone number.

After you have successfully connected a single computer to the Internet, you're ready to move on to the next step of connecting a second computer so that the two computers can share an Internet connection.

HOW TO SHARE AN INTERNET CONNECTION

You have just seen how you can connect a single computer to the Internet using a cable modem, DSL, or dial-up connection. Now let's look at how to connect two or more computers in a small network so they can share this one Internet connection. We're first going to build the two setups shown in Figure 5-24. In Figure 5-24a, two computers are connected with a single crossover network cable, and in Figure 5-24b, a switch or hub is used to connect three or more computers in a small network. In both setups, the host computer has the direct connection to the Internet and no router is used.

Windows Vista **Internet Connection Sharing (ICS)** is designed to manage these types of connections. Using ICS, the host computer stands as a gateway between the network and the Internet and ICS manages the gateway. These types of connections, which don't use a router as a gateway, were popular when routers were quite expensive. Now that routers are relatively inexpensive, one computer serving as a gateway to the Internet for other computers is not as popular as it once was.

In the following sections, you'll learn how to physically set up the equipment and then how to configure Windows for the setup.

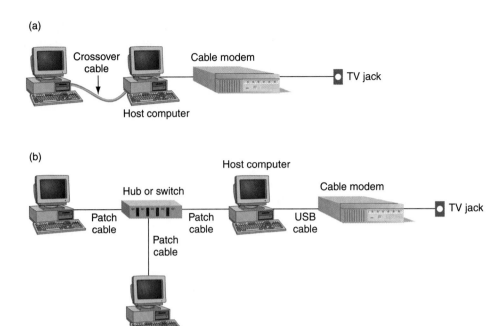

Figure 5-24 Two or more networked computers can share a single Internet connection

TWO COMPUTERS AND A CROSSOVER CABLE

Let's first look at how to set up Figure 5-24a, where a single cable connects two computers. Looking at Figure 5-24a, you can see two cables coming from the host computer. The cable on the right connecting to the cable modem can be a network cable or a USB cable. It would be best if you use a USB cable for this connection so that your one network port on your host computer is free to be used to connect to the other computer. However, if you really want to use a network cable between the host computer and the cable modem, you could install a second network card to provide this port. (If you are not trained to work inside a computer case, have someone who is trained do the installation for you.) You can also use a DSL modem or phone line for this setup.

Now let's turn our attention to connecting the two computers, assuming each has a network port available for the connection. There are two types of network cables: a patch cable and a crossover cable. A patch cable (also called a straight-through cable) is used to connect a computer to a switch or other network device. A crossover cable is used to connect a computer to another computer or connect a switch or hub to another switch or hub. The difference between a patch cable and a crossover cable is the way the transmit and receive lines are wired in the connectors at each end of the cables. A crossover cable has the transmit line and the receive line reversed so that one computer reads off the line that the other computer writes to.

A patch cable and a crossover cable look identical and have identical connectors. The best way you can tell them apart is to look for the label imprinted on the cable, as shown in Figure 5-25. Using a crossover cable, connect each end to the network ports on your two computers.

THREE OR MORE COMPUTERS AND A SWITCH OR HUB

In Figure 5-24b, a hub or switch is used so that you can network three or more computers. Switches are faster than hubs, don't cost much more, and are mostly replacing them. A switch is faster because of the way it manages traffic. A switch sends incoming traffic out to only the one computer for which the data is intended, rather than to all computers it connects to. A

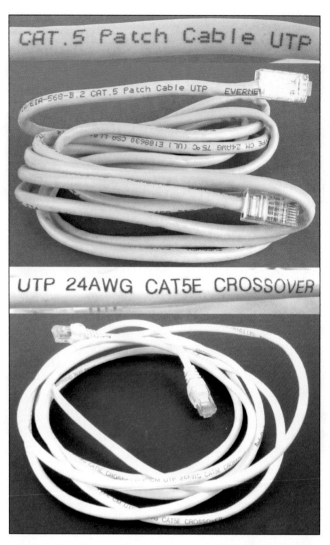

Figure 5-25 Path cables and crossover cables look the same, but are labeled differently

hub, on the other hand, sends incoming traffic out to all ports except the one that sent the message. Figure 5-26 shows a hub and Figure 5-27 shows a switch. Choose and then buy the device based on how many ports you want it to have. Most hubs or switches will also have an uplink port. An uplink port is used to connect the device directly to a router or another switch or hub for more complex networks. Connect the switch or hub to each computer in your network using patch cables.

ASSIGN A UNIQUE NAME TO EACH COMPUTER

Each computer in your network needs to have a unique name. Also, because your computers will be sharing resources, they need to be assigned to the same workgroup. To change the computer name and workgroup name for each computer on your network, do the following:

1. Click **Start**, right-click **Computer**, and select **Properties**. The System window opens showing the current computer name and workgroup (see Figure 5-28). Click **Change settings**.

> **Note**
>
> One way to improve network performance is to replace older hubs on the network with switches.

5

Figure 5-26   A hub is a pass-through device to connect PCs on a network

Figure 5-27   An eight-port switch by Netgear

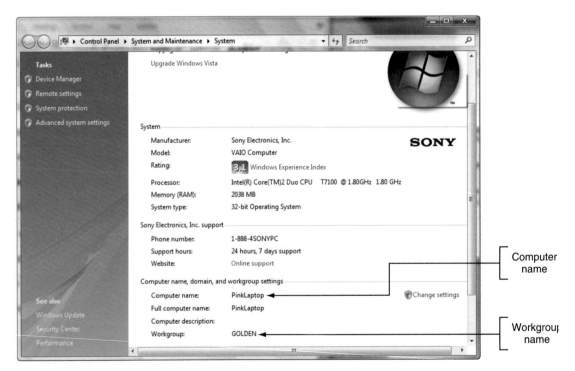

Figure 5-28   The System window shows the computer name and workgroup

2. In the System Properties window, click **Change** (see Figure 5-29) and enter the computer name and workgroup name. Use the same workgroup name for all computers that you intend to share resources. If some computers in your network are using Windows 98/Me, make the computer name no more than 15 characters.

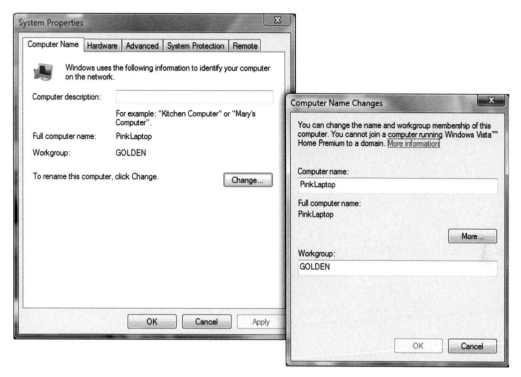

Figure 5-29   Give each computer in your workgroup a unique name

3. Click **OK** to close the Computer Name Changes box, and then click **Apply** in the System Properties box. Click **OK** to close the System Properties box. Reboot your PC.

CONFIGURE WINDOWS TO SHARE AN INTERNET CONNECTION

You're now ready to configure Windows on all computers so that they can share the Internet connection. Do the following:

1. On your gateway computer (the one connected directly to the Internet), open the Network and Sharing Center and click **Manage network connections**. The Network Connections window opens. Right-click the connection that you want to

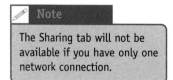

Note

The Sharing tab will not be available if you have only one network connection.

share, select **Properties** from the shortcut menu, and respond to the UAC box. In the Properties box, click the **Sharing** tab (see the left side of Figure 5-30).

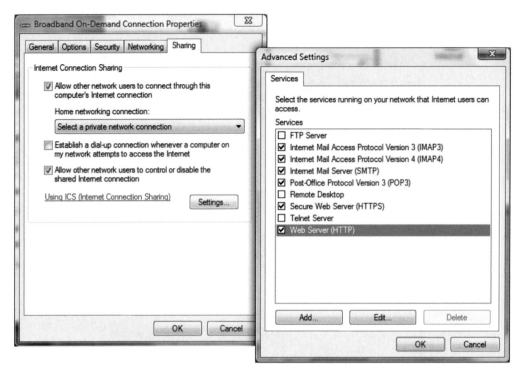

Figure 5-30 Allow others on your network to use this Internet connection

2. Check **Allow other network users to connect through this computer's Internet connection**. You can check the second box if you want to allow users on the network to be able to control the shared connection.

3. Click **Settings** to open the Advanced Settings window shown in the right side of Figure 5-30. Select the services that you want to allow Internet users to access on your network. A dialog box appears; click **OK** to close the box. Do this for each service you want to share.

4. Click **OK** twice to close both boxes.

The disadvantage of this type of shared connection is that the host computer must always be running for another computer on the network to reach the Internet. Another disadvantage is this network is not as secure as it would be if we had a hardware firewall installed. Both these problems can be solved by using a router in our network. How to use a router on a network is covered later in the chapter.

However, before we turn our attention to routers, there's one more step we need to cover. When computers are networked together, it's nice to be able to share files, folders, printers, and other devices among all computers. So let's turn our attention to how to share resources on a network.

CONFIGURING COMPUTERS TO SHARE RESOURCES ON A NETWORK

In this section, you'll learn how to share folders, files, applications, printers, and even an entire hard drive. Remember that computers configured to share resources should each have a unique name on the network and all belong to the same workgroup.

Now let's get started with sharing resources with others in your workgroup.

SHARING FILES, FOLDERS, AND APPLICATIONS

When you open the Network window (see Figure 5-31), you can drill down to see shared files, folders, and printers on your network. You can copy files from one computer to another, use shared applications installed on one computer from another computer, and share printers. Also notice in the left pane of Figure 5-31, the Public folder, which is located at \Users\Public. Microsoft encourages you to put files in this Public folder that will be shared on the network so that your private user data folders are better protected.

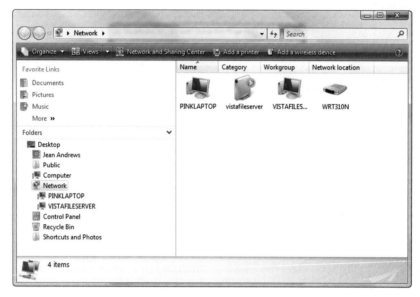

Figure 5-31 View and access shared resources on the network using the Network window in Windows Vista

Before you can share resources on a network, you need to verify that network sharing options are enabled. Do the following:

1. Open the Network and Sharing Center (see Figure 5-32) and verify the following:

   ◢ **File sharing** is turned on.
   ◢ If you want to share the Public folder on the network, turn on **Public folder sharing**.
   ◢ If you want the added protection of requiring that all users on the network must have a valid user account and password on this computer, turn on **Password protected sharing**.
   ◢ If you want to share a printer connected to this PC with others on the network, turn on **Printer sharing**.

2. In the Network and Sharing Center, click **Manage network connections**. In the Network Connections window, right-click the network connection, select **Properties** from the shortcut menu, and respond to the UAC box. In the Properties dialog box, verify that **File and Printer Sharing for Microsoft Networks** is checked.

5

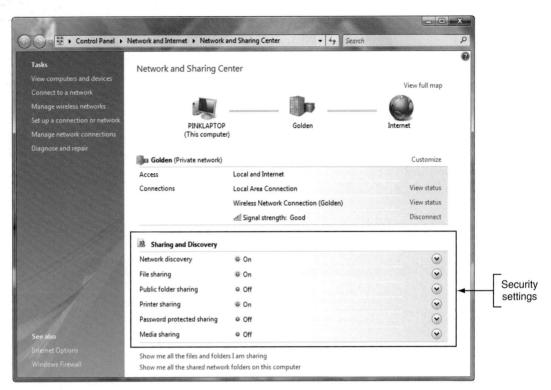

Figure 5-32 Use the Network and Sharing Center window to verify the computer is set to share resources

You are now ready to share folders across the network. Follow these steps:

1. Using Windows Explorer, choose a folder to share and right-click it. Select **Share** on the shortcut menu. The File Sharing window opens as shown in Figure 5-33.

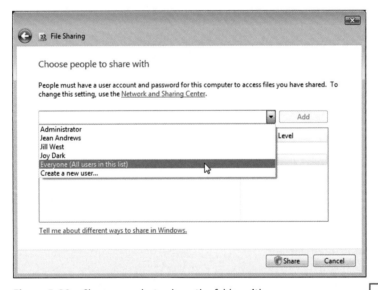

Figure 5-33 Choose people to share the folder with

2. To see a list of users for this computer, click the down arrow in the drop-down box near the top of the window. To allow all users in the list access to the folder, select **Everyone** (**All users in this list**) and click **Add**. You also have the option to select individual users.

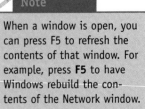

Note

When a window is open, you can press F5 to refresh the contents of that window. For example, press **F5** to have Windows rebuild the contents of the Network window.

3. When a user is added to the list, the user is given the Reader permission (see Figure 5-34). To see other permission levels, click the down arrow beside **Reader** and select the level you want. The levels are described in Table 5-1.

4. To close the File Sharing box, click **Share** and respond to the UAC box. There will now be a two friends icon on the folder, indicated that it is being shared.

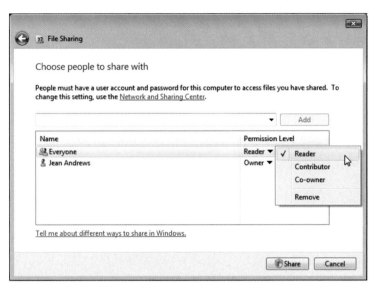

Figure 5-34 Change the permission level of a user

Permission Level	Description
Reader	Can read but not write to the contents of the folder and its subfolders
Contributor	Can write files and read existing files but cannot change existing files put there by others.
Co-owner	Has full control over the folder in the same way the owner does, but is not identified as the folder owner.

Table 5-1 Permission levels for files and folders in Windows Vista

5

SHARING A PRINTER

When you turn on Printer sharing in the Network and Sharing Center window, all printers connected to this computer are automatically shared. If you want to share one printer but not another, you can turn on Printer sharing and then turn off sharing a specific printer. To change the sharing status of a specific printer, in the Control Panel under Hardware and Sound, click **Printer**. Right-click the printer you want to share, and select **Sharing** from the shortcut menu. The printer's Properties dialog box opens, as shown in Figure 5-35. If the box, Share this printer, is grayed out, the box will contain a button named Change sharing options. Click the button and respond to the UAC box. You can then uncheck **Share this printer**. Click **OK** to close the printer Properties box.

 Note

Applications can also be shared with others in the workgroup. If you share a folder that has a program file in it, a user on another PC can double-click the program file in the Network window and execute it remotely on his or her desktop. This is a handy way for several users to share an application that is installed on a single PC. Before sharing an application, first verify that the copyright license you own for the application gives rights for multiple user access. In most situations, you must pay extra for these rights.

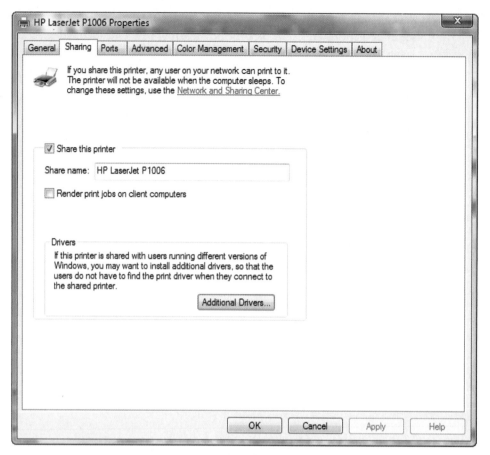

Figure 5-35   Change the sharing status for a specific printer

MAPPING A NETWORK DRIVE

A network drive map is one of the most powerful and versatile methods of communicating over a network. By using Network File System (NFS) client/server software, the network drive map makes one PC (the client) appear to have a new hard drive, such as drive E, that is really hard drive space on another host computer (the server). To set up a network drive, follow these steps:

1. On the host computer, share the drive or folder on a drive to which you want others to have access.

2. On the remote computer that will use the network drive, click **Start**, right-click **Computer**, and select **Map Network Drive**.

3. The Map Network Drive dialog box appears, as shown in Figure 5-36. Select a drive letter from the drop-down list.

4. Click **Browse** and locate the shared folder or drive on the host computer. Click **OK** to close the Browse For Folder dialog box. Alternately, you can type the host computer name and shared folder name in the Folder box like this: **\\Taylor-PC\Budget**, where *Taylor-PC* is the computer name and *Budget* is the name of the shared folder. This method might work when the Browse method fails to find the shared resource.

> **Note**
>
> If a network drive does not work, go to the Network window, and verify that the network connection is working properly.

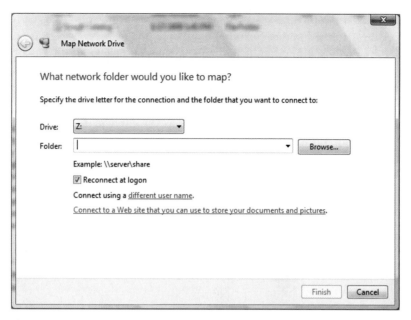

Figure 5-36 Mapping a network drive to a host computer

5. Click **Finish** to map the drive. The folder on the host computer now appears as one more drive in Windows Explorer on your computer.

WHAT IF YOU DON'T WANT TO SHARE?

If you're concerned about others on your network getting to information on your computer, you can do some things to make sure your PC is secure. Your selection from the list below depends on the degree of security you need:

▲ *Action 1: Assign a public profile to the network connection.* Using the Network and Sharing Center window, change the profile of the network to public. Others on the network will not be able to see your computer or any of its resources.

▲ *Action 2: Disable File sharing.* In the Network and Sharing Center window, when File sharing is not checked, others cannot see your files and folders even though they can use a shared printer if printer sharing is turned on.

▲ *Action 3: Share a folder with some but not others.* To control which users have access to a folder, using the Properties box for that folder, select specific users rather than allow sharing for everyone.

▲ *Action 4: Hide a shared folder.* If you want to share a folder, but don't want others to see the shared folder in their Network window, add a $ to the end of the folder name. Others on the network can access the folder only when they know its name. For example, if you name a shared folder MyPrivateFolder$, in order to access the folder a user must enter \\*Computername*\MyPrivateFolder$ in the Start Search dialog box on the remote computer.

USING A ROUTER ON YOUR NETWORK

So far in the chapter, you've seen how one computer can connect to the Internet using a dial-up or broadband connection and also how this host computer can share that connection with others on a LAN. Two major disadvantages of this setup are that the host computer must always be turned on for others on the network to reach the Internet and the fact that security for your network is not as strong as it could be if you were to use a hardware firewall. Also, access to the Internet for other computers might be slow because of the bottleneck caused by the host computer. Installing a router can help solve all these problems.

Recall from the last chapter that a router is a device that manages traffic between two networks. In Figure 5-37, you can see how a router, instead of the host computer that you learned about earlier in the chapter, stands between the ISP network and the local network. The router takes the place of the host computer as the gateway to the Internet and also serves as a hardware firewall to protect your network. Note in the figure that computers can connect to the router directly or by way of one or more switches.

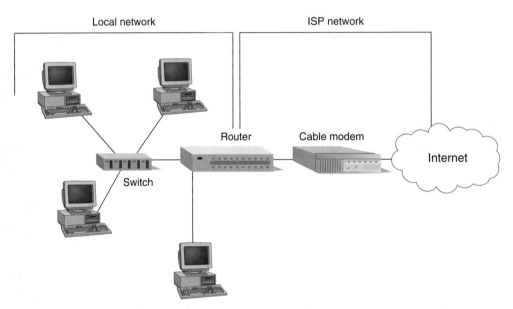

Figure 5-37 A router stands between a local network and the Internet and manages traffic between them

ADVANTAGES OF USING A ROUTER

The advantages of using a router rather than a host computer are:

▲ *Advantage 1*: The host computer will not be a bottleneck to slow down performance for other computers using the Internet.
▲ *Advantage 2*: Internet access is not dependent on the host computer being up and running.
▲ *Advantage 3*: The router can also serve as a hardware firewall device, which provides better protection than a software firewall. In addition, a router can limit access to the Internet. This added security provided by a router is probably the most important reason to use a router for an Internet connection.
▲ *Advantage 4*: The router can provide additional features—such as a DHCP server, switch, or wireless access point—not available on a host computer.

Three companies that make routers suitable for small networks are D-Link (*www.dlink.com*), Linksys (*www.linksys.com*), and NetGear (*www.netgear.com*). An example of a multifunction router is the Wireless-N Gigabit Router by Linksys shown in

Figure 5-38 and Figure 5-39. It has one port for the broadband modem and four ports for computers on the network. The router is also an 802.11b/g/n wireless access point having multiple antennae to increase speed and range using Multiple In, Multiple Out (MIMO) technology. The antennae are built in.

Figure 5-38 The Wireless-N Gigabit router by Linksys has built-in wireless antennae and can be used with a DSL or cable modem Internet connection

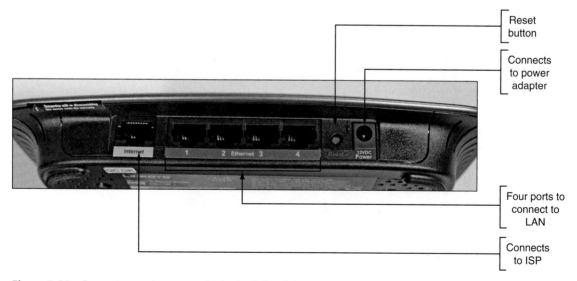

Figure 5-39 Connectors and ports on the back of the Linksys router

> **Note**
>
> A DHCP (Dynamic Host Configuration Protocol) server serves up IP addresses to computers on the network each time a computer attempts to initiate a connection to the network and requests an IP address. With a DHCP server on the network, computers can use dynamic IP addressing so that you don't have to assign and keep up with unique IP addresses for each computer.

The router shown in Figure 5-38 is typical of many brands and models of routers used in a small office or small home network to manage the Internet connection. This router is several devices in one:

▲ *Function 1*: As a router, it stands between the ISP network and the local network, routing traffic between the two networks.

▲ *Function 2*: As a switch, it manages four network ports that can be connected to four computers or to a switch or hub that connects to more than one computer.

▲ *Function 3*: As a proxy server, all computers on the network route their Internet requests through this proxy server, which stands between the network and the Internet using NAT.

▲ *Function 4*: As a DHCP server, all computers can receive their IP address from this server.

▲ *Function 5*: As a wireless access point, a computer can connect to the network using a wireless device. This wireless connection can be secured using four different wireless security features.

▲ *Function 6*: As a firewall, unwanted traffic initiated from the Internet can be blocked.

▲ *Function 7*: As an Internet access restriction device, the router can be set so that Internet access is limited.

> **Note**
>
> A proxy server adds protection to a network because it stands in proxy for other computers on the network when they want to communicate with computers on the Internet or computers at the ISP (such as DNS servers or mail servers). The proxy server presents its own IP address to computers outside the LAN and does not allow these outside computers to know the IP addresses of computers inside the network. This substitution of IP addresses is done using the Network Address Translation (NAT) protocol.

In the small office setting pictured in Figure 5-40, a router connects to four network jacks that are wired in the walls to four other jacks in the building. Two of these remote jacks have switches connected that accommodate two or more computers.

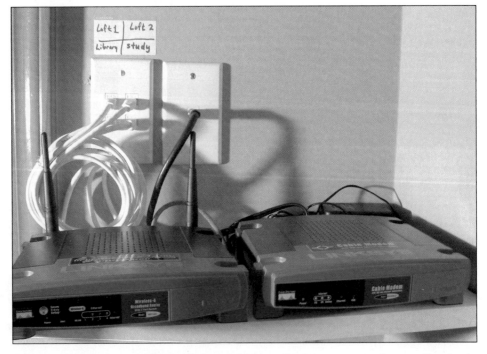

Figure 5-40 A router and cable modem are used to provide Internet access for a small network

Note

The speed of a network depends on the speed of each device on the network. Routers, hubs, switches, and network adapters currently run at three speeds: Gigabit Ethernet (1,000 Mbps or 1 Gbps), Fast Ethernet (100 Mbps), or Ethernet (10 Mbps). If you want your network to run at the fastest speed, make sure all your devices are rated for Gigabit Ethernet. Very few networks today use 10 Mbps Ethernet, and Gigabit Ethernet is slowly replacing Fast Ethernet as the most popular standard.

INSTALLING AND CONFIGURING A ROUTER

To install the router, if your router comes with a setup CD, run the setup program on one of your computers on the network (it doesn't matter which one). Follow the instructions on the setup screen to disconnect the cable or DSL modem from your host computer and connect it to the router. Next, connect the computers on your network to your router. A computer can connect directly to a network port on the router, or you can connect a switch or hub to the router. Plug in the router and turn it on.

You'll be required to sign in to the utility using a default password. The first thing you want to do is reset this password so that others cannot change your router setup.

The setup program will take you through the process of configuring the router. After you've configured the router, you might have to turn the cable or DSL modem off and back on so that it correctly syncs up with the router. If you don't get immediate connectivity to the Internet on all PCs, try rebooting each PC. More about how to fix networking problems is covered at the end of this chapter.

Now let's look at how this Linksys router is configured, which is typical of what you might see for several brands and models of small office or home office routers. Firmware on the router (which can be flashed for updates) contains a configuration program that you access using a Web browser from anywhere on the network. In your browser address box, enter the IP

Caution

Changing the router password is especially important if the router is a wireless router. Unless you have disabled or secured the wireless access point, others outside your building can use your wireless network and might bog down your Internet connection. If they guess the default password to the router, they can change the password to hijack your router. Also, your wireless network can be used for criminal activity. When you first install a router, before you do anything else, change your router password and disable the wireless network until you have time to setup and test the wireless security.

address of the router (for our router, it's 192.168.1.1) and press **Enter**. The main Setup window appears, as shown in Figure 5-41. For most situations, the default settings on this and other screens should work without any changes.

Using this setup screen, under Internet Setup, you can change the host name and domain name if they are given to you by your ISP, or leave them blank, which most often is the case. Under Network Setup, you can configure the DHCP server. Notice in the figure that the router can serve up to 50 leased IP addresses beginning with IP address 192.168.1.100.

5

You can also disable the DHCP server if you want to use static IP addressing on your network or you already have another DHCP server on the network.

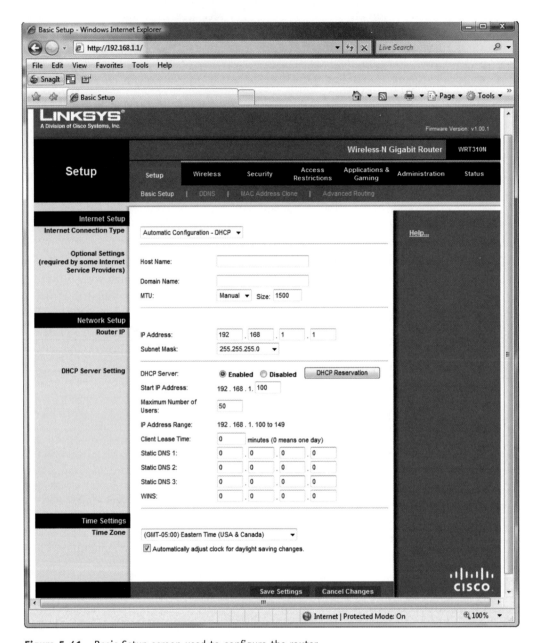

Figure 5-41 Basic Setup screen used to configure the router

CONFIGURE EACH PC FOR DYNAMIC IP ADDRESSING

Configure each PC on your network to use dynamic IP addressing. At each computer, do the following:

1. In the Network and Sharing Center window, click Manage network connections. In the Network Connections window, right-click the **Local Area Connection** icon and select **Properties**. The properties window opens. Select **Internet Protocol Version 4 (TCP/IPv4)** and click **Properties**. Refer to Figure 5-20, shown earlier in the chapter.

2. Select **Obtain an IP address automatically** and **Obtain DNS server address automatically**. Click **OK** to close each window.

HOW TO SECURE A SMALL NETWORK

The Internet is a nasty and dangerous place infested with hackers, viruses, worms, and thieves. Knowing how to protect a single PC or a LAN is an essential skill for someone responsible for this equipment. Recall that the three most important things you can do to protect a single computer or network are to:

▲ Use a software or hardware firewall.
▲ Run antivirus software and keep it current.
▲ Keep Windows updates current so that security patches are installed as soon as they are available.

In earlier chapters, you learned how to use AV software, how to keep Windows updated, and how to use Windows Firewall. In this section, you will learn about hardware firewalls, how to set them for maximum security, and how to let down your shields so that if you want to allow someone on the Internet to get to your network, you can.

The best firewall solution is a hardware firewall that stands between a LAN and the Internet (see Figure 5-42). For most home and small-office LANs, a router is used as a hardware firewall. Note that some DSL devices are also routers and include embedded firewall firmware.

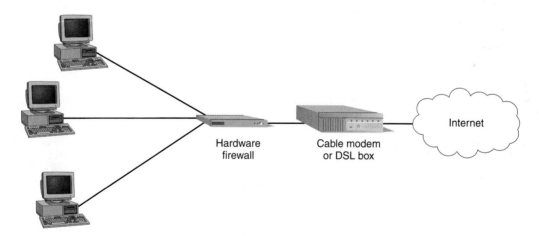

Figure 5-42 A hardware firewall protects the local network by standing between it and the Internet

A hardware or software firewall can function in several ways:

▲ *Function 1*: Firewalls can filter data packets, examining the destination IP address or source IP address or the type of protocol used (for example, TCP or UDP).
▲ *Function 2*: Firewalls can filter ports so that outside clients cannot communicate with inside services listening at these ports. Certain ports can be opened, for example, when your network has a Web server and you want Internet users to be able to access it.

> **Note**
>
> TCP is the primary TCP/IP protocol used by Internet applications such as Web servers, browsers, and e-mail servers and clients for communication. These types of applications use the TCP protocol because TCP guarantees data delivery. TCP sends a delivery confirmation message back to the sender for each data transmission. If the sender does not receive the confirmation, the data is resent. UDP, on the other hand, does not guarantee data delivery because it sends the data without confirmation. UDP is used by applications such as streaming video where speed is more important than accuracy. UDP is also used as a utility protocol to manage network traffic. TCP is like a guaranteed delivery service and UDP is more like a best-effort delivery service and a traffic cop.

▲ *Function 3*: Firewalls can block certain activity that is initiated from inside the network—such as preventing users inside the firewall from using applications like FTP over the Internet.

▲ *Function 4*: Some firewalls can filter information such as Web content inappropriate for children or employees, and can limit the use of the Internet to certain days or times of day.

As an example of configuring a hardware firewall, let's see how the Linksys router's firewall can be configured to protect the network. You can use this information as a guide to configuring another router because, although the exact steps might vary, the basic principles will be the same.

To configure security on the firewall, using the firmware utility shown in Figure 5-41, click the **Security** link. The window shown in Figure 5-43 appears. The most important setting on this window is to enable SPI Firewall Protection. SPI (stateful packet inspection) examines each data packet and rejects those unsolicited by the local network. Enabling this feature prevents your network from being detected or accessed from others on the Internet without an invitation.

Figure 5-43 Configure the router's firewall to prevent others on the Internet from seeing or accessing your network

You can set policies to determine how and when users on your network can access the Internet. To do that, click **Access Restrictions**. The window shown in Figure 5-44 appears, allowing you to set policies about the day and time of Internet access, the services on the Internet that can be used, and the URLs and keywords that are not allowed.

Figure 5-44 Configure the router's firewall to limit Internet access from within the network

Too much security is not always a good thing. There are legitimate times you want to be able to access computers on your network from somewhere on the Internet, such as when you're hosting an Internet game or a Web site. To allow communication initiated from the Internet past your firewall, use the Applications & Gaming tab shown in Figure 5-45 to specify the application you are using, the ports that you want open, and the IP address of the computer on your network that you want the communication routed to. To make this port forwarding work, the computer on your network must have a static IP address so that the router knows where to send the communication. You must also lease a static IP address from your ISP so that people on the Internet can find you. Most ISPs will provide you a static IP address for an additional monthly fee.

Caution

Remember that you should always change the password to your router's setup utility. Default passwords for routers are easily obtained on the Web or in the product documentation. This is especially important for wireless routers.

5

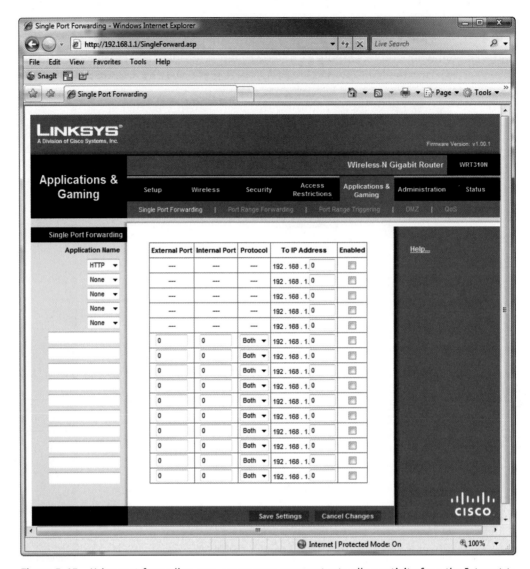

Figure 5-45 Using port forwarding, you can program your router to allow activity from the Internet to initiate a session with a computer inside the network on a certain port using a static IP address

Be aware that when you use port forwarding, your network is more vulnerable because you are allowing external users directly into your private network. For better security, turn on port forwarding only when you know it's being used. In addition, make sure the computer that is receiving outside communication is using all the appropriate security measures discussed in Chapter 4. In fact, to be on the safe side, recognize that every computer on your network is more vulnerable and be careful to secure each one.

USING AND SETTING UP WIRELESS NETWORKS

Wireless LANs are becoming more and more popular, and if a notebook computer doesn't come equipped with a wireless adapter, many people want to install one so they can surf the Web from public hotspots. This section is all about how to use a public wireless network. When using wireless LANs, know that they tend to be slower than wired networks, especially when they are busy. You also need to be aware that wireless LANs don't always provide good security, and public wireless LANs are the least secure of all.

The most popular wireless technology is called WiFi, although its official name is 802.11. Four grades of WiFi are in use: 802.11a, 802.11b, 802.11g, and 802.11n. The latest, 802.11n, is the fastest and is backward compatible with 802.11b and 802.11g. These standards use a frequency range of 2.4 GHz in the radio band and have a range of about 100 meters. 802.11b/g/n has the disadvantage that many cordless phones use the 2.4-GHz frequency range and might cause network interference. 802.11n uses multiple antennas supporting multiple data streams to increase overall bandwidth and range. 802.11n currently runs at up to 140 Mbps and higher throughput is expected in the future; 802.11g runs at up to 54 Mbps, and 802.11b runs at up to 11Mbps. To know that a wireless device supports the latest standards, look for 802.11b/g/n on the package. Also know that some manufacturers of wireless devices are able to improve on the 802.11 standards when the wireless devices in the wireless LAN are all made by the same manufacturer and all use the same bonding techniques.

Wireless connections using 802.11b/g/n can be made with a variety of devices, four of them shown in Figure 5-46. Notice in the figure the different types of antennae.

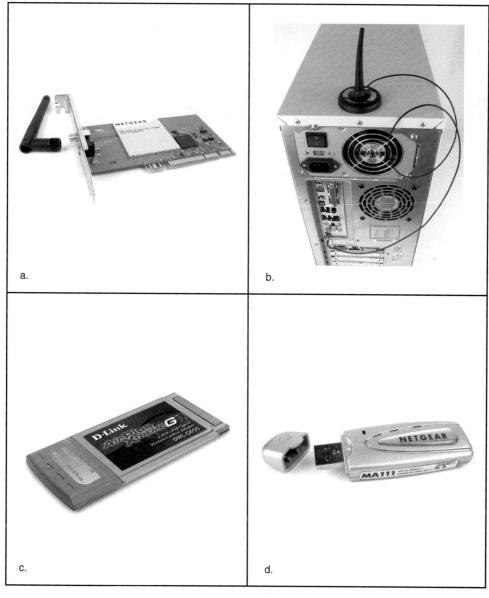

a.

b.

c.

d.

Figure 5-46 Four different types of wireless network cards: (a) wireless NIC that fits in a PCI slot; (b) onboard wireless NIC with an antenna that can be moved about; (c) PC Card wireless NIC with embedded antenna; and (d) wireless NIC that uses a USB port on a desktop or notebook computer

5

Wireless devices can communicate directly, such as from one PC to another (called Ad Hoc mode), or they can connect to a LAN by way of a wireless **access point (AP)**, which is called infrastructure mode. Access points, such as the Linksys router shown earlier in the chapter in Figure 5-38, are placed so that client computers can access at least one access point from anywhere in the covered area. When computers use an access point, they communicate through the access point instead of communicating directly. Later in the chapter, you'll learn how to set up a wireless access point. But first, let's see how to connect to a public hotspot.

HOW TO CONNECT A NOTEBOOK COMPUTER TO A WIRELESS PUBLIC HOTSPOT

When using a public wireless hotspot, know that whatever you send over the network might be read by others. Also, unless you protect your computer by using strong firewall settings, your computer might get hacked. Here are the steps to connect to a public hotspot for a laptop that has embedded wireless ability and how to protect your computer on that network:

1. Turn on your wireless device. For some laptops, that's done by a switch on the keyboard (see Figure 5-47) or on the side of the laptop.

Figure 5-47   Turn on the wireless switch on your laptop

2. Using your mouse, hover over or double-click the network icon in your notification area. Vista reports that wireless networks are available (see Figure 5-48).

Figure 5-48   Windows reports that wireless networks are available

3. Click **Connect to a network**. A list of available networks appears (see Figure 5-49).

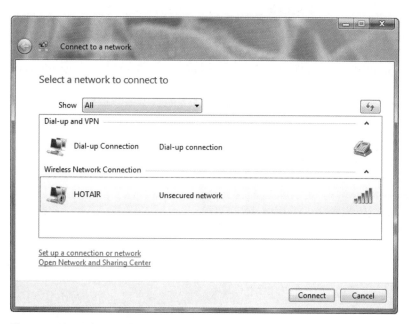

Figure 5-49   Select a wireless network

4. If you select an unsecured network, Vista warns you about sending information over it. Click **Connect Anyway**.

5. Vista reports the connection is made using the window in Figure 5-50. If you are comfortable with Vista automatically connecting to this network in the future, check **Save this network**. Close the window. If you hover your mouse pointer over the

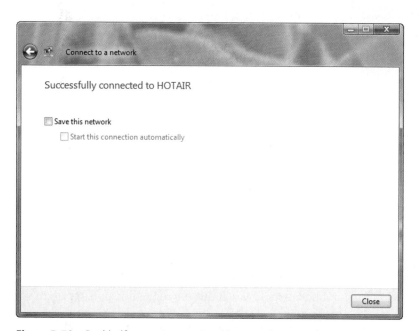

Figure 5-50   Decide if you want to save this network connection

5

network icon in the notification area or double-click it, you can see the network you are connected to (see Figure 5-51).

6. To verify firewall settings and check for errors, open the Network and Sharing Center window (see Figure 5-52). Verify that Vista has configured the network as a public network and that Sharing and Discovery settings are all turned off. In the figure, you can see there is a problem with the Internet connection from the HOTAIR network to the Internet.

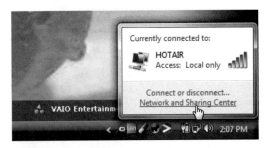

Figure 5-51 Find out the network you are connected to

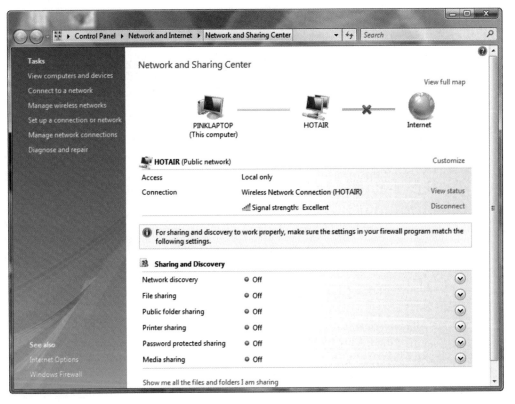

Figure 5-52 Verify that your connection is secure

7. Open your browser to test the connection. For some hotspots, a homepage appears and you must enter a code or agree to the terms of use (see Figure 5-53).

When selecting a public hotspot, watch out for rogue hotspots trying to spoof you. For example, suppose you sit down at a coffee shop with your laptop to surf the Web. When you try to connect to the free hotspot provided by the coffee shop, you see two unsecured hotspots available. One is named JoesCoffeeShop and the other is named FreeInternet. Most likely the first one is provided by the coffee shop and is the one to choose. However, if

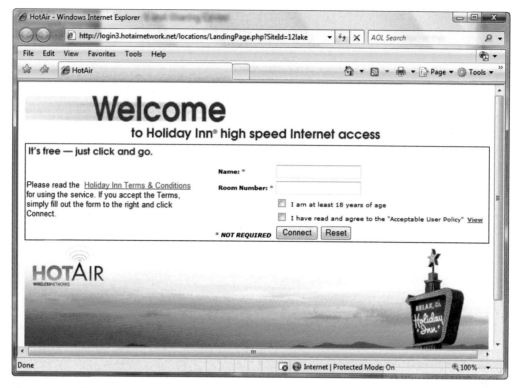

Figure 5-53 This hotspot requires you agree to the terms of use

you're not sure, ask an employee. The danger in connecting to unknown hotspots is that malware and hackers might be waiting for unsecured computers to connect.

Another precaution you can take to protect data you send over a public hotspot is to encrypt your e-mail transmissions. To do that, you can download encryption software and install it into your e-mail client software. Most encryption software products use a method called Public Key Encryption, which is explained in Figure 5-54. Before you can send an encrypted message to someone, that person must first make available to you her public key. Note, however, that only she has the private key that is used to decrypt the message. Encryption software must be installed on both the sender's and receiver's e-mail client. One popular encryption software product is PGP (stands for Pretty Good Privacy) by PGP Corporation (*na.store.pgp.com/desktop_email.html*).

HOW TO CONNECT TO A PRIVATE WIRELESS NETWORK

When connecting to a private and secured wireless access point, you must provide the information that proves you have the right to use the network. If the network is protected with an encryption key, when you first attempt to connect, a screen similar to that in Figure 5-55 appears so that you can enter the key. It is also possible that a private and secured wireless access point has been configured for MAC address filtering in order to control which wireless adapters can use the access point. Check with the network administrator to determine if this is the case; if necessary, give the administrator the adapter's MAC address to be entered into a table of acceptable MAC addresses.

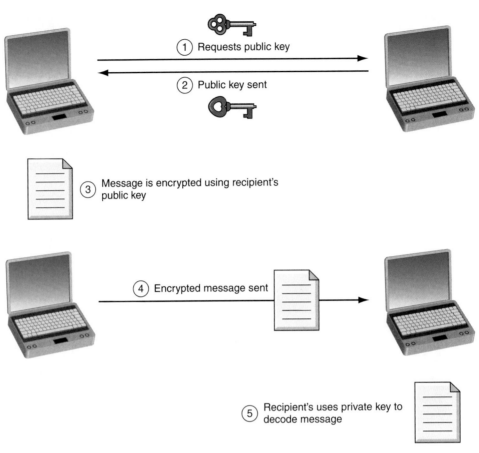

Figure 5-54 Public key encryption uses two keys: the recipient's public key to encrypt the message and her private key to decrypt it

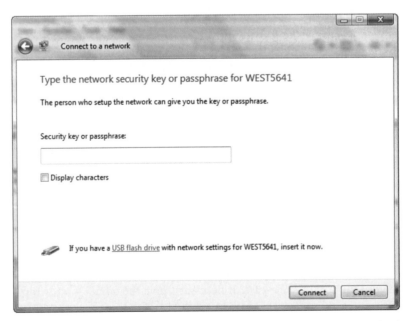

Figure 5-55 To use a secured wireless network, you must know the encryption key

To know the MAC address of your wireless adapter, for an external adapter, you can look on the back of the adapter itself (see Figure 5-56) or in the adapter documentation. Also, if the adapter is installed on your computer, you can open a command prompt window and enter the command **ipconfig /all**, which displays your TCP/IP configuration for all network connections. The MAC address is called the Physical Address in the display (see Figure 5-57).

Figure 5-56 The MAC address is printed on the back of this USB wireless adapter

Figure 5-57 Use the ipconfig /all command to display TCP/IP configuration data

HOW TO SET UP YOUR OWN WIRELESS NETWORK

Setting up your own wireless network involves buying a wireless access point and configuring it and your wireless computers for communication. The key to successful wireless networking is good security. This section first looks at what you need to know about securing a wireless network and then shows how to choose the equipment you'll need and how to set up a wireless network.

SECURITY ON A WIRELESS LAN

Wireless LANs are so convenient for us at work and at home, but the downside of having a wireless network is that if we don't have the proper security in place, anyone with a wireless computer within range of your access point can use the network—and, if they know how, can intercept and read all the data sent across the network. They might even be able to hack into our computers by using our own wireless network against us. For all these reasons, it's terribly important to secure your wireless network.

Securing a wireless network is generally done in four ways:

▲ *Method 1: Disable SSID broadcasting*—Normally, the name of the access point (called the SSID) is broadcast so that anyone with a wireless computer can see the name and use the network. If you hide the SSID, a computer can see the wireless network, but can't use it unless the SSID is entered in the wireless adapter configuration. Disabling SSID broadcasting is normally not used when data encryption is used.

▲ *Method 2: Filter MAC addresses*—A wireless access point can filter the MAC addresses of wireless NICs that are allowed to use the access point. This type of security prevents uninvited guests from using the wireless LAN, but does not prevent others from receiving data in the air. Also, knowledgeable users can hack through MAC address filtering, and it is, therefore, considered a weak security measure.

▲ *Method 3: Data encryption*—Data sent over a wireless connection can be encrypted. The three main protocols for encryption for 802.11 wireless networks are WEP (Wired Equivalent Privacy), WPA (WiFi Protected Access), and WPA2 (WiFi Protected Access 2). With any of these protocols, data is encrypted using a firmware program on the wireless device and is only encrypted while the data is wireless; the data is decrypted before placing it on the wired network. With WEP encryption, data is encrypted using either 64-bit or 128-bit encryption keys. (Because the user can configure only 40 bits of the 64 bits, 64-bit WEP encryption is sometimes called 40-bit WEP encryption.) Because the key used for encryption is static (it doesn't change), a hacker who spends enough time examining data packets can eventually find enough patterns in the coding to decrypt the code and read WEP-encrypted data. WPA encryption, also called TKIP (Temporal Key Integrity Protocol) encryption, is stronger than WEP and was designed to replace it. With WPA encryption, encryption keys are changed at set intervals. The latest and best wireless encryption standard is WPA2, also called the 802.11i standard or AES (Advanced Encryption Standard). When buying wireless devices, be sure the encryption methods used are compatible!

▲ *Method 4: Virtual private network (VPN)*—A VPN requires a password for entrance and encrypts data over both wired and wireless networks. The basic difference between WEP or WPA encryption and VPN encryption is that VPN encryption applies from the user's PC all the way to the VPN gateway on a corporate network. Data stays encrypted the entire trip over wired or wireless networks or the Internet. A VPN uses a technique called tunneling, in which a packet of data is encrypted as shown in Figure 5-58. The encryption methods used by VPN are stronger than WEP or WPA and are the preferred method when transmitting sensitive data over a wireless connection. VPNs are set up at the corporate level and are beyond the scope of this chapter.

CHOOSING A WIRELESS ACCESS POINT

When selecting a wireless access point, look for the ability to use all the security measures listed in the previous section. Also, be sure the access point supports 802.11 g/n and possibly 802.11b if you plan to use 802.11b legacy wireless adapters. And, as always, before you buy, search the Internet to read hardware reviews about the device. Only buy a

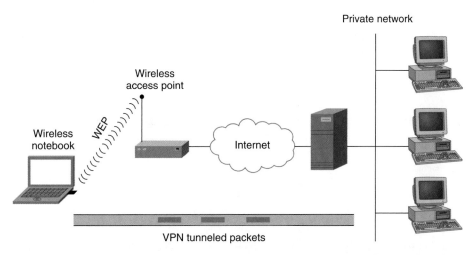

Figure 5-58 With tunneling, packets can travel over a wireless LAN and the Internet in a virtual private network (VPN), but WEP or WPA applies only to the wireless connection

device that consistently gets good reviews. If you're also in need of a wireless adapter to use for the computers that will use your wireless networks, for best results, try to find adapters and an access point made by the same manufacturer.

Some desktop computers come equipped with a wireless adapter, such as the one in Figure 5-46b, that can be configured as a client on a wireless network or as the access point of a wireless network. A wireless access point can also be a stand-alone device such as the one in Figure 5-59 by D-Link. The device supports 802.11g/n and contains a four-port Gigabit switch to connect up to four devices to your wireless network. An access point can also serve other purposes, such as the Linksys multifunctional router shown earlier in Figure 5-38.

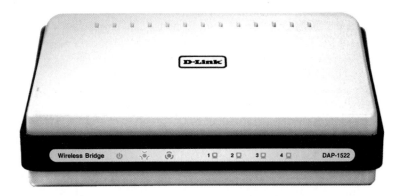

Figure 5-59 Xtreme N Duo Wireless Bridge/Access Point by D-Link

CONFIGURE AND TEST YOUR WIRELESS NETWORK

To install a stand-alone access point, position it in the center of where you want your hotspot and plug it in. It will have a network or USB cable that you can connect to your wired network or to a computer so that you can configure the access point. Run the setup CD that comes with the access point and look for these items on the menus to configure it:

1. Look for a way to select the channel the access point will use, the ability to change the SSID of the access point, and the ability to disable SSID broadcasting.

Figure 5-60 shows these three settings for one Linksys access point. Figure 5-61 shows how a wireless computer sees a wireless access point that is not broadcasting its SSID. This computer would not be able to use this access point until you entered the SSID in the configuration window shown in Figure 5-62.

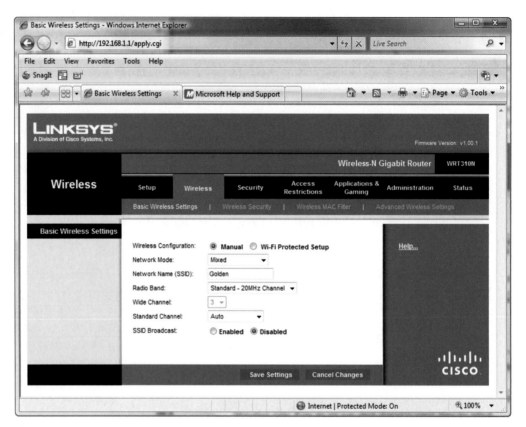

Figure 5-60 Look for the ability of the access point to disable SSID broadcasting

Figure 5-61 A wireless computer shows it has located three access points, but one is not broadcasting its SSID

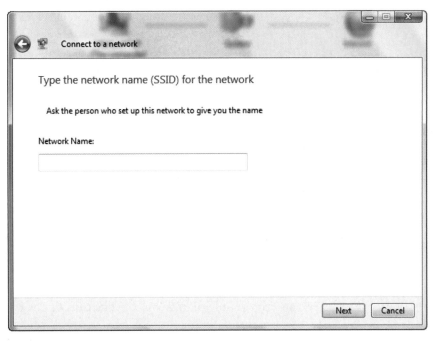

Figure 5-62 Enter the SSID of a wireless network that is not broadcasting its SSID

2. To configure data encryption on your access point, look for a wireless security screen similar to the one in Figure 5-63 where you can choose between several WEP, WPA, or RADIUS encryption methods. (RADIUS stands for Remote Authentication Dial-In User

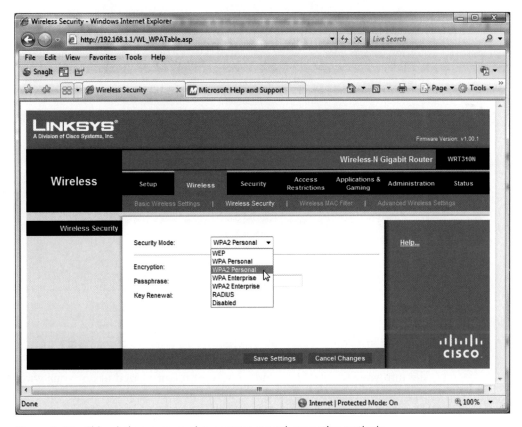

Figure 5-63 This wireless access point supports several encryption methods

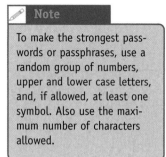

Note

To make the strongest passwords or passphrases, use a random group of numbers, upper and lower case letters, and, if allowed, at least one symbol. Also use the maximum number of characters allowed.

Service and uses an authentication server to control access.) WPA2 Personal is the one to choose unless one of your wireless adapters doesn't support it. Enter the passphrase for encryption on this same access point screen. When you connect a PC to this network, you'll need to enter the same passphrase (see Figure 5-50 earlier in the chapter).

3. Look for MAC filtering on your access point, similar to the screen in Figure 5-64. On this access point, you can enter a table of MAC addresses and decide if this list of MAC addresses is to be used to prevent or permit use of the access point.

4. Save all your settings for the access point and test the connection. To test it, on one of your wireless computers, follow directions given earlier in the chapter to connect to a hotspot, entering the passphrase when requested. If you don't see the network in the list of wireless networks, try moving your access point or the computer. If you still can't get a connection, remove all security measures and try again. Then restore the security features one at a time until you discover the one causing the problem.

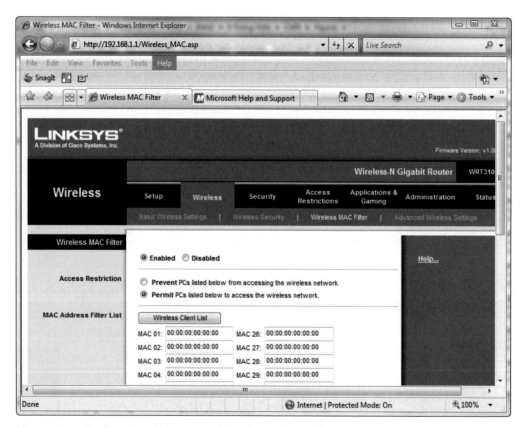

Figure 5-64   Configure how the access point will filter MAC addresses

We've just configured your wireless access point to use several security features. Is it really necessary to use them all? Well, not really. Encryption is essential to keep others from hacking into your wireless data and to prevent unauthorized use of your wireless LAN. For most situations, that's all you need. For added protection, you can disable SSID broadcasting or filter MAC addresses.

FIXING NETWORK PROBLEMS

If you have problems connecting to the network, you can follow the guidelines in this section. First, here are some symptoms of network problems:

▲ *Problem 1*: You cannot make a connection to the network.

▲ *Problem 2*: The Network window does not show any other computers on the network.

▲ *Problem 3*: Device Manager shows a yellow exclamation point or a red X beside the name of the network adapter.

▲ *Problem 4*: In the Network and Sharing Center window, you see a red X over the network icon.

▲ *Problem 5*: Lights on the network adapter, switch, hub, or router are not lit. There are at least two lights on a network adapter: one stays on steadily to let you know there is a physical connection, and another blinks to let you know there is activity (see Figure 5-65). If you see no lights, you know there is no physical connection between the network adapter and the network. This means there is a problem with the network cable; the card; or the hub, switch, or router that the PC connects to. Similar lights display on the hub, switch, or router for each network port.

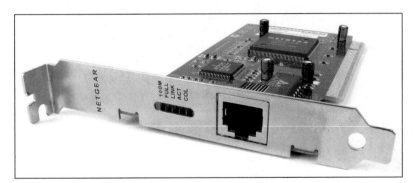

Figure 5-65 Lights on the back of a network adapter can be used for troubleshooting

Sometimes you might have trouble with a network connection due to a TCP/IP problem. Windows TCP/IP includes several diagnostic tools that are useful in troubleshooting problems with TCP/IP. The most useful is **ping (packet internet groper)**, which tests connectivity by sending a signal to a remote computer. If the remote computer is online and detects the signal, it responds. Use the ipconfig command to test the TCP/IP configuration. Try these things to test TCP/IP configuration and connectivity:

1. Try to release the current IP address and lease a new address. To do this, open the Network and Sharing Center window, click **Diagnose and repair**. Alternately, you can open an elevated command prompt window and use these two commands: **ipconfig/release** followed by **ipconfig/renew**.

2. Determine whether other computers on the network are having trouble with their connections. If the entire network is down, the problem is not isolated to the PC you are working on. Check the switch, hub, or router controlling the network.

3. Look for problems with the TCP/IP configuration. Open a command prompt window by entering **cmd** in the Start Search dialog box. Then enter **ipconfig/all** at the command prompt. (Refer to Figure 5-57.) If the TCP/IP configuration is correct

5

and an IP address is assigned, then the IP address, subnet mask, and default gateway appear along with the adapter address. For dynamic IP addressing, if the PC cannot reach the DHCP server, then it assigns itself an IP address. This is called IP autoconfiguration and the IP address is called an Automatic Private IP Address (APIPA). The ipconfig command shows the IP address as the Autoconfiguration IPv4 Address, and the address begins with 169.254 (see Figure 5-66). In this case, suspect that the PC is not able to reach the network or the DHCP server is down.

Figure 5-66 The network connection was not able to lease an IP address

4. Next, try the loopback address test. At a command prompt, enter the command **ping 127.0.0.1** (with no period after the final 1). This IP address always refers to your local computer. It should respond with a reply message from your computer. If this works, TCP/IP is likely to be configured correctly. If you get an error, then assume that the problem is on your PC. Check the installation and configuration of each component, such as the network card and the TCP/IP settings. Remove and reinstall each component, and watch for error messages, writing them down so that you can recognize or research them later as necessary. You might need to uninstall and reinstall the TCP/IP component. Compare the configuration to that of a working PC on the same network.

5. Next, ping the IP address of your default gateway. If it does not respond, then the problem may be with the gateway or with the network to the gateway.

6. Now try to ping the host computer you are trying to reach. If it does not respond, then the problem may be with the host computer or with the network to the computer.

7. If you have Internet access and substitute a domain name for the IP address in the ping command, and ping works, then you can conclude that DNS works. If an IP address works, but the domain name does not work, the problem lies with DNS. Try this command: **ping www.course.com**.

8. Make sure the network adapter and its drivers are installed by checking for the adapter in Device Manager.

9. Try uninstalling and reinstalling the network adapter drivers. If the drivers still install with errors, try downloading new drivers from the Web site of the network card manufacturer. Also, look on the installation CD that came bundled with the adapter for a setup program. If you find one, uninstall the adapter and run this setup program.

10. Some network adapters have diagnostic programs on the installation CD. Try running the program from the CD. Look in the documentation that came with the adapter for instructions on how to install and run the program.

11. Check the network cable to make sure it is not damaged and that it does not exceed the recommended length for the type of network you are using.

12. Connect the network cable to a different port on the switch, hub, or router. If that doesn't help, you may have a problem with the cable or the adapter itself. Uninstall the adapter drivers, replace the adapter, and then install new drivers.

13. Check to see whether you have the most current version of your motherboard BIOS. The motherboard manufacturer should have information on its Web site about whether an upgrade is available.

14. When a network drive map is not working, first check the Network window and verify that you can access other resources on the remote computer. You might need to log on to the remote computer with a valid user account and password.

>> CHAPTER SUMMARY

▲ The four most popular ways to connect to the Internet are cable modem, DSL, dial-up, and, for remote locations, satellite. Dial-up is the slowest but least expensive method.

▲ To set up a network, even as simple as one computer connecting to the Internet, it helps to know that network communication must happen at three levels: the hardware level, the OS level, and the application level.

▲ Network addressing at the hardware level is by MAC addresses, network addressing at the OS level is by IP address, and network addressing at the application level is by port numbers. All three levels of communication and addressing are at work when you use the Internet.

▲ When connecting to the Internet using cable modem, your cable modem connects to the TV jack and uses the TV cable company broadband service. DSL uses the phone lines coming to your house. Cable modem does not interfere with your TV reception. DSL, when properly configured, does not interfere with your telephone service.

▲ TCP/IP is a suite of protocols used by the Internet and most networks. Configuring TCP/IP is done using the Properties window of your network connection in the Network and Sharing Center window.

▲ An ISP can use static or dynamic IP addressing. To use static IP addressing, you need to know the default gateway and DNS servers provided by your ISP.

▲ When a PC is connected directly to the Internet, the PC can share the Internet connection. Windows Vista uses Internet Connection Sharing (ICS) to manage the connection on the host computer.

▲ The simplest of all networks is two computers connected by one crossover cable.

▲ A switch or hub is used to connect three or more computers in a network.

5

◢ To eliminate a host computer for your Internet connection, you can use a router that stands between the modem and the network.

◢ When you open the Network window, you can drill down to see shared files, folders, and printers on your network. A network drive is a convenient way to share a folder or entire hard drive with others on a network.

◢ A router often serves multiple purposes, for example, being a switch, firewall, proxy server, and wireless access point.

◢ To allow a computer on the network protected by a firewall to receive communication initiated by a computer on the Internet, configure the firewall for port forwarding.

◢ The most popular wireless technology is called WiFi, although its official name is 802.11. Four grades of WiFi are 802.11a, 802.11b, 802.11g, and 802.11n.

◢ A wireless access point can secure a wireless network by using one or more of these methods: data encryption, not broadcasting its SSID, filtering MAC addresses, and supporting a virtual private network (VPN).

◢ Tools to use to solve networking problems include ping and ipconfig.

>> KEY TERMS

access point (AP)   A device connected to a LAN that provides wireless communication so that computers, printers, and other wireless devices can communicate with devices on the LAN.

crossover cable   A network cable used to connect two PCs into the simplest network possible. Also used to connect two hubs or switches.

default gateway   A computer or other device on a network that acts as an entry point, or gateway, to another network.

DNS (Domain Name System) server   A computer that matches up domain names with IP addresses.

Internet Connection Sharing (ICS)   A Windows 98/Me/XP and Vista utility that manages two or more computers connected to the Internet.

network drive map   Mounting a drive to a computer, such as drive E, that is actually hard drive space on another host computer on the network.

patch cable   A network cable that is used to connect a PC to a hub, switch, or router.

ping (packet internet groper)   A Windows and Unix command used to troubleshoot network connections. It verifies that the host can communicate with another host on the network.

Public folder   The folder in the %*SystemDrive*%\Users folder that is intended to hold data that users share on the computer or network.

subnet mask   Four numbers separated by periods (for example, 255.255.255.0) that, when combined with an IP address, indicate what network a computer is on.

WEP (Wired Equivalent Privacy)   A data encryption method used by wireless networks whereby data is encrypted using a 64-bit or 128-bit key. It is not as secure as other methods because the key never changes. Compare to WPA.

WPA (WiFi Protected Access)   A data encryption method used by wireless networks that uses the TKIP (Temporal Key Integrity Protocol) protocol. Encryption keys are changed at set intervals. Compare to WEP and WPA2.

WPA2 (WiFi Protected Access 2)   A data encryption standard compliant with the IEEE 802.11i standard that uses the AES (Advanced Encryption Standard) protocol. WPA2 is currently the strongest wireless encryption standard.

>> REVIEWING THE BASICS

1. What Windows Vista component can be used to share an Internet connection with other computers on the LAN?

2. What protocol is commonly used to log on to the ISP with a username and password to make an on-demand broadband connection?

3. What Windows Vista command can be used to display a network adapter's MAC address?

4. When using a cable modem to connect to the Internet, the data transmission shares the cabling with what other technology?

5. If two wireless computers are directly communicating with one another, what type of connection are they using?

6. What is the maximum transfer rate that can be obtained by using the 802.11g standard?

7. What are four ways a wireless network can be secured?

8. When a browser sends a request to a Web server, what port address is normally used?

9. How many bits are in a MAC address?

10. Why does your ISP need to know the MAC address of your cable modem or DSL modem?

11. What is a default gateway?

12. Does it matter which TV jack in your house should be used by your cable modem? Why or why not?

13. What two methods can an ISP use to assign your computer or router an IP address?

14. Why are no two MAC addresses the same?

15. Which data encryption is stronger, WPA or WEP?

16. Why is it important to use some type of data encryption on a wireless network?

17. What type of server is used to translate domain names to IP addresses?

18. What is the difference between a patch cable and a crossover cable?

19. What TCP/IP command tests for connectivity between two networked devices?

20. Give two examples of broadband technology.

>> THINKING CRITICALLY

1. You are trying to connect to the Internet using a Windows Vista dial-up connection. You installed a modem card and tested it, so you know it works. Next, you create a dial-up connection icon in the Network and Sharing Center window. Then you double-click the icon and the Connect dialog box opens. You click Dial to make the connection. An error message appears saying, "There was no dial tone." What is the first thing you do?

    a. Check Device Manager for errors with the modem.

    b. Check with the ISP to verify that you have the correct phone number, username, and password.

    c. Check the phone line to see if it's connected.

    d. Check the properties of the dial-up connection icon for errors.

2. You connect to the Internet using a cable modem. When you open your browser and try to access a Web site, you get the error: "The Web page you requested is not available offline. To view this page, click Connect." Select two explanations and their solutions that are reasonable and might work. Select two explanations and solutions that are not reasonable and explain why they won't work.

    a. The browser has been set to work offline. On the File menu, verify that Work Offline is not checked.

    b. The connection to the cable modem is down. In the Network and Sharing Center, click view status for the LAN connection and select Diagnose.

    c. Windows Firewall is enabled on your PC. Disable it.

    d. The cable modem is not working. Go to Device Manager and check for errors with the cable modem.

3. You work in the Accounting Department and have been using a network drive to post Excel spreadsheets to your workgroup file server as you complete them. When you attempt to save a spreadsheet to the drive, you see the error message: "You do not have access to the folder 'J:\'. See your administrator for access to this folder." What should you do first? Second? Explain the reasoning behind your choices.

    a. Ask your network administrator to give you permission to access the folder.

    b. Check the Network window to verify that you can connect to the network.

    c. Save the spreadsheet to your hard drive.

    d. Using Windows Explorer, remap the network drive.

    e. Reboot your PC.

>> HANDS-ON PROJECTS

PROJECT 5-1: Networking Two Computers

Practice your networking skills by doing the following:

1. Using a crossover cable and two computers, connect them together in a network. Configure the two PCs for static IP addressing. What two IP addresses did you use?

2. Share the C:\Users\Public folder on the first PC so that the second PC can move files in and out of the folder. How did you do this?

3. Secure the C:\Users\Public folder on the second PC so that it cannot be seen by the first PC. How did you do this?

PROJECT 5-2: Researching Switches

Find four Web pages advertising switches that meet these criteria:

1. Find two switches by different manufacturers that support Gigabit Ethernet and have at least five ports.

2. Find two switches by different manufacturers that support Fast Ethernet and have at least five ports.

3. Compare the features and prices of each switch. Which brand and type of switch would you recommend for a small network? Why?

PROJECT 5-3: Researching a Wireless LAN

Suppose you want to set up a wireless LAN in your home. Currently you access the Internet using a cable modem that's connected to your desktop computer. Your notebook computer does not have wireless but it does have a USB port and a PC Card slot. You want to be able to connect your notebook to the Internet using wireless. Do the following to research the equipment you need to buy:

1. Print three Web pages showing different choices for a wireless access point.

2. Print three Web pages showing different choices for the wireless adapter for your notebook.

3. Which access point and adapter would you select for your wireless LAN? Why?

PROJECT 5-4: Researching Routers

Research routers to find the best one to use on a small network of five computers that connect to the Internet using DSL. Do the following:

1. Print a Web page of one router that can also serve as a wireless access point.

2. Print a Web page of another router that supports Gigabit Ethernet.

3. Print a Web page of another router that has at least four ports for computers to connect to.

4. Print a Web page of another router that is a wireless access point, has at least four ports, and supports Gigabit Ethernet.

5. Compare prices. Which router is the least expensive? Which router would you recommend? Why?

PROJECT 5-5:   Practicing Using Ipconfig

Ipconfig can be a useful tool to find out information about the current TCP/IP configuration and to release and renew an IP address. However, sometimes it requires an elevated command prompt. Do the following to practice using the command and find out when the elevated command prompt window is required:

1. Open a standard command prompt window and execute this command: **ipconfig /all**

2. Execute the command **ipconfig /release**. What error message do you get?

3. Open an elevated command prompt window and execute the command again. What is the result?

4. Execute the command **ipconfig /renew**. What is the result?

5. Close both command prompt windows.

>> REAL PROBLEMS, REAL SOLUTIONS

REAL PROBLEM 5-1:   Firewalling Your Home Network

At first, Santiago had only a single desktop computer, an ink-jet printer, and a dial-up phone line to connect to the Internet. Then, his wife, Maria, decided she wanted her own computer. Later they both decided it was time for a broadband connection to the Internet and chose cable. So now, their home network looks like that shown earlier in Figure 5-24a. Santiago chose to use a crossover cable to connect the two computers, and the cable modem connects to Santiago's computer using a USB cable.

Both computers are constantly plagued with pop-up ads and worms, so Santiago has come to you for some advice. He's heard he needs to use a firewall, but he doesn't know what a firewall is or how to buy one. You immediately show him how to turn on Windows Firewall on both Vista PCs, but you know he really needs a better hardware solution. What equipment (including cables) do you recommend he buy to implement a hardware firewall? Also consider that his daughter, Sophia, has been begging for a notebook computer for her birthday, so plan for this expansion. By the way, Sophia has made it perfectly clear there's no way she'll settle for having to sit down in the same room with her parents to surf the Web, so you need to plan for a wireless connection to Sophia's bedroom.

REAL PROBLEM 5-2:   Teaching Yourself About Windows Meeting Space

Using the Windows Help and Support window, search for information on Windows Meeting Space. Describe the tool. When would you want to use it? What can you do with Windows Meeting Space? Set up and test the tool with a friend on a network connection.

CHAPTER 6

Hardware and Application Errors

In this chapter, you will learn:

- About some general guidelines and tools for solving computer problems
- About strategies you can use to deal with hardware problems
- How to approach and solve a problem with an application

This chapter is about how to fix a problem with a hardware device or an application. It's impossible in one chapter to cover every hardware and application problem you might run across. Instead, the first part of the chapter shows you the general approaches, tools, and strategies to use when faced with these types of problems. Then later sections give an example or two of common hardware and application problems to demonstrate how these solutions can be applied.

⌘ **Focus Problem**

"My applications or devices give errors, won't work, won't install, or won't uninstall."

HOW TO APPROACH AND SOLVE ANY COMPUTER PROBLEM

Let's first look at some general troubleshooting guidelines that apply to solving problems with both hardware and applications. Then we'll turn our attention to the tools you need: the physical tools such as a simple screwdriver, and the software tools available in Vista and other sources.

GENERAL TROUBLESHOOTING GUIDELINES

Here are some guidelines intended to help you become a good computer troubleshooter and zero in on the source of a problem in as few steps as possible:

◢ *Guideline 1: Make backups before making changes.* Whether you are working on hardware or software, always back up important data before working on a computer. I could tell you some pretty sad stories about how not making backups resulted in a lot of pain and misery. But just take my word for it—make backups!

◢ *Guideline 2: Approach the problem systematically.* Start at the beginning and walk through the situation in a thorough, careful way. This one rule is valuable. Remember it and apply it every time. If you don't find the solution to the problem after one systematic walk-through, then repeat the entire process. Check and double-check to find the step you overlooked the first time. Most problems with computers are simple, such as a loose cable or circuit board. Computers are logical through and through. Whatever the problem, it's also logical through and through. First, try to reproduce the problem, and then try to figure out whether it is a hardware or software problem.

◢ *Guideline 3: Divide and conquer.* This rule is the most powerful. Isolate the problem. In the overall system, remove one hardware or software component after another, until the problem is isolated to a small part of the whole system. Here are a few examples of applying this rule:

  ◢ *Example 1*: Boot into Safe Mode to prevent unnecessary device drivers and applications from loading.

  ◢ *Example 2*: If a computer won't boot, to figure out if the problem is related to the hard drive or to other vital hardware components, try to boot from the Windows Vista setup DVD. If that works, then you know the problem has to do with the hard drive.

  ◢ *Example 3*: If you're not sure whether the problem is with Windows or a hardware device such as a USB wireless adapter, try using the adapter on another computer. If the problem follows you, you know the adapter is at fault. If the adapter works on this computer, then you know the problem is with the first computer. It might be Windows or it might be the USB port itself, but you're zeroing in on the culprit.

◢ *Guideline 4: Don't overlook the obvious.* Ask simple questions. Is the computer plugged in? Is it turned on? Is the monitor plugged in? Most solutions to problems are so simple that we overlook them because we expect the problem to be difficult. Don't let the complexity of computers fool you. Most problems are easy to fix. Really, they are!

▲ *Guideline 5: Check simple things first.* It is more effective to first check the components that are easiest to replace. For example, if the video does not work, the problem may be with the monitor or the video card. When faced with the decision of which one to exchange first, choose the easy route: exchange the monitor before the video card.

▲ *Guideline 6: Do your own investigating.* This rule is the hardest to follow, because there is a tendency to trust anything in writing and assume that people are telling you exactly what happened. But documentation is sometimes wrong and people don't always describe events as they actually happened, so do your own investigating. For example, if the user tells you that the system boots up with no error messages, but that his application still doesn't work, boot for yourself. You never know what the user might have overlooked.

▲ *Guideline 7: Test all components that might affect the problem.* Be thorough in your testing. Test all hardware components related to the problem, check the Windows configuration, and use whatever testing tools are available, both hardware and software. Use Event Viewer and Device Manager to check for errors and for configuration problems. Many manufacturers offer diagnostic software to test their products, and Windows includes a few tools of its own.

▲ *Guideline 8: Become a researcher.* Following this rule is the most fun. When a computer problem arises that you can't easily solve, be as tenacious as a bulldog. Read, search the Web, make phone calls, ask questions, and then read more, search more, make more phone calls, and ask more questions. Take advantage of every available resource, including online help, the Internet, documentation, technical support, and books such as this one. Learn to use a good Web search engine such as Google. Use it to search on an error message, problem, application error, or hardware device. Also, check out *groups.google.com*. There are a bunch of computer groups listed with problems, ideas, solutions, and discussions. What you learn will be yours to take to the next problem. This is the real joy of computer troubleshooting. If you're good at it, you're always learning something new.

▲ *Guideline 9: Write things down.* Keep good notes as you're working. They'll help you think more clearly. Draw diagrams. Make lists. Clearly and precisely write down what you're learning. Later, when the entire problem gets "cold," these notes will be invaluable.

▲ *Guideline 10: Reboot and start over.* This is an important rule. Fresh starts are good for us and uncover events or steps that we might have overlooked. Take a break and get away from the problem. Begin again. And, when you do start fresh, carefully question any assumptions that you made along the way which might have led you down a wrong fork in the road. For example, did a particular error message cause you to *assume* the problem was caused by the OS when it might have been hardware related?

▲ *Guideline 11: Establish your priorities.* This rule can help make for a satisfied customer. Decide what your first priority is. For example, it might be to recover lost data, or to get the PC back up and running as soon as possible. When practical, ask the user or customer for advice about setting your priorities.

▲ *Guideline 12: Keep your cool and don't rush.* In an emergency, protect the data and software by carefully considering your options before acting and by taking practical precautions to protect software and OS files. When a computer stops working, if unsaved data is still in memory or if data or software on the hard drive has not been backed up, look and think carefully before you leap! A wrong move can be costly. The best advice is not to hurry. Carefully plan your moves. Read the documentation if you're not sure what to do, and don't hesitate to ask for help. Don't simply try something, hoping it will work, unless you've run out of more intelligent alternatives!

▲ *Guideline 13: Don't assume the worst.* When it's an emergency and your only copy of data is on a hard drive that is not working, don't assume that the data is lost. Much can be done to recover data. If you want to recover lost data on a hard drive, don't write anything to the drive; you might write on top of lost data, eliminating all chances of recovery.

▲ *Guideline 14: Know your limitations and be honest.* After you've done all you know to do, you might find it necessary to pass the problem on to someone with more expertise. Also, if you make a mistake or don't know an answer to a question, be honest with the user. In fact, I've discovered one of the keys to successful help-desk support is to say, "I don't know, but I'll find out."

▲ *Guideline 15: Know your starting point.* Before trying to solve a computer problem, know for certain that the problem is what the user says it is. If the computer does not boot, carefully note where in the boot process it fails. If the computer does boot to an OS, before changing anything or taking anything apart, verify what does and what doesn't work, preferably in the presence of the user.

▲ *Guideline 16: Begin by asking the user to describe the problem in detail.* Don't jump right in and begin trying this or that until you first get whatever information you can from the user. One really important fact only the user can tell you is whether valuable data on the hard drive is not backed up. If that is true, you need to know that and you need to take precautions to protect the data. For some good questions to ask the user, see Chapter 1. After you have interviewed the user, if possible, ask the user to reproduce the problem while you watch. Sometimes this reveals that the problem is caused by user error.

WHAT'S IN YOUR PHYSICAL TOOL BOX?

If you're serious about learning to fix computer problems, you can buy some pretty sophisticated PC repair tool kits, but what you really need are just a few simple tools such as those in Figure 6-1.

Figure 6-1 PC repair tools can be simple and not too expensive

You might want to accumulate the following tools and put them in a handy box or container of some sort:

▲ Pen and paper for taking notes
▲ Paper cups for organizing screws as you work
▲ Antistatic ground bracelet
▲ Flashlight
▲ Flat-head screwdriver and Phillips-head screwdriver
▲ Tweezers for picking pieces of paper out of printers and for picking up screws dropped in tight places

▲ Plastic ties to tie power cords together inside the case to keep cords out of the way of fans and to improve circulation; you'll also need some wire cutters to cut off long tie ends

▲ Can of compressed air to blow dust off components; too much dust can cause a system to overheat

▲ Needle-nose pliers for holding objects in place while you screw them in (especially those pesky nuts on cable connectors)

▲ Diagnostic software or antivirus software on CD such as PartitionMagic, Norton AntiVirus by Symantec (*www.symantec.com*), or the Ultimate Boot CD compiled by Victor Chew and available at *www.ultimatebootcd.com*

▲ Diagnostic card, also called a POST card

▲ IDE to USB and SATA to USB adapters

The last two items need a little explanation. Neither of them is essential for PC trouble-shooting, but in some situations, they're a great help.

A **diagnostic card** costs from $25 to $100 and can be used to display error codes at startup to diagnose a startup problem with hardware. Figure 6-2 shows a diagnostic card by MSD (*www.msdus.com*). Just stick the card in an empty PCI slot, turn on the system, and read the numeric code displayed on the LED readout on the card. The code is generated by the motherboard BIOS, which can tell you which device caused the boot to halt.

Figure 6-2   A diagnostic card displays BIOS error codes at startup

Internal hard drives use one of two types of cables and connectors to connect the drive to the motherboard: an IDE connector and cable (the older method) or SATA connector and cable (the newer, faster method). An **IDE to USB adapter** (see Figure 6-3) or a **SATA to USB adapter** (see Figure 6-4) costs less than $30 and is extremely handy when a hard drive won't boot but still has valuable data on it. You can remove the hard drive from its computer and use another working computer to try to recover the data. Using one of these adapters, connect the hard drive to the working computer using its USB port. If the drive works at all, you might be able to recover the data from the drive.

The adapter kit might or might not include the power adapter. If it is missing, you can connect the power port on the drive to a power cable coming from the power supply inside the computer case. Also, some adapter kits, such as the one in Figure 6-3, include a smaller connector used for laptop hard drives. How to use all these adapters to recover data from a hard drive that will not boot is covered in Chapter 7.

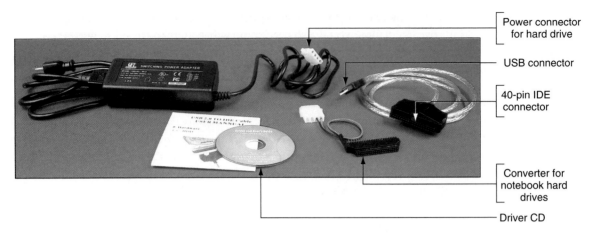

Figure 6-3 Use an IDE to USB converter to recover data from a failing IDE hard drive

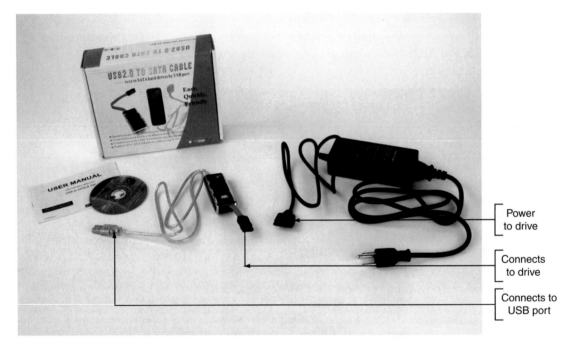

Figure 6-4 Use a SATA to USB converter to recover data from a drive using a SATA connector

WHAT'S IN YOUR VIRTUAL TOOL BOX?

Your virtual tool box is probably more important than your physical tool box. In this part of the chapter, you'll learn about software tools that can help you zero in on and fix both hardware and software problems. In the following sections, you'll learn how CMOS setup, Device Manager, Event Viewer, and other software utilities can help you troubleshoot a computer problem.

CMOS SETUP

CMOS setup can help with problems concerning basic hardware components in a system, including motherboard ports and expansion slots, hard drives, optical drives, floppy drives, and tape drives. These components are detected by the startup BIOS and reported on the BIOS setup screens during the boot. Because the data reported and edited on these screens is stored on a CMOS chip on the motherboard, these setup screens are commonly called CMOS setup.

To access CMOS setup, look for a message onscreen when you first turn on the PC that says "Press DEL for setup," "Press F8 for CMOS setup," "Press F2 to access setup," or something similar. When you press that key, you enter the CMOS setup utility stored on the motherboard. The menus are arranged differently for each type of BIOS utility. For example, in Figure 6-5 you can see the main menu for one CMOS setup. Using this screen, you can change the system date and time and view the drives recognized by the system. Notice in the figure that two hard drives and one CD/DVD drive are installed.

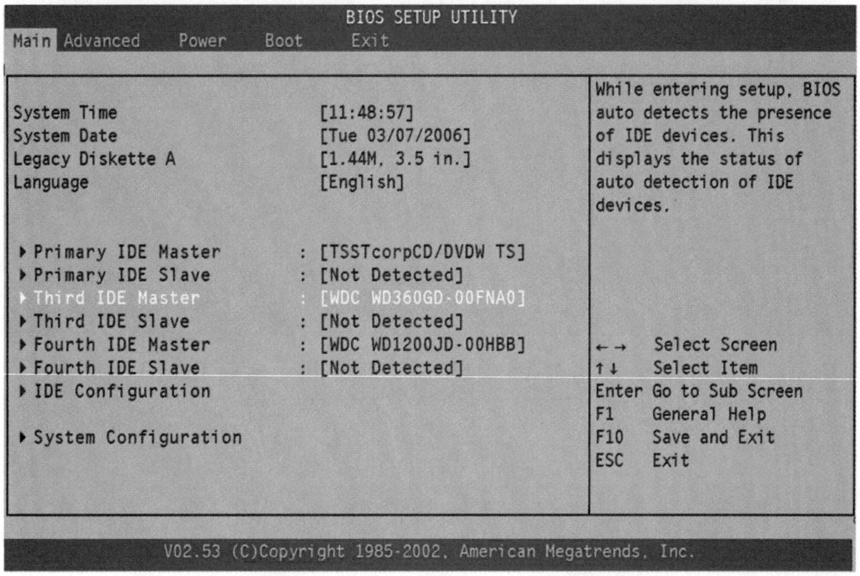

Figure 6-5 In CMOS setup, you can view installed drives and change system date and time

However, in another example, the drives are listed on an advanced screen in the utility. Using the arrow keys, you can navigate to this advanced screen shown in Figure 6-6 where CMOS setup reports one SATA hard drive and one CD drive are installed.

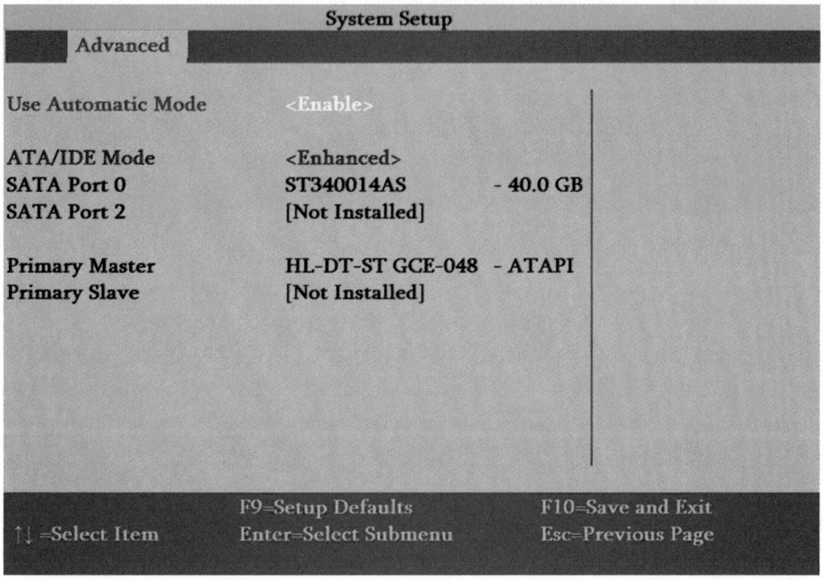

Figure 6-6 A CMOS setup screen with one hard drive and one CD-RW drive installed

The CD drive appears as the Primary Master, which means that it is using an IDE connector rather than a SATA connector, which the hard drive is using. Incidentally, since I keep mentioning IDE and SATA connectors on a motherboard, I thought you might like to see what they look like in Figure 6-7 and Figure 6-8. Today's motherboards are likely to have at least one IDE connector and two or more SATA connectors.

Figure 6-7 This motherboard has a blue primary IDE connector and a black secondary IDE connector. The blue connector is used first.

Figure 6-8 This motherboard has four SATA connectors. The red connectors are used first.

Other devices that are recognized by CMOS setup can be found on other screens. For example, take a look at the CMOS setup screen in Figure 6-9. Using this screen you can enable or disable some of these devices. Know that, for ports and expansion slots, CMOS setup recognizes the port or slot, but not the device or expansion card using that slot. Any device that shows up in CMOS setup should also be listed in Device Manager. However, not all devices listed in Device Manager are listed in CMOS setup.

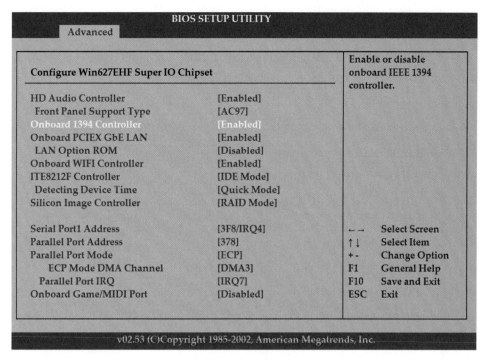

Figure 6-9 In CMOS setup, you can disable and enable motherboard ports and other components

DEVICE MANAGER

Device Manager (devmgmt.msc) is the main Windows tool for managing hardware. Using it, you can disable or enable a device, uninstall it, update its drivers, and undo a driver update (called a driver rollback). Device Manager reports errors about a device on the General tab of the device Properties box and offers solutions (see Figure 6-10). Most hardware is listed in Device Manager, but not all. Included in the missing devices are printers and some USB and FireWire devices. You learned to use Device Manager in previous chapters.

EVENT VIEWER

Event Viewer (eventvwr.msc), showing in Figure 6-11, organizes and views the event logs of many activities that are tracked about applications, security, and the system and can help find information about a problem with both hardware and software. Event Viewer gives a lot of information to wade through, but if you know where to look, it can be a great help when solving intermittent hardware problems or problems with security breaches. It can also help you decide if a problem is caused by hardware or software.

For example, on our network, we have a file server where several people in the office update Microsoft Word documents stored on the server. For weeks people complained about these Word documents getting corrupted. We downloaded the latest patches for Windows and Microsoft Office and scanned for viruses thinking that the problem might be with Windows or the application. Then we suspected a corrupted template file for building the Word documents. But nothing we did solved our problem of corrupted Word documents. Then one day someone thought to check Event Viewer on the file server. Event Viewer had faithfully been recording errors when writing to the hard drive. What we had suspected to be a software problem was, in fact, a failing hard drive, which was full of bad sectors. We replaced the drive and the problem went away.

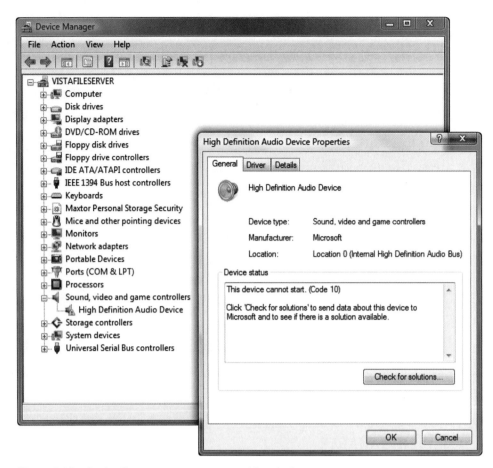

Figure 6-10 Device Manager reports an error with a device

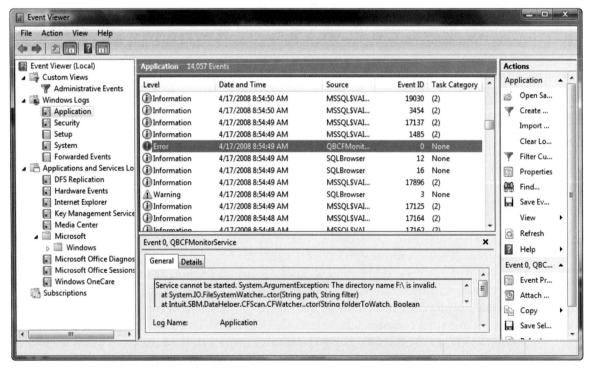

Figure 6-11 Event Viewer reports problems with applications, services, security, and hardware

To access Event Viewer, click **Start** and enter **Event Viewer** in the Start Search box, then respond to the UAC box. By clicking the triangles on the far left of the Event Viewer window you can drill down to various categories of event logs kept by Event Viewer. Look under Hardware Events for reports of warnings and errors caused by hardware devices. This log can help you smoke out the source of intermittent and catastrophic errors.

PRINTERS WINDOW

Use the Printers window to install and uninstall a printer, configure it, share it, and manage its print queue. For example, to install a new printer, in Figure 6-12, click **Add a printer**. If you are having problems with a document printing, one thing you can do is clear out the print queue to start fresh. To do that, double-click the printer in the Printers window. The printer window opens, listing the print queue for this printer. To cancel all documents in the queue, click **Printer** and select **Cancel All Documents** (see Figure 6-13). To cancel a single document, right-click the document and select **Cancel** from the shortcut menu.

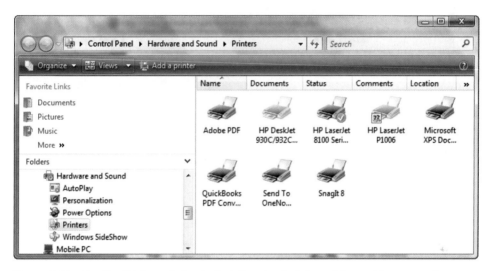

Figure 6-12   Use the Printers window to install and uninstall a printer and to manage its print queue

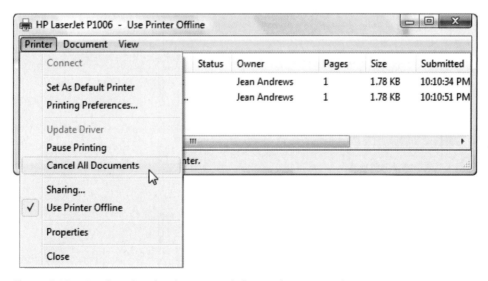

Figure 6-13   Use the printer's print queue window to clean out a print queue

Also, when troubleshooting printer problems, if you want to find out if your PC is communicating with the printer independently of your applications, you can print a test page. To do that, in the Printers window, right-click the printer and select **Properties** from the shortcut menu. The printer properties window opens (see Figure 6-14). Click **Print Test Page**.

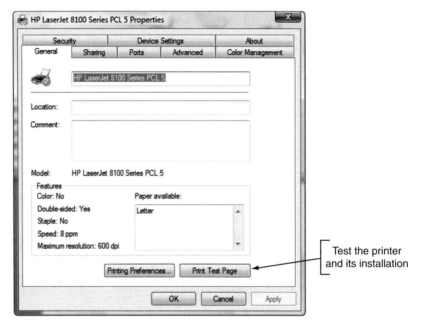

Test the printer
and its installation

Figure 6-14   Print a test page to verify that the PC
can communicate with the printer

Printing goes faster when applications send print jobs to a print queue (called spooling) rather than sending them directly to the printer. However, you can eliminate the print spool as the source of a problem by trying to print directly to the printer. To do that, on the **Advanced** tab of the printer **Properties** window, select **Print directly to the printer** (see Figure 6-15) and try again to print from the application.

Figure 6-15   Eliminate printer spooling as a source of
the problem

PROGRAMS AND FEATURES WINDOW

Printers, scanners, USB or FireWire devices, and some other devices don't show up in Device Manager. For these devices, you can use the Programs and Features window to uninstall the software for the device, including its device drivers. Later in the chapter, you'll see an example of how to do this using a USB device. And, for problems with applications, use this window to repair or uninstall the application. It's also used to uninstall some Internet Explorer add-ons.

SYSTEM RESTORE

If you have a problem with installing or updating a device or application, or if a problem arises and you don't understand its source, you can use System Restore to return to a previous point in time before the problem occurred. For example, if you install a USB device that does not appear in Device Manager and now Windows gives errors when you boot, use System Restore to undo the installation. Remember from Chapter 2, to start System Restore, click **Start**, point to **All Programs**, click **Accessories**, click **System Tools**, click **System Restore**, and respond to the UAC box. Using the System Restore window in Figure 6-16, selecting the recommended restore point is most likely your best option to undo the most recent change to your system.

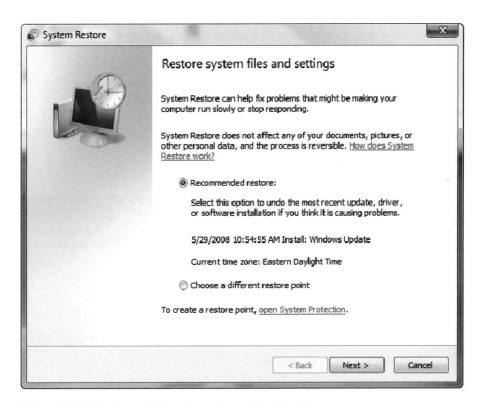

Figure 6-16 Use System Restore to undo recent system changes

PROBLEM REPORTS AND SOLUTIONS

Use the Windows Vista Problem Reports and Solutions tool to deal with an immediate hardware or software problem and use its history feature to help you understand the history of a specific problem or the general history of problems with the system. When a problem occurs, Vista Error Reporting displays an error screen and invites you to check for a solution. If the problem is so drastic a STOP error occurs (known as the Blue

Screen of Death—BSOD for short), the error screen appears on the next restart. For example, after a STOP error occurred on one system and the system was restarted, the screen in Figure 6-17 appeared. If the user clicks **Check for solution**, Microsoft displays information about the problem and its solution. Figure 6-18 shows another example on a different computer which occurred when a graphics driver written for Windows XP was installed on a Vista system.

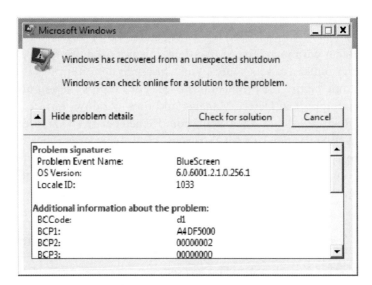

Figure 6-17 Windows reports information about an error

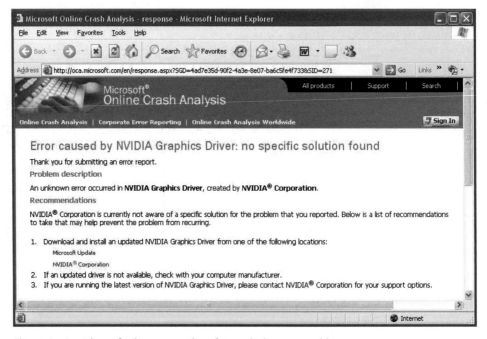

Figure 6-18 Microsoft gives suggestions for a solution to a problem

To see a list of information and possible solutions that have not yet been applied for known problems, click **Start**, click **All Programs**, click **Maintenance**, and click **Problem Reports and Solutions**. The Problem Reports and Solutions window in Figure 6-19 appears. Click on an item in the list to get more details and possibly apply the solution. Click **Check for new solutions** to send information to Microsoft and possibly find new solutions to known problems. These new solutions to old problems appear with the red word "New" in the figure.

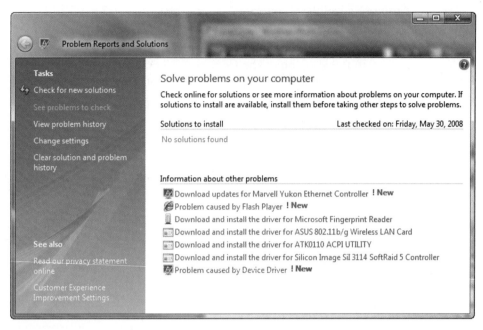

Figure 6-19 Known problems and solutions

To see a history of past problems, click **View problem history**; the window in Figure 6-20 appears. Problems are ordered by category. Click on a problem to see details about the problem. This window is a great tool if you need to understand the history of problems on a computer that you are troubleshooting.

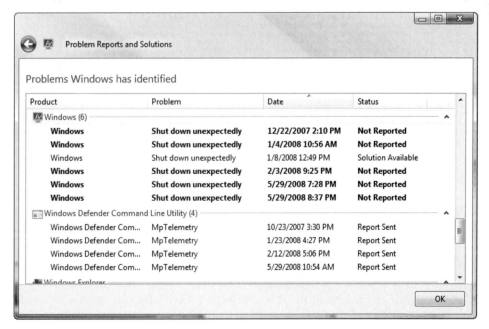

Figure 6-20 Use the Problem Reports and Solutions tool to view a history of past problems

RELIABILITY MONITOR

Another tool that can give you a history of previous problems with a system is the Reliability Monitor. This tool can give you the history of a problem, what has recently happened to the system, and how the system has performed in the past. Follow these steps to learn to use Reliability Monitor:

1. Click **Start**, right-click **Computer**, select **Manage** from the shortcut menu, and respond to the UAC box. The Computer Management console opens. Under System Tools, expand **Reliability and Performance** and then expand **Monitoring Tools**. Click **Reliability Monitor**. The Reliability Monitor pane opens as shown in Figure 6-21.

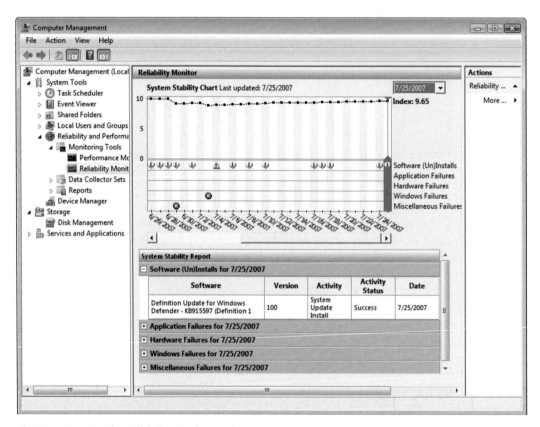

Figure 6-21 Use the Reliability Monitor tool to investigate a history of events on this computer

2. Click a day in the chart to see details about that day in the lower area of the pane. The monitor is tracking five types of events as shown in the pane (Software, Application, Hardware, Windows, and Miscellaneous Failures). To see details for each type event, click the + sign to the left of the event type. By selecting days in the chart where warnings and errors are marked by red circles and yellow triangles in the chart, you can quickly get a pretty good idea as to what has been happening with the system in the last few weeks. This information can be invaluable to help you understand the history and source of a computer hardware or software problem.

DATA COLLECTOR SETS

When you have a problem with the system but don't have a clue about what's causing it, there's another Vista tool that might help. You can use the Data Collector Set utility to collect data about the system and report that data to you in ways that can help you zero in on a problem's source. These reports can also be useful when checking the performance of critical devices such as the hard drive or memory. To see how the tool works, follow these steps:

1. From the Computer Management console, expand **Reliability and Performance**, expand **Data Collector Sets**, and then click **System**. The four categories under System appear in the middle pane as shown in Figure 6-22.

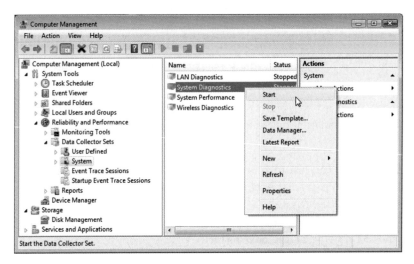

Figure 6-22 Four categories from which you can collect data to analyze

2. To collect data in one of these four categories, right-click it and select **Start** from the shortcut menu as shown in the figure. Wait while data is collected and then fills the middle pane. In our example, we're using System Diagnostics.

3. To view the system diagnostics data as a report, right-click **System Diagnostics** in the left pane and select **Latest Report** from the shortcut menu. The report for one system shows in Figure 6-23, which reports the system is experiencing excessive paging and needs more memory.

MEMORY DIAGNOSTICS

Errors with memory are often difficult to diagnose because they can appear intermittently and might be mistaken as application errors, user errors, or other hardware component errors. You can quickly identify a problem with memory or eliminate memory as the source of a problem by using the Vista **Memory Diagnostics** tool. It tests memory for errors and works before Windows Vista is loaded. The diagnostic test can be initiated using one of these four methods:

▲ *Method 1*: If Windows Error Reporting detects that memory might be failing, the utility will prompt the user to test memory on the next reboot. If the user agrees by clicking **Check for problems the next time you start your computer**, then diagnostic tests are run on the next restart. After the Windows desktop loads, a bubble message appears giving the test results. If the test shows that memory is giving errors, have the memory modules replaced.

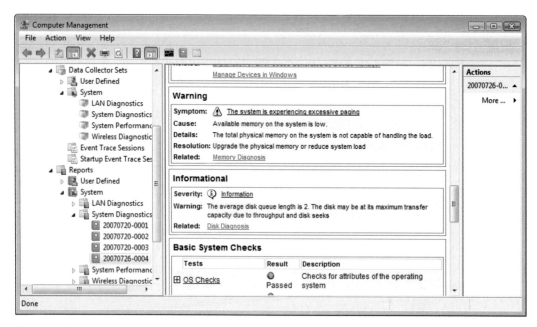

Figure 6-23   Reported results of collecting data about System Diagnostics

▲ *Method 2*: You can test memory at any time using the command prompt. To do so, click **Start, All Programs, Accessories, Command Prompt**. The Command Prompt window opens (see Figure 6-24). Type **mdsched.exe**, press **Enter**, and respond to the UAC box. In the dialog box that appears, also shown in the figure, you can choose to run the test now or on the next restart.

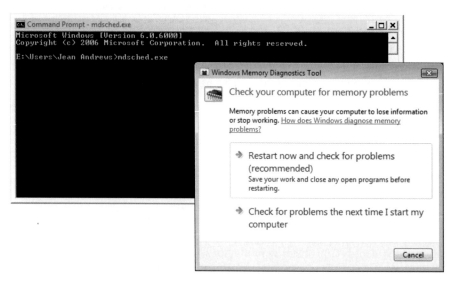

Figure 6-24   Use the mdsched.exe command to test memory

▲ *Method 3*: When troubleshooting a failed system, if the Windows Vista desktop cannot load, you can run the memory diagnostic test from the Windows Vista boot menu. This menu normally displays with a dual-boot configuration so you can select the OS to load. If you are not using a dual boot machine, you can force the menu to display by pressing the space bar during the boot. The resulting menu appears as shown in Figure 6-25. Use the Tab key to highlight the option **Windows Memory Diagnostic** and press **Enter**.

Figure 6-25 Force the Windows Boot Manager menu to display by pressing the space bar during the boot

▲ *Method 4*: For any computer that has a DVD drive, you can run the test using the Windows Vista DVD even if the computer is using a different OS than Vista:

1. Boot from the Vista DVD. On the window that appears, select your language preference and click **Next**.
2. On the opening menu of the Vista DVD, click **Repair your computer**, as shown in Figure 6-26.

Figure 6-26 Opening menu when you boot from the Vista DVD

3. The System Recovery Options window appears (see Figure 6-27). Click **Windows Memory Diagnostic Tool**.

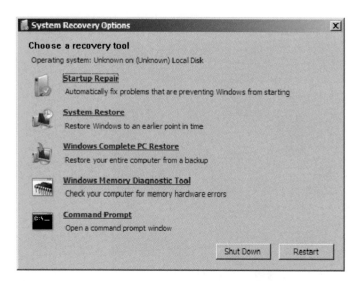

Figure 6-27 Test memory using the System Recovery Options menu

4. On the next window, click **Restart now and check for problems (recommended)**. The system will reboot and the memory test will start.

When the Vista desktop refuses to load but you can boot from the hard drive to the Vista boot menu, use Method 3. If you cannot boot from the hard drive or if Vista is not installed on the drive, use Method 4.

SYSTEM FILE CHECKER

A hardware or application problem might be caused by a corrupted Vista system file. That's where System File Checker might help. System File Checker is a Windows Vista utility that protects system files and keeps a cache of current system files in case it needs to refresh a damaged file. To use the utility to scan all system files and verify them, first close all applications and then enter the command **sfc /scannow** in an elevated command prompt window (see Figure 6-28). If corrupted system files are found, you might need to

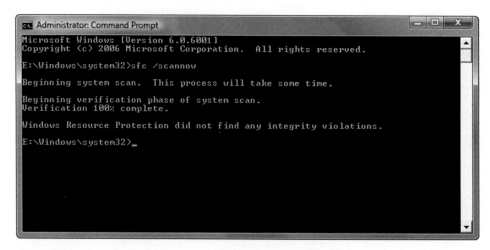

Figure 6-28 Use System File Checker to verify Vista system files

provide the Vista setup DVD to restore the files. If you have problems running the utility, try the command **sfc/ scanonce**, which scans files immediately after the next reboot.

CHKDSK

Recall from Chapter 1 that the Chkdsk utility can be used to check a hard drive for errors. If files are occasionally getting corrupted or applications are giving errors, the problem might be a failing hard drive. Remember that you can use Chkdsk from an elevated command prompt or from the drive Properties box. At a command prompt, the command is **chkdsk C: /r.**

DRIVER VERIFIER

For hardware problems, Driver Verifier (verifier.exe) is a Windows utility that runs in the background to test drivers for problems as they are loaded and running. When a problem occurs, a STOP error is generated so you can identify the problem driver. The tool is useful for smoking out intermittent problems that are not easily detected by other means.

To use Driver Verifier to monitor drivers, follow these steps:

1. Click **Start**, enter **verifier.exe** in the Start Search box, press **Enter**, and respond to the UAC box. The Driver Verifier Manager window opens (see Figure 6-29).

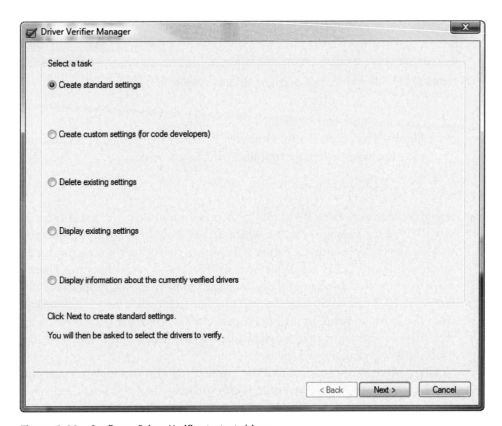

Figure 6-29 Configure Driver Verifier to test drivers

2. Select **Create standard settings** and click **Next**. The window in Figure 6-30 appears.

3. Depending on what you suspect to be the problem with your hardware, you need to select which type of drivers to monitor (unsigned drivers, older drivers, all drivers, or specific drivers that you can select from a list that appears on the next screen). If you are not sure which ones, to be on the safe side, select **Automatically select all drivers installed on this computer**. (When you do that, the Next in the window changes to

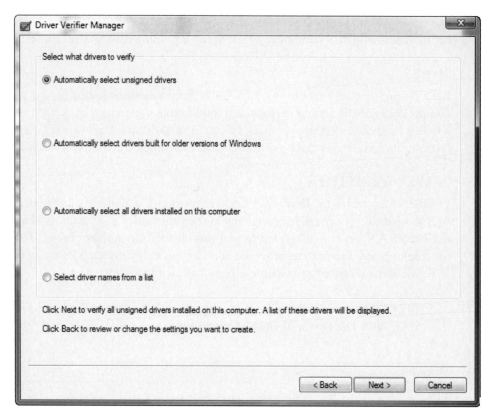

Figure 6-30 Select which type of drivers for Driver Verifier to test

Finish.) Then click **Finish**. However, be aware that the more drivers the utility monitors, the more system performance will be affected.

4. Restart the system.

Driver Verifier puts extra stress on the drivers it monitors, which can cause a STOP error. The STOP error message tells you which driver caused the error, thus identifying a driver with problems. For example, Figure 6-31 shows a STOP error screen caused during startup by the driver, mrv8ka51.sys. Which device does this driver belong to? There are several ways to get at that information; one way is to look at the file Properties box. First find the file in the C:\Windows\System32\drivers folder. Right-click the file and select **Properties** from the shortcut menu. In the file Properties box, select the **Details** tab, which shows that this driver file belongs to the wireless adapter (see Figure 6-32). The next step to fix the problem is to update the driver.

After Driver Verifier has located the problem, to turn it off, click **Start**, enter **verifier.exe** in the Start Search box, press **Enter**, and respond to the UAC box. The Driver Verifier Manager window opens (refer to Figure 6-29). Select **Delete existing settings** and click **Finish**. Click **OK** and restart your computer.

If Driver Verifier runs for a few days and has still not found the problem, it probably will not help you. Turn it off so it will not continue to degrade system performance.

By the way, remember that STOP error I just described that happened during startup? With normal Vista settings, if a STOP error occurs during startup, the system displays the error screen for a moment and then automatically restarts the system, which can result in an endless cycle of restarts, which is exactly what happened in this example with the wireless adapter problem. I got around the problem by booting the system into Safe Mode, which

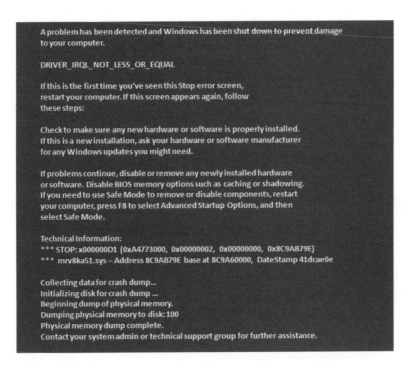

A problem has been detected and Windows has been shut down to prevent damage to your computer.

DRIVER_IRQL_NOT_LESS_OR_EQUAL

If this is the first time you've seen this Stop error screen, restart your computer. If this screen appears again, follow these steps:

Check to make sure any new hardware or software is properly installed. If this is a new installation, ask your hardware or software manufacturer for any Windows updates you might need.

If problems continue, disable or remove any newly installed hardware or software. Disable BIOS memory options such as caching or shadowing. If you need to use Safe Mode to remove or disable components, restart your computer, press F8 to select Advanced Startup Options, and then select Safe Mode.

Technical Information:
*** STOP: x000000D1 (0xA4773000, 0x00000002, 0x00000000, 0x8C9AB79E)
*** mrv8ka51.sys – Address 8C9AB79E base at 8C9A60000, DateStamp 41dcae0e

Collecting data for crash dump...
Initializing disk for crash dump ...
Beginning dump of physical memory.
Dumping physical memory to disk: 100
Physical memory dump complete.
Contact your system admin or technical support group for further assistance.

Figure 6-31 This blue screen STOP error message identifies the driver file causing a problem

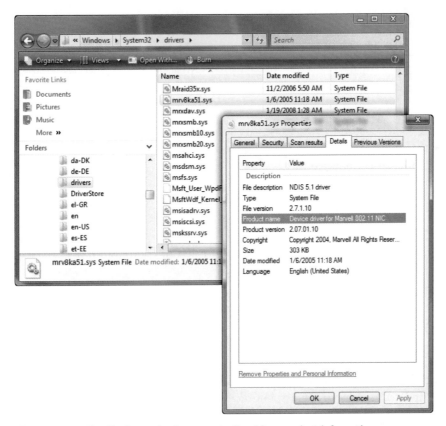

Figure 6-32 The file Properties box reports the driver product information

did not load Driver Verifier, and, therefore, allowed the Windows desktop to load. Then I changed the setting that caused Vista to automatically restart. Here's how to do that:

1. Click **Start**, right-click **Computer**, and select **Properties** from the shortcut menu.

2. In the System window (see upper part of Figure 6-33), click **Advanced system settings** and respond to the UAC box.

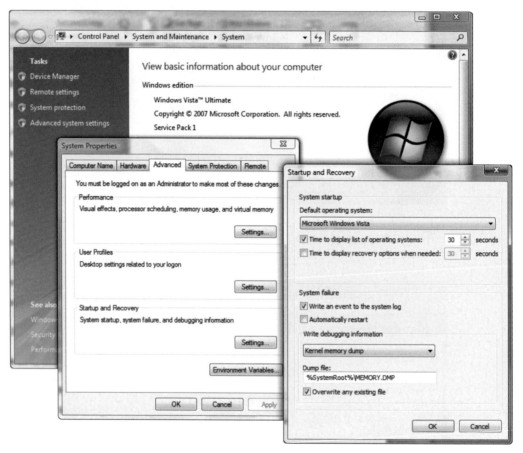

Figure 6-33 Use the Startup and Recovery box to change the way Vista responds to a STOP error during startup

3. In the System Properties box (see lower left of Figure 6-33) in the Startup and Recovery section, click **Settings**.

4. In the Startup and Recovery box (see lower right of Figure 6-33), uncheck **Automatically restart**. Click **OK** twice to close both boxes. Then close the System window.

Next, I restarted the system normally. This time the STOP error remained frozen on screen so I could read it. After I wrote down the information I needed, I restarted the system again in Safe Mode and this time stopped Driver Verifier. Then I restarted Vista normally, located the driver, and updated it. A lot of restarts, but the process did find the driver causing the problem.

UTILITIES BUNDLED WITH A HARDWARE DEVICE

Many devices come with diagnostic utilities included on the setup CD. Sometimes these utilities are installed when you install the device, and sometimes you need to launch the utility from the setup CD. When you have problems with a device, look for this utility either in the Start, All Programs menu or on the setup CD. Use it to test and diagnose problems with the device.

FIXING PROBLEMS WITH HARDWARE

Let's begin learning about how to solve hardware problems by looking at some software tools useful for solving hardware problems and some general guidelines for approaching these problems. Then we'll look at a few typical hardware problems and how to solve them.

This section addresses hardware problems that don't prevent Windows from starting. If you cannot start Windows at all, then move on to Chapter 7, "Resurrecting the Dead."

GUIDELINES FOR SOLVING A HARDWARE PROBLEM

Now let's look at some general guidelines to solve a hardware problem:

▲ *Guideline 1: Check the simple things first.* I know I'm beginning to sound repetitive on this point, but I really feel compelled to say it again. Most computer problems are simple and easy to solve. Check the simple things: Is the external device plugged in and turned on? Are the data cable connections solid at both ends? For sound, is the volume knob turned up? Is there a wall light switch controlling the power, and is it turned on? Is the power strip you're using plugged in and turned on? For expansion cards and memory modules, are they seated solidly in their slots?

▲ *Guideline 2: Check that CMOS setup and Windows recognize the device with no errors.* For a device that should be recognized by startup BIOS, go into CMOS setup and make sure the device is correctly detected and is enabled. Also check Device Manager to verify that the device is enabled and Windows thinks the device should be working. If you see errors in Device Manager, these errors must be resolved before you continue. For devices that don't appear in Device Manager—such as a scanner, printer, or some USB or FireWire devices—use the utility program that came bundled with the device to check for errors. You should find the program on the **Start, All Programs** menus. For printers, also use the Printers window to check for problems.

▲ *Guideline 3: Consider recent changes.* What hardware or software changes have you or someone else recently made? Maybe the change affected something that you have not yet considered. Once I installed a hard drive, turned on the system, and got beep code errors during the power-on self test (POST). I opened the case and checked the drive and connections. It all looked fine, so I tried to boot again with the same results. The second time I opened the case, I discovered that I had bumped a memory module while closing the case. Reseating the module solved my problem.

▲ *Guideline 4: Update device drivers.* A hardware device such as a network adapter, USB device, modem, or printer requires device drivers to work. Device drivers are installed at the time the device is installed and these drivers can come from the device manufacturer or, for some devices, you can use the Microsoft drivers included with Windows. Manufacturers often update their drivers, and Windows Update sometimes includes these updates. However, for best results, download driver updates from the manufacturer's Web site. When you're having a problem with the device, try updating the drivers with the latest versions available. First, download the driver files to your hard drive. Then, in Device Manager, right-click the device and select **Properties** from the shortcut menu. The device properties window opens. Click the **Driver** tab and then click **Update Driver**. The Update Driver Software wizard starts up, as shown in Figure 6-34. Click **Browse my computer for driver software**. On the next screen, you can point to the location of the drivers you have downloaded. If you don't like the results of the update, you can click **Roll Back Driver** (shown in Figure 6-34) to undo the update.

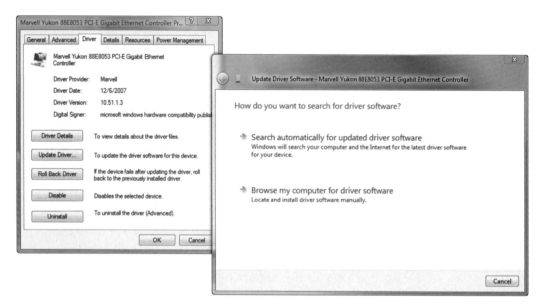

Figure 6-34 Update the device's drivers using the Update Driver Software wizard

◢ *Guideline 5: Try moving the device to a different port or connector.* For external USB devices, try a different USB port. For internal devices, try moving the device to a different expansion slot or connecting it to a different connector on the motherboard. Perhaps the current connector or port is bad, disabled, or not configured correctly.

◢ *Guideline 6: Try reinstalling the device.* To get a clean start with a device, you can uninstall it and start over. In Device Manager, right-click the device and select **Uninstall**. Then reboot the PC. When Windows starts, it should detect a new hardware device and launch the Found New Hardware Wizard. Then you can install the device drivers again. Did the Found New Hardware Wizard launch? If not, the device might be bad or the port it is using might be bad or disabled. You'll see an example of how to deal with a bad port in the next section, "Fixing Problems with USB Devices."

◢ *Guideline 7: Check the manufacturer's documentation.* When installing a device, sometimes the device will not work unless you run the setup CD for the device *before* you physically install the device. (This is sometimes true of internal modem cards, network adapters, and USB devices.) To know the right order, read the manufacturer's documentation. You should also find troubleshooting guidelines there for the device and how to use any diagnostic software the manufacturer offers. Also, the manufacturer's Web site should have a support section including FAQs about the device. When all else fails, I've often found my solution there.

FIXING PROBLEMS WITH USB DEVICES

A USB problem I once encountered started when a friend plugged her USB wireless adapter into her notebook computer. The notebook paused for a moment and then her screen looked like the one in Figure 6-35. Each time she tried again, she got the same result.

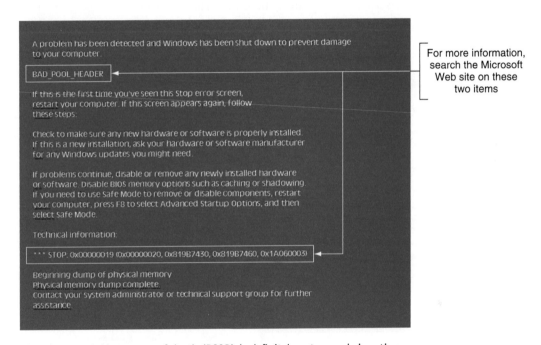

Figure 6-35 A blue screen of death (BSOD) is definitely not a good sign; time to start troubleshooting

If you are having a problem with a USB device, the source of the problem might be:

- ◢ *Source 1*: The device or its device drivers might be bad or corrupted.
- ◢ *Source 2*: The USB port might be bad or disabled or the USB port drivers might be corrupted.
- ◢ *Source 3*: Too many unpowered USB devices might be drawing down too much power from the USB hub.
- ◢ *Source 4*: The USB cable might be too long (hi-speed USB cables should not exceed 16 feet, 5 inches and regular USB cables should not exceed 9 feet, 10 inches).
- ◢ *Source 5*: Too many USB devices connected per USB controller (unlikely since you can connect up to 127).
- ◢ *Source 6*: Vista might be the problem. When Microsoft released a Vista update recently, many reported problems with USB devices. Check the Microsoft Web site if you suspect

this or a similar problem might apply to you and look for a patch. For more information, see the Microsoft Knowledge Base Article 941600 at *support.microsoft.com.*

To isolate and fix a problem with a USB device, the first step is to decide if the problem is with the USB device, the USB port, the USB hub or cabling, or Vista. Follow these steps:

1. Try another device on the same USB port. If this device works, then you know the port is good.

2. If no USB device works using this port, then turn your attention to solving the problem with the port. The port might be damaged, disabled in CMOS setup, or the port drivers might be bad. First go into CMOS setup and verify that the USB port is enabled.

3. Windows might have a problem with the USB controller. Look in Device Manager for the USB controllers listed (see left side of Figure 6-36). Remember, the controllers shown here represent only the USB ports, not the devices using the ports. Make sure the USB controllers are enabled and Windows reports no errors.

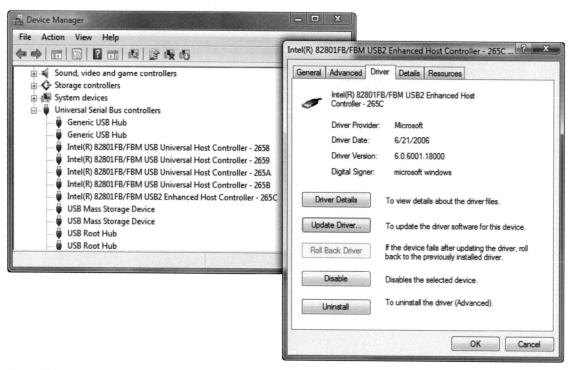

Figure 6-36   Device Manager reports information about USB ports, but not USB devices

4. When did the problem start? If the device was working and now does not, consider whether a Windows update might have caused the problem. Check the Microsoft support site (*support.microsoft.com*) for information and a fix.

5. Try updating the drivers for the USB controller. Windows has its own USB drivers, but if the USB port comes directly off your motherboard, you can try using the drivers supplied with your motherboard. Look for a drivers CD that came bundled with your motherboard and use it to update the USB controller drivers. To update these drivers, right-click a USB controller in Device Manager and select **Properties** from the shortcut menu. The controller Properties box opens. Click the **Driver** tab (see right side of Figure 6-36). Click

Update Driver and the Hardware Update Wizard launches. Follow the directions in the wizard to point to the drivers on CD or your hard drive and complete the installation. Later, if you decide the update does not work for you, you can undo it by clicking **Roll Back Driver** on this same Properties window.

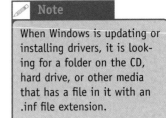

> **Note**
>
> When Windows is updating or installing drivers, it is looking for a folder on the CD, hard drive, or other media that has a file in it with an .inf file extension.

6. If you still can't get the USB port to work, try flashing the BIOS on the motherboard. Don't attempt to flash the BIOS unless you are an experienced technician or have some expert help. To flash BIOS, go to the Web site for the motherboard manufacturer to download the BIOS update and install it. However, be really careful to make sure you've got the right update, and if the update process gives you the option, be sure to create a backup of your old configuration so you can undo the update if necessary. Updating your BIOS with the wrong update can make your entire system not work.

7. Consider that the port might be physically damaged. To solve that problem, you can use CMOS setup to disable it and install an expansion card in a PCI slot to provide USB ports. You can also replace the motherboard, although this is more complicated and expensive; it might not be worth the effort or expense.

After you know the USB port is working, do the following to solve the problem with the USB device:

1. The USB device might be bad. To eliminate that as the problem, try installing the device on another PC. If it works, then you know the problem is not the device. If it doesn't work, the problem might still be with the device drivers and not the device. Also, some older USB devices were picky about the order in which USB devices were installed. Try removing all other USB devices except this one.

2. To solve a problem with corrupted device drivers, first try uninstalling and reinstalling the device. To do that, find the device listed in the Programs and Features window. For example, in Figure 6-37, the driver software for the M-Audio Fast Track USB sound recorder appears. To uninstall the software, select it, click **Uninstall** and follow the directions on screen. Then, to clear out the registry, restart the system. Next, run the setup utility on the CD that came bundled with the device to reinstall it. Watch for errors in the installation routine.

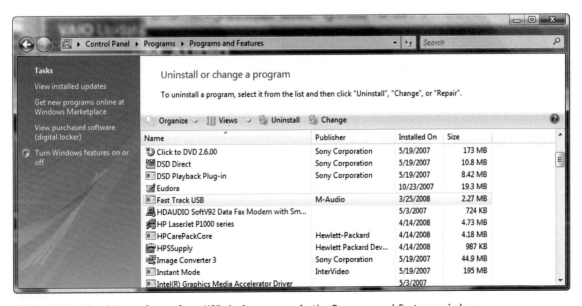

Figure 6-37 The driver software for a USB device appears in the Programs and Features window

3. Check the Web site of the device manufacturer for updated drivers. Download the drivers to your hard drive. For most USB devices, to install these drivers, first uninstall the existing drivers and then double-click the downloaded file. See the Web site for specific instructions.

4. Look in your **Start, All Programs** menu for a utility to manage the device. It might have diagnostic software you can use. Make sure the utility has the device configured correctly.

5. The problem might be with the application software that is controlling the device. For example, if you are having problems trying to use a USB scanner, try scanning using a different application.

6. After you've tried all this and the problem is still not solved, I think it's time to assume your USB device is just not working. Replace it with a new one.

By the way, back to my friend and her USB wireless adapter: We tried another USB device on her notebook, and it worked fine, so we assumed the problem was not the USB port or controller. So next, we tried plugging in the wireless adapter on another computer. The Found New Hardware Wizard launched and we began installing the drivers. Partway through the installation: Poof! Blue screen of death. Just to make sure the drivers were not the problem, we downloaded new drivers from the adapter manufacturer and started fresh. When we got the same results, we decided to toss the adapter and buy her a new one.

FIXING PROBLEMS WITH APPLICATIONS

Problems with applications might be caused by the application, the hardware, the operating system, the data, other applications in conflict with this one, or the user. Several Vista troubleshooting tools—including Windows Error Reporting, Windows Update, System File Checker, Reliability Monitor, Event Viewer, and others—can help you discover the source of the problem. We'll first look at some general guidelines to solving application problems and then look at an example or two of how these guidelines can be applied.

GENERAL APPROACHES TO SOLVING APPLICATION PROBLEMS

Problems with applications can arise from a variety of sources. Here are twenty useful tips to help you sort things out and get to the root of problems with applications and to fix them:

▲ *Tip 1: Ask the user to reproduce the problem while you watch.* Many problems with applications are caused by user error. Watch carefully as the user shows you the problem. If you see him making a mistake, be tactful and don't accuse. Just explain the problem and its solution. It's better to explain and teach rather than fix the problem yourself, so the user learns from the experience.

▲ *Tip 2: Try a reboot.* Reboot the system and see if that solves the problem.

▲ *Tip 3: Suspect a virus is causing a problem.* Scan for viruses and check Task Manager to make sure some strange process is not interfering with your applications.

▲ *Tip 4: Windows update might solve the problem.* When Microsoft is aware of application problems caused by Windows, it sometimes releases a patch to solve the problem. Make sure Windows updates are current.

▲ *Tip 5: Allow Windows to provide a solution.* If Windows Error Reporting displays a window similar to the one shown earlier in Figure 6-17, follow through for a solution by clicking **Check for solution** and apply any recommended solutions. After the problem has happened, you can still apply solutions by using the Problem Reports and Solutions window shown earlier in Figure 6-20.

▲ *Tip 6: Another application might be interfering.* Close all other applications. Another application might be corrupted or have a data file open that this application needs.

▲ *Tip 7: You might be low on system resources.* Close all other applications. Check Task Manager to make sure you have unnecessary processes closed. If you must run more than one application at a time, you can increase the priority level for an application that is not getting its fair share of resources. To do that, on the **Processes** tab of Task Manager, right-click the application and select **Set Priority**. Then increase the priority level. This setting applies to the current session only. Also, consider that your system might be running low on memory. For good performance, Windows Vista needs at least 1 GB of RAM. For great performance, use even more than that.

▲ *Tip 8: Verify Windows system files.* Corrupted Windows system files can cause application errors. To have Windows verify system files and replace a bad one with a good one, use the System File Checker (sfc.exe) utility. You learned how to use the utility earlier in the chapter.

▲ *Tip 9: The problem might be bad memory.* Following directions given earlier in the chapter use the Memory Diagnostics tool to test memory. If it finds errors, have the memory modules replaced.

▲ *Tip 10: Use Event Viewer to look for clues.* The Event Viewer Windows logs might give clues about applications and the system, and the Hardware Events log might give clues about related hardware problems.

▲ *Tip 11: Use the Reliability Monitor to look for clues.* The Reliability Monitor might help you discover the source of the problem. Look for errors with other applications or with key hardware components such as the hard drive. Hard drive errors often appear as an application error.

▲ *Tip 12: Use the Chkdsk command to check the hard drive.* To eliminate the hard drive as the source of an application error, use the Chkdsk command to check the drive. Recall the command is **chkdsk C: /r** and must be executed from an elevated command prompt.

▲ *Tip 13: Download updates or patches for the application.* Software manufacturers often publish updates or patches for their software to address known problems. You can go to the software manufacturer's Web site to download these updates and get information about known problems.

▲ *Tip 14: Verify that the application is digitally signed.* Although applications that are not digitally signed can still run on Vista, a digital signature does verify that the application is not a rogue application and that it is certified as Vista-compatible by Microsoft. To view the digital signature, in Windows Explorer, find the program filename (most likely in a subfolder of the Program Files folder), right-click the filename, and select **Properties** from the shortcut menu. Select the **Digital Signatures** tab and click **Advanced** (see Figure 6-38). If the Digital Signatures tab is missing, the program is not digitally signed.

▲ *Tip 15: Uninstall and reinstall the application.* Sometimes an application gives problems because the installation gets corrupted. You can try uninstalling and reinstalling the application. However, in doing so you might lose any customized settings, macros, or scripts.

▲ *Tip 16: Run the application as an administrator.* The application might require that the user have privileges not assigned to the current account. Try running the application with administrator privileges. To do that, right-click the application icon on the desktop or the application name in the **All Programs** menu, and select **Run as administrator** from the shortcut menu (see Figure 6-39). If this fixes the problem, to make this setting permanent, use Windows Explorer: Locate the program filename (most likely in a subfolder of the Program Files folder), right-click it, and select

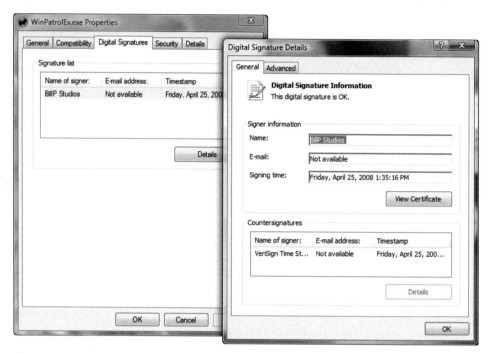

Figure 6-38 This program is digitally signed

Figure 6-39 To elevate an application's privileges, run the application as an administrator

Properties from the shortcut menu. Then click the **Compatibility** tab and check **Run this program as an administrator** (see Figure 6-40). Click **Apply** and then close the Properties box.

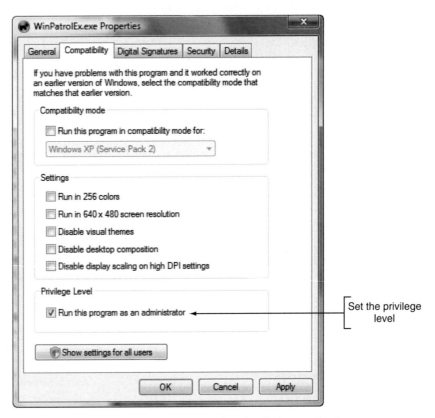

Figure 6-40 Permanently change the privilege level of an application

▲ *Tip 17: Install the application as an administrator.* By default, Vista does not allow Standard accounts to install applications. To install software, first log onto the system as an administrator.

▲ *Tip 18: Consider data corruption.* It might appear that the application has a problem when the problem is really a corrupted data file. Try creating an entirely new data file. If that works, then suspect that previous errors might be caused by corrupted data. You might be able to recover part of a corrupted file by changing its file extension to .txt and importing it into the application as a text file.

▲ *Tip 19: Try restoring default settings.* Maybe a user has made one too many changes to the application settings. Try restoring all settings back to their default values. This might solve a problem with missing toolbars and other functions.

▲ *Tip 20: Consider whether an older application is having compatibility problems with Vista.* Some older applications cannot run under Vista or run with errors. Here are some steps you can take to fix the problem:

1. Go to the Windows Vista Compatability Center Web site at *www.microsoft.com/ windows/compatibility* and search for the application. The site reports problems and solutions for known legacy software. For example, when you search on the application WinPatrol, you find that Version 11 is not compatible with Vista, but Version 14

is compatible (see Figure 6-41). If the application is known to not be compatible with Vista, try to replace or upgrade the software.

2. Try running the application in compatibility mode. To do that, on the **Compatibility** tab of the program file **Properties** box shown earlier in Figure 6-40, check **Run this program in compatibility mode for:**. Then in the dropdown menu, select the operating system that the application was written to run under. Click **Apply** and close the **Properties** box.

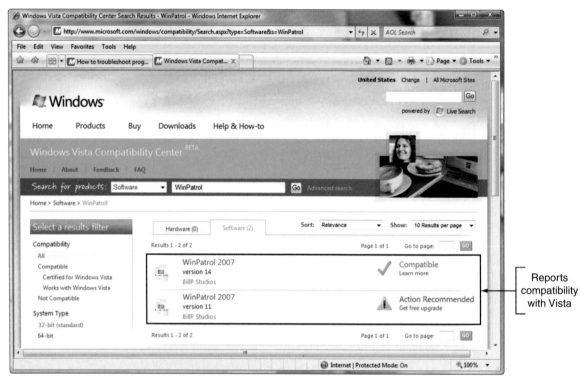

Figure 6-41 Microsoft tracks software and hardware compatible with Vista

FIXING INTERNET EXPLORER

Let's take a look at some things you can do to solve problems with an application most users have on their desktop, Internet Explorer. When application problems occur, our first instinct is to restart the system. However, before you do the restart, make sure you understand the problem that is currently displayed on the screen so that you know how to reproduce it after the restart. And another concern before you restart: If you are concerned that the source of the problem might be a failing OS or hard drive, find out if you need to save data to another media that is only saved on the hard drive. The system might not boot after you restart and saving the data then will be more complicated. So, after you examine the problem and back up the data, restart the system.

When you restart the system, log on as an administrator and verify whether the problem still exists. If it does, begin troubleshooting by following these steps:

1. *Verify that you have Internet access.* Before you assume the problem is with Internet Explorer, verify that the local network is working and you have Internet access. Can you access resources on the local network? Next try to use an application other than IE

that requires Internet access. For example, can you download e-mail using Windows Mail? Open a command prompt window and try to ping a web site. For example, try this command: **ping www.course.com**. If the ping command does not work, then treat the problem as a network problem. Network troubleshooting is covered in Chapter 5.

2. *Verify that all Vista updates are current.* Windows Vista considers Internet Explorer and Windows Mail (formerly Outlook Express) program files to be part of the full set of Windows system files. Therefore, updates to Windows Vista include updates to these apps, and these updates might solve the problem. You learned how to update Windows in Chapter 1.

3. *Using updated antivirus software, scan the system for viruses.* If your AV software finds malware, scan again to make sure the system is infection free.

4. *Use the Error Reporting feature of Vista to search for solutions.* Following instructions given earlier in the chapter, open the Problem Reports and Solution window to search for problems that pertain to Internet Explorer and apply any solutions not yet implemented.

5. *Verify that other applications are not causing the problem.* Other applications might be in conflict with IE. Close all other open applications and check Task Manager to make sure all are closed.

If the problem still persists, then follow the instructions given next where you'll learn to eliminate add-ons, IE history, IE settings, the cache index, and corrupted OS files as sources of the problem.

ELIMINATE ADD-ONS AS THE SOURCE OF THE PROBLEM

Most Internet Explorer problems are caused by add-ons. You can temporarily disable all add-ons so they can be eliminated as the source of a problem. Follow these steps:

1. Restart the system and verify that the problem still exists.

2. Click **Start, All Programs, Accessories, System Tools,** and **Internet Explorer (No Add-ons)**. (Alternately, you can enter **iexplore.exe –extoff** in the Start Search box.) Internet Explorer opens showing the information bar message in Figure 6-42.

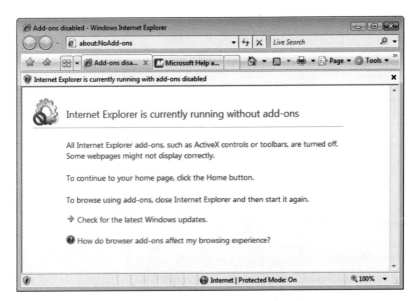

Figure 6-42   Internet Explorer is running with no add-ons

3. Check to see if the problem has disappeared. If it has disappeared, then you can assume the source of the problem is an add-on. You can next try enabling one add-on after another until you discover the one giving the problem.

4. To return Internet Explorer to run with add-ons, close the IE window and then open IE as usual.

To enable and disable specific add-ons, do the following:

1. Open Internet Explorer. Click **Tools,** point to **Manage Add-ons,** and click **Enable or Disable Add-ons** (see Figure 6-43). The Manage Add-ons window opens as shown in Figure 6-44.

Figure 6-43   Manage add-ons using the Tools menu of Internet Explorer

Figure 6-44   Use the Manage Add-ons window to disable or delete add-ons

2. The window displays currently loaded add-ons. From the drop-down list, select **Add-ons that have been used by Internet Explorer**. Then disable all add-ons in the list by selecting each add-on and clicking **Disable**. Beginning at the top of the list, enable the first add-on and check to see if the problem returns.

3. Continue to enable one add-on after another until the problem returns. You have now identified the add-on with the problem.

4. To uninstall the add-on, for ActiveX controls, select it in the Manage Add-ons box and click **Delete**. For other add-ons, open the Programs and Features window. Select the add-on and then click **Uninstall** (see Figure 6-45).

Figure 6-45 Uninstall Internet Explorer add-ons using the Programs and Features window

5. If you believe you need the add-on, to install it, navigate the browser to the Web site that uses the add-on. For example, when you navigate to the site shown in Figure 6-46, an information bar appears asking permission to install an add-on. Click the bar and then click **Run ActiveX Control** to install the add-on. Alternately, if you know the Web site of the add-on developer, you can go there to download the add-on and install it.

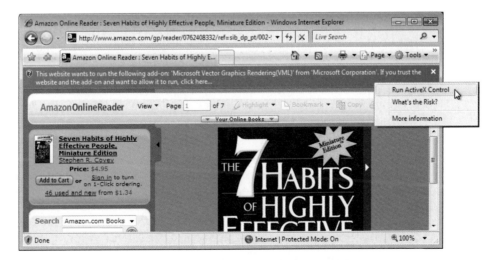

Figure 6-46 Internet Explorer is asking permission to install an add-on

CLEAN THE BROWSER HISTORY

The IE problem might be caused by a corrupted browser history, which might prevent access to particular Web sites or using Internet Explorer in general. Also, deleting the browser history is a good best practice to protect your privacy when you are finished using Internet Explorer on a public computer. To clean the history, follow these steps:

1. In Internet Explorer, click **Tools** and **Internet Options**. The Internet Options dialog box appears as shown on the left in Figure 6-47.

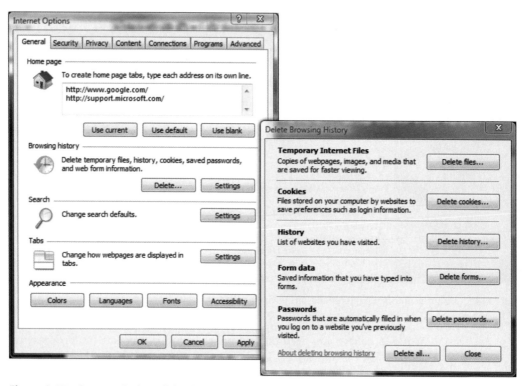

Figure 6-47   Internet Options dialog box

2. Under Browsing history, click **Delete**. The Delete Browsing History dialog box appears as shown in the right of Figure 6-47. You can select particular items to delete or click **Delete all** to clean out the entire browsing history. When using a public computer, definitely click **Delete all** to completely delete history files.

3. When solving a specific problem with Internet Explorer, you might want to be more discriminating because deleting Cookies and Passwords might cause an inconvenience. Try deleting in this order: Delete files, Delete history, Delete forms, and Delete passwords. Verify that the problem still exists after each deletion.

If the problem still persists, before you delete cookies, you can save your cookies so that, if cookies are not the source of the problem, you can restore them. To save your cookies, do the following:

1. In the Internet Explorer menu bar, click **File** and then click **Import and Export**. The Import/Export Wizard opens. Click **Next**.

2. On the next window (see Figure 6-48), select **Export Cookies** and click **Next**. (Notice in this window, you can also export and import favorites and feeds as well as import cookies.)

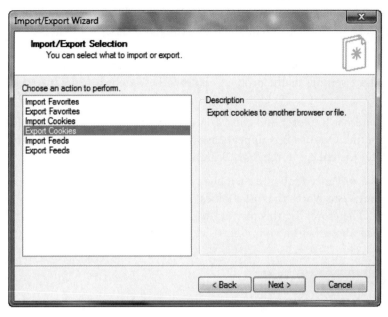

Figure 6-48 Choose to export cookies

3. On the next window (see Figure 6-49), select the location and name of the text file and click **Next**. Confirm the operation and click **Finish** to complete the wizard. Click **OK** to close the box that appears when exporting is completed.

You are now ready to delete cookies. After you delete the cookies, if the problem is still not resolved, use the Import/Export Wizard to import cookies back into Internet Explorer, which restores your cookies.

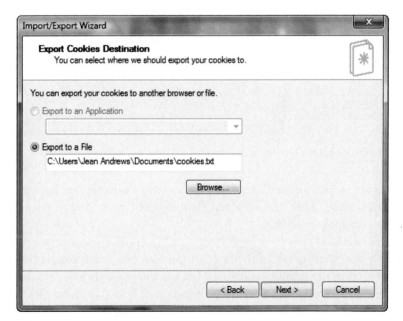

Figure 6-49 Select the path and name of the export file

RESET INTERNET EXPLORER SETTINGS

After you have eliminated add-ons and the browser history as the source of the problem, the next step is to eliminate IE settings. There are two approaches to doing that: resetting IE to default settings (all customized settings are lost and all add-ons are deleted), or the less drastic approach of manually changing one setting at a time, searching for the one that might be causing the problem.

If Internet Explorer does not use many customized settings, resetting IE is the quickest way to eliminate settings as the problem. Follow these steps to reset Internet Explorer:

1. Open Internet Explorer and click **Tools**. From the Tools menu, select **Internet Options**. The Internet Options box appears as shown earlier in Figure 6-47. (Alternately, you can enter **inetcpl.cpl** in the Start Search box.)

2. Click the **Advanced** tab and then click **Reset** (see Figure 6-50). Note in the box on the right that Vista warns that all cookies, passwords, toolbars and add-ons will be deleted. Therefore, use this method with caution and consider exporting cookies as described above before you reset. Click **Reset** to compete the task.

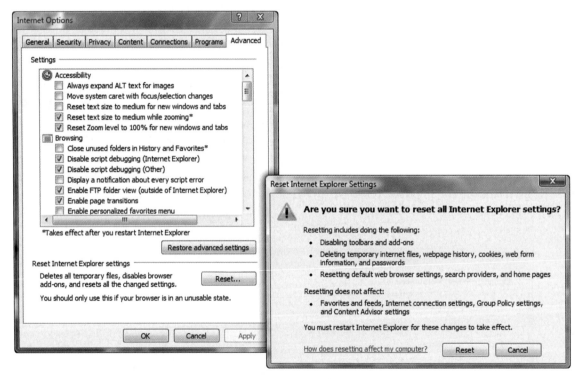

Figure 6-50 Reset Internet Explorer customized settings and add-ons

If you don't want to lose all the IE settings, you can try changing one setting at a time until you identify the culprit. Here are a few tips that might help. Be sure to restart IE and test for a fix after you apply each one:

▲ *Tip 1*: On the Security tab of the Internet Options box, click **Default level** to reset the security level to the default setting (see left side of Figure 6-51).
▲ *Tip 2*: For problems with a specific Web site, on the Security tab, click **Trusted sites** and then click **Sites**. In the Trusted sites box (right side of Figure 6-51), add the site to the trusted zone.

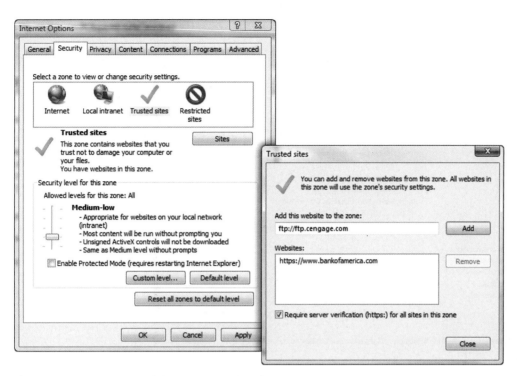

Figure 6-51 Security tab of the Internet Options box

▲ *Tip 3*: On the Advanced tab of the Internet Options box (refer back to Figure 6-50), scroll down the list looking for a specific setting that might apply to your problem. If you're not sure of a setting, you might compare the advanced settings to those on a working computer.

▲ *Tip 4*: Reset all advanced settings by clicking **Restore advanced settings**.

▲ *Tip 5*: On the Privacy tab, click **Default**. (Default will be gray if default settings are already applied.)

▲ *Tip 6*: For Windows Vista Business, Enterprise, and Ultimate editions, check Group Policy to make sure a policy is not overriding a setting in the Internet Options box. Recall from Chapter 2 that you access the Group Policy Editor console using the gpedit.msc command. In the console, Internet Explorer polices can be found under either the Computer Configuration or the User Configuration. To view policies that apply directly to Internet Explorer, expand the Administrative Templates folder, the Windows Components folder, and the Internet Explorer folder. When you select a policy folder in the left pane, policy settings appear in the right pane. Look for policies that display a state other than *Not configured*, such as the one shown in Figure 6-52.

> **Note**
>
> Another way to find out what Group Policies have been applied to a computer or a user is to use the gpresult command in an elevated command prompt window. See Appendix C for details.

REPAIR A CORRUPTED CACHE INDEX

Sometimes IE problems are caused by a corrupted index file in the cache folder. To solve the problem, you need to delete the hidden file index.dat. The easiest way to delete the file is to delete the entire IE cache folder for the user account that has the problem. The next time the user logs on, the folder will be rebuilt. To delete the folder, first make sure you're logged onto the system using a different account that has administrative privileges. The folder you want to delete is C:\Users*username*\AppData\Local\Microsoft\Windows\Temporary Internet Files. You will not be able to delete the folder if this user is logged on.

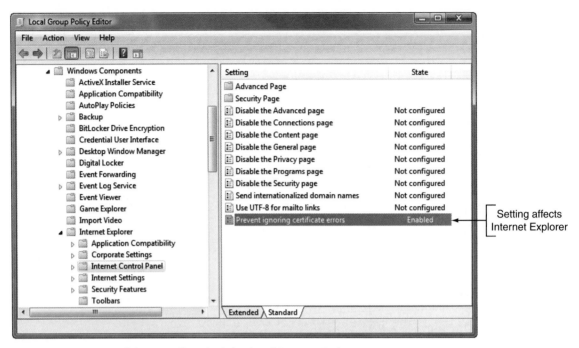

Figure 6-52 Group policies can affect the behavior of Internet Explorer

REPAIR INTERNET EXPLORER

If you still have a problem with IE and you are certain the problem is not with the network or with Internet access, follow the steps listed below to repair Internet Explorer. However, know that each step is progressively more drastic than the next and you might find that, in using the method described, you change other Windows configuration settings and components. Therefore, after you try a step, check to see if your problem is fixed. Don't move on to the next step unless your problem is still present.

Note

The Microsoft Web site at *http://support.microsoft.com* and many other Web sites offer solutions and tips about Internet Explorer. One site I especially like is Sandi Hardmeier's at *http://inetexplorer.mvps.org*. Look there for a bunch of other Internet Explorer problems and solutions.

1. *Use the Windows Vista System File Checker (sfc.exe) to check Windows system files and replace corrupted ones.* You learned to use this utility earlier in the chapter.

2. *Upgrade Internet Explorer 7 to Internet Explorer 8.* At the time of this writing, Internet Explorer 8 has just been released in Beta version. (A Beta version of software is the first, not-fully-tested release of software.) However, by the time you are reading this, IE 8 should be fully tested and ready to go. Consider going to the Microsoft Web site (*www.microsoft.com*) and downloading and installing IE 8, which hopefully might solve your problem.

3. *Run Internet Explorer in Safe Mode with Networking.* Press F8 at startup to display the Advanced Boot Options menu and select Safe Mode with Networking from the menu. If Internet Explorer works in Safe Mode, then you can assume the problem is not with IE but with the operating system, device drivers, or other applications that load at startup which are conflicting with IE. In this situation, approach the problem as a Windows problem rather than an Internet Explorer problem.

4. *Repair a corrupted Windows Vista installation.* If Internet Explorer refuses to work, even in Safe Mode with Networking, you can assume that the Vista installation is corrupted. There are several methods and tools to troubleshoot Windows, all discussed in the next chapter. As you read the next chapter, look for ways to repair Windows Vista that require the least amount of work and make the fewest drastic changes to your system.

> **Note**
>
> Because Internet Explorer is an integrated component of Windows Vista, you cannot uninstall and install it again as you can regular applications. If IE gets corrupted and you don't want to mess with your Windows installation to fix the problem, one way you can solve the problem is to abandon IE and use Firefox by Mozilla as your Web browser. Go to the Mozilla Web site (*www.mozilla.com/firefox*) shown in Figure 6-53, then download and run the installer. If IE is not working and you can't get to the Mozilla Web site, use another computer to download the Firefox file and burn the file to a CD, then use the CD to install Firefox on your computer.

Figure 6-53 Use Firefox as your web browser

>> CHAPTER SUMMARY

◢ Problems with computers can be divided into those that occur during the boot and those that occur after the boot.

◢ When first approaching a computer problem, always take the necessary precautions to protect any data on the hard drive that is not backed up.

◢ Approach computer problems systematically, checking the simple things first, researching all available sources of information, and establishing your priorities. Begin problem solving by asking the user questions.

◢ Learn to ask the user questions that help you understand the nature of the problem, the user's priorities, and the history behind the problem.

◢ Software tools that can help with hardware problems include CMOS setup, Device Manager, Event Viewer, the Printers window, the Programs and Features window, System Restore, Problem Reports and Solutions, Reliability Monitor, Data Collector Sets, Memory Diagnostics, System File Checker, Chkdsk, Driver Verifier and utilities that come bundled with devices.

◢ When solving a hardware problem, check the simple things first, and check CMOS setup, Device Manager, and Event Viewer for errors. Also try updating device drivers and reinstalling the device.

◢ USB devices, FireWire devices, and printers don't show up in Device Manager and require slightly different troubleshooting strategies than other hardware devices.

◢ For devices that use ports, consider that the problem might be with the device or the port that it is using. The problem can be hardware related or related to the device drivers for the device or port.

◢ For problems with applications, you can allow Windows to provide a solution, try uninstalling and reinstalling the application, verify windows system files, run the application under a different account, download patches, and restore the application to default settings.

>> KEY TERMS

Data Collector Set A Vista tool in the Computer Management console used to collect data about different aspects of the system and present that data in a report that can help you identify the source of a computer problem.

diagnostic card An expansion card that can be used to display error codes at startup to diagnose a startup problem with hardware.

IDE to USB adapter An inexpensive device that allows you to connect an IDE hard drive to a USB port. It can help you recover data from an IDE drive that will not boot.

Memory Diagnostics A Vista tool that tests memory before Vista is loaded. This tool can be launched from the Error Reporting utility, the command prompt (mdsched.exe), the Vista boot menu, or the Vista setup DVD.

Reliability Monitor A Vista tool in the Computer Management console that can report the past history of problems on the computer, including the history of Software, Application, Hardware, Windows, and Miscellaneous Failures.

SATA to USB adapter An inexpensive device that allows you to connect a SATA hard drive to a USB port. It can help you recover data from a SATA drive that will not boot.

System File Checker A Windows Vista utility (sfc.exe) that protects system files and keeps a cache folder of current system files in case it needs to refresh a damaged file.

>> REVIEWING THE BASICS

1. When you have a problem with a USB device, what is the simplest way to determine that the USB port is good?

2. When you have a problem with a USB device, what is the simplest way to determine that the USB device is not causing the problem?

3. How can you determine that device drivers loaded at startup are not interfering with an application that is having problems?

4. What is the command used for testing memory?

5. If you are not sure which device is causing a video problem—the monitor or the video card—which one should you exchange first? Why?

6. What type of device that, when installed, is not listed in CMOS setup, Device Manager, or the Printers window?

7. What is the term used to describe undoing a driver update?

8. What Windows tool can you use to uninstall a USB device?

9. What Windows tool can you use to uninstall a printer?

10. What Windows tool can you use to uninstall a network card?

11. What Windows tool can you use to restore the Windows system to a previous point in time before a device was installed?

12. What Windows tool can you use to update your video drivers?

13. What symbol does Device Manager use to indicate a device is not working?

14. If the USB controller on your motherboard is damaged, what can you do so that your system can support USB devices?

15. What level of permission must a user account have to install software?

16. What causes most of the problems with Internet Explorer?

17. If the index file in the IE cache folder gets corrupted, what is the easiest way to fix the problem?

18. List four types of devices that do not appear in Device Manager.

19. If a computer won't boot, to figure out if the problem is related to the hard drive or other vital hardware component, what would be the first step?

20. What is another name for a Windows Stop error?

>> THINKING CRITICALLY

1. As a helpdesk technician, list four good detective questions to ask if a user calls to say, "My PC won't boot."

2. Starting with the easiest procedure, list four things to check if you plug in a USB scanner and the computer does not recognize the scanner.

3. Someone calls to say he has attempted to install a modem, but the modem does not work. List the first three questions to ask.

4. An application refuses to load, giving an error about a file not being accessible. Select from the following steps the ones that might solve the problem. Then order the selected steps in the correct order for troubleshooting. Explain how each selected step might solve the problem.

   a. Uninstall the application
   b. Reinstall the application
   c. Create a restore point
   d. Restart the computer
   e. Log onto the system using an administrator account

5. Reword the following questions that might be asked when interviewing a user over the telephone so as not to antagonize him or her.

   a. Did you drop your laptop?
   b. Did you forget to recharge the laptop battery?
   c. You say the problem is that Microsoft Word is giving an error, but do you really know how to use that application?

>> HANDS-ON PROJECTS

PROJECT 6-1:   Investigating Solutions for a Damaged USB Port

Suppose you have determined that one of your USB ports is damaged. Check CMOS setup on your computer. Is it possible to disable one port without disabling all of them? How much will it cost to buy a PCI card to provide extra USB ports? Give the URL or print the Web page showing your answer.

PROJECT 6-2:   Diagnosing Notebook Computer Problems

Suppose you spend much of your day diagnosing problems with notebook computers. Newer notebooks have a mini-PCI slot that works in a similar way to PCI slots on desktop systems. Search the Internet for a diagnostic card that you can use in a mini-PCI slot that can help you diagnose hardware problems with notebooks. Print the Web pages showing your findings. Which diagnostic card would you choose to buy and why?

PROJECT 6-3:   Support for Your Installed Hardware and Software

Do the following to find out what kind of support and replacement parts are available for your computer:

1. Make a list of all the installed hardware components on your computer that are considered field replaceable components, including the motherboard, processor, power supply, optical drive, hard drive, and memory.

2. Search the Web for the device manufacturer Web pages that show what support is available for the devices, including any diagnostic software, technical support, and device driver updates.

3. Print a Web page showing a replacement part for each device that fits your system. If possible, show the exact match for a replacement part.

4. Make a list of all installed applications on your computer.

5. For each application, print a Web page showing the support available on the software manufacturer's Web site for the application.

PROJECT 6-4: Help with Notebook Hard Drives

As a notebook computer troubleshooter, you find all too often that people bring you notebook computers that have corrupted Windows installations and hard drives containing valuable data that is not backed up. Search the Internet for a device to help you quickly recover the data. Look for an IDE to USB adapter that can accommodate a 2.5" IDE notebook hard drive. Print Web pages showing your findings.

>> REAL PROBLEMS, REAL SOLUTIONS

REAL PROBLEM 6-1: Finding an Unknown Device (Challenging Real Problem)

Someone has come to you for help with their computer. They are unable to connect to the Internet and are not sure why. After some investigation you realize that they have just replaced the network adapter, but have lost the driver CD for the adapter and its documentation. Windows does not recognize the device type and there is no model information on the device itself. To find the correct drivers, you need to know the exact brand and model of the device. Use the following steps to retrieve this information. By following these steps, you'll learn to use the Ultimate Boot CD, which can be a valuable utility to add to your PC repair kit.

1. Go to the Ultimate Boot CD download page at *www.ultimatebootcd.com/download.html* and read the directions about creating the Ultimate Boot CD. The CD is created using an ISO image. An ISO image is a file that contains all the files that were burned to an original CD or DVD. This ISO image is then used to create copies of the original CD or DVD. The process has three steps: (1) Download the ISO image as a compressed, self-extracting .exe file, (2) Decompress the compressed file to extract the ISO file having an .iso file extension, (3) Use CD burning software to burn the CD from the ISO image.

2. Now that you understand the process, follow directions to download to your hard drive a compressed and self extracting executable (.exe) file containing the ISO image. The current version of the Ultimate Boot CD as of the printing of this book is Version 4.1.1 and the file to download is ubcd411.exe.

3. Double-click the downloaded file to execute it and extract the ISO image. (For Version 4.1.1, the new file will be named ubcd411.iso.)

4. You'll need software to burn the ISO image to the CD. (Do not just burn the .iso file to the CD. The software extracts the files inside the ISO image and burns these files to the CD to create a bootable CD holding many files.) The Ultimate Boot CD Web site suggests some free CD burning software that support ISO images. Download and execute one of these products to burn the ISO image to the CD. Using a permanent marker, label the CD "Ultimate Boot CD" and include the version number that you downloaded.

5. Boot the computer from the CD and find a tool that will retrieve the brand and model number of the NIC (network adapter). What software on the CD did you decide to use?

6. Use the program to find the make and model number of the NIC installed in your system and write down this information.

7. Using the acquired information, search the Internet for the correct driver.

8. Does this driver match the driver installed on your system?

9. Answer the following questions about other programs on the Ultimate Boot CD:

   a. Some antivirus software report that some programs on the Ultimate Boot CD are viruses. Search the Ultimate Boot CD Web site for the name of one of these programs. What is its name and what is the purpose of the program? Is the program truly a virus?

   b. Name one other program on the Ultimate Boot CD that you believe will be useful when troubleshooting. Describe what the program does.

REAL PROBLEM 6-2:   Fixing a PC Problem

This project should be fun and extremely useful. Make yourself available to family and friends who have computer problems. For the first three problems you face, keep a record that includes this information:

1. Describe the problem as the user described it to you.

2. Briefly list the things you did to discover the cause of the problem.

3. What was the final solution?

4. How long did it take you to fix the problem?

5. What would you do differently the next time you encounter this same problem?

Resurrecting the Dead

When a computer refuses to boot or the Windows desktop refuses to load, it takes a cool head to handle the situation gracefully. What helps more than anything else is to have a good plan so you don't feel so helpless. This chapter is designed to give you just that—a plan with all the necessary details, so that you can determine just what has gone wrong and what to do about it. Knowledge is power. When you understand what is happening and you know what to do, the situation doesn't seem nearly as hopeless.

In this chapter, you'll learn how to use a variety of tools to face a boot problem caused by either software or hardware. You'll also learn what to do to recover data that is lost or corrupted. Before we get into the how-to, however, you need to know a little about what has to be in good working order so that a Vista computer can successfully boot. You also need to know about the Vista tools that can help you solve problems with startup. So let's start the chapter with a discussion of what has to work for Vista to start error free.

UNDERSTANDING HOW A VISTA COMPUTER STARTS UP

A Windows Vista system has successfully started when you can log onto Windows and the Windows desktop is loaded. To successfully start, a computer needs the bare-bones minimum of hardware and software. If one of these hardware or software components is missing, corrupted, or broken, the boot fails. We begin this part of the chapter by looking at the essential hardware components for a successful boot, and then you'll learn about the essential Vista components needed to load the Vista desktop. Then you'll learn about the steps toward a successful boot.

BARE-BONES HARDWARE NEEDED TO BOOT A SYSTEM

Here is the list of essential hardware components listed in the order they are used to boot the system:

1. The central processing unit (CPU)

2. The motherboard

3. A chip embedded on the motherboard that holds the BIOS (Basic Input-Output System) or firmware embedded on the chip; this BIOS, called **startup BIOS**, is used to control the initial startup processing

4. Memory

5. The keyboard

6. A video card or video chip embedded on the motherboard (called an onboard video chip)

7. A boot device, such as a hard drive with an OS installed, a CD drive with bootable CD, a USB device that contains a bootable OS, or a floppy drive with bootable floppy

8. A power supply with electrical power

A healthy hard drive formatted for a standard desktop computer or laptop contains the elements in the following bulleted list (these elements are shown in Figure 7-1). All of the elements in the list must be present for Windows to load.

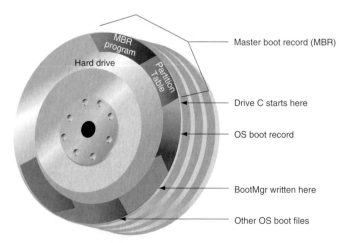

Figure 7-1   Components at the beginning of the hard drive necessary to boot

◢ *The MBR.* The very first item written at the beginning of the drive in the first 512-byte sector is called the **master boot record (MBR)**. This sector contains the master boot program, a tiny, yet incredibly essential program that the BIOS uses to find the OS on the drive. Without this program, you can't boot from the hard drive. The sector also contains the partition table, which is a table that maps out what partitions are on the drive, where on the drive they are located, and which partition is the active partition—the one the MBR program looks to for an OS.

◢ *The OS Boot Record.* The first 512-byte sector of the active partition is called the **OS boot record**, or **boot sector**, and is used to help the MBR find and load the OS, which is normally stored on drive C. Unless a technician changes it, the active partition is always the first partition on a hard drive, which makes the OS boot record the second sector on the drive. (Which partition is the active partition can be changed using Disk Management.) In Microsoft documentation, the active partition is called the system partition.

◢ *Drive C containing OS boot files.* Most often, Windows is installed on drive C. Windows Vista stores files in the root directory of drive C, in the C:\Boot folder, and in the C:\Windows folder and its subfolders. The next section of the chapter covers all of these files.

> **Note**
>
> Vista offers two options as to how a hard drive is configured: basic disks and dynamic disks. Most desktop and laptop computers use a basic disk configuration. Using a basic disk, you can create new partitions, delete partitions, and extend or shrink existing partitions. A second choice for the disk configuration is dynamic disks, which are used on file servers in an enterprise environment where massive data is stored on multiple hard drives. With dynamic disks, you can span a volume across more than one physical hard drive to create larger or faster volumes. Basic disks are easier to configure and use and should be your choice unless you have good reason to do otherwise.
>
> You can also choose between two disk partitioning systems: MBR and GPT. Using the MBR system, you can have up to four partitions on a hard drive, although one of them can be an extended partition with multiple volumes. The GPT (Globally unique identifier Partition Table) disk partitioning system can support up to 128 partitions, and these partitions can be larger than MBR partitions. The GPT system is more reliable than the MBR system because it keeps a backup partition table on the drive in the event the primary partition table is damaged. Also, the GPT system more accurately reports the position of the partition space mapped to cylinders on the drive, which makes it a more reliable system. The advantage the MBR system has is that it is recognized by every Windows operating system, but the GPT system is only recognized by 64-bit Windows XP, Windows Vista, and Windows Server 2003 and higher. To use the GPT system for your bootable hard drive, your computer motherboard must contain an EFI or UEFI chip rather than the traditional BIOS chip. In this chapter, we focus on the MBR system, which is by far the more common system.

> **Note**
>
> EFI (Extensible Firmware Interface) and UEFI (Unified EFI) are two standards for the interface between firmware on the motherboard and the operating system. The standards are intended to replace the legacy BIOS standards and improve on processes for booting, handing over the boot to the OS, and loading device drivers and applications before the OS loads. For more information on either standard, see the UEFI consortium at *www.uefi.org*.

FILES NEEDED TO START WINDOWS VISTA

Table 7-1 lists the files necessary to start Windows Vista. The MBR sector and the OS boot sector are included in the table to complete the list of software components needed to load Vista. Vista startup is managed by two files: the **Windows Boot Manager (BootMgr)** and the **Windows Boot Loader (WinLoad)**. Vista configuration data is stored in the Vista Boot Configuration Data file (BCD). Also notice in Table 7-1 that the BootMgr file and the BCD file are stored in the system partition (the active partition) and the other files are stored in the boot partition. For most installations, the system partition and the boot partition are the same (drive C).

Component or File	Path	Description
MBR	First sector of the hard drive called the master boot record	Contains the partition table and the master boot program used to locate the OS boot program in the OS boot record of the system partition.
OS boot record	First sector of the system partition (most likely drive C)	Contains short program to locate and load the bootloader program, BootMgr.
BootMgr	Root directory of system partition (C:\)	Windows Boot Manager manages the initial startup of the OS.
BCD	\Boot folder of the system partition (C:\Boot)	Boot Configuration Data file contains boot parameters.
WinLoad	%systemroot%\System32* (C:\Windows\System32)	Windows Boot Loader loads and starts essential Windows processes.
Ntoskrnl.exe	%systemroot%\System32 (C:\Windows\System32)	Vista kernel
Hal.dll	%systemroot%\System32 (C:\Windows\System32)	Dynamic-link library handles low-level hardware details
Smss.exe	%systemroot%\System32 (C:\Windows\System32)	Sessions Manager file responsible for loading user mode graphics components
Csrss.exe	%systemroot%\System32 (C:\Windows\System32)	Win32 subsystem
Winlogon.exe	%systemroot%\System32 (C:\Windows\System32)	Logon process
Services.exe	%systemroot%\System32 (C:\Windows\System32)	Service Control Manager starts and stops services
Lsass.exe	%systemroot%\System32 (C:\Windows\System32)	Authenticates users
System registry hive	%systemroot%\System32\ Config\System (C:\Windows\System32\ Config\System)	Holds data for the HKEY_LOCAL_MACHINE key of the registry
Device drivers	%systemroot%\System32\Drivers (C:\Windows\System32\Drivers)	Drivers for required hardware

Table 7-1 Software components and files needed to start Windows Vista

* In Microsoft documentation, the name and location of the folder where Windows system files are stored is referred to as *%systemroot%*, and most likely is C:\Windows.

Don't be confused with the terminology here. It is really true that, according to Windows Vista terminology, the Windows OS is on the boot partition, and the boot record is on the system partition, although that might seem backward. The PC boots from the system partition and loads the Windows Vista operating system from the boot partition. The system partition contains the files that tell a computer where to look to start Windows. The boot partition contains the \Windows folder where system files are located. Most of the time the boot partition and the system partition are the same partition (drive C). The only time they are different is in a dual boot configuration. For example, if Vista has been installed in a dual-boot configuration with Windows XP, the system partition is most likely drive C (where Windows XP is installed), and Vista is installed on another drive, such as drive E, which Vista calls the boot partition. The PC boots from drive C and then loads Vista system files stored on drive E in the E:\Windows folder.

The Vista **Boot Configuration Data (BCD) file** is structured the same as a registry file and contains configuration information about how Vista is started. Here is the type of information contained in the BCD file:

- ◢ Settings that control BootMgr and WinLoad
- ◢ Settings that control WinResume.exe, the program that resumes Vista from hibernation
- ◢ Settings that start and control the Windows Memory Diagnostic program (\Boot\MemTest.exe)
- ◢ Settings that launch Ntldr to load a previous OS in a dual boot configuration Settings to load a non-Microsoft operating system (such as the Mac OS or Linux)

STEPS TO START A VISTA COMPUTER

Now let's look at the steps to start a Windows Vista computer. Several of these steps are diagrammed in Figures 7-2 and 7-3 to help you visually understand how the steps work.

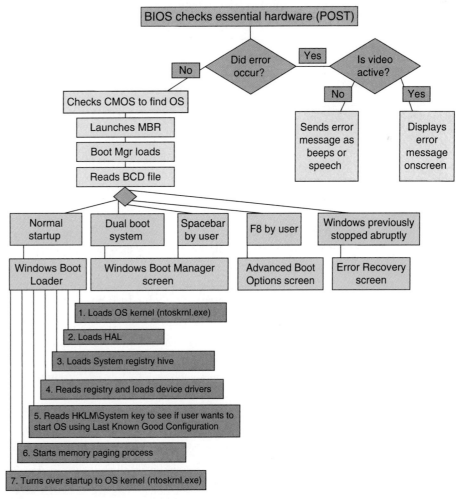

Figure 7-2 Steps to booting the computer and loading Vista

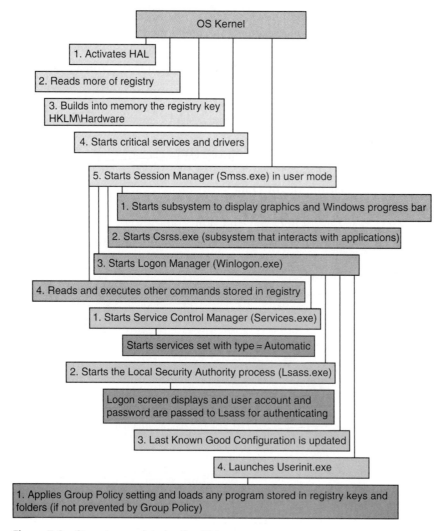

Figure 7-3 Steps to complete loading Vista

Study these steps carefully because the better you understand startup, the more likely you'll be able to solve startup problems.

1. Startup BIOS first checks all the essential hardware components to make sure they're working and displays its progress onscreen. (The computer is sometimes configured to show a manufacturer's logo or welcome screen instead.) If it has a problem and the video system is working, it displays an error message. If video is not working, BIOS might attempt to communicate an error with a serious of beeps (called beep codes) or speech (for speech-enabled BIOS). The process of BIOS checking hardware is called POST (Power-On Self Test).

2. After POST, the BIOS turns to CMOS setup to find out to which device it should look to find an operating system. One of the settings stored in CMOS is the boot sequence, which is a list of devices such as a CD drive, floppy drive, USB device, or hard drive, arranged in the order they should be searched for a bootable OS. The BIOS looks to the first item in the list for storage media that contains an OS to load and, if it doesn't find a bootable OS, moves to the next item in the list. You can change the boot sequence in CMOS setup. Usually the OS is loaded from the hard drive.

3. The BIOS finds and launches the small program in the master boot record (MBR) of the hard drive. This program points to the BootMgr program stored in the root of the system partition. BootMgr is launched.

4. BootMgr starts in 16-bit mode and switches the processor to 32-bit or 64-bit mode. (Starting in 16-bit mode is necessary because all processors start in 16-bit mode, also called real mode.)

5. BootMgr reads the BCD file. The next step, one of five, depends on these factors:

   ▲ *Option 1*: For normal startups that are not dual booting, no menu appears and BootMgr finds and launches Windows Boot Loader (WinLoad).
   ▲ *Option 2*: If the computer is set up for a dual-boot environment, BootMgr displays the Windows Boot Manager screen, as shown in Figure 7-4, with other installed operating systems listed under the Microsoft Windows Vista entry.

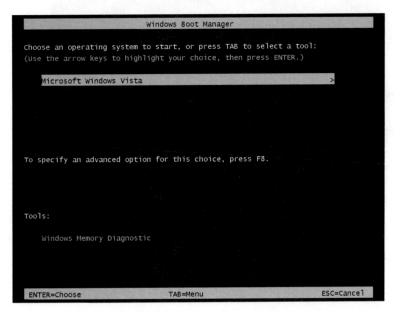

Figure 7-4 Press the spacebar to force the Windows Boot Manager window to appear

   ▲ *Option 3*: If the user presses F8, BootMgr displays the Advanced Boot Options screen, as shown in Figure 7-5.

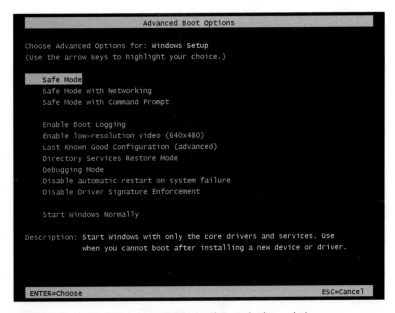

Figure 7-5 Press F8 to see the Advanced Boot Options window

◢ *Option 4*: If the user presses the spacebar, the Windows Boot Manager screen appears.

◢ *Option 5*: If Windows was previously stopped abruptly, the Windows Error Recovery screen (see Figure 7-6) appears.

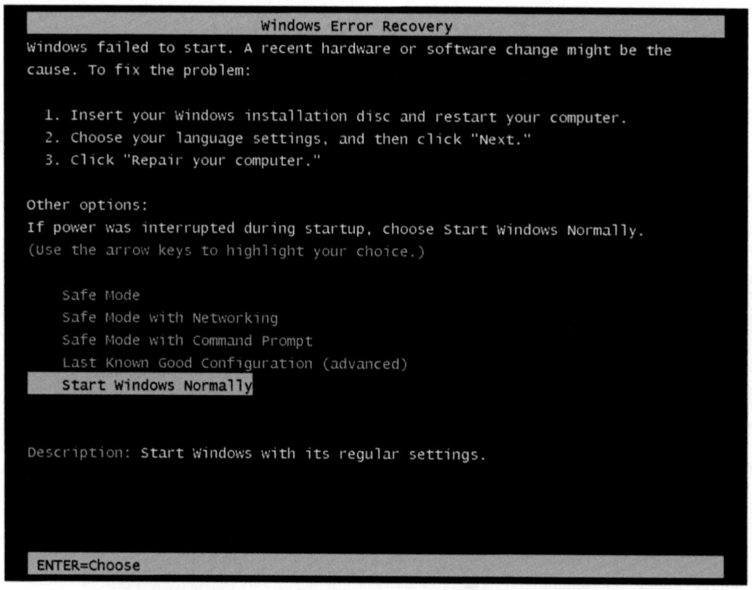

```
                    Windows Error Recovery
Windows failed to start. A recent hardware or software change might be the
cause. To fix the problem:

  1. Insert your Windows installation disc and restart your computer.
  2. Choose your language settings, and then click "Next."
  3. Click "Repair your computer."

Other options:
If power was interrupted during startup, choose Start Windows Normally.
(Use the arrow keys to highlight your choice.)

    Safe Mode
    Safe Mode with Networking
    Safe Mode with Command Prompt
    Last Known Good Configuration (advanced)
    Start Windows Normally


Description: Start Windows with its regular settings.



ENTER=Choose
```

Figure 7-6 This window appears if Windows has been abruptly stopped

6. For normal startups, WinLoad loads into memory the OS kernel, Ntoskrnl.exe, but does not yet start it. WinLoad also loads into memory the hardware abstraction layer (Hal.dll), which will later be used by the kernel.

7. WinLoad loads into memory the system registry hive (C:\Windows\System32\Config\System).

8. WinLoad then reads the registry key just created, HKEY_LOCAL_MACHINE\SYSTEM\Services, looking for and loading into memory device drivers that must be launched at startup. The drivers are not yet started.

9. WinLoad reads data from the HKEY_LOCAL_MACHINE\SYSTEM key that tells the OS if the user wants to start the OS using the Last Known Good Configuration.

10. WinLoad starts up the memory paging process and then turns over startup to the OS kernel.

11. The kernel (Ntoskrnl.exe) activates the HAL, reads more information from the registry, and builds into memory the registry key HKEY_LOCAL_MACHINE\HARDWARE, using information that has been collected about the hardware.

12. The kernel then starts critical services and drivers that are configured to be started by the kernel during the boot. Recall that drivers interact directly with hardware and run in kernel mode, while services interact with drivers. Most services and drivers are stored in C:\Windows\System32 or C:\Windows\System32\Drivers and have a .exe, .dll, or .sys file extension.

13. After all services and drivers configured to load during the boot are started, the kernel starts the Session Manager (Smss.exe), which runs in user mode.

14. Smss.exe starts the part of the Win32 subsystem that displays graphics and the Windows **progress bar** displays on the screen (see Figure 7-7). When you see the progress bar, you know the Windows kernel has loaded successfully.

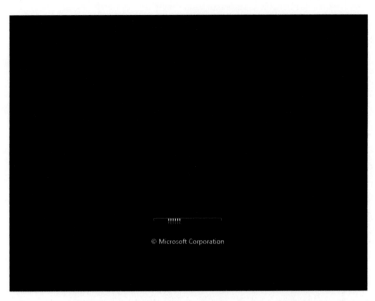

Figure 7-7 The progress bar indicates that the Windows graphics
subsystem is running and the kernel has successfully loaded

15. Smss.exe then starts Csrss.exe, which also runs in user mode. Csrss.exe is the Win32
subsystem component that interacts with applications.

16. Smss.exe starts the Logon Manager (Winlogon.exe) and reads and executes other
commands stored in the registry, such as a command to replace system files placed
there by Windows Update.

17. Winlogon.exe starts the Service Control Manager (Services.exe). Services.exe starts all
services listed with the startup type of Automatic in the Services console.

18. Winlogon.exe starts the Local Security Authority process (Lsass.exe). The logon
screen appears (see Figure 7-8), and the user account and password are passed to the
Lsass.exe process for authenticating. The Last Known Good Configuration information in the registry is updated.

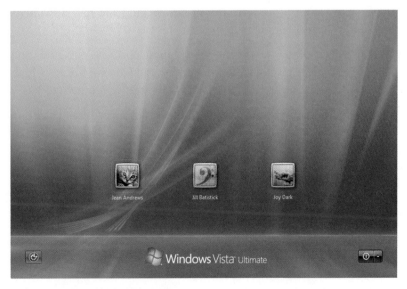

Figure 7-8 Windows Vista logon screen

19. Winlogon.exe launches Userinit.exe and the Windows desktop (Explorer.exe).

20. Userinit.exe applies Group Policy settings and any programs not trumped by Group Policy that are stored in these registry keys and folders:

- HKLM\Software\Microsoft\Windows\CurrentVersion\Runonce
- HKLM\Software\Microsoft\Windows\CurrentVersion\Policies\Explorer\Run
- HKLM\Software\Microsoft\Windows\CurrentVersion\Run
- HKCU\Software\Microsoft\Windows NT\CurrentVersion\Windows\Run
- HKCU\Software\Microsoft\Windows\CurrentVersion\Run
- HKCU\Software\Microsoft\Windows\CurrentVersion\RunOnce
- *Systemdrive*\ProgramData\Microsoft\Windows\Start Menu\Programs\Startup
- *Systemdrive*\Users*username*\AppData\Roaming\Microsoft\Windows\Start Menu\Programs\Startup

The Windows startup is officially completely when the Windows desktop appears and the wait circle disappears.

With this basic knowledge of the boot in hand, let's turn our attention to the Windows Vista tools that can help you solve problems when Vista refuses to load.

VISTA TOOLS TO HELP SOLVE STARTUP PROBLEMS

Some of the Windows tools used in this chapter were first mentioned in Chapter 2, and are only summarized here. When facing a startup problem, generally you can approach the problem by using the following strategy, which is designed to apply the least intrusive fix:

1. Use the Last Known Good Configuration on the Advanced Boot Options menu to recover from a recent change to the Vista configuration. This method works well when a device or application has just been installed or a Windows setting has been changed that is causing a startup failure.

2. Use the Startup Repair process in the Windows Vista Recovery Environment to repair corrupted Vista system files needed to boot.

3. Use System Restore to restore the Vista configuration to a previous point before the problem occurred.

4. Use Safe Mode on the Advanced Boot Options menu to allow you to start Vista with a minimum configuration. In Safe Mode, you can scan for viruses, disable a component or program, check the hard drive for errors, and perform other tasks to solve the problem.

5. Use the Command Prompt in the Windows Vista Recovery Environment to repair more drastic Vista problems that prevent the system from booting into Safe Mode.

6. Perform an in-place upgrade of Windows Vista to completely reinstall Vista without affecting user preferences or data stored on the hard drive.

7. Perform a Windows Complete PC Restore to restore the entire hard drive to the way it was at the time the last Complete PC Restore backup was made.

8. Reformat the hard drive and reinstall Windows Vista. Use this option as a last resort when all the above options fail. It will not work if the hard drive is faulty.

Generally, when solving any computer problem, you want to try the least invasive solution first so as to make as few changes to the system as possible. So keep that in mind as you learn about these tools. Also, the order in which you use tools and techniques might change based on what you know about recent events, how the system is customized, or your observations of error messages and the behavior of the system. In short, a general troubleshooting strategy should be considered a suggestion, not rules set in stone.

In this part of the chapter, we'll first learn about the tools listed above and then we'll discuss in more depth the strategy concerning when to use which tool or technique. Now let's look at these tools: the Last Known Good Configuration and the Windows Recovery Environment which contains Startup Repair, System Restore, Command Prompt, and Complete PC Restore. Then we'll give a quick summary of Safe Mode, which you learned about in previous chapters. Details about upgrading and installing Windows Vista are covered in Appendix E.

Note

As always, when faced with a computer problem, remember to first ask yourself or another user, "Is your data backed up?" If not, then focus on the data first and then the startup problem.

Caution

In this chapter, I often refer to the Windows Vista setup DVD. If you have a notebook computer or a brand-name computer such as a Dell, IBM, Lenovo, or Gateway, be sure to use the manufacturer's recovery CD instead of a regular Windows Vista setup DVD. This recovery CD has drivers specific to your system, and the Windows Vista build might be different from that of an off-the-shelf Windows Vista setup DVD. For example, Windows Vista Home Premium installed on a notebook computer might have been built with all kinds of changes made to it by the notebook manufacturer and is, therefore, different from the Windows Vista Home Premium that you can buy in a retail store.

LAST KNOWN GOOD CONFIGURATION

Recall that the registry settings collectively called the Last Known Good Configuration are saved in the registry each time the user successfully logs onto the system. If your problem is caused by a bad hardware or software installation and you get an error message the first time you restart the system after the installation, using the Last Known Good, can, in effect, undo your installation and solve your problem. Do the following:

1. While the BIOS is finishing up and just before Windows begins to load, press **F8**. The Advanced Boot Options menu appears (see Figure 7-9). If the problem is so severe that

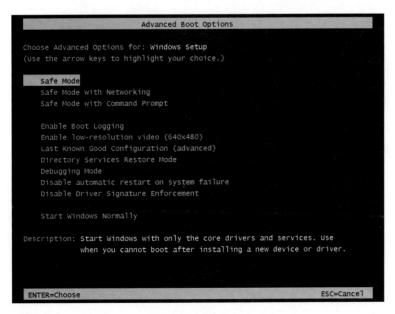

Figure 7-9 Press F8 to see the Advanced Boot Options menu

this menu does not appear, then the next step is to boot from the Vista setup DVD and use Windows RE to recover the system.

2. Select **Last Known Good Configuration** (your most recent settings that worked) and press **Enter**. The system will reboot.

Remember, the Last Known Good registry settings are saved each time a user logs on to Vista. Therefore, it's important to try the Last Known Good early in the troubleshooting session before it's overwritten. (However, know that if you log onto the system in Safe Mode, the Last Known Good is not saved.) If the Last Known Good doesn't work, your next option is the Startup Repair process in the Windows Recovery Environment.

THE WINDOWS RECOVERY ENVIRONMENT (WINDOWS RE)

The Windows Vista Recovery Environment (RecEnv.exe), also known as Windows RE, is an operating system launched from the Vista DVD that provides a graphical and command line interface. Our goal in this section is to help you become familiar with Windows RE, and in later sections of the chapter, you'll learn to use it to solve startup problems. Follow these steps to start up and explore Windows RE:

1. Using a computer that has Windows Vista installed, boot from the Vista setup DVD. (To boot from a DVD, you might have to change the boot sequence in CMOS setup to put the optical drive first above the hard drive.) The screen in Figure 7-10 appears. Select your language preference and click **Next**.

Figure 7-10   Select your language preference

2. The Install Windows screen appears as shown in Figure 7-11. Click **Repair your computer**. The recovery environment (RecEnv.exe) launches and displays the System Recovery Options dialog box (see Figure 7-12).

3. Select the Vista installation to repair and click **Next**.

Figure 7-11   Launch Windows RE after booting from the Vista DVD

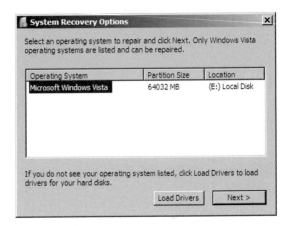

Figure 7-12   Select an installation of Vista to repair

4. The System Recovery Options window in Figure 7-13 appears listing recovery options.

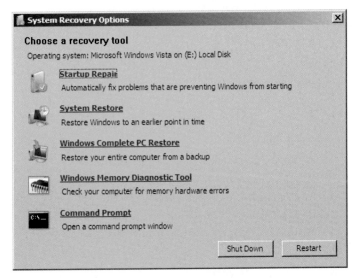

Figure 7-13   Recovery tools in Windows RE

5. The first tool, Startup Repair, can automatically fix many Windows problems including those caused by a corrupted BCD file and missing system files. You can't cause any additional problems by using it and it's easy to use. Therefore, it should be your first recovery option when Vista refuses to load. Click **Startup Repair** and the tool will examine the system for errors (see Figure 7-14).

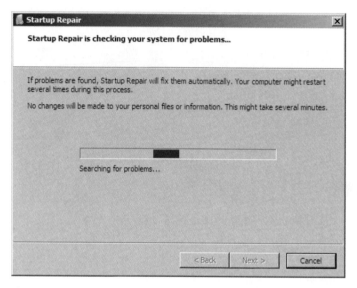

Figure 7-14 Startup Repair searches the system for problems it can fix

6. Based on what it finds, it will suggest various solutions. For example, it might suggest you use System Restore or suggest you immediately reboot the system to see if the problem has been fixed (see Figure 7-15).

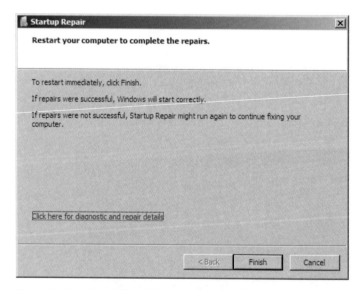

Figure 7-15 Startup Repair has attempted to fix the problem

7. To see a list of items examined and actions taken by Startup Repair, click **Click here for diagnostic and repair details.** The dialog box showing the list of repairs appears as shown in Figure 7-16. A log file can also be found at C:\Windows\System32\LogFiles\ SRT\SRTTrail.txt.

8. System Restore in the System Recovery Options window works the same as Windows Vista System Restore from the desktop to return the system to its state when a restore

point was made. Click **System Restore;** a list of restore points appears (see Figure 7-17). Select the most recent restore point to make the least intrusive changes to the system.

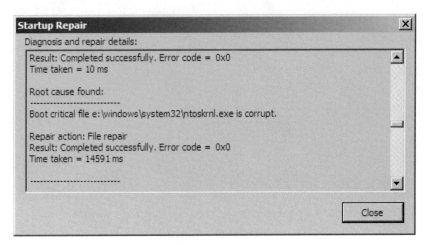

Figure 7-16   Details of actions taken by Startup Repair

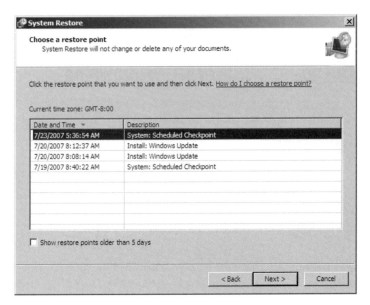

Figure 7-17   Select the most recent restore point to make fewer changes to the system

9. Windows Complete PC Restore can be used to completely restore drive C and possibly other drives to their state when the last backup of the drives were made. The backups are made using Complete PC Backup, which you learned about in Chapter 4. When you use Complete PC Restore, everything on the hard drive is lost because the restore process completely erases the drive and writes to it the OS, user information, applications, and data as they were captured at the time the last Complete PC Backup was made. Therefore, before using Complete PC Restore, consider how old the backup is. Perhaps you can use it to restore drive C and then boot into Windows, reinstall applications installed since the last backup, and use other backups of data more recent than the last Complete PC Backup was made to restore the data.

10. Use the Windows Memory Diagnostic Tool, which you learned to use in the last chapter, to test memory.

11. Click **Command Prompt** to open a command prompt window (see Figure 7-18). You can use this window to repair a corrupted Vista system or recover data. Commands to use in this window are covered later in the chapter.

Figure 7-18 The command prompt window resembles the Windows XP Recovery Console

12. As you use a tool in the System Recovery Options window, be sure to reboot after each attempt to fix the problem to make sure the problem has not been resolved before you try another tool. To exit the Recovery Environment, click **Shut Down** or **Restart**.

THE COMMAND PROMPT WINDOW IN WINDOWS RE

Use the command prompt window in Windows RE when graphical tools available in Windows RE fail to solve the Vista problem. In the following subsections, we'll look at some commands that are helpful when solving boot problems. Appendix C lists more commands that can be used in a command prompt window opened from the Vista desktop; some of these commands can be used in the Windows RE command prompt window.

COMMANDS TO REPAIR SYSTEM FILES, BOOT RECORDS, AND PARTITIONS

Table 7-2 lists some commands that can help you repair a system. To get helpful information about a command, enter the command followed by /?, such as **bcdedit /?**.

Command Line	Description
Bootrec /scanOS	Scans the hard drive for Windows installations not stored in the BCD
Bootrec /rebuildBCD	Scans for Windows installations and rebuilds the BCD
Bcdedit	Manually edits BCD; be sure to make a copy of the file before you edit it
Bootrec /fixboot	Repairs the boot sector of the system partition
Bootrec /fixmbr	Repairs the MBR
Diskpart	Manages partitions and volumes; use these commands within Diskpart:

Table 7-2 Commands used in the command prompt window of Windows RE to repair system files and the file system

Command Line	Description
	• *List disk*—Lists installed hard drives
	• *List partition*—Lists partitions on selected drive
	• *Select disk*—Selects a hard drive
	• *Select partition*—Selects a partition on the selected drive
	• *Active*—Makes the selected partition the active partition
	• *Inactive*—Makes the selected partition inactive
Bootsect	Repairs problems with dual booting PCs
Chkdsk c: /r	Repairs errors on drive C

Table 7-2 Commands used in the command prompt window of Windows RE to repair system files and the file system (*Continued*)

COMMANDS TO RESTORE THE REGISTRY

If key registry files are corrupted or deleted, the system will not start. You can use the Windows RE command prompt window to restore registry files using those saved in the C:\Windows\System32\Config\RegBack folder. This RegBack folder contains partial backups of the registry files put there after a successful boot. Use the commands in Table 7-3 to restore the registry files.

 Note

For a complete list of Diskpart commands, go to the Microsoft support site (*support.microsoft.com*) and search on "DiskPart Command-Line Options."

Command Line	Description
1. c:	Makes drive C the current drive
2. cd \windows\system32\config	Makes the Windows registry folder the current folder
3. ren default default.save ren sam sam.save ren security security.save ren software software.save ren system system.save	Renames the five registry files
5. cd regback	Makes the registry backup folder the current folder

6. copy default
    c:\windows\system32\config
copy sam
    c:\windows\system32\config
copy security
    c:\windows\system32\config
copy software
    c:\windows\system32\config
copy system
    c:\windows\system32\config
	For hardware problems, first try copying just the System hive from the backup folder to the registry folder and then reboot. For software problems, first try copying just the Software hive to the registry folder, and then reboot. If the problem is still not solved, try copying all five hives to the registry folder and reboot.

Table 7-3 Steps to restore the Windows Vista registry

SAFE MODE ON THE ADVANCED BOOT OPTIONS MENU

On the Advanced Boot Options menu, before you try Safe Mode, first try Safe Mode with Networking so you have access to your local network and the Internet to help you fix the problem (for example, to download updates to your AV software). If Safe Mode with Networking doesn't work, try Safe Mode. Here's a list of things you can do in Safe Mode to recover the system:

1. When Safe Mode first loads, if Windows senses the problem is drastic, it gives you the opportunity to go directly to System Restore. Use System Restore unless you know exactly what it is you need to do to solve your problem.

2. If you suspect a virus, scan the system for viruses. You can also use Chkdsk to fix hard drive problems. Your hard drive might be full; if so, make some free space available.

3. Use Device Manager to uninstall or disable a device with problems or to roll back a driver.

4. Use Msconfig to disable unneeded services or startup processes. Recall from Chapter 2 that you can use Msconfig to disable many services and startup processes, and then enable them one at a time until you discover the one causing the problem.

5. If you suspect a software program you have just installed, use the Programs and Features window to uninstall it.

6. You can also use System Restore from within Safe Mode to restore the system to a previous restore point.

After you try each fix, reboot the system to see if the problem is solved before you do the next fix.

TROUBLESHOOTING STARTUP PROBLEMS

This section is written as step-by-step instructions for problem-solving so that you can use it to solve a boot problem by following the steps. Each step takes you sequentially through the boot process and shows you what to do when the boot fails at that point in the process. Therefore, your first decision in troubleshooting a failed boot is to decide at what point in the boot the failure occurred. Then your next decision is to decide which tool to use to fix the problem that will be the least invasive. The idea is to make as few changes to your system as possible in order to solve the problem without having to do a lot of work to return the system to normal (such as having to reinstall all your applications). And, as with every computer problem, if user data is at risk, you need to take steps to back up the data as soon as possible in the troubleshooting process.

To determine where in the boot process the failure occurred, we'll focus on these three startup stages of the boot:

▲ *Stage 1: Before the progress bar.* When you see the Microsoft progress bar appear, you know the Windows kernel, including all critical services and drivers, has loaded. Any problems that occur before the progress bar appears are most likely related to corrupt or missing system files or hardware. Your best Vista tools to use for these problems are Startup Repair and System Restore.

7

◢ *Stage 2: After the progress bar and before logon.* After the progress bar appears, user mode services and drivers are loaded and then the logon screen appears. Problems with these components can best be solved using Startup Repair, the Last Known Good Configuration, System Restore, Safe Mode, Device Manager, and Msconfig.

◢ *Stage 3: After logon.* After the logon screen appears, problems can be caused by startup scripts, applications set to launch at startup, and desktop settings. Use Msconfig to temporarily disable startup programs. Other useful tools to solve the problem are Software Explorer and Safe Mode.

Now let's take a closer look at how to address problems at each of these three stages.

PROBLEMS AT STAGE 1: BEFORE THE PROGRESS BAR APPEARS

As always, first check with the user to find out if important data is on the hard drive and not backed up. Make every effort to copy the data to a safe location before you start troubleshooting the original problem. How to recover data from a system that refuses to boot is covered later in the chapter.

Remember, if the progress bar has not yet appeared, some portions of the Vista kernel and critical drivers and services to be started by the kernel have not yet started. Therefore, the problem is with hardware or these startup files. Hardware that might be failing include the power supply, motherboard, CPU, memory, hard drive, video, or keyboard. If any one of these devices is not working, the error is communicated using beep codes, or using onscreen or voice error messages—and then the computer halts.

In the following subsections are some symptoms you might see when a hardware problem is present, and what you can do about the problem. As you perform each troubleshooting step, be sure to restart the system to see if the problem is solved before you apply the next step.

SYMPTOM 1: THE SCREEN IS BLANK

If you see absolutely nothing on the screen, check that the system is getting power and the monitor is plugged in and turned on. Can you hear the spinning fan or hard drive inside the computer case? Are lights on the front of the case lit? If not, suspect that power is not getting to the system. Check that the system is not in standby mode or hibernation: Try waking up the system by pressing any key or a special standby key on laptops, or by pressing the power-on button. Is the monitor totally without lights, or is the screen blank but the LED light on front of the monitor is lit? If the LED light is lit, try rebooting the system. If the LED light is not lit, check that power is getting to the monitor. Is it turned on?

Try trading the monitor for one you know is good. If you can hear a spinning drive and see lights on the front of the computer case and know the monitor works, the video card might be bad or not seated properly in its slot, the memory might be bad, the video cable might be bad, or a component on the motherboard might have failed.

SYMPTOM 2: THE COMPUTER DOES NOT APPEAR TO HAVE POWER

If you can't hear the spinning drive or see lights on the front of the case, suspect the electrical system. Check power connections and switches. The power supply might be bad or connections inside the case might be loose.

SYMPTOM 3: AN ERROR MESSAGE APPEARS BEFORE VISTA STARTS

Recall that when you first turn on a system, system BIOS takes control, checks essential hardware devices, and searches for an OS to load. If it has a problem while doing all that and the video system is working, it displays an error message onscreen. If video is not working, it might attempt to communicate an error with a series of beeps (called beep codes) or speech (for speech-enabled BIOS).

For messages displayed onscreen that apply to nonessential hardware devices such as DVD drives or floppy drives, you might be able to bypass the error by pressing a key and moving forward in the boot. However, for errors with essential hardware devices such as the one shown in Figure 7-19, focus your attention on the error message, beep code, or voice message describing the problem. For example, notice in Figure 7-19 that the hard drive should have been recognized as the Primary Master device, but it is missing from the list. If you don't know what the error message or beep codes mean, you can search the Web site of the motherboard manufacturer or do a general search of the Web using a search engine such as Google.

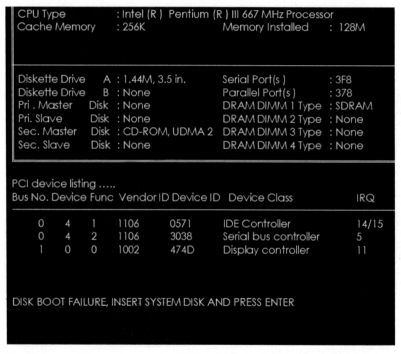

Figure 7-19 This error message at POST indicates a hardware problem

SYMPTOM 4: BIOS CANNOT ACCESS THE HARD DRIVE

Error messages generated by startup BIOS that pertain to the hard drive can be caused by a variety of things. Here is a list of text error messages that indicate that BIOS could not find a hard drive:

- ◢ Hard drive not found
- ◢ Fixed disk error
- ◢ Disk boot failure, insert system disk and press enter
- ◢ No boot device available

The problem might be a physical problem with the drive, the data cable, power, or the motherboard. Start with checking CMOS setup to verify that CMOS detected the drive correctly. If the drive was not detected, check the autodetection setting. (Chapter 6 shows sample CMOS setup screens for these hard drive settings.) If autodetection is turned off, turn it on and reboot. Your problem might be solved. If startup BIOS still doesn't find the drive, power down the system, unplug it, and open the case. Physically check the hard drive power and data cable connections at both ends. Sometimes cables work their way loose. Be careful not to touch circuit boards or the processor as you work and to protect the system against static electricity, wear an anti-static bracelet that is clipped to the computer case.

Here is a list of error messages that indicate the BIOS was able to find the hard drive but couldn't read what was written on the drive or could not find what it was looking for:

▲ Invalid boot disk or Inaccessible boot device
▲ Invalid drive specification
▲ Invalid partition table
▲ No operating system found, Missing operating system, Error loading operating system
▲ Couldn't find bootmgr or bootmgr is missing

For these error messages, you need to boot from the Windows Vista setup DVD, but first check CMOS setup to make sure the boot sequence lists the DVD drive before the hard drive.

USE CMOS SETUP TO SET THE BOOT SEQUENCE

To access CMOS setup, reboot the PC and look onscreen for a message such as "Press DEL for setup" or "Press F2 for BIOS settings" or something similar. Press that key and the CMOS setup utility loads. Find the screen, such as the one in Figure 7-20, that lets you set the boot sequence. The boot sequence is the order of devices to which BIOS looks to find an OS to load. Make sure that the DVD drive and the floppy drive are listed before the hard drive so that you can force the system to boot from the Windows Vista setup DVD or from a floppy disk. Save your settings and exit CMOS setup.

The next step is to try to boot from the Windows Vista setup DVD.

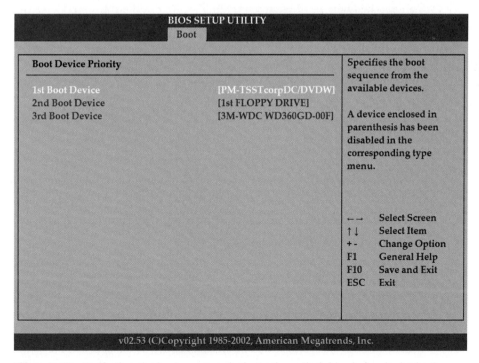

Figure 7-20 Verify that the boot sequence looks to the optical drive before it checks the hard drive for an operating system

CAN YOU BOOT FROM THE WINDOWS VISTA SETUP DVD?

Now that you have made sure that CMOS setup is configured to boot first from the DVD drive before it turns to the hard drive, you can try to boot from the Windows Vista setup DVD. If you cannot boot from this disc, the problem is not just the hard drive. Study the error message and solve the immediate hardware problem. It's possible the hard drive and the optical drive have failed, but the floppy drive might still work. If you have a DOS or Windows 9x startup floppy disk, you can try booting from the floppy. If you can boot from the floppy, then you have proven the problem is with both the hard drive and the DVD drive.

If you are able to boot from the Vista DVD, the window shown earlier in Figure 7-10 appears. If you see this window, you have proven that the problem is isolated to the hard drive. Now the trick is to find out exactly what is wrong with the drive and fix it.

CAN WINDOWS RE FIND THE VISTA INSTALLATION?

At this point, click **Next** in Figure 7-10 and then click **Repair your computer** to attempt to launch Windows RE. The first thing Windows RE does is attempt to locate a Vista installation on the hard drive (refer to Figure 7-12). If it cannot locate the installation, but CMOS setup recognizes the drive, then the drive partitions and file systems might be corrupted. If Windows RE does locate the installation, the problem is more likely to be limited to corrupted or missing system files or drivers.

As you attempt each fix in the following list, be sure to restart the system after each step to find out if the problem still exists or has changed:

1. Run Startup Repair. This process can sometimes fix drastic problems with system files and boot records.

2. Run System Restore. The process won't help if the file system is corrupted.

3. Restart the system and press **F8** during the boot to launch the Advanced Boot Options menu, shown earlier in the chapter in Figure 7-5. If the boot menu does not appear, chances are the problem is a corrupted boot sector. If the boot menu appears, chances are the BCD file or other startup files are the problem. If you do see the menu, enable boot logging and reboot. Then check the boot log (\Windows\ntbtlog.txt) for the last entry, which might indicate which system file is missing or corrupt. (If the hard drive is at all accessible, your best chance of viewing the boot log file is to use the command prompt window and the Type command.)

4. If the boot menu does not appear, return to Windows RE, launch the command prompt window, and attempt to repair the boot sector. Try these commands: **bootrec /fixmbr** and **bootrec /fixboot**. Also try the **Diskpart** command followed by the command **list volume**. Does the OS find the system volume? If not, the entire partition might be lost.

5. If the boot menu does appear, return to Windows RE, launch the command prompt window, and attempt to repair the BCD file. Try this command: **bootrec /rebuildbcd**.

6. Try to repair a corrupted file system by using the command prompt window and the **chkdsk c: /r** command.

7. When startup files are missing or corrupt, sometimes Vista displays an error message similar to the one shown in Figure 7-21, which names the file giving the problem. You can replace the file by going to a healthy Vista computer and copying the file to a removable media. Then, on the problem computer, boot to Windows RE, open the command prompt window, and rename the original file so you will not overwrite it with the replacement and can backtrack if necessary. Then copy the replacement file to the hard drive.

8. Try using the command prompt window to access drive C. If you can get to a C prompt, use the **DIR** command to list folders and files. If you see a good list, check the

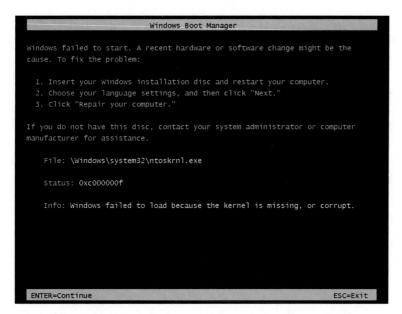

```
                        Windows Boot Manager

Windows failed to start. A recent hardware or software change might be the
cause. To fix the problem:

   1. Insert your Windows installation disc and restart your computer.
   2. Choose your language settings, and then click "Next."
   3. Click "Repair your computer."

If you do not have this disc, contact your system administrator or computer
manufacturer for assistance.

    File: \Windows\system32\ntoskrnl.exe

    Status: 0xc000000f

    Info: Windows failed to load because the kernel is missing, or corrupt.




ENTER=Continue                                            ESC=Exit
```

Figure 7-21 Windows Vista might display a screen similar to this one
when a critical startup file is missing or corrupt

log file, C:\Windows\System32\LogFiles\SRT\SRTTrail.txt, for clues. If you cannot get a good list of contents of drive C, most likely the Vista installation is destroyed beyond repair. Before you address the problem of a corrupted Vista installation, make every effort to copy data to another media by using commands given earlier in the chapter.

OPTIONS TO RECOVER FROM A CORRUPTED VISTA INSTALLATION

If you are not able to repair the corrupted installation using the techniques in the previous list, your next step is to consider what options are available to restore the system. Your options depend on backups available. Here are your choices to restore a corrupted installation:

▲ *Option 1*: If you have a Complete PC backup, use it to restore the system to the last backup. If data is on the hard drive that has not been backed up, make every effort to copy this data to a safe place before you restore the system.
▲ *Option 2*: If you don't have a Complete PC backup but you do have backups of the data on the hard drive, install Windows Vista on the partition, formatting the hard drive during the installation. You'll need to install all applications again and then restore the data.
▲ *Option 3*: If you don't have a Complete PC backup and you also don't have backups of the data on the drive (worst case scenario), try to copy the data and then perform a reinstallation of Windows Vista. Even if you cannot copy the data, you might be able to recover it after the reinstallation. If you have data on the same partition as Vista, don't format during the Vista installation.

STEPS TO REINSTALL WINDOWS VISTA

Follow these steps to reinstall Vista when the OS refuses to boot and there is important data on the drive:

1. Boot from the Vista DVD and select **Install now** from the opening menu. Follow directions onscreen to install the OS.

2. When given the opportunities, enter the product key and accept the license agreement. For the type of installation, select **Custom** (**advanced**).

3. When asked where you want to install the OS, select the partition on which Vista is installed.

Vista setup will move all folders of the old installation into the \Windows.Old folder, including the \Windows, \Users, and \Program Files folders. A fresh, clean installation of Vista will then be installed in the \Windows folder. If you suspect the hard drive might be failing or need reformatting, immediately save all important data to a removable media and reinstall Windows Vista a second time, this time reformatting the hard drive. If you believe the hard drive is healthy, then follow these steps to get things back to their original order:

1. Run Chkdsk to fix errors on the drive.

2. Install all applications and device drivers.

3. Create all user accounts and customize Vista settings. Then copy all user data and other folders from the \Windows.Old folder to the new installation.

4. To free up disk space, delete the \Windows.Old folder. To do that, using the Disk Cleanup utility in the Properties box for drive C, select **Previous Windows installations** (see Figure 7-22). Note that this option will not be available if the \Windows.Old folder does not exist.

Appendix E contains more information about installing Windows Vista.

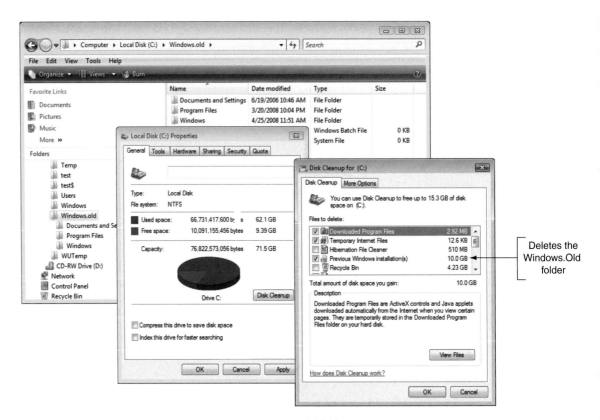

Figure 7-22 Free up disk space by deleting the Windows.Old folder

REINSTALLING VISTA ON A LAPTOP OR BRAND-NAME COMPUTER

If you have a laptop or a brand-name computer such as a Gateway, Dell, or IBM, most likely the manufacturer has set up a hidden partition on the hard drive that can be used to recover the Windows installation. During startup, you'll see a message onscreen such as

"Press F2 to recover the system" or "Press F11 to start recovery." When you press the appropriate key, a menu should appear that gives you two options: one repairs the Windows installation, saving user data, and the other reformats drive C and restores your system to the way it was when purchased. First, try to save user data before you attempt the destructive recovery. If neither method works, the hidden partition might be corrupted or the hard drive might be physically damaged.

If the recovery process stored on the hard drive doesn't work, try to use the recovery CD that came bundled with your computer to repair the installation. If you don't have the recovery CD, you might be able to buy one from the computer manufacturer. For notebook computers, you really must have this recovery CD to reinstall Windows because the device drivers on the CD are specific to your notebook. If you cannot buy a recovery CD, you might be able to download the drivers from the notebook manufacturer's Web site. Download them to another computer and burn them to a CD that you can use on the notebook to install drivers.

PROBLEMS AT STAGE 2: AFTER THE PROGRESS BAR APPEARS AND BEFORE LOGON

When you see the Microsoft progress bar appear during the boot, you know the Windows kernel has loaded successfully, critical drivers and services configured to be started by the kernel are running, and the Session Manager (Smss.exe) running in user mode has started the Win32 subsystem necessary to provide the graphics of the progress bar. If the logon screen has not yet displayed, most likely the problem is caused by a corrupted driver or service that is started after the kernel has finished its part of the boot. Your general attack plan to fix the problem is to isolate and disable the Windows component, service, or application causing trouble. However, if user data is on the hard drive not backed up, do what you can to copy that data to another media before you focus on the problem at hand.

Follow these steps:

1. Launch Windows RE from the Vista setup DVD and run **Startup Repair** from the Recovery Environment. It can't do any harm, it's easy to use, and it might fix the problem.

2. Reboot and press **F8** to launch the Advanced Boot Options menu. Then select the **Last Known Good Configuration**. It's important to try this option early in the troubleshooting process, because you might accidentally overwrite a good Last Known Good with a bad one as you attempt to log on with the problem still there.

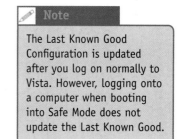

Note

The Last Known Good Configuration is updated after you log on normally to Vista. However, logging onto a computer when booting into Safe Mode does not update the Last Known Good.

3. In Windows RE, run **System Restore**. Select the latest restore point. If that doesn't fix the problem, try an earlier one.

4. Try booting into **Safe Mode**. If you don't know the source of the problem, here are some things you can try to discover the source and hopefully solve the problem:

   ◢ *Step 1*: Immediately run antivirus software to eliminate a virus as the problem.
   ◢ *Step 2*: Run **Chkdsk c: /r** to check and repair the hard drive.
   ◢ *Step 3*: Examine all the logs in Event Viewer for errors that might point to the problem.

▲ *Step 4*: Use Software Explorer and Msconfig to stop any applications just installed. Then uninstall and reinstall the application.

▲ *Step 5*: Use Device Manager to check for hardware errors and disable any devices just installed. If you have just updated a driver, roll back the driver.

▲ *Step 6*: Open an elevated command prompt window and use the System File Checker (SFC) tool to search for and replace corrupted system files. The command **sfc /scannow** searches for and replaces corrupted system files. Be sure to restart the system after this command is finished. You'll learn more about the SFC tool in a project at the end of this chapter.

▲ *Step 7*: Rename the \Windows\Ntbtlog.txt file to keep it from being overwritten so you can view it later.

5. Boot to the Advanced Boot Options menu and select **Enable Boot Logging**. Windows starts, logging information to the log file \Windows\Ntbtlog.txt. Every driver that is loaded or not loaded is written to the file (see Figure 7-23).

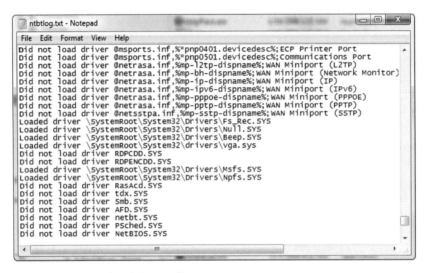

Figure 7-23 Sample Ntbtlog.txt file

6. Compare the Ntbtlog.txt file to the one that was created in Safe Mode. If the boot failed, look at the last entry in the Ntbtlog.txt file that was generated. Find that entry in the one created while booting into Safe Mode. The next driver listed in the Safe Mode Ntbtlog.txt file is likely the one giving problems.

7. The easiest way to view the logs is to boot into Safe Mode and view the files with Notepad. If you can't boot into Safe Mode, you can still view the file using the command prompt window in the Recovery Environment. Try replacing the program file listed last in the log or disabling the device or service. If that doesn't work, then you'll need to dig a little deeper to identify the culprit. Here are some tips for identifying a device or service causing the problem:

▲ *Tip 1*: Try to boot into Safe Mode. Then use Msconfig to disable all nonessential services and devices. Reboot normally. If the problem goes away, you can enable one after another until you find the one causing the problem.

▲ *Tip 2*: In Safe Mode, examine Event Viewer Application logs, Security logs, and System logs for errors.

▲ *Tip 3*: In Safe Mode, use System Information (msinfo32.exe) to find the program filenames of drivers and services. Useful information can be found at these locations: Services in the Software Environment group and Problem Devices in the Components group.

▲ *Tip 4*: Compare the entries in the Ntbtlog.txt file when booting in Safe Mode to the entries when booting normally. Consider that the culprit might be any item that is loaded for a normal boot but not loaded for Safe Mode. Disable each driver one at a time until the problem goes away.

▲ *Tip 5*: If the computer will not boot into Safe Mode, compare the Ntbtlog.txt file to one created on a similar computer booted into Safe Mode. Look for a service or driver listed as loaded on the good computer that is not loaded or is missing on the bad computer.

8. After you believe you've identified the problem service or device, if you can boot into Safe Mode, first use Device Manager to disable the device or use the Services console to disable the service. Then reboot, and, if the problem goes away, restore the program file and enable the driver or service.

9. If you cannot boot into Safe Mode, open the command prompt window of the Recovery Environment. Then back up the registry and open the Registry Editor using the regedit command. Drill down to the service or device key. The key that loads services and drivers can be found in this location: HKEY_LOCAL_MACHINE\System\CurrentControlSet\Services

10. Disable the service or driver by changing the Start value to 0x4. Close the Registry Editor and reboot. If the problem goes away, use the Copy command to replace the program file, and restart the service or driver.

PROBLEMS AT STAGE 3: AFTER WINDOWS LOGON

Problems that occur after the user logs onto Windows are caused by applications or services configured to launch at startup. Programs can be set to launch at startup by placing their shortcuts in startup folders, by Group Policy, or by software installation processes.

Do the following to disable programs put in startup folders:

1. Use Msconfig to temporarily disable the programs in the startup folders. These folders are:

   ▲ C:\Users*username*\AppData\Roaming\Microsoft\Windows\Start Menu\Programs\Startup

   ▲ C:\ProgramData\Microsoft\Windows\Start Menu\Programs\Startup

2. If the problem goes away, one of these startup programs is the problem. Move first one after the other to a different folder until the problem is fixed.

You can use Group Policy (gpedit.msc) to manage startup programs. But know that if the computer belongs to a domain, policies set at the domain level override any local policies. Generally, if you belong to a domain, the administrator manages all policies at the domain level. However, for a standalone computer or one that belongs to a workgroup, you can follow these steps:

1. Click **Start**, in the **Start Search** box, enter **gpedit.msc**, press **Enter**, and respond to the UAC box. The Group Policy console opens.

2. Drill down to **Computer Configuration, Administrative Templates, System,** and **Logon.** A list of Logon policies appears in the right pane (see Figure 7-24). To change an entry, double click it; its Properties box appears as shown in Figure 7-25. If the policy is enabled, you can disable it by clicking **Disabled,** clicking **Apply,** and then clicking **OK.**

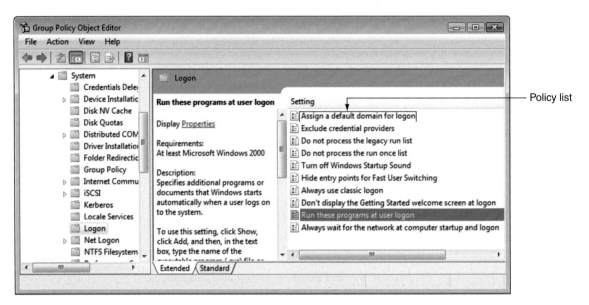

Policy list

Figure 7-24 The list of policies that affect the logon event

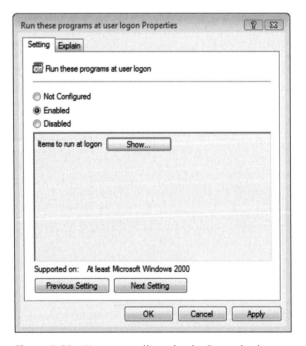

Figure 7-25 Manage a policy using its Properties box

3. Now drill down and check the entries in the **User Configuration, Administrative Templates, System,** and **Logon** policies. During startup, policies in the Computer Configuration are applied first, followed by policies in the User Configuration, so you must check both areas.

To permanently remove a startup program, do one of the following:

▲ From Control Panel, use the Programs and Features window to uninstall an application.
▲ Remove the entry from a startup folder or from Group Policy.
▲ Use the Services console to disable a service.
▲ Use Software Explorer (as discussed in Chapter 1) to remove or disable an entry in the startup programs list.

Table 7-4 summarizes some error messages including stop errors you might encounter during the boot and what to do about them. Stop errors occur when the Windows kernel encounters an error in a kernel mode process, which most likely points to a hardware or driver problem.

Error or Error Message	Description and What to Do
Non-system disk or disk error Replace and press any key when ready	Startup BIOS could not find a boot device. Check CMOS setup for the boot sequence and try to boot from another device.
Invalid partition table Error loading operating system Missing operating system	MBR record is damaged or the active partition is corrupt or missing. Use the repair commands from the Windows RE command prompt window.
An application launched at startup that gives errors or takes up resources	Use Software Explorer to remove it from the list of startup programs.
Stop 0xc0000034 or The Windows Boot Configuration Data file is missing required information	The C:\Boot\BCD file is corrupted or missing. Use the Startup Repair tool in Windows RE or the Bootrec command.
Stop 0x0A or IRQL_NOT_LESS_OR_EQUAL	Caused by a driver or service making an illegal access to memory. Try the Last Known Good Configuration. Then look for an incompatible driver or service.
Stop 0x1E or KMODE_EXCEPTION_NOT-HANDLED	A bad driver or service has performed an illegal action. Look for corrupted or bad drivers or services. Try updating firmware.
Stop 0x24 or NTFS_FILE_SYSTEM	Suspect a failing hard drive or bad third-party disk utility tools.
Stop 0x2E or DATA_BUS_ERROR	A hardware problem most likely caused by failing memory or a corrupted hard drive.
Stop 0x50 or PAGE_FAULT_IN_NONPAGED_AREA	Caused by failing memory or bad software. Test memory using the Memory Diagnostic tool.
Stop 0x7B or INACCESSIBLE_BOOT_DEVICE	Windows cannot access the hard drive. This is probably caused by installing bad or incorrect hard drive drivers.
Stop 0xFE or BUGCODE_USB_DRIVER	Caused by corrupted USB drivers. Update the motherboard drivers for the USB ports.
Any other Stop error that occurs during startup	Other Stop errors are most likely caused by a corrupted registry, a system file is missing or damaged, or a device driver is missing or damaged. Use the Startup Repair tool and then examine the log file it creates at C:\Windows\System32\LogFiles\Srt\Srttail.txt.
Any Stop error that occurs during a Vista installation	See the Microsoft Knowledge Base article 935806 for a list of Stop errors during installation and what to do about them.

Table 7-4 Error messages during startup and what to do about them

HOW TO RECOVER LOST DATA

When data is lost or corrupted, you might be able to recover it using Windows tools, third-party software, or commercial data recovery services. This section discusses your options to recover lost data.

RECOVER A DELETED OR CORRUPTED DATA FILE

Here are some things to try to recover a deleted or corrupted data file:

▲ If you have accidentally deleted a data file, to get it back, look in the Recycle Bin. Drag and drop the file back to where it belongs, or right-click the file and click **Restore** on the shortcut menu.

▲ If a data file is corrupted, you can try to use the Recover command. To use the command, the volume on which the file is located cannot be in use. The easiest way to do that is to boot into Windows RE and open a command prompt window. For example, Figure 7-26 shows the command **recover C:\Data\Mydata.txt**. Notice in the figure that the C drive is not the current drive. This is necessary so that the drive is not in use. (Incidentally, technicians sometimes say that a drive not in use is not mounted.)

Figure 7-26   Use the Recover command to recover a corrupted file while the volume on which it is stored is not in use

▲ If an application's data file gets corrupted, go to the Web site of the application manufacturer and search the support section for what to do to recover the file. For example, if an Excel spreadsheet gets corrupted, search the Knowledge Base at *support.microsoft.com* for solutions.

▲ Third-party software can help recover deleted and corrupted files. On the Internet, do a search on "data recovery" for lots of examples. One good product is GetDataBack by Runtime Software (*www.runtime.org*), which can recover data and program files even when Windows cannot recognize the drive. It can read FAT and NTFS file systems and can solve problems with a corrupted partition table, boot record, or root directory.

RECOVER DATA FROM A COMPUTER THAT WILL NOT BOOT

If Windows is corrupted and the system will not boot, recovering your data might be your first priority. One way to get to the data is to remove your hard drive from your computer and install it as a second non-booting hard drive in another system. After you boot up the system, you should be able to use Windows Explorer to copy the data to another medium. If the data is corrupted, try to use data recovery software.

Recall from Chapter 6 that for less than $30 you can purchase an IDE to USB converter kit or a SATA to USB converter kit that includes a data cable and power adapter. You can use the kit to temporarily connect an IDE or SATA hard drive to a USB port on a working computer. Set the drive beside your computer and plug one end of the data cable into the drive and the other into the USB port. (For an IDE drive, a jumper on the drive must be set to the master setting.) The AC adapter supplies power to the drive. The setup is shown in Figure 7-27. There's also a converter kit that can be used for notebook hard drives.

Figure 7-27 To recover data, connect a failing hard drive to a PC using a USB connection

Using Windows Explorer, you can browse the drive and copy data to other media. After you have saved the data, use Disk Management to try to repartition and reformat the drive. You can also use diagnostic software from the hard drive manufacturer to examine the drive and possibly repair it.

USE A DATA RECOVERY SERVICE

If your data is extremely valuable and other methods have failed, you might want to consider a professional data recovery service. They're expensive, but getting the data back might be worth it. To find a service, Google on "data recovery." Before selecting a service, be sure to read up on reviews and perhaps get a recommendation from a satisfied customer.

>> CHAPTER SUMMARY

- ▲ The hardware components required for a successful boot are the CPU, motherboard, power supply, memory, keyboard, video card or onboard video, and a boot device such as a hard drive or CD drive.

- ▲ When you first turn on a system, startup BIOS on the motherboard takes control to examine hardware components and find an operating system to load.

- ▲ If startup BIOS encounters an error, it communicates the problem by a text message onscreen, a series of beeps (called beep codes), or speech (for speech-enabled BIOS).

- ▲ Items on the hard drive essential for a successful boot include the MBR (master boot record), which contains the master boot program and partition table, the OS boot record, and OS boot files in the root directory and in the \Boot folder and the \Windows folder.

- ▲ Vista startup is managed by the Windows Boot Manager (BootMgr) and the Windows Boot Loader (WinLoad).

- ▲ The Boot Configuration Data (BCD) file contains information about settings that control BootMgr, WinLoad, WinResume.exe, and the Windows Memory Diagnostic program, settings that launch Ntldr for loading a previous OS in a dual boot configuration, and settings to load a non-Microsoft operating system.

◢ Windows Vista tools and techniques used to troubleshoot a failed boot include Last Known Good Configuration, Startup Repair, System Restore, Safe Mode, Command Prompt, in-place upgrade of Windows Vista, Complete PC Restore, and reformatting the hard drive and reinstalling Windows.

◢ Startup Repair in the Windows Recovery Environment can automatically fix many Windows problems including those caused by a corrupted BCD file and missing system files. You can't cause any additional problems by using it and it's easy to use. Therefore, it should be your first recovery option when Vista refuses to load.

◢ Last Known Good Configuration can solve problems caused by a bad hardware or software installation by undoing the install.

◢ Use the command prompt window in Windows RE, when the other RE tools fail to solve the problem.

◢ Your first decision in troubleshooting a failed boot is to decide at what point in the boot the failure occurred. Determine if the failure occurred before the progress bar, after the progress bar and before logon, or after logon.

◢ If a hard drive contains valuable data but will not boot, you might be able to recover the data by installing the drive in another system as the second, non-booting hard drive in the system.

>> *KEY TERMS*

Boot Configuration Data (BCD) file   The Windows Vista registry file named BCD that is stored in the \Boot folder of the active or boot partition and holds configuration data used during Windows Vista startup.

boot sector   *See* OS boot record.

master boot record (MBR)   The first 512-byte sector on a hard drive. Contains the partition table and the master boot program, which the BIOS uses to find the OS on the drive.

OS boot record   The second 512 bytes on a drive, used to help the MBR find and load the OS.

progress bar   A graphical bar that appears on the screen during Windows Vista startup. When you see the bar you know that the Windows kernel (ntoskrnl.exe) and all its kernel mode components are running and the Win subsystem running in user mode has started, displaying the progress bar. Up to this point in the boot, all displays have been in text mode.

startup BIOS   Firmware embedded on the motherboard that is used to start up the system.

Windows Boot Loader (WinLoad)   The Windows Vista startup program named WinLoad that is stored in the \Windows\System32 folder of the boot partition (most likely drive C). The program is responsible for loading into memory essential Windows components including the Vista kernel program, Ntoskrnl.exe.

Windows Boot Manager (BootMgr)   The Windows Vista startup program named BootMgr that is stored in the root directory of the active or system partition (most likely C:\) that is responsible for beginning Windows Vista startup. It reads the BCD file and then searches for and loads the Windows Boot Loader (WinLoad).

Windows RE   *See* Windows Vista Recovery Environment

Windows Vista Recovery Environment   A recovery OS loaded from the Vista setup DVD that includes both graphical and command-line interfaces. Tools available in the environment are Startup Repair, System Restore, Windows Complete PC Restore, Windows Memory Diagnostic Tool, and the Command Prompt. Also called *Windows RE*.

>> REVIEWING THE BASICS

1. Is the BootMgr file stored in the boot partition or the system partition?

2. Where is the master boot record (MBR) located?

3. What is the first thing that BIOS checks?

4. What are the two types of disk partitioning systems that can be used with Vista?

5. Which registry hive is loaded first during the Vista boot?

6. Which key do you press to launch the Advanced Boot Options window during Windows startup?

7. What is the name of the log file created when you enabled boot logging from the Advanced Boot Options startup menu?

8. List the location of one of the program startup folders.

9. What are the two main components of the MBR?

10. What is the name of the folder that is created, where files from an old installation are moved during a reinstall of Vista?

11. What is the purpose of the hidden partition used by many of the brand-name computer companies?

12. The DIR command is used to list what items?

13. What can be used to set the boot sequence?

14. If registry files are corrupted or deleted, you can use the Windows RE command prompt to restore the registry files saved in what location?

15. What is the Bootrec /fixboot command used for?

16. What command can be used to manually edit the BCD?

17. What information is contained in the C:\Windows\System32\LogFiles\SRT\ SRTTrail.txt file?

18. At what point in the boot is the Last Known Good Configuration saved?

19. When is it appropriate to use dynamic disks with Windows Vista?

20. Where is the Vista boot configuration data stored?

>> THINKING CRITICALLY

1. You have important data on your hard drive that is not backed up and your Windows installation is so corrupted you know that you must repair the entire installation. What do you do first? Why?

    a. Use System Restore.
    b. Make every attempt to recover the data.
    c. Perform an in-place upgrade of Windows Vista.
    d. Reformat the hard drive and reinstall Windows Vista.

2. Windows Vista refused to start and the error message says something about the WinLoad program file being missing. Which action is the best way to fix the problem? Why?
    a. Boot from the Vista DVD and use the command prompt windows to copy the WinLoad file from a working PC to this PC.
    b. Boot from the Vista DVD and use the Startup Repair tool.
    c. Use the latest Complete PC backup to restore the system.
    d. Boot into Safe Mode and restore the program from backup.

3. An error message displays during Vista startup before the progress bar appeared about missing services program files. You try to boot into Safe Mode, but get the same error message. Next, you use the Vista DVD to boot into the Recovery Environment. Select the best two tasks to fix the problem and order them correctly.
    a. Use System Restore to restore the system to a previous restore point.
    b. Use the command prompt to disable and then replace the service.
    c. Use Startup Repair.
    d. Use Complete PC Restore.

>> HANDS-ON PROJECTS

PROJECT 7-1:　Practicing Solving Boot Problems

This project is best done on a lab computer rather than your personal computer. Unplug the computer, open the case, and disconnect the data cable to your hard drive. Turn the computer back on and boot the system. What error message did you see? Now reboot using your Windows Vista setup DVD. Try to load the Recovery Environment. What error messages did you receive, if any? Power down your computer, unplug it, and reconnect your hard drive. Reboot and verify that Windows Vista loads successfully.

PROJECT 7-2:　Practicing Using the Recovery Environment

Boot from the Vista DVD and launch the Recovery Environment. Then do the following:

1. Execute the Startup Repair Process. What were the results?

2. Execute System Restore. What is the most recent restore point? (Do not apply the restore point.)

7

3. Using the command prompt window, open the Registry Editor. What command did you use? Close the editor.

4. Using the command prompt window, copy a file from your Documents folder to a flash drive. Where you able to copy the file successfully? If not, what error message(s) did you receive?

PROJECT 7-3:   Using Ntbtlog.txt

Compare an Ntbtlog.txt file created during a normal boot to one created when booting into Safe Mode. Note any differences you find.

PROJECT 7-4:   More Practice with Windows RE

Using Windows Explorer, rename the BootMgr file in the root directory of drive C. Reboot the system. What error message do you see? Now use Windows RE to restore the BootMgr file. List the steps taken to complete the repair.

PROJECT 7-5:   Problem-solving Using the Microsoft Knowledge Base

You are trying to clean up a hard drive to free some disk space. You notice the hard drive has a C:\Windows.Old folder that uses 10 GB. However, in the Disk Cleanup dialog box, you don't see the option to delete Previous Windows Installations. Using the Microsoft support site (*support.microsoft.com*), find the Knowledge Base Article that allows you to manually delete the folder. Answer these questions:

1. What is the Article ID for this article?

2. What are the three command lines needed to delete the folder?

3. Explain the purpose of each of the three commands, and explain the purpose of each parameter in the command line.

>> REAL PROBLEMS, REAL SOLUTIONS

REAL PROBLEM 7-1:   Digging Deeper into System File Checker

The System File Checker tool can be used to find and replace corrupted Vista system files. The tool keeps a log of its actions, and, if it cannot replace a corrupted file, you can find that information in the log file. Then you can manually replace the file. Locate the Microsoft Knowledge Base Article 929833 at the *support.microsoft.com* site. Do whatever research is necessary to understand the steps in the article to manually replace a corrupted file and answer these questions:

1. What are other parameters for the sfc command besides /scannow?

2. Explain the purpose of the findstr command when finding the log file.

3. Can a filename other than sfcdetails.txt be used in the findstr command line? Explain your answer.

4. What is the purpose of the edit command?

5. Explain the purpose of the takeown command when replacing a system file.

6. Explain why the icacls command is needed in the process.

7. List some ways that you can locate a known good copy of the corrupted system file.

REAL PROBLEM 7-2:   Fixing a PC Problem

This project should be fun, extremely useful, and give you an opportunity to find out just how much you have learned so far from this book. Make yourself available to family and friends who have problems with their computers. For the first three problems you face, keep a record that includes this information:

1. Describe the problem as the user described it to you.

2. Briefly list the things you did to discover the cause of the problem.

3. What was the final solution?

4. How long did it take you to fix the problem?

5. What would you do differently the next time you encounter this same problem?

Useful Web Sites and Other Resources

Tables A-1 through A-7 list important URLs alphabetically within each table.

BIOS MANUFACTURERS AND SUPPLIERS OF BIOS UPDATES

When looking for a BIOS upgrade for your desktop or notebook computer, the most reliable source is the Web site of the motherboard or notebook manufacturer.

Company	URL
Abit	www.abit-usa.com
American Megatrends, Inc. (AMI)	www.ami.com
Asus	www.asus.com
Dell	www.dell.com
Driver Guide (database of firmware, drivers, and documentation)	www.driverguide.com
Driverzone by Barry Fanion	www.driverzone.com
eSupport.com (BIOS upgrades)	www.esupport.com
Gateway	www.gateway.com
Hewlett-Packard and Compaq	www.hp.com
IBM	www.ibm.com
Lenovo (includes IBM ThinkPads)	www.lenovo.com, www.pc.ibm.com/us
Marco Volpe	www.mrdriver.com
NEC	www.nec-computers.com
Packard Bell	www.packardbell.com
Phoenix Technologies (First BIOS, Phoenix, and Award)	www.phoenix.com
Toshiba	www.toshiba.com
VIA Technologies	www.viatech.com
Wim's BIOS	www.wimsbios.com

Table A-1   Bios manufacturers and suppliers of BIOS updates

MOTHERBOARD MANUFACTURERS, REVIEWERS, AND SUPPLIERS

Company	URL
Abit	www.abit.com.tw
American Megatrends, Inc. (AMI)	www.megatrends.com or www.ami.com
Amptron	www.amptron.com
ASUS	www.asus.com
A-Trend	www.atrend.com
Chaintech	www.chaintech.com.tw
Dell	www.dell.com
DFI	www.dfiweb.com
ECS	www.ecs.com.tw or www.ecsusa.com
EpoX	www.epox.com
Famous Tech	www.magic-pro.com.hk
First International Computer of America, Inc.	www.fica.com or www.fic.com.tw
FreeTech	www.freetech.com
Gateway	www.gateway.com
Gigabyte Technology Co., Ltd.	www.gigabyte.com.tw
IBM	www.ibm.com
Intel Corporation	www.intel.com
Lenovo (includes IBM ThinkPad notebooks)	www.lenovo.com
MicroStar	www.msicomputer.com
Motherboards.org	www.motherboards.org
NEC	www.nec-computers.com
Panasonic	www.panasonic.com
PC Chips	www.pcchips.com.tw
Shuttle	www.shuttle.com
Soyo	www.soyo.com
Supermicro	www.supermicro.com
Tyan	www.tyan.com

Table A-2   Motherboard manufacturers, reviewers, and suppliers

HARD DRIVE MANUFACTURERS

Company	URL
Excelstor	www.excelstor.com
Fujitsu America, Inc.	www.fujitsu.com
IBM	www.ibm.com
Hitachi	www.hitachigst.com
Iomega (removable drives)	www.iomega.com
Maxell Corporation	www.maxell.com
Maxtor Corporation	www.maxtor.com
Quantum Corporation	www.quantum.com
Samsung	www.samsung.com
Seagate Technology	www.seagate.com
Sony	www.sony.com
Western Digital	www.wdc.com

Table A-3 Hard drive manufacturers

TROUBLESHOOTING PCS AND TECHNICAL INFORMATION, INCLUDING HARDWARE REVIEWS

Company	Description	URL
CNET, Inc.	Technical information and product reviews	www.cnet.com
Computing.NET	Technical information	www.computing.net
EdScope, LLC	Technical information and hardware reviews	www.basichardware.com
GetDataBack by Runtime Software	Data recovery software	www.runtime.org
Hardware Central by Jupitermedia	Technical information and hardware reviews	www.hardwarecentral.com
How Stuff Works	Explanations of how computer hardware and software work	www.howstuffworks.com
Inboost.com	Performance information	www.inboost.com
Jupitermedia	Hardware reviews	www.earthwebhardware.com/computers
Microsoft	Windows support and Microsoft applications support	support.microsoft.com
MicroSystems Development Technologies	POST diagnostic cards, port test software, loop-back plugs, floppy drive diagnostic tools	www.msdus.com
MK Data	Tons of technical information	www.karbosguide.com

Table A-4 Troubleshooting PCs and technical information, including hardware reviews

Company	Description	URL
Motherboards.org	Aggregate site on motherboards; includes hardware reviews	www.motherboards.org
Norton SystemWorks by Symantec	PC maintenance and troubleshooting software suite includes Norton AntiVirus, Norton Utilities, Norton GoBack, CheckIt Diagnostics, and System Optimizer	www.symantec.com
PartitionMagic by Symantec	Manages a hard drive, including resizing and copying partitions	www.symantec.com
PC World	Technical information and hardware reviews	www.pcworld.com
SiSoftware Sandra	Benchmarking, diagnostic, and tune-up software	www.sisoftware.co.uk
SpinRite by Gibson Research	Data-recovery software	www.grc.com
The Elder Geek	Solutions for Windows, hardware, network, Internet, and system problems; includes downloads	www.theeldergeekvista.com
Tom's Hardware Guide	In-depth technical information	www.tomshardware.com
Uniblue	Utility software to solve Windows problems	www.liutilities.com
Webopedia by Jupitermedia	Encyclopedia of computing terms	www.webopedia.com
Windows Sysinternals	Diagnostics, repair, and data recovery for hard drive, network, and more.	technet.microsoft.com/en-us/sysinternals
ZD Net Help	Technical information and downloads	www.zdnet.com

Table A-4 Troubleshooting PCs and technical information, including hardware reviews (continued)

VIRUS DETECTION, REMOVAL, AND INFORMATION

Product or Site	Description	URL
AntiVirus by Trend Micro (for home use)	Anitvirus software for home use	www.trendmicro.com
AVG Anti-Virus by Grisoft	Antivirus software	www.grisoft.com
Command Antivirus	Antivirus software and virus information	www.authentium.com
ESafe by Aladdin Knowledge Systems, Ltd.	Antivirus software	www.esafe.com
ESET NOD32 Antivirus	Antivirus software	www.eset.com
F-Prot by Frisk Software International	Antivirus software available as shareware	www.f-prot.com
F-Secure Anti-Virus	Virus information and antivirus software	www.f-secure.com
NeatSuite by Trend Micro (for networks)	Antivirus software for networks	www.trendmicro.com
Norman Virus Control	Sophisticated antivirus software	www.norman.com
Norton AntiVirus	Antivirus software	www.symantec.com
Virus Bulletin	Virus information	www.virusbtn.com
VirusScan by McAfee	Antivirus software	www.mcafee.com
Windows Live OneCare	Antivirus, antispyware, and firewall software	onecare.live.com

Table A-5 Virus detection, removal, and information

HELP WITH WINDOWS TROUBLESHOOTING AND WINDOWS DRIVERS

Site	URL
Computing.NET	www.computing.net
The Driver Guide	www.driverguide.com
DriverUpdate.com	www.driverupdate.com
Driverzone by Barry Fanion	www.driverzone.com
HelpWithWindows.com	www.helpwithwindows.com
Hermanson, LLC	www.windrivers.com
Marco Volpe	www.mrdriver.com
Microsoft Support	support.microsoft.com and technet.microsoft.com
PC Pitstop	www.pcpitstop.com
Windows IT Library	www.windowsitlibrary.com
Windows User Group Network	www.wugnet.com

Table A-6 Help with Windows troubleshooting and Windows drivers

NOTEBOOK COMPUTER MANUFACTURERS

Manufacturer	URL
Acer America	global.acer.com
Apple Computer	www.apple.com
Dell Computer	www.dell.com
eMachines by Gateway	www.emachines.com
Fujitsu/Fuji	www.fujitsu.com
Gateway	www.gateway.com
Hewlett-Packard and Compaq	www.hp.com
Lenovo (includes IBM ThinkPads)	www.lenovo.com
Micron Electronics	www.mpccorp.com
NEC	www.nec.com
Sony (VAIO)	www.sonystyle.com
Toshiba America	csd.toshiba.com
WinBook	www.winbook.com

Table A-7 Notebook computer manufacturers

APPENDIX B

Entry Points for Startup Processes

This appendix contains a summary of the entry points that can affect Windows startup. The entry points include startup folders, Group Policy folders, the Scheduled Tasks folder, and registry keys. For an explanation of each entry point, see Chapter 2.

Programs and shortcuts to programs are stored in these startup folders:

- ◢ C:\Users*username*\AppData\Roaming\Microsoft\Windows\Start Menu\Programs\Startup
- ◢ C:\ProgramData\ Microsoft\Windows\ Start Menu\ Program\Startup

Scripts used by Group Policy are stored in these folders:

- ◢ C:\WINDOWS\System32\GroupPolicy\Machine\Scripts\Startup
- ◢ C:\WINDOWS\System32\GroupPolicy\Machine\Scripts\Shutdown
- ◢ C:\WINDOWS\System32\GroupPolicy\User\Scripts\Logon
- ◢ C:\WINDOWS\System32\GroupPolicy\User\Scripts\Logoff

Scheduled tasks are stored in this folder:

- ◢ C:\Windows\ System32\Tasks

Registry keys known to affect startup are as follows:

- ◢ HKLM\Software\Microsoft\Windows\CurrentVersion\RunOnce
- ◢ HKLM\Software\Microsoft\Windows\CurrentVersion\RunServiceOnce
- ◢ HKLM\Software\Microsoft\Windows\CurrentVersion\RunServicesOnce
- ◢ HKCU\Software\Microsoft\Windows\CurrentVersion\RunOnce
- ◢ HKCU\Software\Microsoft\Windows\CurrentVersion\Policies\Explorer\Run
- ◢ HKLM\Software\Microsoft\Windows\CurrentVersion\Policies\Explorer\Run
- ◢ HKLM\Software\Microsoft\Windows\CurrentVersion\ShellServiceObjectDelayLoad
- ◢ HKLM\Software\Microsoft\Windows\CurrentVersion\Run
- ◢ HKCU\Software\Microsoft\Windows NT\CurrentVersion\Windows

- HKCU\Software\Microsoft\Windows NT\CurrentVersion\Windows\Run
- HKCU\Software\Microsoft\Windows\CurrentVersion\Run
- HKLM\Software\Microsoft\Windows\CurrentVersion\RunServices
- HKLM\System\CurrentControlSet\Control\Session Manager
- HKCU\Software\Microsoft\Command
- HKCU\Software\Microsoft\Command Processor\AutoRun
- HKCU\Software\Microsoft\Windows\CurrentVersion\RunOnce\Setup
- HKCU\Software\Microsoft\Windows NT\CurrentVersion\Windows\load
- HKLM\Software\Microsoft\Windows NT\CurrentVersion\Windows\AppInit_DLLs
- HKLM\Software\Microsoft\Windows NT\CurrentVersion\Winlogon\System
- HKLM\Software\Microsoft\Windows NT\CurrentVersion\Winlogon\Us
- HKCR\batfile\shell\open\command
- HKCR\comfile\shell\open\command
- HKCR\exefile\shell\open\command
- HKCR\htafile\shell\open\command
- HKCR\piffile\shell\open\command
- HKCR\scrfile\shell\open\command

Other ways in which processes can be launched at startup:

- Services can be set to launch at startup. To manage services, use the Services Console (services.msc).
- Device drivers are launched at startup. For a listing of installed devices, use Device Manager (devmgmt.msc) or the System Information Utility (msinfo32.exe).

Windows Vista Commands

This appendix contains a list of some of the most useful Windows Vista commands that can be used in a normal or elevated command prompt window or from the command prompt in the Windows Vista Recovery Environment. This list is not comprehensive and might not contain all available parameters that can be used with each command. For help with a command, enter the command with /? after it, as in attrib /?.

For more information about a command, see the Microsoft Technet Web sites at *technet.microsoft.com/en-us/library/cc772390.aspx* or *technet.microsoft.com/en-us/library/bb490913.aspx*.

ASSOC

Purpose: Displays the association assigned to a given file extension. This association determines which program is launched when you double-click a file that has the specified file extension. When you use assoc without parameters, the command displays a list of all the current file name extension associations.

Parameters:

.ext	The file name extension.
filetype	The file type to associate with the specified file name extension.

Examples:

assoc	Displays a list of file extensions and the file type associated with these extensions. For example, for the text file extension, .txt, the display is .txt=txtfile.
assoc .doc	Displays the current file type association for the file name extension .doc.
assoc .doc=	Removes the file type association for the file name extension .doc. (Be sure to use a space after the equal sign.)
assoc .doc=txtfile	Assigns the text file association to the file extension .doc.

ATTRIB

Purpose: Displays or changes the read-only, archive, system, and hidden attributes of a file. If a file has a hidden or system attribute, you must remove these attributes before you can change the **r** or **a** attributes of the file. Wildcard characters are allowed in the command line.

Parameters:

+h or −h	Sets or removes the hidden-file attribute.
+r or −r	Sets or removes the read-only status of the file.
+s or −s	Sets or removes the system status of the file.
+a or −a	The archive attribute marks a file as having been changed since the last backup.
/s	Includes subdirectories found within the specified path.
/d	The command is applied to directories.

Examples:

attrib +h +r *filename.ext*	Makes the file a hidden, read-only file.
attrib −h −r *filename.ext*	Unhides the file and removes read-only status.
attrib *filename.ext*	Displays the file's attributes.
attrib +a c:\data*.doc /s	Turns on the archive attribute for all files with a .doc file extension in the C:\data folder and its subfolders.

CD OR CHDIR

Purpose: Changes the current or default drive and directory.

Parameters:

/d	Changes the current drive and directory.
drive:	Drive to display or change.
path	Drive and directory that you want to change to.
..	Makes the parent folder the current folder.

Examples:

cd e:\backup	Makes the backup directory on drive E the current directory.
cd \	Makes the root directory (for example, C:\) the current directory.
cd ..	Moves up the directory tree one level.
cd /d c:\data	Makes drive C the current drive and makes C:\data the current directory.

CHKDSK

Purpose: Examines a hard drive or disk for lost and cross-linked clusters and repairs them. An elevated command prompt is required.

Parameters:

volume	The drive letter or volume name of the drive.
/f	Fixes file errors on the drive. The drive must be locked, which means no files on the drive are open.
/v	Verbose mode displays file names as they are checked.
/r	Fixes file errors on the drive and recovers data from bad sectors on the drive.
/i	Used with NTFS, performs a quick check by checking only index entries.

Examples:

chkdsk d:	Checks drive D for lost and cross-linked clusters and reports errors found.
chkdsk d: /f	Checks drive D and attempts to fix errors.

CONVERT

Purpose: Converts a FAT drive or volume to the NTFS file system. Files and directories on the drive are not altered.

Parameters:

volume	The drive letter or volume name to be converted.
/fs:ntfs	Converts the drive to NTFS.
/v	Verbose mode displays details during the conversion.
/nosecurity	After the conversion, files can be accessed by all users.
/x	Closes all files before the conversion (called dismounting the drive).

Examples:

convert c: /fs:ntfs /v	Converts drive C to NTFS in verbose mode.

COPY

Purpose: Copies a file or group of files from one location to another. Wildcard characters can be used.

Parameters:

/d	Encrypted files being copied are written as decrypted files.
/v	Verifies that the copied files are written correctly.
/y	Does not prompt before overwriting a file.
source	The location of the file or files to be copied.
destination	The location where the file or files are written.

Examples:

copy myletter.txt document.txt/v	Copies myletter.txt to document.txt in the current drive and directory and verifies that the file is written correctly.
copy spring.txt + summer.txt report.txt	Combines the files spring.txt and summer.txt into the file report.txt.
copy *.doc c:\data\report	Copies all files with the .doc extension into the C:\data\report folder

DEL OR ERASE

Purpose: Deletes a file or group of files. You can use more than one filename separated by spaces, commas, or semicolons.
Parameters:

/p	Prompts for confirmation before deleting a file.
/f	Forces deletion of read-only files.
/s	Deletes files from current directory and its subdirectories.
/q	Quiet mode does not prompt you before deleting.
/a	Deletes files with specified attributes.

Examples:

del myfile.*	Deletes all files in the current directory with the filename myfile.
del *.txt /a +a	Deletes all files with the .txt file extension that have the archive attribute set.

DIR

Purpose: Displays a list of files and subdirectories in a directory.
Parameters:

/p	Lists files and subdirectories and their sizes a page at a time.
/q	Lists file ownership information.
/w	Lists files and subdirectories in a wide-screen format.
/d	Lists in wide-screen format, and files are sorted by column.

Examples:

dir c:	**Lists all files and directories in the root directory of drive C.**
dir c: /p /w	**Lists all files and directories in the drive C root directory, one page at a time across the screen.**
dir c:\temp*.txt	**Lists all files and directories in the C:\temp folder that have a .txt file extension.**

DRIVERQUERY

Purpose: Displays a list of installed device drivers and their properties.
Parameters:

/v	**Shows detailed driver information.**
/si	**Displays digital signatures for signed drivers.**

Examples:

driverquery	**Lists installed device drivers for this computer.**
driverquery /si	**Lists digital signatures for installed device drivers.**

EDIT

Purpose: A text editor that is handy to use at a command prompt when editing text files.
Parameters:

/b	**The editor displays in black and white.**
/r	**Loads the file in read-only mode.**

Examples:

edit textfile.txt	**Edits the file textfile.txt in the current directory. If the file does not exist, it is created.**

EXIT

Purpose: Exits the command prompt window. When used at a command prompt, the command has no parameters.

FIND

Purpose: Searches a file or group of files for the specified string of text.
Parameters:

/c	**Counts the number of lines in a file or files that contain the specified string.**
/n	**Displays the line number in the file where the string is located.**
/i	**The specified search string is not case-sensitive.**

Examples:

find "book" bookreport.txt	**Lists all lines from bookreport.txt that contains the string "book".**

FORMAT

Purpose: Writes a file system to a disk so that it can accept Windows files.
Parameters:

/fs:*filesystem*	**The file system to use: FAT, FAT32, NTFS, or UDF.**
/v:*volumename*	**Assigns a volume name to the drive.**
/q	**Quick format rewrites the file table and root directory of a drive that has been previously formatted.**
/c	**For NTFS only, the new drive will be compressed.**
/x	**Closes all files on the drive before it is formatted (called dismounting the drive).**

Examples:

format e: /fs:NTFS	**Formats drive E using the NTFS file system.**
format f: /fs:FAT32 /q	**Performs a quick format of drive F using FAT32.**

GETMAC

Purpose: Displays the MAC address of all installed network adapters. The command has no parameters.

GPRESULT

Purpose: Displays the Resultant Set of Policy (RSoP) information about a user or computer. Use this command to find out what Group Policy settings are in effect. Requires an elevated command prompt window.

Parameters:

/r	Displays summary data.
/v	Displays verbose or detailed data.
/ scope user|computer	Displays data for user or computer. If this parameter is not used, both are displayed.

Examples:

gpresult /r	Displays summary data for user and computer.
gpresult /v /scope computer	Displays detailed data about policies that apply to the computer.

HELP

Purpose: Provides information about commands. If used without parameters, the help command lists commands with short descriptions of the commands. It does not provide information for network commands.

Parameters:

command	The command to be described.

Examples:

help convert	Gives information about the convert command.
convert /?	Gives information about the convert command.

HOSTNAME

Purpose: Displays the name of the local computer. This command has no parameters.

IPCONFIG

Purpose: Displays, releases, and renews the IP address, subnet mask, and default gateway for each TCP/IP connection.

Parameters:

/all	Displays detailed host information.
/release	Releases or clears all of the adapter's TCP/IP settings including the IP address.
/renew	Renews all of the adapter's TCP/IP settings including leasing a new IP address.

Examples:

ipconfig	Displays IP address, subnet mask, and default gateway for all TCP/IP connections.
ipconfig /all	Shows detailed information for all TCP/IP connections.
ipconfig /renew	Renews all TCP/IP settings for network adapters.

LABEL

Purpose: Changes, removes, or creates a name or label assigned to a volume or drive.
Parameters:

volume	The drive letter of the volume.
label	The name of the volume. (Also called the volume label.)

Examples:

label e:backup_drive	Changes the volume name for drive E to backup_drive.
label	Removes the volume name from the current drive.

MKDIR OR MD

Purpose: Makes or creates a directory.
Parameters:

drive	Drive where the new directory is to be created.
path	Name and location of the new directory.

Examples:

mkdir \documents\reports	Creates a directory named documents with a subdirectory named reports.
mkdir c:\data	Creates a directory on drive C named data.

MOVE

Purpose: Moves a file or group of files from one location to another. The command is similar to copy followed by delete.
Parameters:

/y	Does not prompt you before overwriting an existing file.
/-y	Does prompt you before overwriting an existing file.
source	Path and name of the file or files to move.
destination	Path where the destination files are to be moved. When moving a single file, the destination can contain a path and filename.

Examples:

move \data*.doc \documents\reports\	Moves all files with the .doc extension from the \data directory to the \documents\reports\directory.
move myfile.txt \documents\yourfile.txt	Moves myfile.txt to the \documents folder and renames the file to yourfile.txt.

NETSTAT

Purpose: Displays information about the current TCP/IP network connections.
Parameters:

-a	**Displays all connections and listening ports.**
-e	**Displays Ethernet information and may be combined with the –s option.**
-n	**Displays information about active connections.**
-s	**Displays information organized by protocol.**

Examples:

netstat –e -s	**Shows both the Ethernet data and data organized by protocols.**
netstat –a	**Shows all connections and listening ports.**

PING

Purpose: Verifies connectivity between two devices that are using TCP/IP.
Parameters:

-t	**Causes the ping to continue until interrupted.**
-a	**Performs a reverse name resolution on the destination IP address.**
-n	**The number of echo requests to be sent; the default is 4.**
targetname	**The target host, which can be an IP address or host name.**

Examples:

ping google.com	**Sends an echo request message to google.com. If the request is received, a reply message will be displayed with the IP address of google.com.**
ping –a 10.0.99.100	**Pings destination 10.0.99.100 and displays its host name.**

RECOVER

Purpose: Recovers data from bad sectors on a drive. Wildcard characters are not allowed. You can recover only one file at a time and the drive must first be locked. The easiest way to lock the drive is to use the recover command in the Recovery Environment.
Parameters:

drive:\path\filename	**The location and name of the file to recover.**

Examples:

recover d:\myfiles\contacts.doc	**Recovers the file contacts.doc in the myfiles directory on drive D.**

REN OR RENAME

Purpose: Renames a file, a group of files, or a directory.
Parameters:

drive:\path\filename1	The location and name of the file or files you want to rename.
filename2	The new name of the files or directory.

Examples:

ren *.txt *.docx	Changes all files with the .txt file extension in the current directory to have the .docx file extension.
ren docs1 docs2	Changes the name of the docs1 directory to docs2.

RMDIR OR RD

Purpose: Removes or deletes a directory.
Parameters:

drive:path	The location of the directory to delete.
/s	Deletes the directory and all subdirectories, including files.
/q	Does not ask for a confirmation before the deletion.

Examples:

rmdir /s \oldfiles	Deletes the oldfiles directory and all subdirectories and files in it.

TASKKILL

Purpose: Ends a process or process tree.
Parameters:

/pid *processID*	The process ID of the process to be ended.
/f	The process is forced to end.
/t	Ends the specified process and all its child processes.

Examples:

taskkill /pid 1285	Ends the process with process ID 1285. You can use Task Manager to find out the process ID of a process.
taskkill /pid 1285 /pid 1297	Ends the processes with process IDs 1285 and 1297.
taskkill /f /pid 1285	Forcefully ends the process with process ID 1285.

TRACERT

Purpose: Maps the route a packet takes through the network, from the local machine to a remote destination.

Parameters:

target name	Name or IP address of the target.
-d	Does not resolve addresses to hostnames.
-h maximum hops	Sets the maximum number of hops that can be used to search for the target machine.
-w timeout	Sets the timeout in milliseconds to wait for a reply.

Examples:

| tracert microsoft.com | Maps the route a packet takes to the destination microsoft.com. |
| tracert –d google.com | Maps the route a packet takes to google.com, but only IP addresses are listed and not hostnames. |

VER

Purpose: Displays the version number of the operating system. This command has no parameters.

VERIFY

Purpose: A setting that determines if Windows will tell you that your files are written correctly to a disk.

Parameters:

| on off | Switches the verify setting on or off. |

Examples:

Verify on	Turns the verify setting on. Windows will now tell you whether subsequent commands are correctly writing files to the disk.

VOL

Purpose: Displays the name and serial number of a volume or drive. This command has no parameters. Use the label command to change the volume or drive name.

How Windows Vista Works

In this appendix, we're going to the back rooms of Windows operation so that you can understand how Windows works on the inside. With that understanding comes tremendous power! Once you understand a problem, solving it becomes easy and even fun. In fact, problems with Windows can become a game of mastering mind over matter. You truly can become a master Windows fixer-upper.

So let's begin by walking through a door labeled "Not for the normal user" and into the heart of Windows operations. In this first section, we'll go behind the scenes and see how Windows is put together and how it works.

THE WINDOWS VISTA STRUCTURE

Windows Vista is the most refined, secure, and stable desktop operating system Microsoft has ever created. Most of this stability already existed with Windows XP, and, in fact, the Vista structure greatly resembles that of XP but with some added security features. In this section, you'll learn how Windows Vista is structured and how it is designed to create this stability.

Figure D-1 shows the layout of the many components and subsystems of Windows Vista. Each of the boxes in the figure represents a group of program files assigned to that task. In this appendix, as you learn about system files, services, processes, and threads, this figure can serve as your map to how they all interrelate.

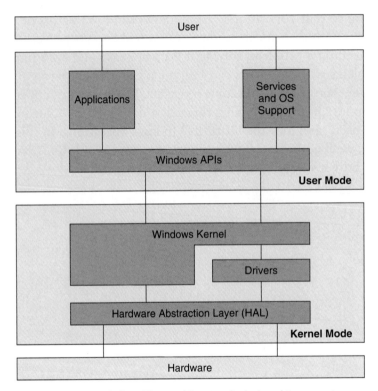

Figure D-1   The Windows Vista architecture is designed to prevent unauthorized interaction between user applications and services and underlying hardware

WHAT THE USER SEES

In this section, I want you to view what the user sees, not as a user but as a Windows expert. Let's look at the Windows desktop with a new awareness of why and how things appear and work as they do.

VIEWING THE WINDOWS DESKTOP

On the surface, the Windows desktop (see Figure D-2) is the interface from which a user can store a document or photograph or launch a program to create and manage files, play a game, or surf the Web. To the user, the Windows desktop is similar to the desktop of a

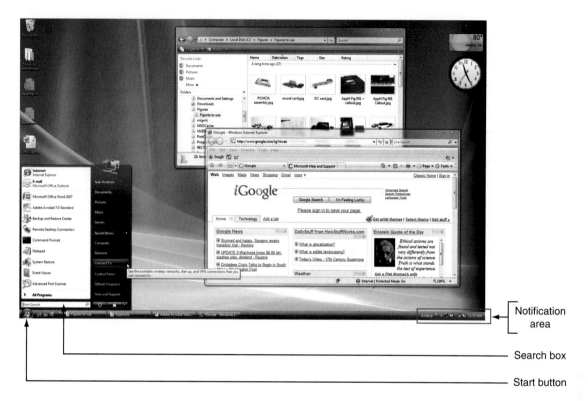

Notification area

Search box

Start button

Figure D-2   The Windows Vista desktop

physical desk; it's a place to put things you're working on or are saving for easy access. A user can place files and shortcuts to programs on the desktop for easy access. The horizontal bar along the bottom of the screen, called the taskbar, can be used to easily switch between open or running programs. The notification area, located on the right corner of the taskbar, displays the time and icons that represent some of the programs that are running in the background. The Start button, located on the left side of the taskbar, provides access to a menu that contains a variety of applications, utilities, and system settings.

UNDERSTANDING THE WINDOWS DESKTOP

On the surface, the Windows desktop is made up of shortcuts, a taskbar, the Start button, and the notification area. All of these items make up the dynamic user interface. Now let's look behind the scenes.

The Windows desktop is created and managed by a single program, explorer.exe. Explorer.exe is a system file located in the C:\Windows folder; we commonly know it as Windows Explorer. Explorer.exe is launched at startup and opens as the Windows desktop. For this reason, explorer.exe is always being used by Windows and cannot be deleted.

Explorer.exe provides the graphical user interface and can be unloaded and loaded very easily. To unload the Windows desktop, you must stop explorer.exe, which causes the desktop and taskbar to disappear. Once this occurs, you can start explorer.exe again, which reloads the Windows desktop. Do the following to unload and load the Windows desktop:

1. Press and hold the **Ctrl-Alt-Delete** keys. If you are on a Windows domain, the Windows Security dialog box opens and you need to click the **Task Manager** button. If you are in a Windows workgroup or not connected to a network, instead of the Windows Security dialog box, you'll see a menu and you need to click **Start Task**

Manager. Regardless of how you got there, when you see the Task Manager window, click the **Processes** tab (see Figure D-3).

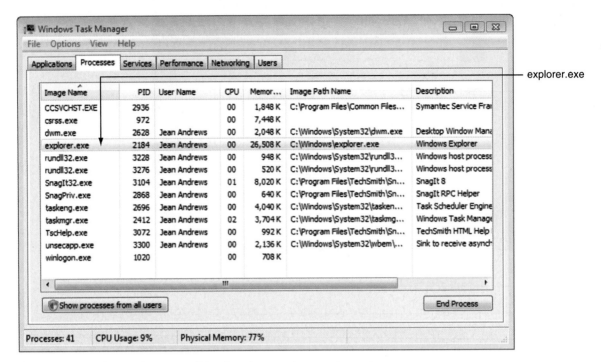

Figure D-3   Windows Task Manager dialog box shows explorer.exe is running

2. Click the **explorer.exe** process and then click the **End Process** button. A warning dialog box appears. Click **End Process** to confirm you really want to do this. All icons on the desktop and the taskbar disappear. You should still see the Task Manager window and the desktop wallpaper.

3. Click the **Applications** tab and then click the **New Task** button. The Create New Task dialog box appears.

4. Type **explorer.exe**, as shown in Figure D-4, and then click **OK**. The Windows desktop reappears.

5. Click **File** and then click **Exit Task Manager** to close the Task Manager window.

In summary, you can think of the Windows desktop, along with its icons and taskbar, as a type of visual presentation of Windows Explorer that is different from the normal

> **Note**
>
> If an application locks up or does not close properly, sometimes you can solve the problem by using Task Manager to stop the program. If this doesn't work, try stopping the explorer.exe program to unload the Windows desktop. Then use Task Manager to reload the desktop. If you still have a problem, then reboot the PC.

Explorer window we're all accustomed to using. Anything you can do on the Windows desktop, such as saving a file or opening an application, can be done using the Windows Explorer window shown in Figure D-5.

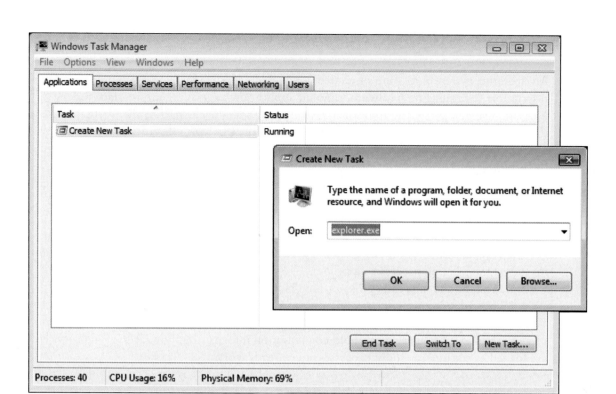

Figure D-4   Loading the Windows desktop

Figure D-5   Windows Explorer can be used to perform many OS functions

UNDERSTANDING WINDOWS COMPONENTS

An operating system is a group of related components used to manage a computer. An OS is responsible for managing hardware, running applications, providing an interface for the user, and managing files and folders. A **system file** is a file that is part of the OS that is used to (1) start the OS; (2) hold configuration information about the OS, software, hardware, and user preferences; or (3) perform one of the many functions of the OS, such as managing the printing process or interfacing with the hard drive. A system file might have an .exe, .dll, .drv, .sys, or .ocx file extension, or it might not have a file extension at all (for example, BootMgr). Many system files are never used and some are used only occasionally. Others run all the time Windows is running and are essential for Windows operations. For example, explorer.exe is a core system file used to display the Windows Vista desktop and is constantly in use. Another example of a system file is spoolsv.exe, which is responsible for managing the printing process to a printer.

To understand the many functions of the OS is to understand the purpose of groups of system files and how they relate to other groups of system files. In fact, the system files *are* Windows. In this section, you'll learn about the two modes that system files run in, examples of system files, how they can hold configuration information, how drivers and services are loaded at startup, and how processes and threads work.

USER MODE AND KERNEL MODE

Looking back at Figure D-1, you can see that some system files run in user mode and some run in kernel mode. The three main categories of system programs that run in user mode are system applications, system services, and Windows APIs. User applications also run in user mode. For our discussion here, the difference between a user application and a user service is that a user application runs in the foreground with a user interface (for example, Windows Explorer) and a user service runs in the background (for example, Windows Defender).

Processes that run in kernel mode have full access to all CPU instructions and full access to memory. Most of these kernel mode processes are written by Microsoft. The exception is device drivers that are written by device manufacturers. Because device drivers have unlimited access to hardware, it's important to only use drivers digitally signed by Microsoft. In fact, the 64-bit version of Windows Vista allows only digitally signed drivers to be installed. An error that occurs with a kernel mode process generates a Stop error, which halts the entire system and requires a restart (see Figure D-6).

User applications and other programs are designated to run in user mode so they can be more closely monitored by the OS to prevent unauthorized access to hardware and to limit the amount of damage they can do if an error occurs. Processes that run in user mode cannot directly access hardware and must make API calls to Windows components, which access hardware in their behalf. When errors occur with user mode processes, the error is handled using Windows Error Reporting. These errors don't require a restart and don't interfere with other running processes.

SOME KERNEL MODE COMPONENTS

In Chapter 7 you learned about the steps to start Windows Vista. Recall that the Vista kernel is loaded first. Then control is given to the Session Manager (smss.exe), which runs in user mode and causes the progress bar to appear. Remember that when the progress bar appears, you know the kernel has loaded successfully.

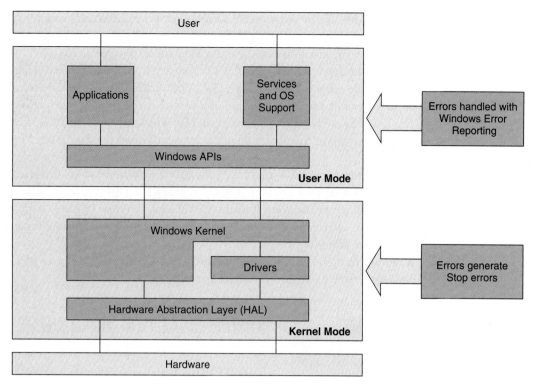

Figure D-6 How errors are handled in user mode and kernel mode

Here are the key Vista kernel mode components:

- ◢ **Components of the kernel and HAL.** Programs used to start the OS include BootMgr and WinLoad. The main kernel program is Ntoskrnl.exe and the HAL program is Hal.dll; both programs stay running as long as Vista is loaded. The kernel and HAL include many other programs as well.
- ◢ **Device drivers.** Device drivers are programs that make the interface between API calls from an application or service and a hardware device. Each command from the OS is translated into the exact command and parameters a device can understand and obey. Some device drivers are supplied when a new device is installed, and some come preinstalled on Windows. An example of a core device driver preinstalled with Windows is the file system device driver, srv.sys. Windows allows certain video card drivers that interface with the video card and with the user to run in kernel mode and user mode so that the driver can better interact with both.

SOME USER MODE COMPONENTS

Recall that the Vista kernel is loaded first and then turns control over to the Session Manager (smss.exe), which loads the user mode components of Vista. Key components are listed here (keep in mind that the list is by no means complete):

- ◢ **The Session Manager (C:\Windows\system32\smss.exe).** This program performs many of the first steps in starting Windows, including opening the page file, starting core Windows processes, and starting the Windows logon program. If errors occur during these key events, smss.exe will terminate the startup, crashing the system.

▲ *The Windows logon program (C:\Windows\System32\Winlogon.exe).* This program oversees the logon process, calling other programs as needed. Programs that it calls include services.exe, lsass.exe, userinit.exe, and explorer.exe.

▲ *The Service Control Manager (C:\Windows\system32\Services.exe).* This program starts up the services component of Windows including the generic service host process (svchost.exe). An example of a service is the print spooler, spoolsv.exe.

▲ *The Local Security Authority program (C:\Windows\System32\Lsass.exe).* This program is responsible for authenticating a password the user types in to log onto the system.

▲ *Logon Application (C:\Windows\System32\Userinit.exe).* This program performs whatever instructions are stored in the registry for this user at logon.

▲ *The Client Server Runtime Process (C:\Windows\system32\Csrss.exe).* This program provides an interface for Windows applications and is responsible for managing most graphics in Windows.

▲ *Windows Explorer (C:\Windows\Explorer.exe).* This program provides the Vista desktop as well as Windows Explorer windows.

> **Note**
>
> In this book, I use C:\Windows as the folder in which Windows is installed. However, keep in mind that Windows might be installed at a different location, such as C:\Winnt or E:\Windows.

SYSTEM FILES THAT HOLD INFORMATION

Most system files are program files that contain programming code, but some system files are used only to hold information. Most of these files are database files and some are text files. Here are some examples:

▲ *Example 1*: The Vista Boot Configuration Data (C:\Boot\BCD) file is a database file that holds Vista startup settings.

▲ *Example 2*: Log files are kept about various events. The logs reported by Event Viewer include the Windows, applications, services, and security logs. One log recorded at startup is C:\Windows\System32\LogFiles\SRT\SRTTrail.txt, which is created by the Startup Repair process. Another startup log is C:\Windows\Ntbtlog.txt, which is kept when you boot into Safe Mode or when you choose Enable Boot Logging on the Advanced Boot Options menu.

▲ *Example 3*: Pagefile.sys is a database file used as virtual memory. Pagefile.sys is a hidden system file stored in the root directory of the drive used for the Windows installation (most likely drive C).

▲ *Example 4*: The five registry files are database files. Their names are Sam, Security, System, Software, and Default; they are stored in the C:\Windows\System32\Config folder. The registry holds configuration information for Windows, hardware, applications, and user preferences.

▲ *Example 5*: Windows settings that apply to a specific user are kept in the database file C:\Users*username*\Ntuser.dat.

The most important Windows component that holds information for Windows is the registry. The registry is a hierarchical database that contains configuration information for Windows, users, software applications, and installed hardware devices. Windows builds the registry from the five registry hives, the current hardware configuration, and the Ntuser.dat database file. The registry is built in memory and remains there until Windows shuts down. During startup, Windows builds the registry and then reads from it to obtain information about the startup process. After Windows is loaded, it continually reads from many of the subkeys in the registry.

The five hives that hold information used to build the registry are stored in the C:\Windows\System32\config folder and are named System, SAM, Security, Software, and Default. If you check the folder, you'll find a .LOG file and a .SAV file for each hive. The .LOG files hold logged information about the hive activity, and the .SAV files are backup copies of each hive created during Windows Vista setup.

Registry data is stored on the hard drive in the five hive files, but when it is loaded into memory, it is organized by keys. The registry is divided into six keys and each serves a specific purpose for the normal functioning of the operating system. Figure D-7 shows the high-level keys displayed by the Registry Editor, and the following bulleted list provides a description of each key:

Figure D-7 The Registry Editor shows the high-level keys of the registry

- ▲ *HKEY_LOCAL_MACHINE (abbreviated HKLM)* is the most important key and contains hardware, software, and security data. The data is taken from four hives: the SAM hive, the Security hive, the Software hive, and the System hive. In addition, the HARDWARE key of HKLM is built when the registry is first loaded based on data collected about the current hardware configuration.
- ▲ *HKEY_CURRENT_CONFIG (abbreviated HKCC)* contains hardware configuration data including Plug and Play information. Some of the data is gathered from the current hardware configuration when the registry is first loaded into memory. Other data is taken from the HKLM key, which gets its data from the System hive.
- ▲ *HKEY_CLASSES_ROOT (abbreviated HKCR)* contains data about applications and associated file extensions. Data is gathered from the HKLM key and the HKCU key.
- ▲ *HKEY_USERS (abbreviated HKU)* contains data about all users and is taken from the Default hive.
- ▲ *HKEY_CURRENT_USER (abbreviated HKCU)* contains data about the current user. The key is built when a user logs on using data kept in the HKEY_USERS key and data kept in the Ntuser.dat file of the current user. The Ntuser.dat file is stored in the C:\Users*username* folder.
- ▲ *HKEY_PERFORMANCE_DATA* is a pass-through placeholder for performance data. This key is used only as a reference point for Windows processes and does not contain data, and therefore is not displayed by the registry editor.

> **Note**
>
> Device Manager reads data from the HKLM\HARDWARE key to build the information it displays about hardware configurations. You can consider Device Manager to be an easy-to-view presentation of this HARDWARE key data.

Figure D-8 shows the way the five keys (also called subtrees) that hold data are built from the five hives stored in the C:\Windows\System32\Config folder. As you can see from the figure, only two root keys have associated hives, HKEY_LOCAL_MACHINE (four hives) and HKEY_USERS (the Default hive). Using the registry editor, you can expand HKEY_LOCAL_MACHINE to see its subkeys, as shown in Figure D-9. The HARDWARE subkey is built from the hardware configuration at the time the registry is loaded into memory. Also notice the other subkeys named after the hives from which data was taken (Sam, Security, Software, and System).

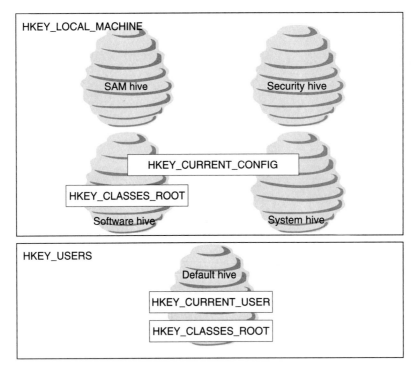

Figure D-8   The relationship between registry subtrees (keys) and hives

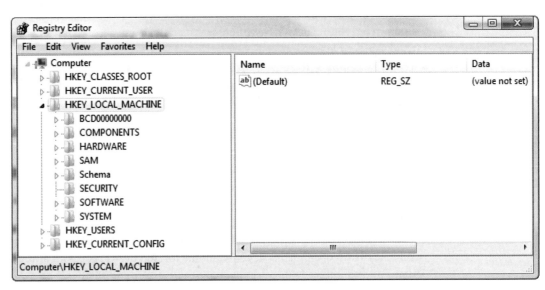

Figure D-9   Windows Registry Editor shows the subkeys of the HKEY_LOCAL_MACHINE key

UNDERSTANDING HOW DRIVERS AND SERVICES ARE LOADED AT STARTUP

Now that you have an understanding of how the registry is put together, let's do a little exploring to see how the drivers and services are loaded from the registry at startup. Recall from Chapter 7 that drivers and some services are loaded while the kernel is loading. After the kernel is loaded, the Services process starts other services. Follow these steps to examine how all this works.

1. Be careful! You're about to open the registry editor to view important keys. Please don't change these registry keys as you work! Click **Start**, enter **regedit** in the Search box, press **Enter**, and respond to the UAC box. The registry editor window opens.

2. Drill down to this key:
   HKEY_LOCAL_MACHINE\SYSTEM\CurrentControlSet\Services.

3. The key contains many subkeys that hold information about services. For example, click the subkey ACPI and the left pane in Figure D-10 shows information about that subkey.

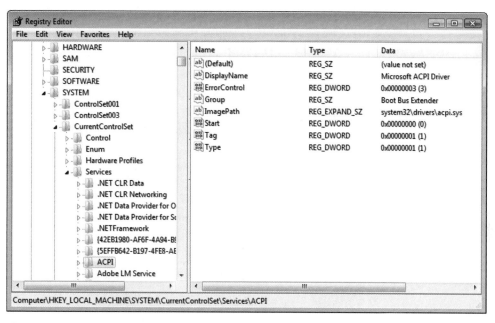

Figure D-10 The Services key lists keys for each installed service

4. To understand how Vista manages a service, it's important to understand the purpose of each name and data value in the right pane of Figure D-10. These items are explained in Table D-1. Note that a service or driver might not use every name in the table.

5. When you compare the list of services and drivers listed under this registry key to the list in the Services console, you'll see that the Services console does not list every item in the key. That's because the Services console manages some services, but not all. To open the Services console, click **Start**, enter **services.msc** in the Search box, press **Enter**, and respond to the UAC box. The Services console opens (see Figure D-11). Notice in the figure that the first service listed is the Adobe LM Service, which is also listed near

Name	Value
DependOnGroup	**Service dependent on the listed item, which must be started first**
DependOnService	**Service dependent on the listed service, which must be started first**
DisplayName	**Describes the service**
ErrorControl	**Identifies what must happen if the driver will not start; possible values are as follows:**
	◢ **0x0 = Continue with startup**
	◢ **0x1 = Record in the System event log and continue with startup**
	◢ **0x2 = Record in the System event log and use the Last Known Good Configuration (LKGC)**
	◢ **0x3 = Record in the System event log and use the LKGC; if the LKGC is already being used, display a Stop error and halt**
Group	**Will start all services or drivers in this group together as a group**
ImagePath	**Path and filename to the service or driver**
ObjectName	**Account that a service logs on with**
Start	**When the service or driver will start; values are as follows:**
	◢ **0x0 = Loaded by BootMgr and started by WinLoad**
	◢ **0x1 = Loaded and started by WinLoad**
	◢ **0x2 = Started by services.exe or smss.exe (listed as Automatic in the Services console)**
	◢ **0x3 = Started manually as needed (listed as Manual in the Services console)**
	◢ **0x4 = Disabled (listed as Disabled in the Services console)**
	◢ **0x5 = Started shortly after startup; these services are not critical to startup and have a delayed start so that the system can more quickly provide a logon screen to user (listed as Automatic, Delayed Start, in the Services console)**
Tag	**The order a driver starts within its driver group**
Type	**Service or driver**

Table D-1 Names and descriptions for values used to manage a service or driver

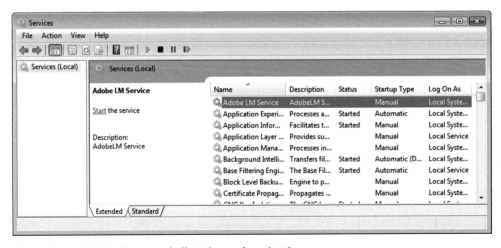

Figure D-11 The Services console lists the services that it manages

the bottom of Figure D-10. This service has a start value of 0x3, meaning it will be loaded on demand. Also notice in Figure D-11 that the ACPI driver is not listed and, therefore, not managed by the Services console. Knowing how to investigate a service or driver in this way can be invaluable when smoking out problems with when or how a process is loaded.

Now let's turn our attention to understanding how Windows works with processes and threads to manage applications and Windows programs running in user mode.

PROCESSES AND THREADS

Put simply, a **process** is a program that is running together with the resources the running program needs (see Figure D-12). When a program is started up, such as when you double-click a program file in Windows Explorer or select a program from the Start menu, the program is copied from the hard drive or other secondary storage media and loaded into memory. It's then executed. A program often starts by telling the OS what other programs or subroutines it needs and what system resources it requires to run. These other programs are also launched, and the system resources (such as memory addresses for the program's data) are assigned to the process. Sometimes a process requires a DLL subprogram after the process has already started. These DLL processes are loaded and unloaded as needed.

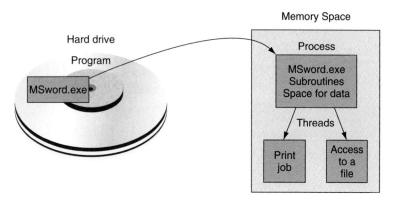

Figure D-12   A process is a running program and its resources

When a process asks the OS to perform a certain task, a thread is created. A **thread** is a task that a process has requested of the OS. For example, a process might request that the OS print a file and then immediately request that another file on the hard drive be opened. In this case, two threads are in progress, as shown in Figure D-12.

When a process starts another process, the two processes are called a process tree. Let's demonstrate what a process tree looks like by using Task Manager. For example, do the following to show how a process tree works under Windows:

1. Enter **cmd** in the Start Search dialog box and press **Enter** to open a command prompt window.

2. In the command prompt window, type **mspaint.exe** and press **Enter**. This opens a Paint window.

3. Click **Start**, point to **All Programs**, click **Accessories**, and then click **Paint**. Another Paint window opens.

4. The first Paint window was opened by the Cmd process, which becomes its parent process. The second Paint window does not have a parent process. Now press **Ctrl-Shift-Esc,** which causes Task Manager to open.

5. On the Applications tab of Task Manager, confirm that three applications are running (see Figure D-13).

Figure D-13   Use Task Manager to view and manage running processes

6. Right-click the **Cmd** process and select **Go To Process** from the shortcut menu. The Processes tab window appears, and the cmd.exe process is selected (see Figure D-14).

7. Right-click the **cmd.exe** process and select **End Process Tree** from the shortcut menu. When the Task Manager message box appears, click **End process tree** to continue. The command prompt window and one of the Paint windows close. The Paint window that is not part of the Cmd process tree remains open.

We've just used Task Manager to demonstrate that processes are often related to parent processes and Windows keeps track of which process is related to which. We've also demonstrated that Task Manager can be a powerful tool when trying to weed through several process trees.

Based on what you've learned so far about Windows and the information presented in the Task Manager window in Figure D-14, it should be apparent that more processes are running in the Windows background than are running in the Windows foreground. Most of these background processes are required in order for Windows Vista to function properly. Some of the programs were started by services that are configured to automatically run when Windows Vista loads. Other programs have created icons in the notification area to

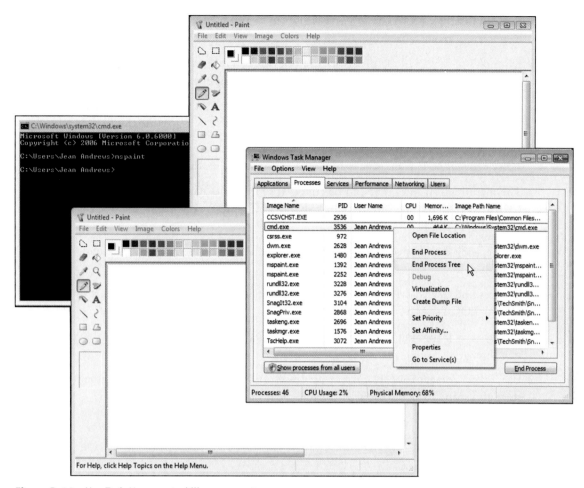

Figure D-14 Use Task Manager to kill a process tree

let the user know they're running and to provide an interface for configuration. Still other programs are launched at startup from other locations.

In order to troubleshoot Windows Vista problems, you must have a strong understanding of what's running and what is really required to run for Windows Vista to function properly. So how can you tell what user mode processes are running on your computer? Use Task Manager. Task Manager can be used to determine the executables that are running and what percentage of system resources they're using. In Chapter 2, you use Task Manager to examine each process that is launched at startup for a clean Windows Vista installation.

>> APPENDIX SUMMARY

- ◢ The Windows Vista architecture is a group of interrelated components that form the interface between the hardware, the user, and applications software.

- ◢ The notification area holds icons that represent running programs and services.

- ◢ The Windows desktop is a presentation made by Windows Explorer that is used to manage files, folders, and programs.

- ◢ Processes run in either user mode or kernel mode. Some processes that serve as a bridge between the two modes can run in both modes.

◢ Errors caused by processes running in user mode are handled by Windows Error Reporting. Errors caused by kernel-mode processes cause Stop errors.

◢ Examples of kernel mode processes are BootMgr, WinLoad, hal.dll, and device drivers. Examples of user mode processes are smss.exe, winlogon.exe, services.exe, and lsass.exe.

◢ A few system files are used to hold information. The registry is stored in five files called hives. The BCD file holds startup settings, and pagefile.sys is used for virtual memory.

◢ Key system files used to create and maintain the Windows environment, services, and subsystems include smss.exe, winlogon.exe, lsass.exe, services.exe, and csrss.exe.

◢ The main registry keys that can be edited are HKEY_LOCAL_MACHINE, HKEY_CURRENT_CONFIG, HKEY_CLASSES_ROOT, HKEY_USERS, and HKEY_CURRENT_USER.

◢ The registry data is stored in five hives named Sam, Security, Software, System, and Default.

◢ Services and device drivers are loaded from the Services subkey which is part of the HKEY_LOCAL_MACHINE key.

◢ A process is a running program together with its resources. A process must have at least one thread.

◢ Use Task Manager to view current processes and how they relate to each other. You can start and stop a process using Task Manager.

>> KEY TERMS

process   A program that is running, together with the resources needed by the running program.

system file   A file that is part of the OS that is used to do one of the following: boot the OS; hold configuration information about the OS, software, hardware, and user preferences; or perform one of the many functions of the OS, such as managing the printing process or interfacing with the hard drive.

thread   A task that a process has requested of the OS.

>> REVIEWING THE BASICS

1. What is the main function of the Windows taskbar?

2. How can you tell that an antivirus program is running in the background by looking at the desktop?

3. What system file loads and manages the Windows desktop?

4. What is the function of the Windows desktop?

5. Which registry key contains Plug and Play information?

6. What is the main kernel program for Windows Vista?

7. What are the five Windows Vista registry hives?

8. Which main registry key contains information about installed hardware?

9. What subkey is used by Device Manager to build information about installed hardware?

10. What is the difference between a process and a thread?

>> THINKING CRITICALLY

1. A Stop error occurs that displays an error message about a service. Is the service running in user mode or kernel mode? Explain your answer.

2. The system locks up. You open Task Manager and find that no applications are running. What should you do next? Explain your answer.

   a. End the Explorer.exe process and restart it.
   b. Unplug the computer. Plug it in again and reboot.
   c. Start Msconfig to diagnose the problem.
   d. Run AV software to scan for viruses.

>> HANDS-ON PROJECTS

PROJECT D-1:   CPU Time Used by Processes

Open Task Manager to view the processes currently running. Click the **Processes** tab. Which process has used the greatest amount of CPU time? Why?

PROJECT D-2:   Using Task Manager to View Processes

Reboot your Windows Vista system and open Task Manager. Under the Processes tab, write down the list of processes or take a screen shot and print it so that you have a printed record of the running processes. Research each process and write a one-sentence description of each.

PROJECT D-3:   Loaded Device Drivers

You can use the System Information utility to view a list of system and signed device drivers currently running. To open System Information, enter **msinfo32.exe** in the Start Search dialog box and press **Enter**. Then expand **Software Environment** and click **System Drivers**. Answer the following questions:

1. What are the two types of system drivers?

2. In what folder are most system drivers stored?

3. What is the filename of the CD-ROM driver?

PROJECT D-4:   Just How Lean Can Windows Get?

Using Task Manager, how many processes can you kill before Windows locks up? Do the following:

1. Make sure no one else is logged onto the system and you've closed important applications, saving any work.

2. Open Task Manager.

3. End all the processes you can. List the processes that refuse to end. Which process reappears after you end it?

4. Ending which process caused the system to begin the shutdown event? (When you end this process, the system shuts down. Restart the system and don't attempt to end this process again. Begin at Step 1 again.)

5. Shut down the system. In this stripped-down state, does Windows Vista shut down with no errors? How did you perform the shutdown?

>> REAL PROBLEMS, REAL SOLUTIONS

REAL PROBLEM D-1:   Researching How Windows Vista Works

This appendix gives you background information on how Windows Vista works, but it's only a good start. Much more information is available on the Microsoft Web site and on other sites. Pose one good question about the material in this appendix that will take your understanding deeper into the internals of Windows Vista. Research the Internet to find your answer. In a classroom environment, report your question and your findings to the class.

APPENDIX E

Installing Windows Vista

Microsoft considers Windows Vista to be an upgrade of Windows XP. If you have adequate hardware resources, Windows Vista is an extremely stable and high-performing OS. Many of us technicians remember the horror days when Windows XP was first released and all the many bugs, errors, and faults it had. It was not until after Windows XP Service Pack 2 was available that support technicians were able to relax and enjoy the OS. However, Microsoft did a much better job of testing Windows Vista, and it was first released relatively bug-free compared to Windows XP. What a relief! Thus you now can simply enjoy learning to use and support a new OS with tons of new features and support techniques and tools.

This appendix explains the several versions of Vista and how to plan a Vista installation and then perform the installation. Then you'll learn how to install hardware and applications, set up user accounts, and customize the Vista desktop.

VERSIONS OF VISTA

Microsoft has released several versions of Vista designed to satisfy a variety of consumer needs. All the versions are included on the Windows Vista setup DVD; the version installed depends on the product key that you enter during the installation. Therefore, upgrading to a better version of Vista can easily be accomplished by using the Windows Anytime Upgrade feature. Here are the Vista versions:

▲ Windows Vista Starter has the most limited features and is intended to be used in developing nations.

▲ Windows Vista Home Basic is similar to Windows XP Home Edition and is designed for low-cost home systems that don't require full security and networking features.

▲ Windows Vista Home Premium is similar to Windows Vista Home Basic but includes additional features such as the Aero user interface.

▲ Windows Vista Business is intended for business users. Computers can join a domain, support Group Policy, and use the Encrypted File System for better security. You can also purchase multiple site licenses using this version. Consumer features not included in Windows Vista Business or Windows Vista Enterprise include Windows Media Center, Movie Maker, DVD Maker, and parental controls.

▲ Windows Vista Enterprise includes additional features over Windows Vista Business. The major additional security feature is BitLocker, which is useful to secure data stored on a hard drive if the drive is stolen. Multiple site licensing is available.

▲ Windows Vista Ultimate includes every Windows Vista feature. You cannot purchase multiple licensing with this version.

The major features for all versions are listed in Table E-1.

Feature	Starter	Home Basic	Home Premium	Business	Enterprise	Ultimate
Aero user interface			X	X	X	X
BitLocker hard drive encryption					X	X
Optional dual processors*				X	X	X
Complete PC backup				X	X	X
Encrypting File System (EFS)				X	X	X
IE parental controls	X	X	X			X
Network and Sharing Center	X	X	X	X	X	X
Scheduled and network backups			X	X	X	X
Tablet PC			X	X	X	X
Windows DVD Maker			X			X
Windows Media Center			X			X

Table E-1 Vista versions and their features

Feature	Starter	Home Basic	Home Premium	Business	Enterprise	Ultimate
Windows Movie Maker			X			X
Windows SideShow			X	X	X	X
Shadow Copy backup				X	X	X
Join a domain				X	X	X
Group Policy				X	X	X
Processor: 32-bit or 64-bit		X	X	X	X	X
Flip 3D display			X	X	X	X
Remote Desktop				X	X	X
Windows Meeting Space			X	X	X	X

Table E-1 Vista versions and their features (*Continued*)
*Core duo processors are allowed for all versions

Here are the minimum hardware requirements for Windows Vista. However, as you consider this list, please note that with the limited memory and video listed in the second and third bullets, you won't be able to see the Aero user interface, which gives a 3-D appearance to Vista windows.

▲ A processor rated at least 800 MHz
▲ 512 MB of RAM
▲ SVGA video
▲ A 20 GB hard drive with at least 15 GB free space
▲ A CD-ROM drive

Note

For best performance, a Vista system needs 2 GB of RAM or more. Also, Vista is most often sold in retail stores on DVD, so having a DVD drive makes your installation easier.

Recommended hardware requirements for Windows Vista are:

▲ A processor rated at least 1 GHz, which can be a 32-bit or 64-bit processor
▲ 1 GB of RAM
▲ A video card or embedded video chip that has at least 128 MB of graphics memory and DirectX 9 support with a Windows Display Driver Model (WDDM)
▲ A 40 GB hard drive with at least 15 GB free space
▲ A DVD-ROM drive
▲ Internet access

INSTALLING VISTA

When you buy a brand-name new PC or laptop, the computer often comes with Vista already installed. For a brand-name computer, this installation might be an Original Equipment Manufacturer (OEM) build of the OS. It is likely the installation files for Vista are stored on a hidden partition on the hard drive in case the Vista installation fails and needs reinstalling. The computer bundle should also include operating system recovery DVDs or CDs to be used in emergencies when the hard drive totally fails you. These recovery discs will most likely include the OEM build of Vista, as well as device drivers and applications preinstalled on this computer.

When you build a computer from scratch, replace a hard drive, or need to upgrade from an older OS to Windows Vista, you will install Windows Vista using a single license version or a volume license version of Windows Vista on DVD or CD (see Figure E-1). Just as with Windows XP, you can copy the Vista installation files from the disc to a file server or to the local hard drive and install the OS from that source.

64-bit version DVD

32-bit version DVD

Figure E-1   Windows Vista Ultimate can be purchased only as a single license version and comes with two DVDs

This part of the appendix covers decisions you need to make before you install Windows Vista; it also covers how to do the actual installation of the OS.

CHOOSING THE UPGRADE, CLEAN INSTALL, OR DUAL BOOT

As with previous versions of Windows, you can install Windows Vista as a clean install, as an upgrade, or as the second OS on a computer in a dual boot configuration. The upgrade version of Windows Vista costs less than the for-a-new-PC version. However, you can use either version to perform a clean install or an upgrade installation.

When you perform a clean install, Vista overwrites any previously installed OS and you get a fresh start. You will need to reinstall any applications, printers, and other hardware peripherals. If you format the hard drive during the installation, all data on the drive is erased. If you don't format the hard drive, user data will be saved, but you'll still need to reinstall applications and peripheral devices. Before you do a clean install, be sure to

> **Note**
>
> Windows Vista is sold to retail customers in three ways: a single license, discounts on additional licenses after you first purchase a single license, and volume licensing. For more information, see Microsoft's Web site at *www.microsoft.com*.

back up all data on the drive and make sure you have available all the application CDs and device drivers. If you don't plan to format the hard drive, be sure to run antivirus software before you begin the installation. If you suspect a virus is present, to be safe, format the hard drive.

When you perform an upgrade to Vista, you carry forward into the Vista installation all installed applications, data, and user settings and preferences. You might also carry forward problems with the previously installed OS, so only do an upgrade if your old OS installation is fairly healthy. And be sure to back up user data and run antivirus software before you install Vista.

When you install Windows Vista as the second OS in a system, called a dual boot configuration, Vista must be installed as the only OS in a partition, and you must install the old OS before you install Vista. You can install Vista in a second partition on a single hard drive or on a second hard drive in the system. One good reason to use a dual boot configuration is that you are not sure your hardware or applications will work under Vista. After you have installed Vista and tested your hardware and software, you can then delete the old OS from the hard drive. How to delete the old OS or to delete the Vista installation is covered in a project at the end of the appendix.

UPGRADE PATHS

You can purchase and use the less expensive upgrade version of Windows Vista if you are upgrading from Windows XP or Windows 2000 to Windows Vista. If Service Pack 2 is applied to Windows XP, you can use Windows Easy Transfer to transfer Windows XP user data and preferences to Windows Vista. Upgrade options are outlined in Table E-2. Notice in the table that even though you can purchase the upgrade version of Vista when upgrading from Windows 2000 or Windows XP 64-bit, you must perform a clean installation of Vista on your PC. You also cannot upgrade from Windows 95/98/Me or Windows NT to Windows Vista.

Old OS	Home Basic	Home Premium	Business	Ultimate
Win XP Professional	Clean install	Clean install	Upgrade	Upgrade
Win XP Home	Upgrade	Upgrade	Upgrade	Upgrade
Win XP Media Center	Clean install	Upgrade	Clean install	Upgrade
Win XP Tablet PC	Clean install	Clean install	Upgrade	Upgrade
Win XP x64	Clean install	Clean install	Clean install	Clean install
Win 2000	Clean install	Clean install	Clean install	Clean install

Table E-2 Upgrade paths to Windows Vista

BEFORE YOU START THE INSTALLATION

Before installing Windows Vista, do the following:

◢ Make sure your computer qualifies for Vista. Check the minimum and recommended hardware configurations listed earlier in the appendix. Check your CPU rating, amount of installed RAM, and hard drive size and free space. Vista comes on a CD or a DVD. Know that you can't install Vista from a DVD if you have a CD drive but not a DVD drive unless the computer is networked to another computer that has a DVD drive.

◢ Make sure your applications will work under Vista. Check the Windows Vista Compatibility site by Microsoft at *www.microsoft.com/windows/compatibility*, which lists software and hardware that qualify for Vista (see Figure E-2). If your application is not listed, check the application's Web site for information about the problem. You might be able to download updates of the application to Windows Vista.

◢ Make sure your hardware devices will work under Vista and that you have the necessary drivers. To verify that your hardware qualifies, click the **Hardware** tab in the lower area of the web page shown in Figure E-2 to search by hardware categories. If you are not sure that essential devices, such as a network card, will install under Vista, you can install Vista as a dual boot so that, if the network card doesn't work under Vista, you can boot into the old OS and still have access to the network.

◢ Decide if you want to perform an upgrade, a clean install, or a dual boot. You cannot install Vista as a dual boot unless you have a second partition to hold Vista.

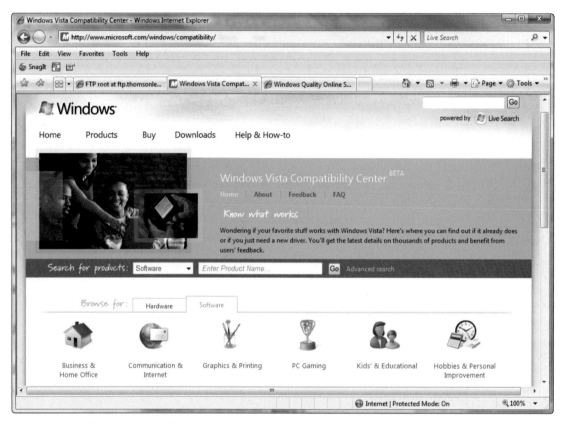

Figure E-2   Verify that your applications and hardware qualify for Vista

PERFORMING A VISTA IN-PLACE UPGRADE

To upgrade from Windows XP to Windows Vista, follow these steps:

1. From the Windows XP desktop, launch the Windows Vista CD or DVD. The opening menu shown in Figure E-3 appears. Click **Install now**.

2. On the next screen, you can choose to allow the setup program to download updates for the installation. If you have Internet access, click **Go online to get the latest updates for installation (recommended)**. Setup will download the updates as shown in Figure E-4. When using this option, you'll need to stay connected to the Internet throughout the installation.

Figure E-3 Windows Vista Setup opening menu

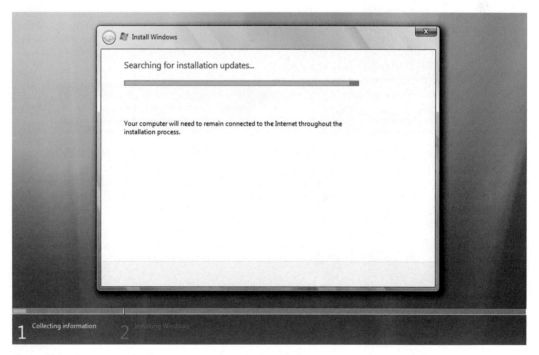

Figure E-4 Setup uses the Internet to update the installation process

3. On the next screen, as shown in Figure E-5, enter the Vista product key. It's printed on a sticker inside the CD or DVD case.

4. On the next screen, accept the license agreement.

5. On the next screen, shown in Figure E-6, select the type of installation you want, either an upgrade or a clean install. Select **Upgrade**.

6. The installation is now free to move forward. The PC will reboot several times. At the end of this process, a screen appears asking for your country, time, currency, and keyboard layout. Make your selections and click **Next**.

> **Note**
>
> Notice in Figure E-5 the checkbox "Automatically activate Windows when I'm online". Normally, you would leave this option checked so that Vista activates immediately. However, if you are practicing installing Vista and intend to install it several times using the same DVD, you might choose to uncheck this box and not enter the product key during the installation. When you do that, you will be prompted to select the version of Vista to install. You can later decide to enter the product key and activate Vista after the installation.

Figure E-5 Enter the product key found inside the Vista CD or DVD case

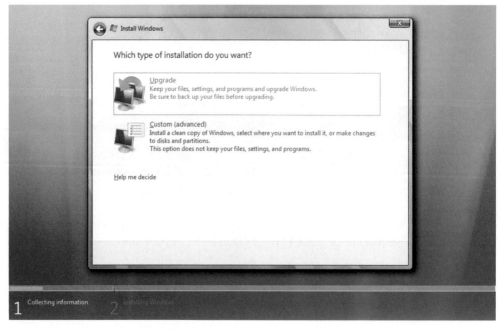

Figure E-6 Select the type of installation you want

7. On the following screens, you are asked to enter a user name, password, computer name, date, and time, and you are asked how you want to handle Windows updates.

8. Finally, Setup checks your computer's performance and then a logon screen appears (see Figure E-7). After you log on, a Welcome window appears (see Figure E-8). The installation is complete.

Figure E-7   Vista logon screen after the installation

Figure E-8   Vista Welcome Center appears after first logon to Vista

> **Note**
>
> If your computer is part of a Windows domain, when Windows Vista starts up, it displays a blank screen instead of a logon screen. To log onto the domain, press Ctrl-Alt-Del to display the logon screen. If you want to log onto the local machine instead of the domain, type **.\username**. For example, to log onto the local machine using the local user account "Jean Andrews", type **.\Jean Andrews**.

PERFORMING A CLEAN INSTALL OR DUAL BOOT

To perform a clean install of Windows Vista or a dual boot with another OS, do the following:

1. Boot directly from the Windows Vista CD or DVD. If you have trouble booting from the disc, go into CMOS setup and verify that your first boot device is the optical drive. Select your language preference, and then the opening menu shown earlier in Figure E-3 appears. Click **Install now**.

2. On the next screens, enter the product key and accept the license agreement.

3. On the next screen, shown earlier in Figure E-6, select the type of installation you want. Choose **Custom (advanced)**.

> **Note**
>
> If your computer refuses to boot from the DVD, verify that your optical drive is a DVD drive. Perhaps it is only a CD drive. If this is the case, you can use another computer on your network that has a DVD drive to read the disc. This computer can act as your file server for the Vista installation on the first PC, or you can copy the installation files on the DVD across the network to a folder on the hard drive of your first PC and install the OS from this folder.

4. On the next screen, you will be shown a list of partitions on which to install the OS. For example, the computer shown in Figure E-9 has two hard drives (Disk 0 and Disk 1), each with one partition. You can choose to install Vista on drive C (only partition on the first hard drive) or drive E (only partition on the second hard drive). For this computer, Windows XP is installed on drive C. If you choose drive C, then you will be

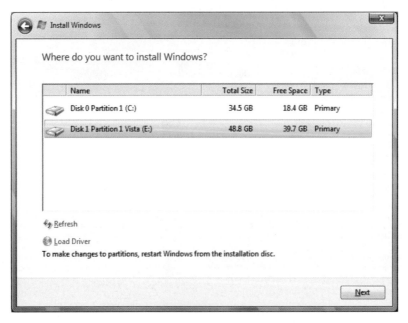

Figure E-9 Select a partition to install Vista in a dual boot environment

performing a clean install on top of Windows XP, erasing XP. If you choose drive E, then you will be installing Vista on the second hard drive and the system will function with a dual boot configuration. Make your selection and click **Next**.

The installation continues the same way as an upgrade installation.

PERFORMING A CLEAN INSTALL USING THE VISTA UPGRADE DVD

A problem sometimes arises when you have purchased a Vista upgrade DVD but you cannot boot your Windows 2000/XP system to start the Vista installation from within Windows 2000/XP. You have two options in this situation. One option is to reinstall Windows 2000/XP and then install Windows Vista as an upgrade. Another option is to use the Vista upgrade DVD to perform a clean install. However, during the Vista installation, when you enter the product key, Vista verifies that the product key is for an upgrade DVD or for-a-new-PC DVD. If you are using an upgrade product key for a clean install, Setup gives an error and stops the installation. The error message is, "To use the product key you entered, start the installation from your existing version of Windows." Follow these steps to get around that error:

1. Boot from the Vista DVD and start the installation. When you get to the installation window that asks you to enter your product key, don't enter the key and uncheck **Automatically activate Windows when I'm online.**

2. A message appears asking you to enter the key. Click **No** to continue. On the next window (see Figure E-10), select the version of Vista you have purchased, check **I have selected the edition of Windows that I purchased**, and click **Next**.

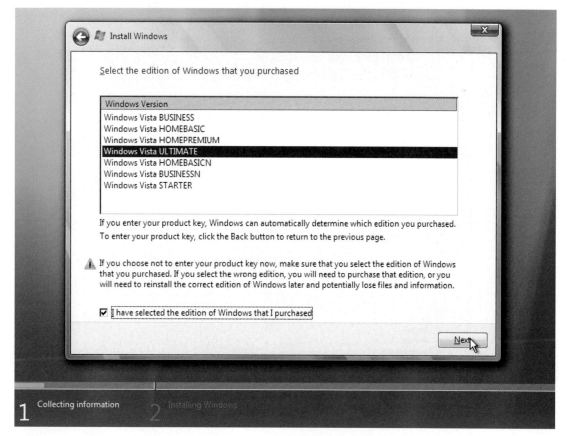

Figure E-10 Installing Windows Vista without entering the product key

3. Complete the installation. You will not be able to activate Vista without the product key.

4. From the Vista desktop, start the installation routine again, but this time as an upgrade. If you get an error, restart the installation. Enter the product key during the installation and Vista will activate with no problems.

WHAT TO DO AFTER THE INSTALLATION

After you have installed Windows Vista, you need to do the following:

1. Verify that you have network access

2. Activate Windows Vista and install updates

3. Install hardware

4. Install applications

5. Create user accounts

6. Customize the Vista desktop and other settings

Let's look at each of these items in detail.

VERIFY THAT YOU HAVE NETWORK ACCESS

When you install Vista, the setup process should connect you to the network and to the Internet, if available. To verify that you have network and Internet access, do the following:

1. Click **Start, Network** to open the Network window (see Figure E-11). You should see other computers and resources on the network in the right pane and you should be able to drill down to see shared resources on these computers.

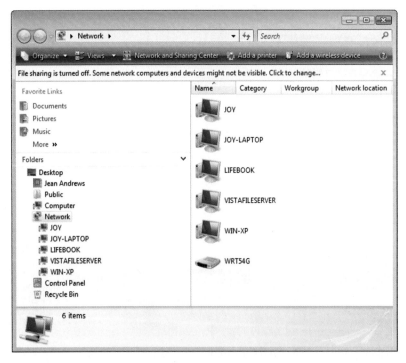

Figure E-11   Use the Network window to access resources on your network

2. If the Network window does not show other computers on your network, first try rebooting the PC. Then verify that the computer, workgroup, or domain names are correct using the System Properties dialog box. Click **Start**, right-click **Computer**, and select **Properties** from the shortcut menu. The System window appears as shown in Figure E-12.

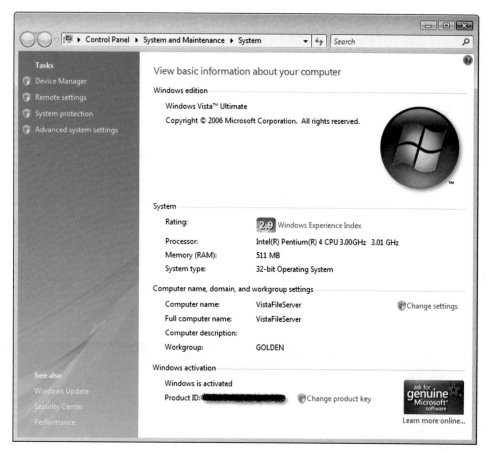

Figure E-12 Use the System window to change computer settings

3. Under *Computer name, domain, and workgroup settings*, click **Change settings** and respond to the UAC box. The System Properties dialog box displays as shown in Figure E-13.

4. To verify that you have Internet access, open **Internet Explorer** and try to navigate to a couple of Web sites.

If you have problems with accessing the network or the Internet, you'll need to dig a little deeper into Vista networking, which is covered in Chapter 5.

ACTIVATE WINDOWS VISTA AND INSTALL UPDATES

After you install Vista, you have 30 days to activate the OS. If you don't activate within the given time, the screen in Figure E-14 displays forcing you to activate Windows, enter or purchase a new product key for the activation, or convert Vista to Reduced Functionality Mode (RFM), which greatly limits what you can do in Windows. After you are in RFM mode, if you activate Vista, it will return to the fully functioning mode.

Figure E-13   Use the System Properties window to change the workgroup name, domain name, or computer name

Figure E-14   Vista informs the user that the activation period has expired

> **Note**
>
> If you need more than 30 days before you activate Windows, you can use this command in a command prompt window: **slmgr –rearm**. Your activation period will be extended an additional 30 days from the day you issue the command. You can use the command three times, at which time Vista will revert to RFM mode.

To see or change the activation status, use the System window: Click **Start**, right-click **Computer,** and select **Properties** from the shortcut menu. The System window appears. Scroll down to the bottom of the window to see the activation status (refer back to Figure E-12). Using Windows XP, you could not change the product key unless you were in the process of activating XP, but with Vista, the product key can be changed at any time. For example, if you discover your product key is a pirated key, you can change it before you activate Vista. If you change the key after Vista is activated, you must activate Vista again, because the activation is tied to the product key and the system hardware. Incidentally, if you replace the motherboard or replace the hard drive and memory at the same time, you must also reactivate Vista.

After Vista is activated, the next step is to update Vista. To download and apply Vista updates, click **Start, All Programs**, and **Windows Update**. The Windows Update window appears as shown in Figure E-15. Click **Install updates** and follow directions on screen.

> **Note**
>
> The Windows Vista DVD includes the Windows Anytime Upgrade feature. Using this feature, if you have purchased Windows Vista Home Basic, Home Premium, or Business versions, you can upgrade them to Vista Ultimate using the same DVD. To do that, go to the Microsoft Web site (*www.microsoft.com*), purchase the upgrade, and download an upgrade program file which includes a new product key. You use the downloaded file and the Vista DVD to install the new version of Windows Vista.

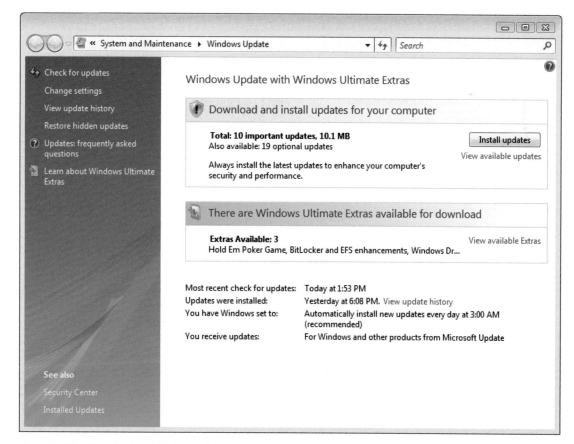

Figure E-15 Download and install updates for your computer

During the Vista installation, you were asked how you want to handle Vista updates. To verify or change this setting, in the left pane of the Windows Update window, click **Change settings**. From the Change settings window, shown in Figure E-16, you can decide how often, when, and how you want Vista to install updates. The recommended setting is to allow Vista to automatically download and install updates daily. However, if you are not always connected to the Internet, your connection is very slow, or you want more control over which updates are installed, you might want to manage the updates differently.

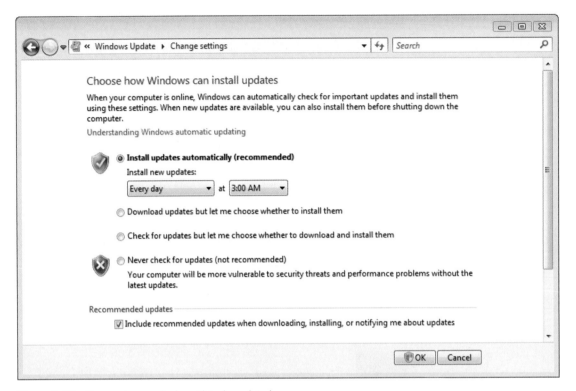

Figure E-16   Manage how and when Vista is updated

INSTALL HARDWARE

You're now ready to install the hardware devices that were not automatically installed during the installation, such as printers, USB devices, and other peripherals. As you install each device, reboot and verify that the software or device is working before you move on to the next item. Let's look at how to install printers and then we'll turn our attention to USB devices.

INSTALLING AND CONFIGURING PRINTERS

Four significant changes in the way Windows Vista handles printing are as follows:

> **Note**
>
> Windows Vista and Windows XP also support two other printer protocols—PostScript and PCL—that both require the printer to format or render a page before printing. Generally, PostScript and PCL are used with high-end printers and XPS and GDI are used with low-end printers.

◢ Windows Vista supports a new and improved printing protocol called XML Paper Specification (XPS). This protocol specifies how a page is formatted (called rendering the page) before the print job is spooled to the printer, and is written using the XML programming language. When you print from an application, Vista uses either GDI or XPS for rendering based on the type of printer driver installed. GDI (Graphics Device Interface) is the rendering protocol supported by Windows XP and earlier versions of Windows.

◢ Local, network, and wireless (including Bluetooth) printers can be installed using the Add Printer Wizard, which is accessed from Control Panel.

◢ Printers connected to print servers on an enterprise network are managed using the Print Management console together with the Printer Migrator utility (to manage print servers). These remote network printers are installed using the Network Printer Installation Wizard. How to use these tools when supporting remote printers and print servers is not covered in this book.

◢ Group Policy can be used to limit and control all kinds of printer-related tasks, including the number of printers that can be installed using the Add Printer Wizard, how print jobs are sent to print servers (rendered or not rendered), which print servers the computer can use, and which printers on a network the computer can use.

Now let's look at how to install a printer. To install a local USB printer, all you have to do is plug in the USB printer and Vista installs the printer automatically. On the other hand, you'll need to follow these steps to install a non-USB local printer or a network printer:

1. For a network printer, make sure the printer is connected to the network and turned on. For a wireless printer, turn on the printer and set the printer within range of the PC. For a parallel port or serial port printer, connect the printer to the PC and turn it on.

2. In Control Panel (see Figure E-17), under Hardware and Sound, click **Printer**. The Printers window opens as shown in Figure E-18.

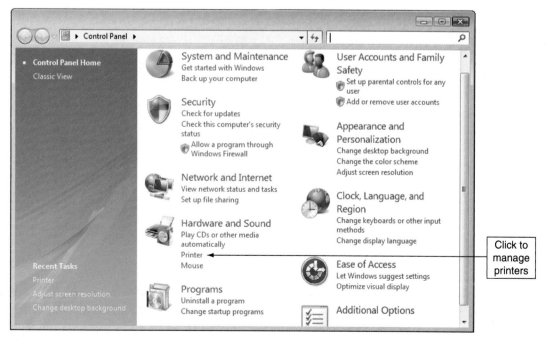

Figure E-17   To install and manage printers, use the Control Panel to access the Printers window

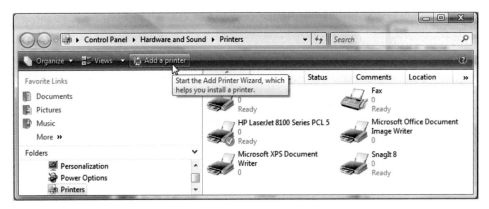

Figure E-18 Use the Printers window to install a new printer

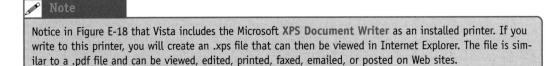

> **Note**
>
> Notice in Figure E-18 that Vista includes the Microsoft **XPS Document Writer** as an installed printer. If you write to this printer, you will create an .xps file that can then be viewed in Internet Explorer. The file is similar to a .pdf file and can be viewed, edited, printed, faxed, emailed, or posted on Web sites.

3. Click **Add a printer**. In the Add Printer window that appears (see Figure E-19), select the type of printer and click **Next**.

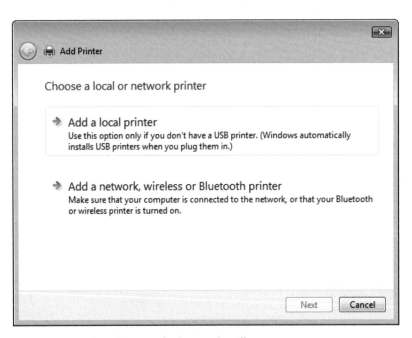

Figure E-19 Select the type of printer to install

4. Vista searches for available printers and lists them. Select the printer from the list and click **Next**. If your printer is not listed, click **The printer that I want isn't listed**. You will then be able to point to the port or IP address of the printer. In Figure E-20, we are installing a network printer identified by its IP address, which is 192.168.1.109.

5. In the next window, shown in Figure E-21, you can change the name of the printer, such as "John's Office Printer", or leave the printer name as is. If this printer will be your default printer, check **Set as the default printer**. Click **Next** to continue.

E

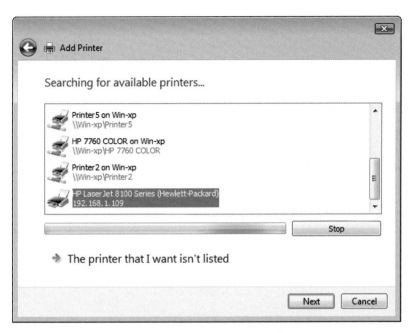

Figure E-20   Select the printer from the list of available printers

Figure E-21   Name the printer and decide if it will be your default printer

6. To test the printer, in the next window, click **Print a test page**. Click **Finish** to complete the installation.

Just as with Windows XP, configuring add-on devices for a printer and setting printer preferences is done using the printer properties window. To access the window, open the Printers window and right-click the printer and select **Properties** from the shortcut menu. To manage the printer queue, double-click the printer icon in the Printers window. For example, in Figure E-22, to empty the printer queue, click **Cancel All Documents** under the Printer menu.

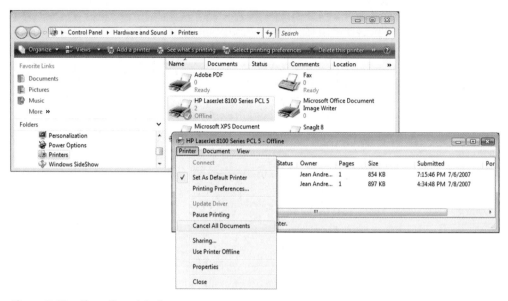

Figure E-22 Clean the printer's queue

INSTALLING OTHER HARDWARE DEVICES

The primary tool for managing hardware in Windows Vista is Device Manager. To access Device Manager, click **Start**, right-click **Computer** and click **Properties** on the shortcut menu. In the System window that appears, in the left pane, click **Device Manager** (see Figure E-23) and respond to the UAC box. Use Device Manager to uninstall devices, update drivers, and troubleshoot problems with devices.

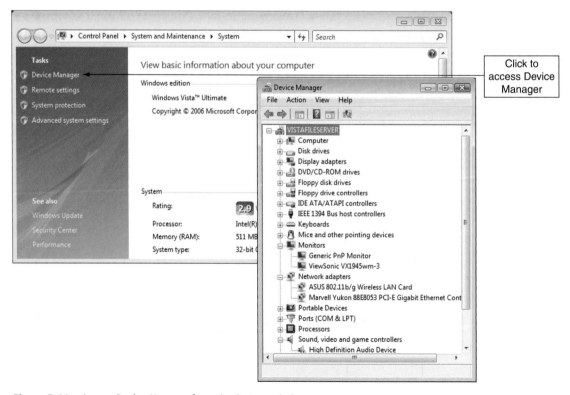

Figure E-23 Access Device Manager from the System window

To install a new hardware device, always read and follow manufacturer directions for the installation. Sometimes you are directed to install the drivers before you connect the device, and sometimes you will first need to connect the device. When you first connect a new device, the Found New Hardware Wizard launches to step you through the installation.

Let's look at one installation example of a Web camera that has a problem:

1. Connect the USB Web camera to the PC and the Found New Hardware Wizard launches showing the window in Figure E-24. Click **Locate and install driver software (recommended)**.

Figure E-24 Opening window of the Found New Hardware Wizard

2. The next window, shown in Figure E-25, indicates Windows could not locate the drivers. If you have downloaded the drivers from the manufacturer Web site or have the drivers on CD, click **Browse my computer for driver software (advanced)**. Locate the drivers and continue with the installation.

3. If you don't have the drivers, click **Check for a solution**. Vista will attempt to help you find the drivers. In Figure E-26, Vista has correctly identified the device and provided a link to the driver download page of Creative Technology, LTD, the camera manufacturer.

4. When you click that link, you are taken to a Web page with a message from Creative saying they will not provide Vista drivers for the camera because the camera is too old. Therefore, this camera cannot work under Windows Vista. (Too bad; it was only a year old.) Incidentally, the lack of drivers for hardware under Vista has been one of the primary complaints against choosing Vista over Windows XP.

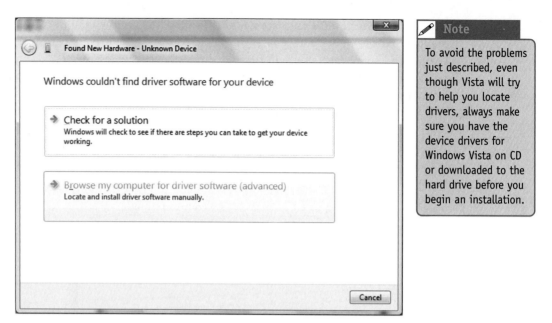

Note

To avoid the problems just described, even though Vista will try to help you locate drivers, always make sure you have the device drivers for Windows Vista on CD or downloaded to the hard drive before you begin an installation.

Figure E-25 Windows could not find drivers for the device

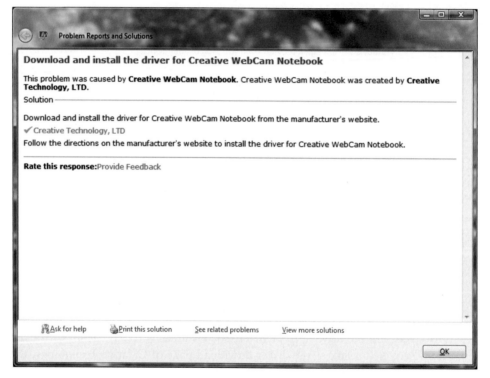

Figure E-26 The Problem Reports and Solutions window gives help to find device drivers

INSTALL APPLICATIONS

As with previous versions of Windows, to install an application, insert the setup CD or DVD and follow directions on screen to launch the installation routine. For software downloaded from the Internet, using Windows Explorer, double-click the program filename to begin the installation. If you are not logged on as an administrator, but need to install the software using administrative privileges, right-click the program filename and select **Run as administrator** from the shortcut menu (see Figure E-27). You'll then need to respond to the UAC box, which will require you enter an administrator password.

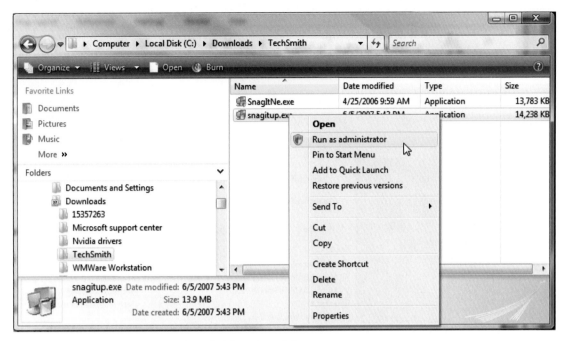

Figure E-27 Execute a program using administrative privileges

In Windows Vista, use the Programs and Features window to manage software. From Control Panel, click **Programs** (see Figure E-17 earlier in the appendix). The list of tools to manage installed programs appears in the left pane of the Programs window shown in Figure E-28.

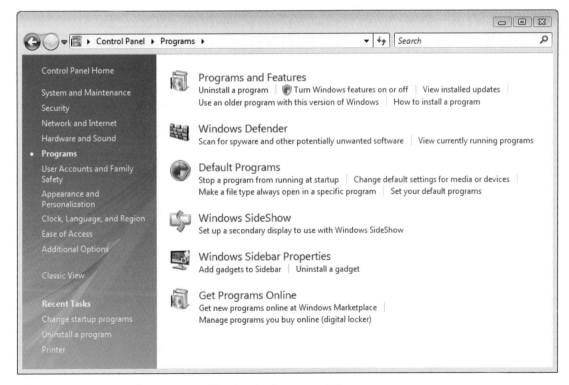

Figure E-28 Manage software on your PC using the Programs window

To see a list of installed programs, under Programs and Features, click **Uninstall a program**. The Programs and Features window shown in Figure E-29 appears. Select a program from the list. Based on the software, the buttons at the top of the list will change. For example, in Figure E-29, the SnagIt8 software offers the option to Uninstall, Change, or Repair the software.

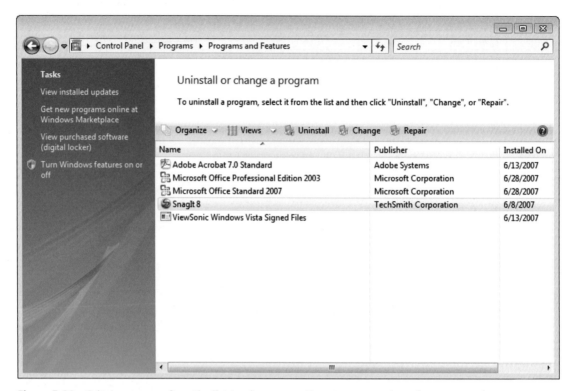

Figure E-29 Select a program from the list to view your options to manage the software

CREATE USER ACCOUNTS

When Vista is first installed, it creates one user account with administrative privileges and the all-powerful Administrator account. (The Administrator account is disabled by default.) Even if you are the single user for a computer, be sure to create at least one other user account for your normal work that has limited power. Malicious software can sometimes take advantage of an administrator account when it is active so it is best to not log on as an administrator for normal day-to-day activities.

In the following sections, you'll learn about new features in Vista for managing user profiles and user data, how to set up a new user account, and how to transfer user data and preferences from another computer to a Vista computer.

HOW VISTA ORGANIZES USER PROFILES AND USER DATA

Using Windows Vista, when you set up a user account and the user first logs on, a user profile is created that consists of two general items:

▲ A folder together with its subfolders, which is created under the *%SystemDrive%* \Users folder, for example, C:\Users\Jean Andrews

▲ A registry hive file named Ntuser.dat in the user's folder contains user settings and it maps to the HKEY_CURRENT_USER key of the registry

Using Windows Vista, there are two types of user profiles:

▲ **Local user profiles** are created and used solely on a single computer.
▲ **Roaming user profiles** are stored in the Active Directory on a domain and follow a user from computer to computer on the domain.

As discussed in Chapter 4, Vista has two levels of user accounts:

▲ An administrator account has complete access to the system and can make changes that affect the security of the system and other users.
▲ A standard user can use software and hardware and make some system changes, but cannot make changes that affect the security of the system or other users.

The user folder (for example, C:\Users\Jean Andrews) contains a group of subfolders organized as shown in Figure E-30. This group of folders and subfolders is called the **user profile namespace**. The organization of these subfolders under Vista is cleaner and easier to manage than the organization under Windows XP.

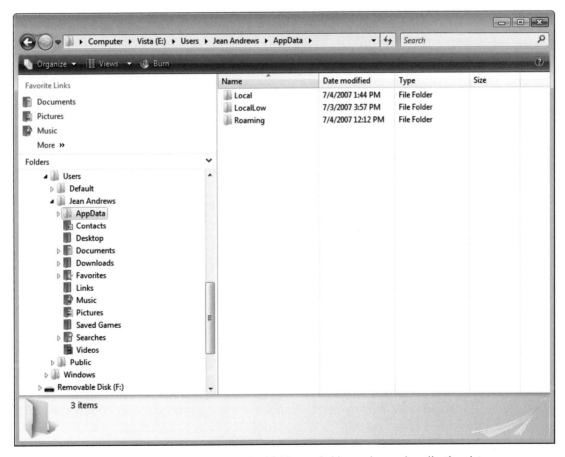

Figure E-30 A user profile contains a folder and subfolders to hold user data and application data

Also notice in Figure E-30 the \Users\Public folder. Microsoft encourages you to put files in this Public folder that will be shared on the network so that your private user data folders are better protected.

SETTING UP A NEW USER ACCOUNT

To set up a new user account, follow these steps:

1. From Control Panel, under User Accounts and Family Safety, click **Add or remove user accounts** and respond to the UAC box. The Manage Accounts window appears, as shown in Figure E-31.

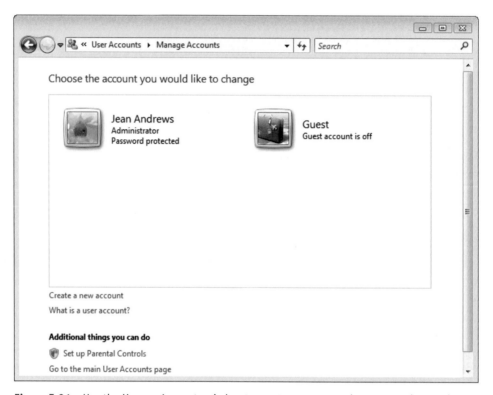

Figure E-31   Use the Manage Accounts window to create accounts and set parental controls

2. Click **Create a new account**. On the Create New Account window shown in Figure E-32, enter the account name and select the type of account (Standard user or Administrator). Then click **Create Account**.

3. The account now displays in the Manage Accounts window. Click the account to see a list of changes you can make to the account. The Change an Account window appears, as shown in Figure E-33. If you want to set a password for the new account, click **Create a password** and enter the password on the next screen.

When using the Vista Business, Enterprise, and Ultimate editions, another way to create and manage accounts is to use the Computer Management console. Follow these steps:

1. To open the console, click **Start**, right-click **Computer**, select **Manage** from the shortcut window, and respond to the UAC box. In the console window (left side of

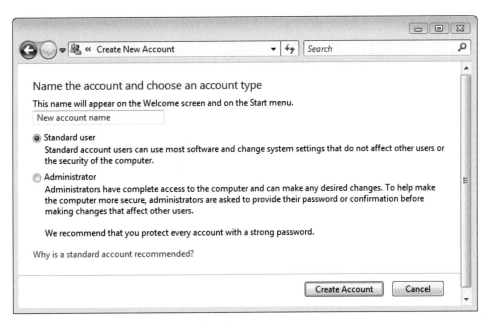

Figure E-32   Name the account and select the account type

Figure E-33   Make changes to an account

Figure E-34), under System Tools, Local Users and Groups, right-click **Users** and select **New User** from the shortcut menu. The New User dialog box appears as shown on the right side of Figure E-34.

2. Fill in the appropriate information and click **Create**. The new Standard account is now listed under Users.

3. To change an account, right-click the account and select **Properties** from the shortcut menu. Using the properties window (see Figure E-35), you can control the password, user groups the account belongs to, and the path to the user's profile. Incidentally, if you want to give Administrator privileges to a Standard account, using the Member Of tab, add the account to the Administrators group.

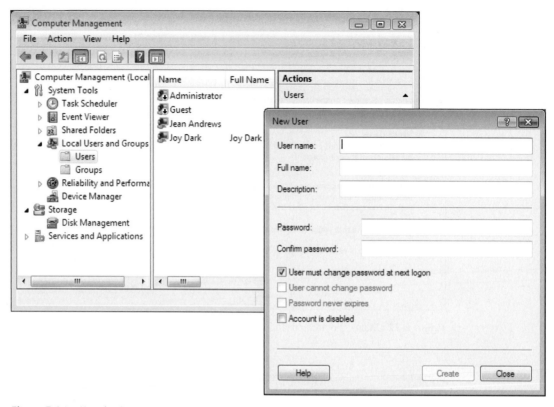

Figure E-34   Use the Computer Management console to create an account

Figure E-35   Use an account properties window to manage the account

TRANSFERRING USER DATA AND PREFERENCES

When you first install Vista on a new computer, you might need to transfer user data and preferences from an old computer to this new Vista computer. Two tools used for this purpose are the User State Migration Tool (USMT) and Windows Easy Transfer.

USMT is an automated tool used in large organizations when Vista is being deployed to multiple computers. Windows Easy Transfer is a manual tool similar to Windows XP Files and Settings Transfer Wizard. Windows Easy Transfer is much easier to use than USMT and the better choice for a few installations. To use it, the old computer (source computer) must be using Windows XP with Service Pack 2, Windows 2000 with Service Pack 4, or Windows Vista.

Follow these steps:

1. On the new Vista computer, click **Start, All Programs, Accessories, System Tools, Windows Easy Transfer,** and respond to the UAC box. The opening window is shown in Figure E-36.

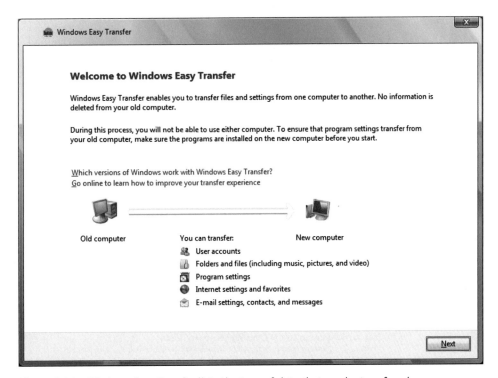

Figure E-36 Windows Easy Transfer lists the type of data that can be transferred

2. The tool is self explanatory and easy to follow. As you work your way through, the utility asks if you are using an Easy Transfer Cable (see Figure E-37). If you don't have the cable, then click **No, show me more options** to transfer data using a network, CD, DVD, USB device, or external hard disk.

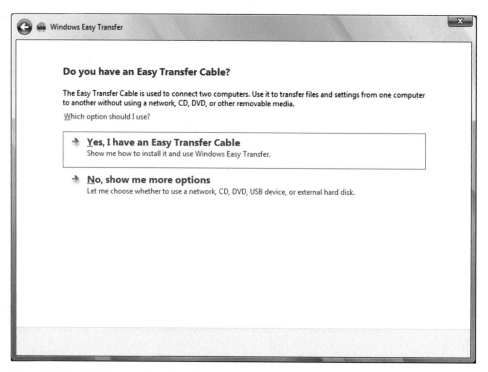

Figure E-37   Tell Windows Easy Transfer what device will be used for the transfer

3. The next window is shown in Figure E-38. If your old computer is a Windows XP or Windows 2000 computer, you'll need to install the Windows Easy Transfer software. In this situation, choose **No, I need to install it now**.

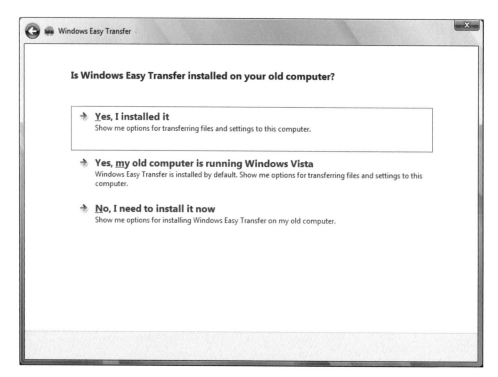

Figure E-38   Is Windows Easy Transfer installed on your old computer?

4. The next window (see Figure E-39) asks how you will install the software. If the two computers are on the same network, select **External hard disk or shared network folder**.

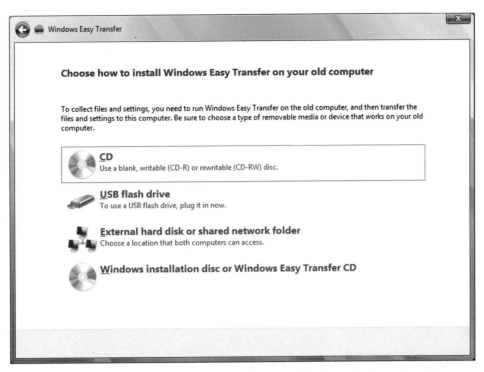

Figure E-39 Choose how you will install the Windows Easy Transfer software on the old computer

5. After the software is installed and running on the old computer, the two computers will be communicating. The next step is to select the files, folders, and other items on the old computer that you want to transfer. The window that appears on the old computer for you to make your selections is shown in Figure E-40.

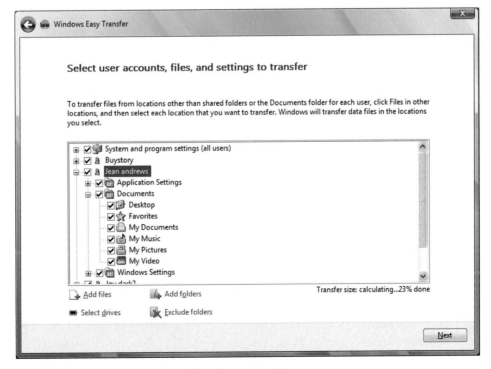

Figure E-40 Select folders, files and settings to transfer

6. After you have made your selections, the transferring begins. When finished, be sure to verify that all is safely transferred before you delete the data on the old computer. In fact, it's a good idea to keep the old computer intact until the user has worked on the new computer for about a month, just in case the user left something important behind.

CUSTOMIZE THE VISTA DESKTOP AND OTHER SETTINGS

To customize the Vista desktop and display settings, first be sure you are logged on under the correct user account, because these settings apply to the currently logged on user. Then in the Control Panel, click **Appearance and Personalization**. In the Appearance and Personalization window shown in Figure E-41, you can make selections to change the desktop background, color scheme, screen resolution, screen saver, desktop theme, taskbar, Start menu, folder options, fonts, and sidebar gadgets so that Windows will look and work the way you want it.

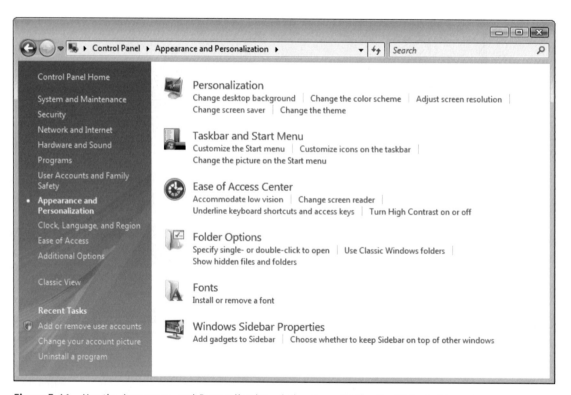

Figure E-41   Use the Appearance and Personalization window to customize the Vista desktop

You can also configure the Start menu using the Taskbar and Start Menu Properties dialog box or from Group Policy. To use the dialog box, right-click **Start** and select **Properties** from the shortcut menu. Using the Notification Area and Toolbars tabs, you can control when icons and toolbars appear in the taskbar (see Figure E-42).

When Vista is first installed, by default, it turns certain software components on and others off. To see how these features are set and change these settings, from Control Panel, click **Programs**. The Programs window appears as shown in Figure E-43. Click **Turn Windows features on or off** and respond to the UAC box. The Windows Features dialog box opens. To expand groups of items, click the plus sign beside a checkbox. Generally, the

Figure E-42 Manage the taskbar using the Taskbar and Start Menu Properties box

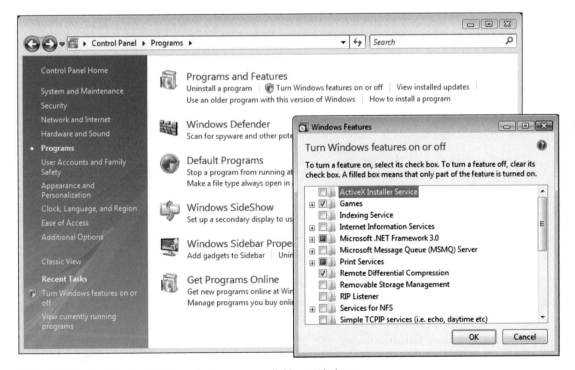

Figure E-43 Control what Windows features are available to Windows

features are set as they should be. However, to meet specific user needs, you might need to turn on Telnet client, Telnet server, FTP server, or some similar seldomly used Windows feature. To get more information about an item, search for it in Windows Help and Support. Check or uncheck a feature to turn it on or off. Click **OK** when you're done.

You should now have Windows Vista configured and functioning as you want it. To finish up, do one last restart and verify that everything is working and looking good. After you have verified everything, it's a good idea to back up the entire volume on which Vista is installed. How to perform a Complete PC Backup is covered in Chapter 4.

>> APPENDIX SUMMARY

▲ Versions of Vista include Starter, Home Basic, Home Premium, Business, Enterprise, and Ultimate.

▲ When installing Vista, you can perform an in-place upgrade, clean install, or dual boot configuration.

▲ You can upgrade to Vista from Windows XP or Windows 2000.

▲ After you have installed Vista, verify that you have network and Internet access, activate and update Windows, install hardware and applications, set up user accounts, and customize Vista user settings.

▲ You have 30 days to activate Vista after it is installed.

▲ Vista supports the XML Paper Specification (XPS) protocol to render pages before they are sent to a printer. XPS documents can be created by Vista and used as PDF files are used.

▲ Non-USB printers are installed from the Printers window accessed from Control Panel. USB printers install automatically.

▲ During the hardware installation process, if Vista cannot locate drivers, it searches the Internet for help.

▲ Applications are managed from the Programs and Features window of Vista, accessed from the Control Panel.

▲ The user profile namespace is created in the %SystemDrive%\Users folder. User settings are stored in the Ntuser.dat hive of the registry.

▲ Two kinds of user profiles are local user profiles and roaming user profiles.

▲ Two types of user accounts are administrator accounts and standard user accounts.

▲ The Public folder is intended to be used for files shared on the network.

▲ User accounts can be managed from the Computer Management console or the Manage Accounts window accessed from Control Panel.

▲ Two tools used to transfer user data and preferences from an older computer to a Vista computer are the User State Migration Tool (USMT) and Windows Easy Transfer. The latter tool is easier to use and appropriate for a few transfers.

▲ Use the Windows Features dialog box to turn Vista features on or off.

>> KEY TERMS

local user profile   A user profile created and used solely on a single computer.

roaming user profiles   A user profile stored in the Active Directory on a domain that follows a user from computer to computer on the domain.

user profile namespace   The folder and its subfolders where user data and preferences are kept. By default, the folder is stored in the %SystemDrive%\Users folder.

Windows Anytime Upgrade   A Vista feature that allows a user to purchase an upgrade to Vista Ultimate after having already purchased a Vista Home edition. A new product key is issued by Microsoft.

Windows Easy Transfer   A Vista feature that allows user data and preferences to be transferred from an old PC to a Windows Vista PC.

Windows Vista Business   A version of Vista intended for business users, which includes support for joining a domain, Group Policy, and Encrypted File System, but does not support Windows Media Center, Movie Maker, DVD Maker, and parental controls.

Windows Vista Enterprise   A version of Vista that includes additional features over Windows Vista Business including BitLocker.

Windows Vista Home Basic   A version of Vista designed for low-cost home systems that don't require full security and networking features.

Windows Vista Home Premium   A version of Vista similar to Windows Vista Home Basic but which includes additional features including the Aero user interface.

Windows Vista Starter   A version of Vista with limited features intended to be used in developing nations.

Windows Vista Ultimate   A version of Vista that includes every Windows Vista feature.

XML Paper Specification (XPS)   A printing protocol by Microsoft used to render a page before it is sent to the printer and expected to replace GDI, an earlier rendering protocol.

XPS Document Writer   A Vista feature that creates a .xps document file that works similar to a .pdf file by Adobe. When printing from an application, the writer appears in the list of printers.

>> REVIEWING THE BASICS

1. Which Vista version includes all features of Vista?

2. What is the minimum amount of RAM necessary to run Windows Vista?

3. After you have installed Vista, how many days do you have before it needs activating?

4. Using Windows Vista, what page formatting protocol is replacing GDI?

5. Using Vista, how do you create an XPS document file?

6. When you first install Vista, what two user accounts are created?

7. What type of user profile is used solely on a single computer?

8. Which folder is the preferred folder to hold user data to be shared on the network?

9. Which two tools can be used to create user accounts?

10. Which two tools can be used to transfer user data and preferences from an old PC to a Vista PC?

>> *THINKING CRITICALLY*

1. After installing Vista on a new computer, which is the easiest way to copy Internet Explorer Favorites from a Windows XP computer to the new Vista computer?

   a. Copy the C:\Documents and Settings*username*\Favorites folder from the XP computer to the C:\Users*username*\Favorites folder on the Vista computer.
   b. Use Windows Easy Transfer.
   c. Use the User State Migration Tool.
   d. Rebuild the Favorites list by navigating to each web site and adding it to Favorites.

2. You have purchased an Upgrade version of Windows Vista Ultimate. You are planning to install Windows Vista on a computer that has Windows XP installed, but the Windows XP installation is seriously corrupted and you cannot boot from the hard drive. What can you do?

   a. Reinstall Windows XP and then install Windows Vista as an upgrade.
   b. Boot from the Vista DVD and perform a clean installation of Windows Vista without activating Vista and then install Vista a second time as an upgrade.
   c. Either a or b will work.
   d. Neither a or b will work. You must purchase For-a-new-PC version of Windows Vista.

>> *HANDS-ON PROJECTS*

PROJECT E-1: Creating User Accounts

On a Windows Vista computer, do the following to explore user accounts:

1. Create a standard account named Jane Doe and an administrator account named Tom Jones.

2. Log onto the system as Tom Jones and then log onto the system as Jane Doe.

3. Logged on as Jane Doe, try to view the folders in the Tom Jones user profile namespace. What error message do you see? Print the screen showing the error message.

4. Now try to open Device Manager. Print the screen showing the UAC box.

PROJECT E-2: Optimize Windows Vista

When Windows Vista runs slowly, you might can improve performance by turning off some of its visual effects. To see how this works, in Control Panel, click System and Maintenance. Then, check your computer's Windows Experience Index base score, Advanced tools, and Adjust the appearance and performance of Windows. When you respond to the UAC box, the Performance Options dialog box appears. Try these three options: Adjust for best appearance, Adjust for best performance, and Let Windows choose what's best for my computer. Which of the three options works best on your system? Why?

PROJECT E-3: Verifying that Your Windows XP System Qualifies for Vista, Part 1

If you have access to a Windows XP computer, verify that all hardware qualifies for Vista. Fill in the following table:

Hardware	Description	Does It Qualify? (Yes/No)
CPU		
Memory		
Hard drive free space		
Optical drive		
Video card and video memory		

PROJECT E-4:   Verifying that Your Windows XP System Qualifies for Vista, Part 2

List all the applications installed on your Windows XP system. Using the Windows Vista Compatibility site at *www.microsoft.com/windows/compatibility/*, search for each application. Does each application qualify? Print web pages to support your conclusions.

>> REAL PROBLEMS, REAL SOLUTIONS

REAL PROBLEM E-1:   Installing Windows Vista

Perform either an in-place upgrade or a clean install of Windows Vista. As you perform the installation, follow all appropriate instructions in the appendix and keep notes as you go. Then answer these questions:

1. For which hardware devices did you need to provide drivers for Windows Vista?

2. Did you encounter any errors during the installation? If so, how did you resolve these errors?

3. How did you install Windows updates after the installation was finished?

4. How long did the installation take?

REAL PROBLEM E-2:   Removing Windows Vista from a Dual Boot Configuration

Joan purchased an upgrade version of Windows Vista Home Edition and installed it in a dual boot configuration with Windows XP on her laptop computer. She discovered after the installation that her laptop manufacturer does not provide Vista drivers for all her laptop components. She has come to you asking for help. You first congratulate her on not upgrading Windows XP to Vista, which would have made it necessary to reinstall XP. In discussing her options, you discover that her desktop computer does qualify for Windows Vista. She is most happy to move the Vista installation to her desktop.

One step in that process is to delete the Vista installation from her laptop. Recall that when Vista installs, it changes the MBR program on the hard drive so that the program searches for Bootmgr rather than Ntldr. The command to reinstate the Windows XP Ntldr program as the boot loader is:

```
C:\Boot\Bootsect.exe -NT52 All
```

The command is executed from an elevated command prompt. Using this command, list the steps to uninstall Windows Vista from Joan's laptop, freeing the hard drive space.

REAL PROBLEM E-3:   Removing Windows XP from a Dual Boot Configuration

Larry wanted to try out Windows Vista without overwriting his Windows XP installation, so he decided to install Vista in a dual-boot configuration with Windows XP. He partitioned his hard drive so that drive D contains Windows Vista and drive C contains Windows XP. Now that Vista is up and working well, he wants to remove Windows XP to increase free space on his drive. Drive C is the active partition, and, therefore, contains the Bootmgr and BCD files. Reorder the steps listed below to remove Windows XP:

1. Delete the C:\Windows folder and other Windows XP folders on drive C.

2. Using the command prompt in the Vista Recovery Environment, use the *Bootrec /fixmbr* command to fix the MBR.

3. Reboot to the Vista Recovery Environment and select the option to repair startup, which reinstalls Bootmgr and builds a new D:\Boot folder.

4. Booting to the Vista Recovery Environment, use the Diskpart command to make drive D the active partition. The Diskpart commands used are *list disk, select disk 0, list partition, select partition 1,* and *active.*

5. Using the command prompt in the Vista Recovery Environment, use the *Bootrec/ rebuildBCD* to build a new BCD file on drive D.

6. Using the command prompt in the Vista Recovery Environment, use the *Bootrec /fixboot* command to fix the boot sector of drive D.

GLOSSARY

This glossary defines the key terms listed at the end of each chapter and other terms related to fixing Windows XP.

access point (AP) A device connected to a LAN that provides wireless communication so that computers, printers, and other wireless devices can communicate with devices on the LAN.

administrator account A type of user account that has complete access to the system and can make changes that affect the security of the system and other users.

Advanced Boot Options Menu A startup menu that lists advanced troubleshooting options used to diagnose Windows startup problems.

adware Software installed on a computer that produces pop-up ads using your browser; the ads are often based on your browsing habits.

API (application program interface) A predefined Windows procedure that allows a program to access hardware or other software.

API call A request made by software to the OS to use an API procedure to access hardware or other software.

BitLocker Drive Encryption A Vista feature that locks down a hard drive if it is stolen. It encrypts the entire system volume and is designed to be used in conjunction with file and folder encryption for high security requirements.

Boot Configuration Data (BCD) file The Windows Vista registry file named BCD that is stored in the \Boot folder of the active or boot partition and holds configuration data used during Windows Vista startup.

boot sector *See* OS boot record.

boot sector virus A virus that hides in one or both of the small programs at the beginning of the hard drive used to initiate the boot of the operating system.

browser hijacker A malicious program that infects your Web browser and can change your home page or browser settings. It can also redirect your browser to unwanted sites, produce pop-up ads, and set unwanted bookmarks.

crossover cable A network cable used to connect two PCs into the simplest network possible. Also used to connect two hubs or switches.

Data Collector Set A Vista tool in the Computer Management console used to collect data about different aspects of the system and present that data in a report that can help you identify the source of a computer problem.

default gateway A computer or other device on a network that acts as an entry point, or gateway, to another network.

device driver A program stored on the hard drive that tells the computer how to communicate with a hardware device such as a printer or modem.

device manager A Windows tool to view and manage installed hardware devices and drivers and the resources they use.

devmgmt.msc The Microsoft Management Console program that launches Device Manager.

diagnostic card An expansion card that can be used to display error codes at startup to diagnose a startup problem with hardware.

dialer Malicious software that can disconnect your phone line from your ISP and dial an expensive pay-per-minute phone number without your knowledge.

diskmgmt.msc The Microsoft Management Console program that launches Disk Management.

DLL (dynamic link library) A group or library of programs packaged into a single program file that can be called on by a Windows application. A DLL file can have a .dll, .fon, .ocx, .drv, .nls, .evt, or .exe file extension.

DNS (Domain Name System) server A computer that matches up domain names with IP addresses.

domain profile The profile settings that Windows Firewall uses when the computer is logged onto a domain and security is managed by the domain controller.

elevated command prompt A command prompt window that allows commands to run at the privileged administrative level.

encrypting virus A type of virus that can continually transform itself so that it is not detected by AV software.

encryption　Used to protect sensitive data, the conversion of data into code that must be translated before it can be accessed.

file virus　A virus that hides in an executable program (for example, .exe, .com, or .sys) or in a word-processing document that contains a macro.

firewall　Software or a hardware device that protects a computer or network from unsolicited communication. A hardware firewall stands between two networks or a computer and a network. A software firewall is installed on a single computer to protect it, and is called a personal firewall.

freeware　Software you can download for free.

guest account　An account that has few privileges and that is normally disabled.

handle　A relationship between a process and a resource it has called into action.

IDE to USB adapter　An inexpensive device that allows you to connect an IDE hard drive to a USB port. It can help you recover data from an IDE drive that will not boot.

infestation　*See* malicious software.

Internet Connection Sharing (ICS)　A Windows 98/Me/XP and Vista utility that manages two or more computers connected to the Internet.

kernel mode　The Windows privileged processing mode that has access to hardware components.

keylogger　A type of spyware that tracks your keystrokes, including passwords, chat room sessions, e-mail messages, documents, online purchases, and anything else you type on your PC. Text is logged to a text file and transmitted over the Internet without your knowledge.

Last Known Good Configuration　Configuration information about the Windows startup process saved in the registry immediately after the user logs on. The information can be used to reconfigure startup when the user chooses this option on the Advanced Boot Options menu.

local user profile　A user profile created and used solely on a single computer.

logic bomb　A type of malicious software that is dormant code added to software and triggered at a predetermined time or by a predetermined event.

logical drive　A portion or all of a hard drive partition that is treated by the operating system as though it were a physical drive. Each logical drive is assigned a drive letter, such as drive C, and contains a file system. Also called a *volume*.

macro　A small sequence of commands, contained within a document, that can be automatically executed when the document is loaded, or executed later by using a predetermined keystroke.

macro virus　A virus that can hide in the small programs embedded in a document file. These small programs are called macros.

malicious software　Any unwanted program that is transmitted to a computer without the user's knowledge and that is designed to do varying degrees of damage to data and software. Types of infestations include viruses, Trojan horses, worms, adware, spyware, keyloggers, browser hijackers, dialers, and downloaders.

malware　*See* malicious software.

master boot record (MBR)　The first 512-byte sector on a hard drive. Contains the partition table and the master boot program, which the BIOS uses to find the OS on the drive.

Memory Diagnostics　A Vista tool that tests memory before Vista is loaded. This tool can be launched from the Error Reporting utility, the command prompt (mdsched.exe), the Vista boot menu, or the Vista setup DVD.

MSconfig.exe　A Windows troubleshooting utility that launches the System Configuration Utility used to reduce startup to essentials.

msinfo32.exe　The Windows utility program that launches the System Information window.

multipartite virus　A combination of a boot sector virus and a file virus. It can hide in either type of program.

network drive map　Mounting a drive to a computer, such as drive E, that is actually hard drive space on another host computer on the network.

open handle　A handle that is still in progress. (A handle is the relationship between a process and a resource it has called into action.)

OS boot record　The second 512 bytes on a drive, used to help the MBR find and load the OS.

partition　A division of a hard drive that can be used to hold logical drives (for example, drive C).

password reset disk　A Windows Vista disk created to be used to reset a password in the event the user forgets the user account password to the system.

patch cable　A network cable that is used to connect a PC to a hub, switch, or router.

phishing　Sending an e-mail message with the intent of getting the user to reveal private information that can be used for identify theft.

ping (packet internet groper)　A Windows and Unix command used to troubleshoot network connections. It verifies that the host can communicate with another host on the network.

private profile The profile settings that Windows Firewall uses when the computer is not logged onto a domain and all active networks (wired and wireless, including Bluetooth) are configured as private networks. The profile uses a medium level of protection. Also see *public profile*.

polymorphic virus A type of virus that changes its distinguishing characteristics as it replicates itself. Mutating in this way makes it more difficult for AV software to recognize the presence of the virus.

port A number assigned to an application or other process on a computer so that the process can be found by TCP/IP. Also called a *port address* or *port number*.

process A Program that is running together with the resources needed by the running program.

process tree A process and all the processes it has launched or other processes beneath it have launched.

progress bar A graphical bar that appears on the screen during Windows Vista startup. When you see the bar you know that the Windows kernel (ntoskrnl.exe) and all its kernel mode components are running and the Win subsystem running in user mode has started, displaying the progress bar. Up to this point in the boot, all displays have been in text mode.

Protected Mode An operating mode used by Internet Explorer to protect the system from malware where files can only be written to the Temporary Internet Files folder and only insignificant registry keys can be changed.

Public folder The folder in the *%SystemDrive%*\Users folder that is intended to hold data that users share on the computer or network.

public profile The profile settings that Windows Firewall uses when Vista recognizes the computer is connected to a public network. This profile offers the highest level of protection. Also see *private profile*.

registry A database designed with a tree-like structure (called a hierarchical database) that contains configuration information for Windows, users, software applications, and installed hardware devices.

Reliability Monitor A Vista tool in the Computer Management console that can report the past history of problems on the computer, including the history of Software, Application, Hardware, Windows, and Miscellaneous Failures.

roaming user profiles A user profile stored in the Active Directory on a domain that follows a user from computer to computer on the domain.

rootkit A type of malicious software that loads itself before the OS boot is complete and can hijack internal Windows components so that it masks information Windows provides to user-mode utilities such as Windows Explorer or Task Manager.

restore point A snapshot of the Windows system settings and configuration, usually made before installation of new hardware or applications. *See also* System Restore.

Safe Mode An Advanced Boot Menu option that loads only the core device drivers needed to operate essential hardware at startup and does not load installed applications or third-party services.

SATA to USB adapter An inexpensive device that allows you to connect a SATA hard drive to a USB port. It can help you recover data from a SATA drive that will not boot.

scam e-mail E-mail sent by a scam artist intended to lure you into a scheme.

script virus A type of virus that hides in a script which might execute when you click a link on a Web page or in an HTML e-mail message, or when you attempt to open an e-mail attachment.

service A program running in the background that provides support to Windows, an application, or a device (for more explanation, see Appendix D).

shareware Software you can download and try before you buy.

spam Junk e-mail you don't ask for, don't want, and which gets in your way.

spyware Malicious software that installs itself on your computer to spy on you. It collects personal information about you that it transmits over the Internet to Web-hosting sites that intend to use your personal data for harm.

standard user A type of user account that can use software and hardware and make some system changes, but cannot make changes that affect the security of the system or other users.

startup BIOS Firmware embedded on the motherboard that is used to start up the system.

stealth virus A virus that actively conceals itself by temporarily removing itself from an infected file that is about to be examined, and then hiding a copy of itself elsewhere on the drive.

subnet mask Four numbers separated by periods (for example, 255.255.255.0) that, when combined with an IP address, indicate what network a computer is on.

system file   A file that is part of the OS that is used to do one of the following: boot the OS; hold configuration information about the OS, software, hardware, and user preferences; or perform one of the many functions of the OS, such as managing the printing process or interfacing with the hard drive.

System File Checker   A Windows Vista utility (sfc.exe) that protects system files and keeps a cache folder of current system files in case it needs to refresh a damaged file.

System Restore   A Windows utility used to create restore points and to restore the system from a restore point.

Taskmgr.exe   The Windows utility program that launches Task Manager.

third-party utility   Software not written by Microsoft that you can install on your system to help solve a Windows problem.

thread   A task that a process has requested of the OS.

tracking cookie   A cookie placed on your PC without your knowledge by a Web site to spy on your surfing habits in order to generate marketing statistics.

Trojan horse   A type of malicious software that hides or disguises itself as a useful program, yet is designed to cause damage at a later time.

user account   The information that defines a Windows Vista user, including username, password, memberships, and rights.

user mode   In Windows, a processing mode that provides an interface between an application and the OS and that has access to hardware resources only through programs running in kernel mode.

user profile namespace   The folder and its subfolders where user data and preferences are kept. By default, the folder is stored in the %SystemDrive%\Users folder.

virus   A malicious program that often has an incubation period, is infectious, and is intended to cause damage. A virus program might destroy data and programs or damage a hard drive's boot sector.

virus hoax   E-mail that does damage by tempting you to forward it to everyone in your e-mail address book with the intent of clogging up e-mail systems or by persuading you to delete a critical Windows system file by convincing you the file is malicious.

virus signature   The distinguishing characteristics of malicious software that are used by AV software to identify a program as malicious.

volume   *See* logical drive.

WEP (Wired Equivalent Privacy)   A data encryption method used by wireless networks whereby data is encrypted using a 64-bit or 128-bit key. It is not as secure as other methods because the key never changes. Compare to WPA.

Windows Anytime Upgrade   A Vista feature that allows a user to purchase an upgrade to Vista Ultimate after having already purchased a Vista Home edition. A new product key is issued by Microsoft.

Windows Boot Loader (WinLoad)   The Windows Vista startup program named WinLoad that is stored in the \Windows\System32 folder of the boot partition (most likely drive C). The program is responsible for loading into memory essential Windows components including the Vista kernel program, Ntoskrnl.exe.

Windows Boot Manager (BootMgr)   The Windows Vista startup program named BootMgr that is stored in the root directory of the active or system partition (most likely C:\) that is responsible for beginning Windows Vista startup. It reads the BCD file and then searches for and loads the Windows Boot Loader (WinLoad).

Windows Easy Transfer   A Vista feature that allows user data and preferences to be transferred from an old PC to a Windows Vista PC.

Windows RE   *See* Windows Vista Recovery Environment

Windows Vista Business   A version of Vista intended for business users, which includes support for joining a domain, Group Policy, and Encrypted File System, but does not support Windows Media Center, Movie Maker, DVD Maker, and parental controls.

Windows Vista Enterprise   A version of Vista that includes additional features over Windows Vista Business including BitLocker.

Windows Vista Home Basic   A version of Vista designed for low-cost home systems that don't require full security and networking features.

Windows Vista Home Premium   A version of Vista similar to Windows Vista Home Basic but which includes additional features including the Aero user interface.

Windows Vista Starter   A version of Vista with limited features intended to be used in developing nations.

Windows Vista Recovery Environment   A recovery OS loaded from the Vista setup DVD that includes both graphical and command-line interfaces. Tools available in the environment are Startup Repair, System Restore, Windows Complete PC Restore, Windows Memory Diagnostic Tool, and the Command Prompt. Also called *Windows RE*.

Windows Vista Ultimate A version of Vista that includes every Windows Vista feature.

worm Malicious software designed to copy itself repeatedly to memory, on drive space, or on a network, until little memory or disk space remains. The attack can result in the system not being able to function.

WPA (WiFi Protected Access) A data encryption method used by wireless networks that uses the TKIP (Temporal Key Integrity Protocol) protocol.

Encryption keys are changed at set intervals. Compare to WEP and WPA2.

WPA2 (WiFi Protected Access 2) A data encryption standard compliant with the IEEE 802.11i standard that uses the AES (Advanced Encryption Standard) protocol. WPA2 is currently the strongest wireless encryption standard.

XML Paper Specification (XPS) A printing protocol by Microsoft used to render a page before it is sent to the printer and expected to replace GDI, an earlier rendering protocol.

XPS Document Writer A Vista feature that creates a .xps document file that works similar to a .pdf file by Adobe. When printing from an application, the writer appears in the list of printers.

INDEX